Writing for Interior Design

Writing for Interior Design

Patricia Eakins

Fairchild Publications, Inc.

New York

Executive Editor: Olga T. Kontzias
Art Director: Adam B. Bohannon
Director of Production: Priscilla Taguer
Development Editor: Sylvia L. Weber
Associate Production Editor: Elizabeth Marotta
Editorial Services: Barbara Chernow
Copy Editor: Sheila Friedling
Interior Design: Susan C. Day
Cover Design: Adam B. Bohannon
Illustrations for Figures 2.3 and 4.13 by Ron Carboni
Illustrations for Figures 1.2, 2.9, and 3.4 by Anthony Jenkins
Cover Art: Corbis

Library of Congress Catalog Card Number: 2004101103

ISBN: 1-56367-279-0
GST R 133004424
Printed in the United States of America

Contents

Preface

Writing for Interior Design grew out of my 20 years' experience leading students in focused undergraduate design programs from basic writing skills to fluency in the range of genres, tones, and styles appropriate for the practices they would soon take up. There simply was no appropriate or adequate textbook. What was available on writing for designers tended to be sketchy and breezy, long on anecdote and short on how-to. Often the assumption has been that designers reading such materials would associate with offices that provide "teams" to create basic presentational materials and hire copywriters to make the argument for the work of the firm. No textbook spoke directly to the needs of entrepreneurial designers in start-up businesses with limited budgets—or for that matter to the needs of designers who compete for advancement within well-established firms—often on the strength of their writing and presentational skills. This book seeks to fill those gaps and to redress the imbalances that are inherent in them.

Because *Writing for Interior Design* addresses matters that have not otherwise been covered widely or consistently well—at least, not in a teaching context—its hands-on approach may be its most important feature from the point of view of students and teachers both. I have done my best to provide a useful range of examples, tips, discussion questions, and exercises at every step of the way.

I have also tried to address the special qualities that designers bring to the act and the art of writing—first and foremost, the confidence and joy my students have in their ability to manipulate color, shape, texture, light, and space. For designers, as for poets, the look of words on the page is part of their meaning.

Important for designers always is the interpenetration of oral and written presentation in all phases of marketing and promotion—the fluidity with which, say, a project description escapes from the written page into the airier state of orality and from orality is distilled once again to written communication.

Today's CAD-literate students will emerge from their design programs to work in fully electronic offices. It is important to acknowledge that, not so much with arcane formulations about the effect of computers on the writing process as with strategies for coping in a language environment that accumulates new possibilities and opportunities for communication without giving up the old ones.

Finally, in teaching writing to designers, it is important to remain alert to the secondary importance that they, as self-defined "visual people," attach to language. While to most writing teachers, words are the ultimate determiners of meaning, many interior designers will agree with the painter Georgia O'Keefe, whose museum in Santa Fe, NM, is approached via walking past the painter's inscribed musings about the imprecision of language:

> The meaning of a word to me is not as exact as the meaning of a color. Colors and shapes make a more definite statement to me than words. I am often amazed at the spoken and written word telling me what I have painted.

Even if colors and shapes do often need to have arguments made for them, to help onlookers understand the nature of what has been painted, most artists and designers would insist that words play a subordinate role—and they are right to so insist. A language-oriented teacher must approach this difference with humility. At the same time, in my years of observation, a writing designer is apt to be not only a more successful designer in worldly terms, but a better one, in artistic terms. This book is written with that hope and from that belief.

Chapters 1 through 3 lay down a foundation for writing designers. Chapter 1 is a primer, focusing on the importance of clear, plain English for the various audiences for whom an interior designer writes. Chapters 2 and 3 focus, respectively, on description and analysis, two types of expository development that are especially important for writing designers. These two chapters emphasize the generative aspects of writing for interior design and its importance in the actual design process, with particular reference to programming.

Chapters 4 through 11 take the student, in roughly chronological order, through the various types of writing associated with getting, administering, and promoting design work.

- In Chapter 4, the student learns to establish a professional identity and present capability.
- Chapter 5 presents a discussion of business development through marketing correspondence, including letter proposals and response to RFQs and RFPs.
- Chapter 6 discusses designer-client agreements, including both letter and form contracts.
- Chapter 7 discusses contracts for construction and fabrication and includes tips for writing specifications for construction and fabrication.
- Chapter 8 discusses writing as it relates to the procurement process for fixtures, furnishings, and equipment, with tips on writing specifications for FF & E.
- Chapter 9 discusses standard business writing strategies within the ongoing life of a design firm.
- Chapter 10 discusses the role of writing in contract administration.
- Chapter 11 examines the role that writing plays in promotion and publicity and the ways that designers use writing to develop their practices.

Chapter 12 represents a return to the beginning, a cycling back to the here and now for the principal readers of *Writing for Interior Design*—students who need to generate résumés and cover letters and to build portfolios that will carry them from the academic world to the work world. There they can put into practice all they have learned from this book in support of the design curricula they have pursued so intensively.

The CD-ROM enclosed in this text allows users to further develop their writing skills. Throughout the text there are references to the CD-ROM indicated by this icon (◎). This icon alerts users to the material that is presented on the CD-ROM including forms, documents, reports, discussion questions, and exercises. Users can input their answers to questions and exercises electronically and create their own personalized documents. There is also an annotated "Webography" of helpful links for interior designers and additional examples of professional writing.

Acknowledgments

Many people have helped with the creation of *Writing for Interior Design*, its instructor's guide, and its CD-ROM, as the project grew from its origins in a syllabus and an inch-and-a-half thick handout packet. I would particularly like to thank Dr. Gary Stephens, Dr. Katherine Williams, and Dr. Catherine Bernard of the New York Institute of Technology (Manhattan Campus), who created the space for my interest in this subject matter to grow. Special thanks for their help with the development of the manuscript are due to Dan Beert, Gail Cain, Bob and Ursula Garrett, Geraldine C. Pontius, and Cynthia Rock.

The book would not have come into being without the faith, skill, and vision of my development editor and friend, Sylvia Weber, or the resourcefulness, conceptual ability, and courage of the late acquiring editor Mary McGarry, who remains a source of inspiration to all who knew her. I am grateful to Olga Kontzias, executive editor, for backing this project from the initial proposal to publication and to the other members of the Fairchild staff whose contributions are evident in the final product: Elizabeth Marotta, associate production editor; Barbara Chernow, editorial services; Adam Bohannon, art director; and Priscilla Taguer, director of production; and Sheila Friedling, copy editor.

The following reviewers of the proposal and manuscript, selected by the publisher, provided helpful suggestions for which I am grateful: Katherine Ankerson, University of Nebraska—Lincoln; Ann Black, University of Cincinnati; Allen Fannin, Syracuse University; Thomas Houser, University of Georgia; Robert Paul Meden, Marymount University; LuAnn Nissen, University of Nevada—Reno; Jill Pable, California State University,

Sacramento; Suzanne Scott, University of Wisconsin, Madison; and Susan Slotkis, Fashion Institute of Technology.

Above all, I would like to thank my husband, Peter Martin, not only for his patience and encouragement during the gestation and writing of this book, but for the benefit of his 30 years of experience with and insight into the world in which interior design projects are actualized.

Patricia Eakins

Audience and Writing Style

Many art lovers cherish the late work of Claude Monet. The French Impressionist's paintings of the water lilies in his pond at Giverny are lush, dreamy, and profoundly spiritual even in reproduction, the means by which many of us know them. If you have never seen the actual paintings, you might be astonished at their dimensions. Each takes up an entire large wall at the Orangerie, in Paris, or at the Museum of Fine Arts in Boston. If a two-inch-square detail adapted from a reproduction of one of the water-lily paintings is accompanied by a note on scale and size, then you as viewer will find it easier to imagine what the actual painting might look like. You might find it even easier to "see" the painting in your mind's eye if the reproduction is accompanied by textual notes containing information such as the title of the painting, the date, some biographical data on Claude Monet, and a quotation from Monet that conveys his artistic philosophy. Not only paintings like Monet's but other kinds of art and design mean more to viewers if they are supported by appropriate textual information. Like other visual arts professionals, interior designers use texts to clarify concepts and explain how to execute them.

Novice interior designers may not think of themselves as natural writers—"I'm a visual person"—but they soon understand that professional practice will involve them in communication with a great many people regarding residential, commercial, corporate, and institutional interiors (Figure 1.1). They will be communicating with

- clients and users of project premises.
- vendors.
- contractors and fabricators.
- collaborating professionals.
- other interior designers.
- members of the press.
- the public-at-large.

Of course, much of what designers have to say is communicated with visual materials, including drawings, photos, boards, and models. These visual materials are supported by a wide variety of written materials, including

Figure 1.1
Interior designers
must communicate
with many
audiences.

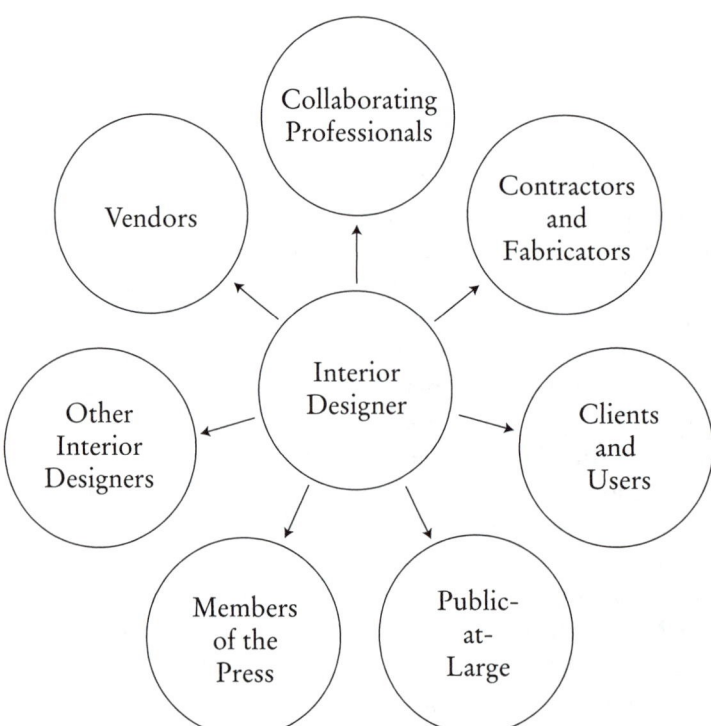

concept statements, project descriptions, press releases, proposals, letters of interest, specifications, and client profiles. Many of these *genres*, or types of writing, are associated with the complex process of getting work. This process can be very competitive for interior designers, arguably more so than for other professionals such as lawyers and doctors. The need to compete puts designers in the position of subtly promoting themselves. Their language imbues their visual concepts with value and meaning so that prospective clients may better understand the domains that have been or could be created for them. Ideally, a designer's language will help clients to know, as Charles Moore has put it, "where they are and by extension who they are."[1] Quite a tall order, especially when you take into account that interior designers also need to spell out precisely for contractors and vendors what is required to execute a given project.

Professional writing for interior designers combines aspects of business writing, advertising, publicity, technical writing, and art-critical writing, the exact mix depending on the purpose to which the writing is to be put. For instance, a proposal may combine strategies of business writing, advertising, and technical writing, while a concept statement may combine strategies of technical writing, advertising, and art-critical writing. Whatever the purpose of a piece of writing, you as a writing interior designer will need to think about the best way to reach a given audience. For an audience of contractors, fabricators, or engineers you will employ the factual, number-based style of specification writing. For an audience composed of prospective clients, you will employ a vivid, figurative style that is suitable for sales and publicity. Although your audience is not usually present at the moment of writing, your sense of its presence affects every writing decision you make. Later in the chapter we look at some style rules that govern all good professional writing. For now, we focus on how your sense of who you are writing for changes the way you write.

Discovering Your Audience

To define the audience for a piece of writing in a meaningful way, it is helpful to ask yourself four basic questions:

- Who will read what I have written?
- What do my readers know about my subject?
- What is the social relationship between my audience and me?
- What is the reading style of my audience?

Who Will Read What I Have Written?

You need to ask not only who your **primary readers** are, but who your **secondary readers** are. For instance, you may be writing a letter proposal with its primary recipient in mind. Suppose that recipient is Hartley Jones, the owner of Hartley's, a restaurant for which your firm would like to be selected to design a new interior. Hartley Jones has taken several restaurants through the renovation process. He is familiar with the technical language of renovation professionals. Moreover, he is a native speaker of American English. You may speak to him in a manner that takes for granted his knowledge of terms such as "coefficient of friction," an important technical standard used in the specification of ceramic flooring tile.[2] However, your proposal will also be read by the proposal's secondary recipient, Zilenka Jones, a recent immigrant from Central Europe. Although she is a bright, capable woman, a computer-graphics artist with a well-developed eye, she has not yet learned to speak English fluently. Her vocabulary is small; apart from the language of computer graphics it is composed mostly of everyday words. Certainly she is unfamiliar with the technical language of renovation professionals.

Since Zilenka's reception of your proposal will influence Hartley's decisions, you may decide to use simpler terminology than *coefficient of friction* in your proposal. You may explain in greater detail than if your only reader were Hartley. He may know that the coefficient of friction is "the ratio of force that maintains contact between an object and a surface and the frictional force that resists the motion of the object."[3] Yet he is unlikely to mind if your proposal states that one tile (with a high coefficient of friction) is less slippery than another (with a low coefficient). Both Joneses will understand that very well!

What Do My Readers Know about My Subject?

The knowledge level of a particular audience may be high in general; yet it is possible that this same audience will be unfamiliar with the subject matter you are presenting. A good example is provided by a legendary oral interaction between a kitchen designer and a client, an affable, intelligent, and very wealthy man whom we will call "Mr. Ridley." As the project—a new kitchen for Mr. Ridley's enormous "summer cottage"—neared completion, it was time to select the finish hardware. "So, Mr. Ridley," said the kitchen designer, "what kind of hinges would you like for your kitchen cabinets?" "What's a hinge?" Ridley replied.

Mr. Ridley may have known a great deal about wines, paintings, fine French food, custom-tailored suits, and the capital markets of Europe, Asia, and the United States. He may have spoken five languages, traveled around the world several times, run a huge corporation, and sat on the boards of museums, foundations, libraries, and charitable organizations. However, he did not know that a *hinge* is a joint that holds two parts together so that one can swing relative to the other. Surely, you may say, he had lived in houses and apartments and worked in offices with doors and cabinets! Indeed, he had, but he had never had any reason to notice the hinges. After all, he never had to oil them if they squeaked! He may never have cooked a meal in any of his kitchens or put away clothes in the closets of any of his bedrooms.

If your audience knows a term or a concept, then it is appropriate to simply present it. For a less knowledgeable audience, it will be necessary to define terms and explain concepts. You may also compare unfamiliar concepts to familiar ones to provide a bridge of understanding. When in doubt, err in the direction of clarification and explanation, but do not routinely tell people more than they need to know.

Explain if you need to, but do not tell people more than they need to know.

What Is the Social Relationship Between My Audience and Me?

Pieces of writing demonstrate a variety of social relationships between writers and audiences. For instance, writing that is directed at an audience of peers may use the language of design and related professions, confident that peer readers will know the meanings of words like *hinge*. Specifications, with their highly controlled meaning and their *imperative*, or command, mode are directed at those who execute design projects. And the graceful, more nuanced tone of concept statements is created to enrich the understanding of clients who commission interior design for various projects and purposes. If you are writing to strangers, your style will be more formal than if you are writing to friends or acquaintances. Social relationship, then, powerfully determines an interior designer's written style.

What Is the Reading Style of My Audience?

In addition to social relationships, a designer as writer must consider the variety of strategies that readers use to assimilate information. Most people use different reading styles at different times, and sometimes readers switch styles within one reading session. Some common reading styles are:

- *Skimming* Reading lightly and quickly to get the main points.
- *Scanning* Reading quickly to find particular information.
- *Searching* Scanning and focusing, in alternation.
- *Receptive Reading* Careful perusal for thorough understanding.
- *Critical Reading* Reading and weighing and musing, so as to evaluate.

For readers who are scanning, skimming, or searching, it is wise to state your purpose for writing very directly, to place clear headings and solid topic sentences at the beginning of paragraphs, to highlight what is important, and to put details into lists. Even receptive, critical readers will appreciate your keeping key words consistent and your use of standard terminology. These more careful readers, however, are willing and able to grasp more elaborate organization, richer detail, and more nuanced presentation of concepts.

Gearing Your Style to Your Audience

Your perception of your audience will determine the tone, style, and syntax of your writing. As you move from your notes and first rough draft to more polished drafts, you will express your sense of audience through decisions about such elements of writing as sentence structure and length, vocabulary, formatting, degree of formality, and level of detail.

Sentence Structure and Length

Depending on the audience, most good professional writing uses a combination of the three basic sentence types: *simple sentence*, *compound sentence*, and *complex sentence*. Good professional writing also uses a mixture of *loose* and *periodic* sentences varied by the occasional *insertion sentence*.

SIMPLE SENTENCES

A sentence may be elegant and lengthy, with multiple subjects, verbs, and modifiers, yet still be a "simple" sentence in grammatical terms if it contains only one *clause*, or subject/verb unit. A good example is the following sentence[4]:

> Underlying *values* and operational *structures* often <u>lie</u> hidden beneath any workplace design.

This simple sentence has a compound subject, *values* and *structures*. It is a simple sentence because it has only one clause. The verb portion of the sentence could also be compounded without changing the "simple" structure of the sentence, for example:

> Underlying *values* and operational *structures* often <u>lie</u> hidden but <u>remain</u> potent beneath any workplace design.

In this altered example, the sentence has two verbs, *lie* and *remain*. Numerous modifiers might also be added to lengthen the sentence without altering the basic simple structure, although the result might be an unnecessarily wordy sentence:

> Complex underlying *values* and intricate operational *structures* often <u>lie</u> completely hidden beneath a seemingly simple workplace design.

Sometimes it is possible—and usually it is desirable—to state complex ideas in simple sentences so that readers are not distracted while they are digesting difficult ideas. Although simple sentences are the easiest for all readers to understand, too many short, simple sentences create a choppy "Dick and Jane" effect. Words of transition may vary the pace and suggest relationships between short sentences. However, it is often better to combine them into compound or complex sentences.

COMPOUND SENTENCES

The compound sentence structure combines two or more *independent clauses*, that is, clauses that could stand alone as simple sentences. Typically the clauses are joined by commas and by conjunctions such as *and*, *but*, *or*, or *nor*. The result is a sentence order that resembles the patterns of ordinary speech. Readers tend to assume that the clauses in a compound sentence are of equal importance. A well-balanced compound sentence contains clauses of similar length and construction, as you can see from the following example[5]:

> Second, her "real" *experience* of the space completely <u>contradicted</u> her "mind's eye" experience, and this *dissonance* <u>made</u> for a very strong, memorable experience.

This sentence contains two clauses joined by the coordinating conjunction *and*, which is preceded by a comma. The subject of the first clause is *experience*, and its verb is *contradicted*. The subject of the second clause is *dissonance*, and its verb is *made*. The two clauses are similar in weight and structure.

Like simple sentences, compound sentences are easy for most people to understand, although their overuse can create a monotonous texture and a singsong rhythm.

COMPLEX SENTENCES

To emphasize the meaning of one clause relative to that of another, a complex sentence subordinates at least one dependent clause (which cannot stand alone) to an independent clause (which can stand alone). Often this is accomplished by having the dependent clause—the one carrying the less important idea—follow a subordinating conjunction such as *when*, *where*, *while*, or *though*.

> When *it* is used systematically, *design* becomes part of the root mechanism for healthy organizational growth and change.[6]

In this example, the main idea is that design can be part of the mechanism for organizational change. The less important idea is the caveat that design must be used systematically to effect change. Complex sentences are suitable for communicating subtle relationships between ideas, or for considering different aspects of an issue. Subordinating some thoughts to others makes your sentences more varied and thus more interesting. It is usually better to put the subordinate clause at the beginning of the sentence, followed by a comma, rather than at the end, although end placement is also possible and is sometimes desirable.

> *Design* becomes part of the root mechanism for healthy organizational growth and change when *it* is used systematically.

Note that no comma comes before a subordinate clause at the end of a sentence.

Complex sentences impart conciseness and rich texture to professional writing, although their overuse turns prose into a dense, impenetrable thicket. Readers may choose not to hack through such a thicket. That is why good writing contains a mixture of simple, compound, and complex sentences. It also contains a mixture of "loose" and "periodic" sentences. The distinction between these two sentence types has to do with whether the major point is presented at the front of the sentence or reserved for the end.

LOOSE SENTENCES

The major point is made near the beginning of a loose sentence and then developed and modified by phrases and clauses. "Loose" does not mean poorly written or lacking in structure. Rather, the term *loose* refers to the relaxed, seemingly natural feel of this sentence order. Those qualities are evident in the following example[7]:

> And *students* throughout this country soon learn to converse comfortably in the arcane but richly fascinating language of architecture that has developed over the centuries.

The subject of this sentence is *students*; the verb is *learn*. The object of the verb—what the students learn—is *to converse comfortably*. Thus, the main idea of this loose sentence is asserted at its beginning. Everything that follows is a *modifier*, a word or phrase that describes a subject or verb.

PERIODIC SENTENCES

By positioning subordinate ideas or modifiers at the beginning of a sentence, a periodic structure reserves the main idea for the sentence's end, thus creating dramatic tension that rises to a climax. The sentence in the following example is periodic.[8]

> By reconstructing a design project from multiple perspectives, this *method* <u>can expose</u> much about the creative process.

Notice that the long prepositional phrase comes at the beginning of the sentence and that the main idea is expressed toward the end. Periodic sentences lend excitement to professional prose style, although your writing would seem to be stilted and artificial if all your sentences were periodic. Good writing usually contains a combination of loose and periodic sentences. Another way to impart variety and interest is through "insertion sentences."

INSERTION SENTENCES

Sometimes a writer alters the normal order of a sentence by inserting a phrase or even a clause where a reader may not expect it.

> The firm was aware of success stories from other fields—such as the Volkswagen Beetle—as well as gaps in the status quo.[9]

Insertion sentences impart a refreshing authenticity to a designer's professional writing, since they seem to spring from the wells of spontaneity that generate creativity in design itself. They can keep readers awake, as can a series of long sentences followed by a short one.

As you work with different types of sentences, the decision to use one or another should not be arbitrary. Your aim is to generate supple prose that places emphasis where it makes the most sense. The pace at which ideas are presented should be varied to suit the speed at which a particular audience can receive them. As you revise a piece of professional writing, read it aloud to see if the sentence structure is varied, interesting, and clear. As you read aloud, you can also check whether your vocabulary is appropriate for the particular audience you are addressing.

Vocabulary

You already know that common words like *window* and *door* are more user-friendly than insider words like *fenestration* (the arrangement, proportioning, and design of windows and doors in a building). Many designers believe that insider words like *fenestration* sound professional, even if a phrase like *windows and doors* would be clearer to nonprofessional readers. This is a misguided belief. In general, it is best to write in the plainest, most direct way that conveys your full meaning to an audience, whether that audience is composed of clients, peers, vendors, contractors, or the public (Figure 1.2). In artful simplicity lies true sophistication.

Yet sometimes the most revealing choice is not a word that is familiar to the general public. For instance, the word *mullion* refers to a slender verti-

Figure 1.2
Speak and write in the plainest, most direct way possible.

cal bar or pier forming a division between the panes of windows, doors, or screens. If such a bar or pier is the subject under discussion, then *mullion* is the simplest way to say what you mean, provided your audience will know what you are talking about. The following sentence from the February 2000 issue of *Architecture* uses the word *mullion*:

> [The designer] wraps the corners of the living room with horizontal bands of wood-framed glass and then erodes the corners by removing the mullions, invoking a favorite detail of Frank Lloyd Wright.

Writing for a magazine geared to an audience of peer designers, the writer of this sentence can be reasonably sure that *mullion* is part of readers' vocabularies. If it were not, a definition or a synonym would be in order. Here is a set of examples that shows another designer/writer—this time, an imaginary one—presenting "mullion" or the simplified idea of a mullion in several different ways.

Technical terms not explained:
Special care has been taken with the milling of the mullions.

Technical terms defined or synonyms provided:
Special care has been taken with the *milling* (custom woodwork) of the *mullions*, the slender vertical bars between the *lights*, or panes, of the windows.

Technical terms replaced with simpler language:
Special care has been taken with the custom woodwork, including the slender vertical bars between the windowpanes.

Even when speaking to sophisticated audiences, do not obscure your meaning with *gobbledygook*, or chunks of abstract jargon. No matter how technical your topic, readers appreciate straightforward prose that has not come unmoored from its subject matter. In this excerpt from "Cookie Architecture" by Paul Goldberger, the well-known design critic seems to be chuckling at the tendency of some fellow critics to suspend elaborate interpretation from slender concrete evidence.[10]

Lorna Doone (Nabisco)
Like the Las Vegas casino that is overwhelmed by its sign, image is all in the Lorna Doone. It is a plain, simple cookie (of shortbread, in

fact), but a cookie like all other cookies—except for its sign. The Lorna Doone logo, a four-pointed star with the cookie's name and a pair of fleur-de-lis-like decorations, covers the entire surface of the cookie in low relief. Cleverly, the designers of this cookie have placed the logo so that the points of the star align with the corners of the square, forcing one to pivot the cookie 45 degrees, so that its shape appears instead to be a diamond. It is a superb example of the ordinary made extraordinary.

In this deft, playful *parody*, or humorous imitation of a writing style, Goldberger expresses both admiration for and dismay at the overly abstract vocabulary of much critical writing, a style reflected in the following sentence from a professional journal:

> These visual oscillations result in a spatial ambiguity that is exaggerated by continual changes in the color and intensity of sunlight streaming in from the three window walls.

As readers, how grateful we are to have slogged through the swamp of oscillating ambiguity! At last we find ourselves in the clear, with sunlight streaming in! Perhaps that is the author's point. Such language may be appropriate for academic readers of theoretical bent. But it is hard to conceive of a practical setting in which writing so overblown would be well received. This style is directed at an audience that has the luxury to read slowly. Most readers today are in a hurry, and they appreciate help in rapidly assimilating the gist of a text. Apart from making judicious word choices, you can help your readers with careful formatting.

Formatting

Like most other textbooks, the one you are currently reading is a good introduction to the art of **formatting**, using the resources of your word-processing program to increase the accessibility and visual coherence of a text so that it is easier to read quickly.

Sometimes the simplest formatting is the most effective. For instance, your word-processing program probably includes three type styles—"normal," (also called roman), *italic*, and **bold**—as well as underlining. With these type styles, you can highlight important words, providing clues to the structure of your writing. Your word processor will also create bulleted and numbered lists as well as tables and charts. These are all examples of formatting, as are *heads* and *subheads*, short lines of text set off to indicate what the passages below them are about. Heads may be located within the text itself or in the margins. Either way, they keep readers on track throughout a document and help them find the information they are looking for.

Other formatting resources include:

- *White space* This is the printer's term for the space on each page where no printing appears. You will find it on every printed page, including this one. Frame your text in white space as you would frame a painting, and use white space to separate elements within the page so as to enhance clarity.
- *Margins* Default margins for word-processed text on standard 8$\frac{1}{2}$-by-11-inch pages are an inch at the top and the bottom of a page and an inch-and-a-quarter at the sides. For the body of professional documents, use "ragged right" margins that are not *justified*, or blocked, on the right-hand side. (You can do this in Microsoft Word by choosing "Align Left" on the formatting toolbar, which also offers you other choices less suitable for most professional writing—"Center," "Align Right," and "Justify.")
- *Header or footers* Long documents should have standard headers or footers that list the abbreviated title of the document, the date of its issue, the author, and so forth. (The View menu of Microsoft Word permits you to create headers or footers that will turn up on every page of a document.)
- *Page numbers* Don't use consecutive page numbers in long documents unless you have no plan to update or revise. Instead, number consecutively within sections of the document.[11]

Formatting accommodates readers who skim and scan and makes a report easier to discuss at meetings. ("Let's take a look at the list on page 2.") Formatting can also make a proposal more accessible to negotiators. ("For that amount of money, I'd like a more elegant upholstery fabric than you specified in paragraph 3.21a.")

By laying out clear choices, formatting also makes advertising and promotional materials immediate and punchy. Notice how such data as item number and price are formatted in standard catalog text—usually as separate items below each block of description. The name of the merchandise item may be in boldface type above the description. Such formatting, as in this catalog entry, provides busy customers with easy, rapid access to data that are central to buying decisions.

ST. GERMAIN CHANDELIER (Figure 1.3)

This dramatic iron chandelier is a reproduction of an early eighteenth-century French campaign original (strictly officer's tent caliber). Its nine arms are suspended around a center orb suspended from a pole and chain. Candle lamps with golden shades cast a warm glow. Takes nine candelabra bulbs, up to 60W max. $28^{1}/_{2}"$ diam., $20^{1}/_{4}"$ H.

#6806.0018 - **$749**[12]

Figure 1.3 St. Germain Chandelier. *Courtesy of Restoration Hardware.*

Too much formatting can be annoying to readers and can present a designer/writer in an unsophisticated light. Beware of fancy fonts and cute typographical devices used for their own sake. Your formatting goal is to enhance the reading experience for a particular audience, not to distract your readers from what you are saying.

A fancy font like Forte is a poor choice for most professional writing.
Choose a plain font like Georgia that is easy to read.
Cute typographical devices spell death to your professionalism.

Formality

Like appropriate formatting, the degree of formality apparent in a piece of professional writing can improve the reading experience of its audience. Standard English can be divided into two broad categories of style, the *formal* and the *informal*, and each has appropriate uses for a designer writing in different situations related to professional practice. For example, e-mail to another designer inquiring about the best time to meet for lunch might be relaxed and chatty in tone, while a proposal for a corporate client might be reserved and deliberate. In both cases, the audience for the communication determines the appropriate writing style.

FORMAL WRITING

A formal writing style is impersonal and objective because the subject matter is more important than the writer's personality. Sentences are often intricate because the writer is presenting complex relationships between ideas. If a formal report or other document is directed at an audience of knowledgeable readers, as is the following excerpt, the vocabulary will be precise and specialized. [13]

> This report will evaluate six ceramic floor tiles in terms of the three most important technical standards: surface wear abrasion (PEI), water absorption, and coefficient of friction.

Formal writing does not use contractions such as *isn't* for *is not*, and it does not use *you* to mean *someone or anyone*. In general, formal writing is polished, well organized, and carefully revised and presented. Its audience is usually outside the design firm that has generated it.

Formal does *not* mean larded with buzzwords and clogged with terms in that pompous language spoken by nobody called *business-ese*. Listed below are some buzzwords you can simply do without.[14] In Table 1.1 are some examples of business-ese with their plain English "translations." Sometimes pompous-sounding words are needed to convey a subtlety of meaning; usually they are not.

Buzzwords to Avoid
Bottom line
Businesswise, profitwise, policywise, anythingwise
Expertise
Impact (used as a verb)
Interface
Optimize, maximize, finalize, utilize, prioritize
Viable
Downsize
Ongoing
Hopefully (when you mean "I hope")
Input
Take this opportunity
We wish to inform you
The undersigned

INFORMAL WRITING

Informal writing is a relaxed and conversational style of writing.

> Don't forget to turn off the lights if you're the last person to leave the office at night.

This style is found in personal letters, in most routine office correspondence, including most e-mail, and to a certain extent in this textbook, which may be characterized as semiformal. For instance, it uses *you* to mean someone or anyone but avoids contractions. Informal writing usually relies on familiar vocabulary words. It reads the way people sound when they speak, although it conforms to the conventions of correct grammar. It is more personal in tone than a formal writing style, although some constraints apply. Slang and dialect are not generally acceptable in informal business writing, although they may be used in personal letters and other private communication.[15] Even in a handwritten note posted on the office coffeemaker describing what will happen if people forget to turn off the power when the glass pot is empty, good spelling is important. After all, a client may visit the office for a conference at any time.

Detail

Be precise in your word choices.

In order to communicate clearly as a designer/writer, you will need to choose the right word to express the smallest detail. If you mean *banister*, a railing at the side of a staircase or balcony to prevent people from falling,

POMPOUS	PLAIN ENGLISH
Additional	More
Advance planning	Planning
Affix your signature	Sign
Aid	Help
Ascertain	Find out
At that time	Then
At the present writing	Now
Commence	Start, begin
Currently	Now
Demonstrates	Shows
Detrimental	Harmful
During the time that	While, when
Employ	Use
Encounter difficulty	Find it hard, have trouble
Enumerate	List
Experience has indicated	We have learned
Facilitate	Make easy
Finalize	End, complete, conclude, close
In conjunction with	With
In the event that	If
In the vicinity of	Near
In view of the fact that	Because, since
Indicate	Show
Inform	Tell, say, let know
Kindly advise	Tell me
Make application for	Apply
Participate	Take part
Peruse	Read
Pursuant to	Following
Provide	Send, give
Regarding	About
Similar to	Like
Sufficient	Enough
Subsequent to	After

Table 1.1
Business-ese:
Pompous Words
and Their Plain
English Equivalents

Table adapted from Gail Cain, Keep It Simple Lists, "Good Business Writing: Helpful Hints" (Handout Packet, 1998), 10–14.

then do not say *baluster*, which means "one of a number of closely spaced supports for a railing." In addition to being precise in your word choices, you need to *support* your meanings adequately for each set of readers.

Support is often defined as evidence for the ideas and concepts you are expressing. It may take the form of descriptive data, illustrations, examples, points of argument, or *analysis* (breakdown into parts). In general, support makes an idea that has been expressed seem real and present for the reader. For instance, in a discussion of existing conditions on the premises of a residential project, you might report that the house was shabby. Your supporting evidence for this view might include the following examples:

- Peeling paint on the walls and ceilings
- Torn, stained upholstery on the sofa and chairs
- Worn spots in the carpeting
- Out-of-date kitchen appliances

How much supporting detail is enough? It depends on your audience and the purpose of your writing. The amount given in the list above is plenty for an informal e-mail from one designer to another about the general condition of the Jones house. However, suppose that the Joneses had bought this charming vintage house on a quick visit to your city. They are now busy winding up their affairs in a city many hundreds of miles away, preparing to move to your city. You have been asked to inventory the conditions needing attention in their new house so that you can prepare estimates, solicit the appropriate bids for repairs and renovations, and propose new furnishings and appliances. You might need to create a list by room of all items in the house requiring attention. Even a partial list for any particular room, such as the following, may contain many more details than the previous brief e-mail:

Downstairs Bathroom

- Floor tiles are missing behind the sink.
- The grout in floor and wall tiles needs to be repaired.
- The toilet seat is cracked and needs to be replaced.
- The medicine cabinet mirror is cloudy, and the cabinet shelves have rusted. The entire unit needs to be replaced.
- A crack has opened in the wall to the left of the door. It needs to be filled and spackled.

- The ceiling paint is scaling. It needs skim-coating before re-painting. (If water damage is discovered, a section of sheetrock may need to be replaced.)
- The enamel on the tub and sink is chipped and has slight cracks on the surface.
- The chrome has worn off the faucets and knobs on the sink and in the tub. The valve in the hot-water faucet is faulty, and the faucet drips. All bathroom fixtures need to be replaced.
- The towel bars and shower-curtain rod are corroded. It may be possible to patch these items with chrome paint.
- The sconces and overhead light are outdated and provide insufficient illumination. The right sconce is inoperative. These fixtures need to be replaced, and the wiring may need to be upgraded.
- No key is available for the antique lock on the bathroom door, but the lock imparts an appealing vintage look to the room. It should be supplemented with a bolt.

This inventory of on-site conditions from a preliminary report to an imaginary client might function as the basis of a scope statement for a later proposal. It is detailed, accurate, and informative, but each item is economically phrased. *Detailed* does not mean wordy. A good rule of thumb is: Tell people only what they need to know, but tell them everything they need to know, given the relationship you have with them and the actions you expect them to take as a result of your communication.

Basic Professional Writing Style

Despite the need to communicate in different ways with different audiences, you as a designer need to develop a fluent basic writing style that expresses your sense of professionalism. Whatever your purpose in communicating, you want your writing to convey dignity, mastery, and excellence. What should your basic style be like?

The Importance of Plain English
Most writing experts nowadays agree that professional business writing should be plain, serviceable English, rather than fancy, flowery English that smacks of *affectation*, "the use of language that is more technical, formal, or showy than is necessary to communicate information to the reader."[16] Much of the writing you do as a working interior designer will not be for the

sophisticated members of your profession whose knowledge of cutting-edge concepts and terms you can take for granted. It will be for prospective clients who are lawyers and homemakers, merchants and accountants, physicians and engineers and bureaucrats and marketing executives. Your writing will be incomprehensible to these individuals if you use too many long, abstract words; too much design jargon; or too many stale, old-fashioned business expressions such as "pursuant to your letter of May 5th."

Write mostly short sentences, each containing one main thought.

SHORT SENTENCES

Gail Cain, who teaches business writing at the University of Sioux Falls in South Dakota, suggests that her students "write to express an idea and not to impress your reader."[17] Like Richard C. Wydick, Cain advocates short sentences. As we have seen, some sentences may be simple in structure, some compound, some complex; some sentences may be loose and some periodic. Whatever their structure, Wydick suggests, they should contain, on average, fewer than 25 words apiece. Most sentences, he advises, should contain only one main thought.[18] If you look at the examples of sentence structure discussed earlier in this chapter, you will see that none is longer than 25 words, and each contains only one main idea; yet all convey a dignified professionalism.

According to Edward P. Bailey, Jr., there is "solid scientific underpinning for the plain English movement" that has been transforming the way that people in fields as diverse as banking, insurance, and health care communicate with one another and with clients or customers. For instance, *psycholinguists* (experts who study the psychological basis of language) have learned that "we all take longer to read less familiar words (like *commence*) than familiar ones (like *begin*). The difference is only a few hundred milliseconds in time—but a lot less strain on the short-term memory. . . . The implication? As writers, we can help our readers by preferring ordinary words."[19] And writing in short sentences! (Later in the chapter, you will learn how to check the plainness of your writing with the Fog Index.)

Write like one human being talking to another.

WRITING LIKE TALKING

Plain-language activists suggest that you write the way you talk, even when writing formally. This can be a frightening thought to those who speak in disconnected sentence fragments, ramble on and on, or pepper their speech with "um"s and "aaah"s. But, says Bailey, "if you imagine a reader in front of you, if you imagine you are actually talking on paper to that reader, the words will come out like the best of speaking—and the best of writing too."[20] Even when writing formally, write like one human being talking to another.

You may already be saying to yourself, "That's all right for informal writing, but it will never work for formal writing." If you are like most people, for instance, you use contractions when you speak. Yet, as we have seen, contractions are not appropriate for truly formal writing, with its distant, objective tone. To keep the vigor, spontaneity, clarity, and directness of plain speech in your formal writing, you might want to try a trick with contractions suggested by Edward P. Bailey. Remember, we are much more likely to write in plain, strong English if we use contractions when we write. So if you need to write a document that is formal in tone, but you want it to have the vigor and vivacity of plain English, write the first draft with contractions, then *de-contract*—that is, remove the contractions—in a subsequent draft as needed.[21]

Simple Guidelines

Gail Cain offers these simple guidelines for business and professional writing:

- Use the active, rather than the passive, voice whenever possible. With the active voice, the reader clearly understands *agency*: who is doing what to whom.

  Active I will call you tomorrow.
  Passive You will be called tomorrow.

- Use the present tense whenever possible. The present tense is more direct and vigorous than other tenses, such as the future; if constructed properly, however, other tenses are, of course, grammatically correct.

  Present Weber Design serves clients' needs.
  Future Weber Design will serve clients' needs.

- Never be afraid of a little humor, but avoid sarcasm and jokes.
- Write complete sentences, rather than fragments. A complete sentence needs a subject and a verb.
  - *Clients* expect.
  - *Designers* deliver.
  - *Contractors* perform.
- Place descriptive words or phrases next to what they describe.
  - *OK* The red room in back is for the boys.
  - *NOT OK* The room in the back which is red is for the boys.
- Place participles near what they describe.
  - *OK* I found the client's letter hidden in his in-basket.
  - *NOT OK* Hidden in his in-basket, I found the client's letter. (Why were you hiding in the client's in-basket?)

- Do not start sentences with numerals. Spell out numbers at the beginning of a sentence.
  - *OK*   On order are 12 Knoll chairs.
  - *ALSO OK*   Twelve Knoll chairs are on order.
  - *NOT OK*   12 Knoll chairs are on order.
- In general, write numbers from zero to ten as words and numbers above ten as figures: one plank, ten planks, 12 planks.
- Place a comma between the day and the year in a date. If the date consists only of a month and a year, no comma is necessary.
  - May 17, 2004
  - May 2004
- Do not hide verbs in long nouns. The verb is the engine of any sentence. Long nouns that end in *-ire*, *-sion*, *-tion*, *-ment*, *-ence*, *-ance*, or *-al* hide the power of verbs. Use the <u>verb itself</u>; not an enclosing noun.
  - *OK*   Consider
  - *NOT OK*   Give consideration to
  - *OK*   Conclude
  - *NOT OK*   Come to the conclusion that
- About 50 percent of the world's population is female. Avoid the use of *he* to mean *someone* or *anyone*. To de-masculinize your writing:
  - Make the subject plural: "Fabricators should. . . ."
  - Write in the command voice: "Wax the countertop. . . ."
  - Replace a pronoun with a noun: "The engineer" rather than "he."
  - Replace *he* with *he or she* or *she or he*.
- Use parallel structure for ideas similar in content and function. This helps the reader recognize the pertinent similarities.[22]
  - *OK*   The contractor will need to sand, polyurethane, and wax the floors.
  - *NOT OK*   The contractor will need to sand, polyurethane, and then the floors should be waxed.

More Advanced Guidelines

As designer writers dealing with complex subject matter, you will need to be aware of complicated writing problems. Important pitfalls to avoid are *nested modifiers*, *elegant variation*, *crutch words*, *empty adverbs*, *telling*, and *fog*.

NESTED MODIFIERS

Savvy writers avoid nested modifiers—piled-up descriptors—because they make it hard for readers to keep track of the sentence's meaning.

> The shiny marble counters in the kitchen, which is painted with high-gloss Benjamin Moore paint, an excellent paint for this application, in Bridal White, a pinkish tint that imparts a warm, suffusing glow, create glare.

The best remedy for a sentence like this is to break it into several sentences that make it easier for readers to track meanings:

> The kitchen is painted with high-gloss Benjamin Moore paint, which is an excellent paint for this application. The color is Bridal White, a pinkish tint that imparts a warm, suffusing glow. Unfortunately, the shiny marble counters create glare.

ELEGANT VARIATION

So-called elegant variation usually occurs when a writer mistakenly believes that it would sound moronic to use the same word for a concept just mentioned. Elegant variation can result in fuzzy sentences like the following:

> The <u>entry</u> to the office suite is dominated by a pair of marble urns that mark the <u>entranceway</u> as an important point of <u>ingress</u> to a powerful financial-services organization.

A reader assumes that a shift in terms signals a shift in meaning. Yet, in this example, the synonyms *entry*, *entranceway*, and *ingress* are used simply to provide elegant variation. The meaning has not shifted, although it takes the reader a moment to realize this. If the writer keeps terms constant—particularly key terms—the meaning will be revealed to the reader without delay. Rewriting a problem sentence will usually clarify meaning:

> The entry to the office suite is dominated by a pair of marble urns that mark the entry as the threshold of a powerful financial-services organization.

Note that one of the synonyms—*ingress*—has been replaced by a word with a slightly different meaning—*threshold*. "Do not be afraid to repeat a word," says Wydick, "if it is the *right* word and if repeating it will avoid confusion."[23] (Of course, you could also replace the second *entry* with the pronoun *it*.)

CRUTCH WORDS

While it is sensible to repeat key terms, you should not lean on crutch words.[24] If the entry to the office suite is <u>dominated</u> by a pair of marble urns, the wall behind the receptionist's desk should not be <u>dominated</u> by an aluminum casting of the corporate logo while the president's office is <u>dominated</u> by his ten-foot mahogany desk.

EMPTY ADVERBS

In conversation, we use adverbs to lend our words instant emphasis: "The Egyptian wing at the Metropolitan Museum of Art in New York is *totally* fabulous." In writing, a flavorless adverb like *totally* will strike readers as inauthentic, immature, and unprofessional. Former *San Francisco Chronicle* book editor Pat Holt[25] elaborates usefully:

> *Actually, totally, absolutely, completely, continually, constantly, continuously, literally, really, unfortunately, ironically, incredibly, hopefully, finally*—these and others are words that promise emphasis, but too often they do the reverse. They suck the meaning out of every sentence.

If you remove *totally* and say "The Egyptian wing of the Metropolitan Museum of Art in New York is fabulous," your point is sharper. If you find a richer way to reveal the impact of the Egyptian Wing, your point is even sharper.

TELLING

Fabulous is one of the many bossy words that dictate what we are to make of an experience without letting on why. They *tell* rather than *show*. In the following example, Pat Holt again elaborates usefully[26]:

> *Handsome, attractive, momentous, embarrassing, fabulous, powerful, hilarious, stupid, fascinating* are all words that "tell" us in an arbitrary way what to think. They don't reveal, don't open up, don't describe in specifics what is unique to the person or event described.

It is not enough to assert the value of an experience; you must demonstrate it. To get your *readers* to conclude that, "the Egyptian Wing must be fabulous," you need to re-create your experience of it. Were you awed by its sheer scope? If so, you need to demonstrate scope, as in the following description[27]:

> The Metropolitan Museum of Art in New York City has one of the best collections of ancient Egyptian art outside Cairo. It contains 36,000 pieces dating from the Paleolithic to the Roman period (300,000 B.C–A.D. Fourth Century). In thirty-two major galleries and eight study galleries, the collection displays the "aesthetic values, history, religious beliefs, and daily life of the ancient Egyptians over the entire course of their civilization."

The more your writing *shows*, rather than tells, the more convincing it will be. According to Pat Holt, "the difference between telling and showing usually boils down to the physical senses. Visual, aural, aromatic words . . . place us in the scene you've created."[28] A collection of facts about the Egyptian wing may be impressive, but to truly engage readers, you need to place them on the scene so they can see what you saw. Here is my own visual impression of a particular work of art in the Metropolitan Museum's Egyptian collection (Figure 1.4):

> The soft but accurate outlines of the little "river horse" convey both hippo-ness and the sweet character of an individual creature known to generations of museum-goers as William. His azure coloring suggests

Figure 1.4
Statuette of a hippopotamus, from the ancient Egyptian art collection of the Metropolitan Museum of Art, New York.
Courtesy of The Metropolitan Museum of Art, Gift of Edward S. Harkness, 1917. Reprinted with permission.

that he is one with his world of water and sky. His small eyes appear relaxed, and his barely visible smile is subtle.

The nineteenth-century critic Ruskin observed that an arts writer begins with the study of the smallest things,[29] such as William's smile. The same might be said of a writer designer, who must cultivate a style that makes full use of the sensory experience revealed in particulars. (In Chapter 2, we look more closely at what it means to write from the senses, particularly the visual sense.)

To show, not tell, write from the senses.

FOG

If you are writing from the senses, you are probably using short words. The long buzzwords listed earlier in this chapter do not describe anything we can see, hear, smell, taste, or feel. Sometimes we need to use words of three or more syllables to describe complex interactions or ideas, but short words are usually clearer. The further your writing gets from the sensory experience of people living in the world, the foggier it will seem to your readers. You can check the clarity of your writing by applying to it the Fog Index[30]:

1. Choose a 100-word passage.
2. Count the words with three or more syllables.
3. Calculate the average number of words in a sentence. (You can do this by counting and noting the number of words in each sentence. Add these numbers and divide the total by the number of sentences to arrive at the average number of words.)
4. Add together the results of the operations performed in steps 2 and 3.
5. Multiply your total by 0.4.
6. The result is your Fog Index.

Writing with a high Fog Index requires many years of education to understand, based on a one-to-one ratio. Thus, a Fog Index of thirty-two would require thirty-two years of schooling to understand! The wise writer-designer will opt for the lowest appropriate Fog Index, even when writing for highly literate professionals. It is a mistake to choose long words because they sound more "educated." If your writing is foggy, replace some of the long words with shorter ones and break up unnecessarily long sentences.[31] Your best-educated readers will appreciate the sophistication of artful simplicity—but your simplicity must be selective.

The Importance of Rich Punctuation

Most plain-English advocates do not believe that punctuation should be simplified. That is because punctuation functions in the same way as traffic signage. It is not really enough to have only two signs, "Stop" and "Right Lane Merges." Traffic signs are also needed to indicate a great many other complex, subtle, and urgent contingencies—for instance, "No Left Turn," "Railroad Crossing," "S Curve Ahead," or "Yield." In the same way, you cannot convey every possible written meaning if you limit yourself to, say, the period and the comma. You also need question marks, colons, dashes, and semicolons, not to mention brackets and parentheses.

Punctuation marks, taken as a whole, form a punctuation system that has a *syntactic* basis—that is, it uses punctuation marks as guides to the grammatical arrangement of words in a sentence. By clarifying syntax, punctuation also clarifies meaning. Since "shifts in syntax tend to coincide with pauses for emphasis or for breath in oral delivery . . . modern punctuation . . . tends to reflect the patterns and rhythms of speech."[32] It therefore makes writing more reader-friendly.

Some people think that knowing punctuation means knowing where to put it in a piece of finished writing—rather like the frosting on an already baked cake. However, for a person who is adept at punctuation, explains Edward P. Bailey, "the words come out differently than for someone who is not"[33]

> People who understand commas, semicolons, periods—and especially colons, dashes, and question marks—produce entirely different sentence structures from people who are not good at punctuation. . . . The result? Better sentences that have the emphasis—and the ideas—in just the right places.

This short introductory guide to professional writing is not the place for a comprehensive review of all the rules governing the use of the various punctuation marks. A good way to learn about them is to build a library of reference books that will help you answer the multitude of questions that may arise about punctuation, grammar, syntax, and writing style.

The following list of reference books should help to get you started[34]:

The American Heritage Dictionary of the English Language, 4th ed. Boston: Houghton Mifflin, 2000. (Available in CD-ROM as well as print format.)

Bernstein, Theodore M., *The Careful Writer: A Modern Guide to English Usage*. New York: Athenaeum, 1977.

The *Chicago Manual of Style*, 15th ed. Chicago: University of Chicago Press, 2003.

Follett, Wilson, and Erik Wensberg. *Modern American Usage: A Guide*, rev. ed. New York: Hill & Wang, 1998.

Fowler, Henry W., *Fowler's Modern English Usage* (Oxford Language Classics Series). London and New York: Oxford University Press, 2003.

Howell, John Bruce. Style Manuals of the English-Speaking World: Guide. Phoenix: Oryx Press, 1983.

The New Oxford American Dictionary. New York and London: Oxford University Press, 2001. (Available with or without CD-ROM.)

Sutcliffe, Andrea, *The New York Public Library Writer's Guide to Style and Usage*. New York: HarperResource, 1994.

The Oxford English Dictionary. 2nd ed. 20 vols. Ed. J. A. Simpson and Edmund S. Weiner. London and New York: Oxford University Press, 1989. (Also available as CD-ROM, edited by John A. Simpson.)

Roget International Thesaurus. 6th ed. Ed. Barbara Ann Kipfer. New York: HarperCollins, 2001. [Dictionary of synonyms.]

Skillin, Marjorie E., and Robert M. Gay. *Words into Type*. 3rd ed. Boston: Pearson PTP, 1974.

Strunk, William, Jr., and E. B. White. *The Elements of Style*, 4th ed. Boston: Pearson Longman, 2000.

Webster's Third New International Dictionary, Unabridged. 3rd ed. Springfield, Mass.: G. & C. Merriam Co., 2002. (Available with CD-ROM.)

If you prefer online dictionaries, you can "own" several useful ones for a small fee. Some good ones are found at:

- www.gurunet.com (Check out the free trial download)
- www.xrefer.com
- www.m-w.com/home.htm (Merriam-Webster online)
- www.bartleby.com (American Heritage Dictionary)

Available for free is a very useful online thesauraus:
http://www.visualthesauraus.com/online/index.html.

Proofread, Proofread, Proofread

Familiarizing yourself with these books and Web sites and others like them will take time, but of course nobody reads them straight through. They are reference publications in which you can clarify any confusion you may have about comma use or whether to call your physician-clients *M.D.s* or *MDs*. These publications are not a replacement for thorough proofreading. Neither is a spellchecker.

By all means, run your spellchecker and your grammar checker on every piece of writing you create in your word-processing program. Some errors are picked up by the checkers, which catch many common misspellings, many duplicate words (*the the*), many overly long sentences, most passive constructions, and the like. However, if you said *its* when you meant *it's*, your checkers may not tell you—or they may alert you to the possibility of an error when you have not in fact made one.

Some grammar checkers do not check for so-called "expletive constructions," those namby-pamby sentences beginning with *there is*, *there are*, or *here is*. Instead, you can do a simple search for *there* with the "find" function of your word processor—and another for *here*. Then it's "a matter of eliminating the expletive construction and . . . saying something useful about the real subject of the sentence."[35]

Avoid expletive constructions.

You need to supplement your computer's proofreading capacities with your own skills and those of a friend whose eye you trust. Above all, root out the bloopers that could make clients question your literacy, your maturity, and your professionalism: sentence fragments, run-together sentences, agreement problems (subject/verb, pronoun/antecedent), and consistency problems with pronouns and verb tense. You might also try reading your writing into a tape recorder, then playing it back to yourself. "Your ears will catch clumsy phrasing and botched sentences before your eyes will."[36] You may not think of yourself as a "natural writer," but over time if you are careful about the shapeliness of sentences, paragraphs, and whole texts, you will find that writing becomes a well-developed skill that you can take pleasure in—not the least because it provides such strong support for your work as an interior designer.

Root out bloopers.

Discussion Questions

1. Is the "plain-English movement" a bane or a blessing for interior designers and others who need to present themselves in a professional manner? How so?

2. How can a designer who is a visual person and loathes writing best function as a professional in a world that requires writing as a support for design work proper?

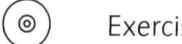 Exercises

1. Conduct brief telephone interviews to ascertain the reading styles of three individuals among your acquaintance whom you have identified as prospective design clients. One may be a family member or friend; one should be an executive or administrator in a corporation, institution, or government agency; the third should be a professional or small-business owner. Prepare a one-minute informal class presentation that summarizes what you learned from these interviews. When everyone in your class has made a similar presentation, discuss as a class-sized group what you learned from the data you collected in the full group of interviews.

2. Find an article in a design magazine or a book about design that contains highly technical language that is unsuitable for a general audience. Rewrite two paragraphs of it so as to render the prose intelligible for ordinary readers.

3. Obtain a specification sheet for a floor covering such as nylon carpet or vinyl asbestos tile (VAT). In no more than three paragraphs, explain the virtues of your floor covering in a direct and personal manner, using contractions to provide conversational directness. Write as if you were talking to an actual client prospect whom you are picturing in your mind. Then de-contract, removing contractions and making any other adjustments needed to turn your first draft into more formal English.

4. Interview a child about the features she would like to see in her dream bedroom. Then translate three of these features into actual specifications that would be clear to a vendor, fabricator, or contractor. For instance, you might write (or find) specifications for a window treatment, a wallpaper, and a carpet.

5. Bring in a published piece of writing that you consider well formatted. Be prepared to deliver a brief oral report (no more than five minutes) expounding its virtues.

Description: The Basis for Writing about Interiors

2

Description is a picture in words, based on personal observation of the characteristics that identify places, things, persons, or processes. Description of places and things—so-called *spatial description*—is of special interest to interior designers because it is the approach underlying all their marketing efforts. *Spatial description* is made up of images that capture sense impressions: the sound, smell, taste, and feel of the subject, but above all its look. Through carefully selected details, the writing designer can generate not only a record or an impression but a mood, an aura, and a range of meaning.

A description can be a relatively impersonal report on what any eye might see, or it can be more personal, reporting what one very special eye sees. The careful observation techniques that support spatial description can also be used to record data about people and processes, and thus to research existing conditions and client needs and aspirations. They can assist the designer with the actual work of design—particularly in the preprogramming and programming phases.

Description and Images

In the days before photographs were commonplace, description was often highly detailed, in order to bring an unseen reality to life in the mind's eye. It was hard for a writer to describe an architectural interior for readers. Some writers conveyed an intense response to highly decorated interiors by imagining the emotions of the figures depicted in the sculptures, murals, and stained-glass windows sometimes found in interior settings. For example, the nineteenth-century writer Henry Adams evokes the spirit and style of Chartres Cathedral[1] by imagining the emotions of the Mother of Christ (Figure 2.1) to whom this elaborate French Gothic cathedral (Figure 2.2) is dedicated:

> The Queen Mother was as majestic as you like; she was absolute; she could be stern; she was not above being angry; but she was still a woman, who loved grace, beauty, ornament—her . . . robes [and]

Figure 2.1
This image shows the *Virgin and Child Enthroned* from the *Life of Christ* lancet window at Chartres Cathedral. In Henry Adams *Mount Saint Michel and Chartres*, the Virgin is personified in a manner that expresses the spirit of Chartres Cathedral. *Reprinted with permission of Corbis/Dean Conger.*

jewels—who considered the arrangements of her palace with attention, and liked both light and colour. . . . She was extremely sensitive to neglect, to disagreeable impressions, to want of intelligence in her surroundings. . . . This church was built for her in [a] spirit of simple-minded, practical, utilitarian faith—in this singleness of thought, exactly as a little girl sets up a doll-house for her favourite . . . doll. Unless you can go back to your dolls, you are out of place here. If you can go back to them, and get rid for one small hour of the weight of custom, you shall see [the cathedral] in glory.

Figure 2.2
Chartres Cathedral.
Reprinted with permission of Corbis Sygma/Giraud Philippe.

This type of description, in which an object is seen as a fictional character, is no longer common. Yet most readers will be familiar with more recent examples of description filtered through a writer's emotional response. For instance, in the following twentieth-century passage, the description is filtered through the dramatic storytelling personality of that "old master" Frank Lloyd Wright. Here is how he described the interior of the research laboratory he designed for the SC Johnson Wax Company[2] (Figure 2.3).

> So we went up in the air around a giant central stack with floors branching from it, having clear light and space all around each floor. All laboratory space was then clear and in direct connection with a duct-system cast in the hollow reinforced-concrete floors, connecting to the vertical hollow of the stack itself.

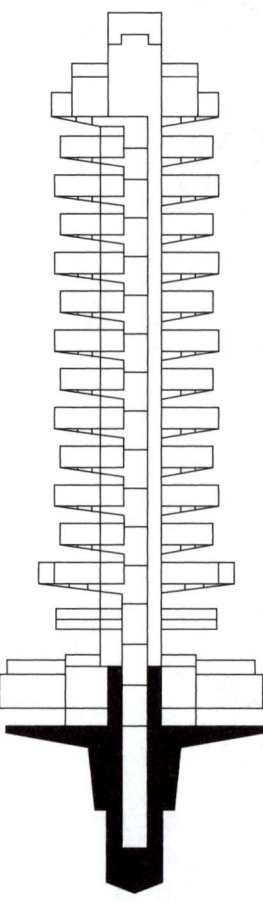

Figure 2.3
This section of the SC Johnson Research Tower shows the floor slabs cantilevered out from the central cove. They look like the branches of a tree. *Reprinted with permission of SC Johnson.*

This seemed to me a natural solution . . . affording all kinds of delightful sunlit, directly related work space. Cantilevered from the giant stack, the floor slabs spread out like tree branches, providing sufficient segregation of departments vertically. Elevator and stairway channels up the central stack link these departments to each other. All utilities and the many intake and exhaust pipes run in their own central utility grooves, arranged like the cellular pattern of the tree trunk.

Wright's "tree" makes the concept and structure of the research laboratory clear to readers; it also ties the design of the building and its interiors to Wright's theories of "organic" design. Thus, he provides a *gloss*, or explanatory comment, on his own creative work—rather like the voice-over in a documentary film. Some designers do not believe that good photos and drawings require any explanation in words. They would have urged Frank Lloyd Wright to let the photographs and drawings speak for themselves.

Yet despite the proverbial wisdom that "one picture is worth a thousand words," pictures do not always speak for themselves. The "duct-system cast in . . . hollow reinforced-concrete floors" that is central to the design of the research laboratory would be invisible in photographs of the finished building. Those who are not professional designers may be unable to interpret drawings and diagrams of the complicated ductwork. In addition, not all members of Wright's audience easily link industrial artifacts like ductwork and concrete floors to the organic notion of a tree. No matter how careful and revealing the drawings and photos generated for any project, they may not be self-explanatory to all the people who need to make decisions based on their understanding of what the images represent. Description such as Wright's can complement and enhance visual imagery, providing a richer and clearer sense of what the images mean.

Description and Vision

The difficulty of seeing the "tree" in Wright's research laboratory points to some fundamental truths about the psychology of seeing. These truths are poignantly explored in nature writer Annie Dillard's remarks on *Space and Sight*, a book by Marius von Senden.[3] Dillard was fascinated by von Senden's writing on the experience of people born blind who suddenly, after corrective surgery, were able to see. But what did they see? A human hand not recognizable as a hand but only as "something bright and then holes." A bunch of grapes seen not as grapes but as "dark, blue and shiny," unsmooth, with "bumps and hollow". The newly sighted people had "no idea of space whatsoever. Form, distance, and size were so many meaningless syllables." One patient confused depth and roundness; another could not figure out how big her mother was, even with the aid of touch. These newly sighted people did not know what to make of the visual information their eyes were taking in. They did not know how to fit the data to labels or names for the data. They saw the world as a "dazzle of color-patches"; and though they named the colors quickly enough, they had a great deal of trouble with the rest of the process called *seeing* that most of us take for granted.

The experience of newly sighted people tells us a lot about how complicated seeing really is. Human eyes are not mirrors that simply reflect what is there. As Nelson Goodman has said, "the eye does not so much mirror as take and make" according to its "needs and prejudices."[4] In large part, we see what corresponds to the ideas of things we already have in our head, although these ideas have at some earlier time been inferred or derived from specific descriptive details. Since ideas about things as well as their physical traits are essential components of the process of seeing, designers must gloss, or interpret, visual imagery with written description and other text to make sure people "get the picture." If they do not already know what they are seeing, they may not know what they are seeing! If we do not tell them what we want them to see, they may see something else.

Tell people what you want them to see so they will not see something else.

You might say that seeing has both an *inductive* and a *deductive* component. The *inductive* part of seeing gathers details and then interprets them, basing ideas on accumulated evidence. The *deductive* part starts with an idea and then looks for evidence to support it. The partnership of these two ways of processing sensory data is built into the complicated act that we call seeing. It is also built into the act of writing about what we see.

The Description Writing Process

In creating a description, you need to respect the natural tension between the "inductive" and "deductive" aspects of vision. You can structure the writing process around this natural tension by observing carefully and taking copious observation notes (inductive), then selecting from the accumulated data what is needed to support the concept(s) you are presenting (deductive). Your concepts may have emerged from your descriptive data or preceded them. For designers, descriptive writing is a process that evolves along with a project.

Respect the tension between the "inductive" and "deductive" aspects of vision.

Beginning with Observation

The goal of a description is to give readers a mental picture of some aspect of reality. To figure out what others need in order to create such a mental picture, the first step is to learn all you can about the subject of the picture. You might begin your description by jotting down notes, free-writing a list of every trait and quality you perceive in the object or objects you are describing. You might jot down your observations of shape, size, materials, color, light, scale, period-style characteristics, and workmanship. As you spend time with your notes and your subject, your observations will become more subtle and more complex. Your first notes toward a description of this book might be something like the following:

- 7 × 9 inches by a certain depth
- Black ink on white pages
- Several different type sizes and fonts
- Many lists and other user-friendly features
- Cover is a certain color, of thicker, shinier paper than the pages
- Contains 12 chapters, an introduction, a certain number of illustrations, an index, and a table of contents

Begin by jotting down notes based on your perceptions.

As you spend more time with the book, examining it from all angles, looking inside as well as out, you will see things you didn't see at first. After a while, your inventory will seem full and rich. It will contain, you might suspect, more than you want to say for any conceivable purpose. So much the better! It's always good for writers to know more than their readers. Your list is a good beginning, but it is not yet a useful description.

Know more than your reader.

Organizing the Description

In order to be coherent, a spatial description needs to be organized according to a principle that corresponds to a path the human eye might take as it passes through or into or around the thing(s) or place(s) you are describing. Some common organizing principles are:

- left to right
- top to bottom (or vice versa)
- outside to inside (or vice versa)
- most important to least important (or vice versa)

When you start writing your first draft, you may want to move from some general statement or definition to particulars. As you begin to write sentences arranging the qualities or traits you have oberved in accordance with the organizing principle you have selected, you can see for yourself how well that principle is working. Your description should move forward steadily, without backtracking. If you need to double back on what you have already written in order to clarify your meaning, then try another principle of organization that permits an unbroken forward momentum.

Keep description
moving forward.

A favorite organizing principle of many interior designers is the *walk-through*, a means of ordering perceptions according to what might be revealed during a stroll through an interior setting. This stroll, or guided tour, begins with entry from the outside and proceeds from there. The walk-through mode accommodates a variety of observations. It also creates a sense of presence in a particular physical space. It allows designers and their clients to imagine living in a newly designed setting that may exist only in *simulation*, that is, as represented in sketch plans and models.

Because a simulation is a possible world, rather than an actual one, the walk-through is not an observation-based description, but an imaginative one that speaks of what living in the space will be like. In the words of Kimberly Dovey, "the aim . . . is to evoke an experience akin to . . . vicarious insideness—the manner in which we experience places secondhand through films, novels, poetry, travel brochures, photographs, and so forth."[5] We might define *vicarious insideness* as the experience of a mental place as if it were a physical reality. It is an experience that may not be available to most readers of plans and other geometric representations, which are created as models of spaces to be constructed. The designer's descriptive language must create the illusion of insideness with rich specifics—detail, detail, detail. It is not enough to say "window." You must give your client an ivy-draped English window of leaded glass or a thermopane picture window that affords a spectacular mountain view.

Let description
create the illusion
of insideness.

The walk-through seems very natural for designers who have been working on their projects 24/7 and in a very real sense have been inhabiting them. Yet the walk-through is not a one-size-fits-all description, suitable for any purpose. Like any other descriptive mode, it has weaknesses as well as strengths. For instance, if it is not combined with another way of organizing descriptive data, it may become repetitious, returning to the subject of, say, floor treatment in each room visited. In truth, no organizing principle will yield a sure-fire outline for creating an all-purpose description. The writer's sense of the purpose of, and audience for, a description helps to create its most economical and coherent structure. You can learn more about how audience affects description by looking at some typical short descriptions geared to different groups of buyers or clients and thus *promotional*—related to sales and publicity—in nature.

Promotional Descriptions

Because the descriptive mode provides a bridge between seeing and saying, it is frequently used to motivate people who may be interested in purchasing design services or a design-related product. Description is therefore found in proposals, letters, brochures, press releases, and most other kinds of writing that a professional design firm is likely to generate. Three typical uses of description to promote enthusiasm, selection, and purchase are found in captions, catalog descriptions, and project descriptions.

Captions

Captions are labels accompanying photos, drawings. and show rooms or museum exhibitions to identify their contents. Captions can direct reader's attention to design elements such as materials, finishes, and structures that cannot be ascertained through direct observation. Captions can also provide important additional information to contextualize what is seen in the image. A canny strategy for effective captioning—or any other description—is to call attention to everything that needs to be included in the mental picture while ignoring what does not. Let us look first at how captions *identify*, *clarify*, and *contextualize* photos and drawings. Then we will switch our focus to captions for show rooms and museum exhibitions.

> Call attention to what needs to be included and ignore what does not.

IDENTIFICATION IN CAPTIONS

Figure 2.4 shows several views of the Gore residence designed by Inscape Studio, accompanied by a *group caption*, that is, one caption for the entire group of photos (color images in Chapter 2 on CD-ROM). The caption reads:

Gore Residence
Adams Morgan, Washington, DC
2001 Residential Renovation
Size: 750 sf

Renovations to this Adams Morgan condo were designed to provide a more open floor plan and add interest to the main spaces. The project was designed to be "green" while keeping in mind a tight budget. The kitchen was opened and reoriented for access to a newly formed living and dining space. These spaces are now oriented around the "clock tower," an orange volume with detailed shelving that contains storage. A small window near the front door provides daylighting and a shelf for keys and wallets. Environmentally friendly features include

Figure 2.4   Gore Residence.
Courtesy of Dan Redmond Photography for Inscape Studio, Architecture + Design

linoleum floors, low-VOC paints, Energy–star rated appliances, and cabinetry with formaldehyde-free cabinetry.

The identity function in the caption is clear: these are pictures of the Gore residence in Washington, D.C. Frequently, photos of different rooms of an interior setting are identified by separate captions, as are any detail photos, but here one caption serves to identify an entire group of closely linked photos. (Professional photographers' credits and copyrights may be written along one side of each photo. See Chapter 11 for more on the designer's use of professional photography.) In addition to serving an identity function, the group caption for the Gore residence provides *clarification* and *contextualization*.

CLARIFICATION IN CAPTIONS

It is sometimes startling to realize how little really is clear from photos and other images. For instance, if the caption for the photos of the Gore residence did not tell you that this is a renovation, how would you know that the photographs do not represent new construction? How would you know the size of the space? It is clear from the largest of the three photos that the floor plan is open (as the caption tells you), but less clear that the kitchen is oriented by access to the living-dining space (which the caption also tells you). You would need to see photos and drawings of the *pre*-renovation space to understand that the floor plan is now "more" open, the living-dining space is "newly formed," and the kitchen has been opened and re-oriented. The caption conveys a sense of the scope of the work in a very economical manner.

CONTEXTUALIZATION IN CAPTIONS

You cannot ascertain from the photos of the Gore residence that the clock tower contains storage space. You can see that the small window provides a shelf—though you might not connect it to keys and wallet. More importantly, you cannot learn from the photo itself that the design is "green" or that it has been completed within a tight budget. Nor could you ascertain that the floors are linoleum, the paints low-VOC, the appliances Energy-star-rated, and the cabinetry made of formaldehyde-free wood. This is not the fault of the photographer. How could anyone photograph "formaldehyde-free"? The images and the caption complement each other to provide a full range of information, written and visual, to anyone looking at pictures and text together. (Note how "open design" and "green design" also serve as organizing concepts.)

A close "reading" of almost any photo and its caption reveals a similar relationship between caption and image, with the caption not only identifying and clarifying, but also providing additional information that contextualizes the images. Shown in Figure 2.5 are a photo and a description of the Kyoto Chair from the online Design Within Reach catalog (www.dwr.com). Without the description that accompanies the photo, you would not be able to tell that the chair is beechwood and available in two finishes, natural or coffee-stained. Nor would you be able to tell, without the caption, that this is a best-selling café chair in Japan and is exclusive to DWR. Nor could you necessarily tell, from looking at the photo, that it has an *unusually* broad back. Some of this information might be conveyed by additional photographs. Yet for this online catalog, the style rule is clearly one photo for each item. In any case, information such as type of wood simply cannot be conveyed by a photo. In order to present to buyers the full range of information needed to reach purchase decisions, a caption needs to supplement the photo.

Figure 2.5
Online Catalog
page for DWR's
Kyoto Chair.
*Courtesy of Design
Within Reach.*

Kyoto Chair

Kyoto Chair
$80

- Add to Order
- Save to My Wish List
- Print this Page
- Email this Page
- Request a swatch

- Best-selling café chair in Japan.
- Solid wood construction.
- Contoured seat for comfort.
- Contract quality.

The Kyoto Chair is so dubbed because it is a best-selling café chair in Japan, a country known for valuing understatement. This clean-looking chair, with its unusual broad back, brings a spare, rustic sensibility to cosmopolitan settings.

Click here to change color.   Click here to enlarge.

coffee   natural

View 6 in Location   View 2 in Detail   View illustration

Material
Natural or coffee-stained beechwood.

Measurements
H 31" D 19" W 15.5" Seat D 15" Seat H 18"

CAPTIONS FOR SHOW ROOMS AND EXHIBITIONS

The captions found on posters or wall placards near show rooms perform the same functions as those that accompany drawings or photos in paper or electronic documents. However, the identification function may be expanded in order to better promote the work of a given design firm. For instance, a caption may provide a brief biography of a designer and an extended description of the work of a firm.

SHOWROOM CAPTIONS

The fixtures, furnishings, and materials used in a showroom may be identified by manufacturer, to give appropriate credit to suppliers with whom a designer has close working relationships. (It is not customary to note the year the design was created unless the showroom re-creates a historic design.)

Usually the promotional purpose of a showroom or showhouse is embedded in a public-spirited and/or educational framework. Accordingly, captions may furnish historical information as part of the viewing context. For instance, beside a period room may be comments on the style of the period and the manner in which it has been interpreted.

EXHIBITION CAPTIONS

A mix of descriptive information similar to that characterizing showroom captions is found in captions near individual display items in a museum setting. These so-called wall captions are replicated or expanded in the catalog created for the exhibition in print or online. The identity function of each caption, or label, may include the dimensions of works displayed, the materials used, and/or the years in which the works were executed. There may be very brief artists' statements, framed as quotations. Because there are often numerous captions in an exhibition, the information in each may be laid out in a list-like manner. The construction of the captions is usually *parallel*—that is, the same kind of information in the same order is listed in each caption, using the same grammatical structure (Figure 2.6).

The tone of description in the individual captions used in a museum setting is customarily quite dry, in keeping with the neutral, educational role of a museum exhibition. (In this kind of writing, avoid promotional adjectives such as "fine" and "excellent" that dictate value.) Because the general public is the audience and each person's time at the exhibition is limited, wall captions, however factual, will not usually be complex or contain highly technical information. The captions in exhibition catalogs may be more elaborate, and the catalog may also contain one or more essays by recognized authorities in appropriate fields that provide insight into the exhibition.

> Use parallel construction in captions.

Group wall captions for an entire exhibition or for a section of the exhibition, known as wall text, may provide a detail-packed overview of a historical period or a design trend. To more actively engage the general public, there is often a strong emphasis on the human factor—with biographical information on important designers or artists featured in the exhibition, a historical overview that emphasizes the role played by these individuals, and a statement of their design or art philosophy. This emphasis is in keeping with a museum show's general mission—to promote the social value of culture and its expression in the various forms on display. An exhibition may also have a more particular mission. For instance, in a flyer for an exhibition of the Targetti Light Art Collection[6] at the Chelsea Art Museum (see Figure 2.6), the mission is stated as follows:

Figure 2.6
Stainless steel,
iron, photograph,
glass, plexiglass,
fluorescent lamps.
*Anne and Patrick
Poirier*, Il sangue
della memoria,
*1999. Courtesy of
Targetti Light Art
Collection,
www.targetti.com.*

ANNE ET PATRICK POIRIER
Born in Marseille in 1941 and in Nantes in 1942, Anne Poirier and Patrick Poirier live and
work in Paris and Trevi (Italy). This piece is dedicated to those who perished in the mass killings
perpetrated in Cambodia between 1970 and 1980. This human drama has not ended and it is
also our responsibility. This red light and this red rose petal must be a memorial to this terrible
episode in the history of the end of the millennium.

The Targetti Light Art is a collection of contemporary artworks commissioned by Targetti, an Italian company based in Florence specialized in architectural lighting, to give tangible form to the expressive potential of artificial light.

Highly specialized museum exhibitions may cater to more limited audiences—for instance, a display of eighteenth-century French wallpapers might be more appealing to an audience of design specialists, historians, and collectors than to the general public. It may be captioned in a more technical manner, with less emphasis on broadly humanistic criteria such as "expressive potential." For additional examples from the Targetti Light Art Collection please see Chapter 2 on the CD-ROM.

Catalog and Ad Descriptions

Like the descriptions found in captions for show rooms or museum exhibitions, descriptions found in commercial catalogs (such as the cut sheet from the Design Within Reach catalog shown in Figure 2.5) are targeted to a specific *audience*, or group of people receiving a communication message. As anyone can discern from the inclusion of price information, a supplier's catalog intends above all to motivate purchase. In the field of interior design, catalog and other promotional description are usually geared either to *retail clients*—consumers—or to *design professionals*, who will specify products for projects.

FOR THE RETAIL CLIENT

Catalog and ad writing for the retail client puts itself in the client's shoes, anticipating the most likely uses of the product. The writer's task resembles a salesperson's, taking the reader on a guided tour, pointing out interesting and appealing features—a process known as "hand selling." However, it is not enough to enumerate the features of a design. The caption writer also needs to make clear the benefits those features offer to the client. For instance, the DWR caption shown in Figure 2.5 contains the following sentence: "This clean-looking chair, with its unusual broad back, brings a spare, rustic sensibility to cosmopolitan settings." The description mentions not only a feature—"clean-looking"—but a benefit—"brings a spare, rustic sensibility to cosmopolitan settings." If you look at the descriptions in any retail catalog, you are likely to see this feature/benefit rhetoric. You may also find it useful to explain the benefits of features when presenting your own design proposals to clients.

A further notable characteristic of the DWR description is its chatty but subtly elevated tone. The fancy flourish of "the Kyoto Chair is so dubbed" sounds like a genial college professor. One can almost "hear" his bow tie! A *persona*—a fictional character similar to those in plays—is created of an authority who wears learning lightly. His references to the broad peasant-like back of the chair, to the role of understatement, and to a "spare, rustic sensibility" all evoke a Zen-related aesthetic that is an important part of Japanese culture. Yet the "professor" does not bear down heavily with facts, names, and dates. His deft hints painlessly educate those who know little about Japan, yet without boring the knowledgeable. Rather than merely selling furniture, the "professor" is kindly sharing an observation about the traditional roots of a contemporary design concept. The voice of the "private professor" flatters retail customers with the implication that their aesthetic understanding may lead them to choose the cultural richness that is expressed in the chair.

FOR THE DESIGN PROFESSIONAL

Catalog description geared to the design professional does not usually speak of the cultural richness of products. Though it may be salted with value-conferring words such as "superb," it mostly speaks in the highly technical manner that is the common language of design professionals. Such an ad may closely resemble specification writing. In this catalog description from Conservation Technology's Web site (www.con-techlighting.com), the text describing Con-Tech's Peak Efficiency Series CTL fixtures is precise and factual, the vocabulary specialized, although the style is not as terse, fragmentary, and imperative as that of specifications (Figure 2.7). Technical language permits the writer to convey information in an economical manner that is quickly read and easily

Figure 2.7
Catalog page for
Con-Tech Lighting's
metal halide HID
track fixture
(CTL1610).
*Courtesy of
Con-Tech Lighting.*

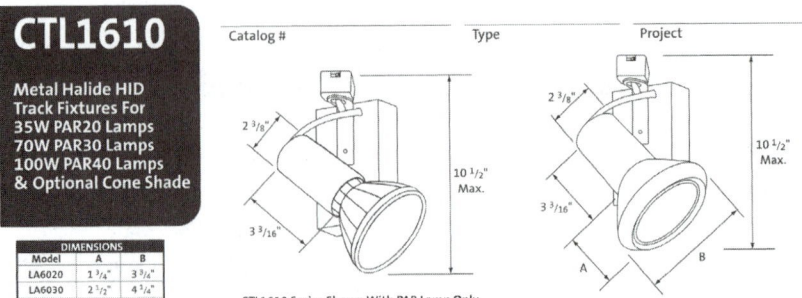

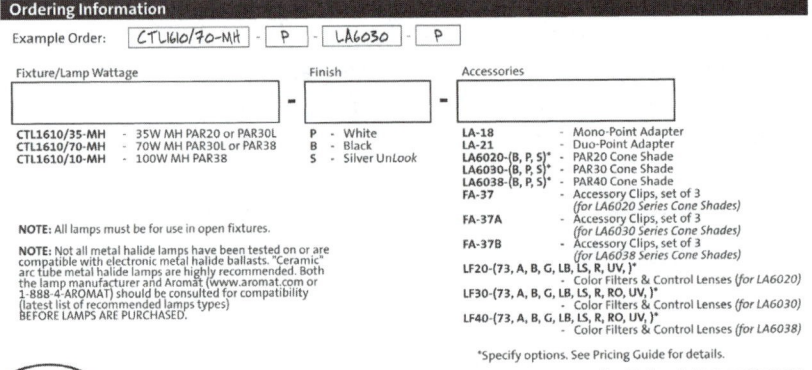

understood by interior design professionals. As in virtually all catalog copy, the focus is very much on the products themselves.

The Con-Tech description uses the passive voice at a number of junctures: "may be mounted," "are spaced," "are pulse rated." The use of the passive voice makes it seem as if the CTL1610 series had designed itself, since we are not told who mounted, spaced, or pulse-rated it. Elsewhere in the ad, the active voice reappears, but the lighting fixture itself continues to be the actor. It "features," "offers," "allows." Whether the voice is active or passive, there is no indication of a person performing an action. This lack of human agency puts the entire focus on the fixtures. (You will note a similar focus in the Kyoto Chair description—no human actors distract prospective purchasers from reading in their own uses for the chair.)

Project Descriptions

Like many vendors' catalog pages, project descriptions prepared by design firms tend to focus resolutely on their subjects, that is, on their completed projects. The implication is that a firm's work speaks for itself so brilliantly that modesty is the only appropriate posture to take. The description of the Gem Plaza project of Pei & Partners shown below is a good example. It is an interesting amalgam of technical and evocative styles, submerging a sense of human agency, as in the Con-Tech ad. The use of numbers, the deployment of insider terms such as *spandrel*, and the impersonal inventory of materials give the Pei description the authority of fact-based technical writing.

I.M. Pei & Partners, Architects and Planners

Project #7224

GEM PLAZA

In an interplay of geometric forms, Gem Plaza combines a rectangle and semi-circle joined by a glass-fronted atrium at a 45-degree angle rising the seven-storey height of the Gem Savings Headquarters building. A two-storey triangular projection housing the Home Savings and Loan Association Headquarters fronts the rectangular wing. The structure is cast-in-place concrete. Spandrel bands of gray Indiana limestone are accented by 10½-inch pink granite sills running beneath the ribbons of clear insulating glass.

The skylit atrium's interior walls of gray ornamental plaster feature alternating diagonal and circular balconies, echoing the building's geometric forms and color. Two pedestrian bridges span the open space at the fourth and sixth levels. The indoor courtyard has a 35-foot-wide glass entry wall and is topped by a square glass pyramid with infills of eight small pyramids, creating prisms of light. The paving, which extends into the atrium from the landscaped plaza, is brown brick bordered by pink granite.

Parking space on grade accommodates 20 cars.

There is no vagueness or unnecessary jargon in the description, and the language is based on careful and accurate observation. It is also very richly and intricately organized. Two clear concepts are presented, those of geometric form and color. Geometric form is embodied in such words as *rectangle*, *semicircle*, *angle*, *triangular*, *rectangular*, *diagonal*, *circular*, and *pyramids*. Color constitutes a repeating refrain: *gray, pink, gray, brown, pink*. The word *glass* is another refrain, repeated four times in this short passage. These artful repetitions convey a disciplined modern aesthetic and an impression of artistic control. They also give the project description a tightly structured unity.

A sentence like "Spandrel bands of gray Indiana limestone are accented by 10½-inch pink granite sills running beneath the ribbons of clear insulating glass" may present an inventory of attributes—and a thorough one at that—but the gracefully organized presentation entices the reader. In the mind's eye, the highly patterned language dances an elegant ballet around the details it presents, creating a sense of animating emotion despite the lack of human presence. The object described, Gem Plaza, seems almost to shimmer, rendering it not only present in the mind's eye but desirable. The shapeliness asserted in the emphasis on geometric form; the delicacy of the gray, pink, and brown color scheme; the sound echoes present in phrases like "spandrel bands," "pink granite sills," "insulating glass," and "brown brick bordered"—all these details work together to fully engage the senses. The language rises to a lyric climax with the phrase "prisms of light."

Of course, real-world prisms are made of glass. Linking unlike objects, this phrase deforms reality as we know it just enough to suggest the transformative nature of design. In shining with a disembodied radiance, the prisms of light connote the power of design to charm and persuade, and ultimately to impart to human life a spiritual dimension. The power of language enhances the power of artfully designed objects themselves, which are presented to clients in glistening representations unsullied by use and age. If the power of this description makes a persuasive marketing statement about the merits of the design firm for which it was written, isn't that the whole point?

Precise and Vivid Description Modes

One might say that the Gem Plaza project description combines the *precise writing* of the Con-Tech ad with the vivid writing of, say, Henry Adams's description of Chartres Cathedral. Frank Lloyd Wright's description of the research laboratory also combines precise writing and vivid writing, and, indeed, both these modes are important in the interior design context as a whole. Precise writing like the Con-Tech description that points directly at objects and avoids associated meanings is said to possess *denotative style*. Vivid writing (like the Kyoto Chair description) that surrounds objects with an aura of meaning is said to possess *connotative style*. Let us examine these two kinds of descriptive writing more closely.

The *denotative style*, along with plans and other contract documents, speaks in one of the two design languages that Kimberly Dovey has written about—that of the builder's world with its geometric sense of space and its requirement for technical exactitude in all matters. The *connotative style* speaks in the language that designers need to use with their clients—that of lived-in space as experienced with the senses.

Denotative Style

As we have seen, denotative style is appropriate for descriptions in which facts and numbers are paramount, descriptions written to facilitate the performance of tasks. A denotative description is based on such mental operations as counting, measuring, weighing, and timing. Writers of denotative descriptions express themselves in a very direct way to ensure that meanings cannot be misinterpreted. When the writer of the Con-Tech ad tells you that "the fixtures may be mounted to track or to outlet boxes via accessory adapters LA-18 mono-point or LA-21 duo-point," nothing is left to the imagination, nor should it be. The descriptions that communicate with contractors and fabricators are deliberately *not* interpretative, as we shall learn in Chapters 7 and 10. They are not intended to support the proliferation of meaning that is a principal tool for a designer who is expressing the value of a concept to a client.

Connotative Style

Used to convey mood and overall flavor, a connotative style deals in auras and hints at meanings beyond the actual words on the page. The truth it describes is one of intuition, emotional resonance, and imagination. As we have seen from the "prisms of light" in the Gem Plaza description, *figures of speech* may be important in this kind of writing, imparting meaning and value to a designer's concepts. A *figure of speech* expresses one thing in terms of another to show an effect beyond what has literally been said. *Metaphor* and its close relative *simile* are among the most commonly used figures of speech. *Metaphor* is language that implies a relationship based on similarity between two things that changes our understanding of either or both of those things. A *simile* is a metaphor in which the word *like* or *as* signals the comparative relationship.

Both metaphor and simile are contained in the excerpt from Frank Lloyd Wright's discussion of his laboratory for the SC Johnson Wax Company. For instance, Wright refers to "floor slabs spread out *like* tree branches" and "utility grooves, arranged *like* the cellular pattern of the tree trunk." "Slabs spread out *like* tree branches" is a simile. So is "grooves arranged *like* the cellular pattern of the tree trunk." The passage speaks of the Johnson laboratory as if it were a tree: "So we went up in the air around a giant central stack with floors branching from it." Here the comparison is clear but there is no *like* or *as*; we are in the presence of metaphor.

A figure of speech closely related to metaphor is *personification*, which represents a thing or abstraction as a person. Henry Adams's description of Chartres Cathedral might be discussed as an example of personification, for in it the Virgin of Chartres is invoked to represent the Gothic style itself.

Some people assume that connotative style is wordier than denotative style, but this is not necessarily so. In nontechnical writing, a well-chosen figure of speech like the phrase "prisms of light" in the Gem Plaza description can create a vivid impression in relatively few words. By means of such figures, designer writers can enlarge the understanding of their clients while conveying a sensory experience of lived-in space.

Generative Writing

Figures of speech are not only important to explain a design that has already been executed. The mental processes that generate figures of speech also play an important role in the design process itself, which, like all creative activity, is based on *explorative reasoning* rather than *linear reasoning*.[7] *Linear reasoning* deals in logical connection—cause and effect, for instance. *Explorative reasoning* is more free-form, as in children's games such as "let's pretend" which encourage spontaneous imagination and bold speculation.

Because of its strength in the imaginative and speculative realms, metaphor lies at the heart of exploratory reasoning and thus of the designer's conceptual process. We know that metaphor operates through *analogy*, a fancy word for comparison. Through it we infer that if things are similar in some respects, they are similar in others. However, metaphor is not the only type of analogy that is relevant to a discussion of generative writing. The problem-solving method known as *synectics*[8] identifies four different types of analogy as generators of creative solutions to design and other problems:

- *Metaphorical* or *symbolic analogy*   Linking the problem to objective and impersonal objects and images

- *Personal analogy*   The problem-solver's identification with part or all of the problem and its solution

- *Direct analogy*   The direct application to the problem of parallel facts, knowledge, technology, principles, and theories

- *Fantasy analogy*   Solving the problem through "what if" solutions

Metaphoric or Symbolic Analogy

The "prisms of light" we saw in the Gem Plaza description are a good example of metaphoric analogy. An image that joins two objective and impersonal objects—prisms and light—creates something fresh that did not exist before. But the prisms of light belong to a description of a completed project. If your problem is a client's bedroom window that is too close to a neighbor's house and you are inspired to find a visual equivalent for the way soothing "white noise" masks intrusive sound, then you are using a metaphor to solve a design problem, asking yourself what "white noise" symbolizes in the visual realm. *Perhaps a lace curtain?*

It isn't enough to conceive of these metaphoric leaps. It is important to put them into words—not just to say them aloud, but to record your creative process in writing. After all, language itself is a symbol system whereby one thing—a group of sounds or a word's shape on the page—stands for another: "lamp" for the real thing glowing before us. "Language," says the writing teacher Peter Elbow, "is the principal medium that allows you to interact with yourself."[9] As a designer, you do that with shapes and colors, of course, but "without a symbol system such as language, it is difficult if not impossible to think about more than one thing at a time, and thus to allow two thoughts to interact."[10]

Elbow extols the creative power of making as many metaphors as you possibly can—too many, if possible. "When you make a metaphor," he explains, "you call something by a wrong name . . . There is . . . a contradiction. You are not just calling a house a house, but rather a playground, a jungle, a curse, a wound, a paradise. Each throws into relief aspects of the house you might otherwise miss. You are seeing one thought or perception through the lens of another . . . new ideas and perceptions result. Connections are loosened so that something may develop or grow in whatever its potential direction."[11] Metaphor is not the only kind of analogy that generates new ideas and perceptions.

Personal Analogy

Actors who use the acting technique known as The Method are using personal analogy. For instance, a young actor who must play an old person might draw on memories of illness or fatigue and their associated physical expressions to create the presence of an old person on stage. In the same way, the interior designer looks for expressions of clients' emotions and feelings. If the client wants a room that makes her toddler feel safe, the designer may list feelings and experiences that the client associates with safety for very young children: "my mother giving me milk and cookies at night," "hearing good old stories like *Pinocchio* and *Sleeping Beauty*," "the sound of grandmother's music box." A child who is old enough to speak will have his or her own ideas—"my lambie," a stuffed lamb. The designer may pick out the white of the lamb and the milk, the fluffiness of the lamb, and the traditional aspect of the old stories, the music box, and the ritual of milk and cookies. These qualities can then be returned to the physical—a white, fluffy rug, a vintage rocking chair—as the design work progresses.

Direct Analogy

When designers research the literature to see how other designers have done things, or return to their training to discover the principals and theories that are relevant to their current projects, they are searching for the direct analogies that will help to generate their designs and explain their concepts. For instance, direct analogy is at work when a client presents a designer with a clipping file and the designer creates a new design that draws on the concepts presented in pictures of existing rooms clipped from magazines and newspapers. If many of the client's photos show traditional rooms filled with landscape art in heavy gold frames and your design features customized wallpaper with a computer-created motif of antique gold frames dancing across a Romantic landscape, then you are drawing on direct analogy. Of course, the process will be richest for you if you write down the design possibilities suggested by the client's clips. Do most of the rooms contain warm colors? Rich textures? Dramatic contrast? A sense of history? As you talk to yourself through writing, you can see how aspects of the rooms represented in the clippings transform one another through interaction.

Fantasy Analogy

"Creativity," R. Guy McGinnis observes, "cannot come from what is already known."[12] Taken to its most extreme, fantasy analogy expresses itself in bizarre images and incongruous juxtapositions—the marriage of an umbrella and sewing machine—such as those we see in surrealism. Fantasy images like these arise involuntarily from the mysterious "dark side" of mental activity. They are the stuff of dreams, daydreams, hallucinations, and psychoses, and they are central to creative problem-solving.

Fantasy analogy may surface in interior design as quirkiness or whimsy, for example, when a child's bedroom contains furniture with animal shapes and wallpaper with scenes of life in a stylized jungle. In addition to being conceptual touchstones for a designer, such images create a sense that a design is unique. Whenever a designer plays "what if," he or she is drawing on fantasy analogy, as in "what if that niche were occupied by a verdigris garden urn full of peacock feathers?" Fantasy analogy might lead a designer to see old things in new ways—to think of the negative as positive (and vice versa), for instance, as when deciding that a chipped, scratched table is "shabby chic." In a similar vein, the designer may reverse assumptions about cause and effect. If the furniture arrangement in a room has been generating the traffic pattern, what would happen if the traffic pattern generated the furniture arrangement—or vice versa?

Fantasy analogy is the purest example of the capacity for language to generate what Peter Elbow has called "fecundity [fertility], novelty, [and] richness."[13] It is analogy at its most explorative. "What if those Queen Anne chairs were covered in shocking pink faux–patent leather and painted black, and set on a zebra-skin rug in front of a wall of marbleized mirrors under a Venetian chandelier with smoked glass prisms before a gilt table with a collection of onyx obelisks and a crystal vase of bright pink peonies?"

The Concept Statement

The fecundity of explorative reasoning must eventually be harnessed to "perspective, structure, and clarity"[14] Analogy bears fruit in concepts, or design ideas, and ultimately in a statement of design mission, the governing concept of a design.

The Role of the Concept Statement

A concept statement is a key tool of the interior design process and is critical to a designer's communication with clients, with other designers, and with the public. In the words of Dan Beert, IIDA, IDEC, a concept statement presents the "big picture," the overall course of action that emerges in response to the issues presented by the client and the client's project.[15] Conceptual writing, the Virginia Institute of Technology tells interior design students, has three functions:

- To state and understand a design problem
- To explore and hypothesize a design solution
- To present and define a design mission

Virginia Tech advises students that conceptual writing differs from other types of writing because of its "intangible subject matter. [You] are writing about ideas."[16] Description moves into the realm of ideas via the process of *abstraction*, which pulls from objects and images their aspects and qualities. By this means, designers may combine relevant analogies. They can think of alternatives based on their understanding of comparable qualities, as shown in Figure 2.8. "Morphological Forced Connections," based on an invention-finding scheme created by Don Koberg and Jim Bagnall.[17] The shading shows the attribute swapping that can result in a new way of thinking about a problem.

Components of a Concept Statement

In Chapter 3, we look more closely at the role of analysis in the multistep process of teasing out concepts. For now, we focus on the complex role of analogy in the concept statement, which can be loosely defined as "a written road map of where your design originated and where your design is going."[18] To function as this kind of road map, a concept statement expresses

Figure 2.8
Morphological
forced connections.

SUBJECT: IMPROVE AN UMBRELLA STAND.
Attributes of existing umbrella stand: cylindrical, ceramic, faux–Chinese decoration— glazed; no compartments.
ALTERNATES:

Cylindrical	Ceramic	Faux-Chinese decoration; glazed	No compartments
Square	Metal	Brushed finish	Grid top creates vertical compartments
Swan-shaped	Wood	Painted	Serrated wing tops create rack and thus horizontal compartments
Spiral	Lucite	Polished	Grid bottom creates vertical compartments

Attributes of new umbrella stand: spiral, metal, painted, no compartments.

Based on an invention-finding scheme created by Don Koberg and Kim Bagnall, Universal Traveler: A Soft-Systems Guidebook to Creativity, Problem-Solving, and the Process of Design *(Los Angeles: William Kaufmann, 1979), as cited in James L. Adams,* Conceptual Blockbusting: A Guide to Better Ideas *(San Fransisco: W. H. Freeman, 1979), 82, 83.*

ideas through the analogy in all of its components: the *idea generator*, the *form-givers*, and the *application*.[19]

THE IDEA GENERATOR

The designer's key analogy, the seed concept, is sometimes known as the *idea generator*. It may connect the design to the client, to a building site, or to a corporate mission.[20] For instance, the example given at the Virginia Polytechnic Institute and State University "Writing Guidelines" Web site shows how sand dunes might generate ideas for a beach-front residence.

Sand dunes are the inspiration for my design.

A statement like this may be true, but it does not really demonstrate how the sand dunes generated the design. It is not yet an effective concept statement.

THE FORM-GIVERS

To effectively communicate a concept, the concept statement must study the idea generator more closely, to discover its form-givers:

The undulating rhythms of the sand dunes found along the Outer Banks of North Carolina are used to reinforce the essential character of the space.

Note that the sand dunes are made specific in this statement: they are not just any sand dunes, but the ones along the Outer Banks. Note, too, that the writing designer now tells us precisely *which* attribute of the sand dunes generated the design idea—not their height, not their sandiness, not the vegetation growing on them, but their "undulating rhythms." Note finally that the mushiness of "inspired my design" has been replaced with a precise design function, "reinforce the essential character of the space," which is, after all, a *beach* house. At every step of the way, then, the writing designer describes the inspiration process "*in terms of* [here analogy comes in] the elements and principles of design." In addition to undulating rhythms, other form-givers might be the play of light and shadows or the movement of dune forms across space. "Sand dunes are not the central premise here, but the design qualities *inherent* to the sand dunes are."[21]

When the designing writer introduces multiple form-givers into a concept statement, it gains even more power to explain a complex design process:

The sand dunes found along the Outer Banks of North Carolina reveal several design relationships that are used to guide the design of the space. Focusing on the undulating rhythms of the dunes to reinforce the essential character of the space, the architectural and interior elements eloquently express the play of light and shadow that complement the horizontal movement of form through space.

Rich as this statement is, however, it is not yet a fully formed concept statement.

THE APPLICATION

In a full-fledged statement, the designing writer goes on to say *how* the form-givers are *revealed* in the design. For instance, according to the Virginia Tech mentors, "components of the design may include the architectural elements and details of the space, aspects of spatial and furniture layout," lighting design, and "surface materials and finishes."[22] From form-giving, then, the sand dune concept statement might move to application as follows:

Subtle, curvilinear lines define the dominant architectural interior forms such as the stair, loft, and built-in furniture. These lines are further integrated into the interior details of moldings, trim, and hardware. However, in order to establish contrast and relief within the space, [the] window[s] . . . and freestanding furniture are given a low, horizontal orientation, . . . echoing the coastal horizon. Materials are chosen for their appropriateness, incorporating a variety of texture and color that reflects the coastal environment.[23]

You will find the entire concept statement, including the generator, the form-givers, and the application in the following text:

The sand dunes found along the Outer Banks of North Carolina reveal several design relationships that are used to guide the design of the space. Focusing on the undulating rhythms of the dunes to reinforce the essential character of the space, the architectural and interior elements eloquently express the play of light and shadow that complement the horizontal movement of form through space. Subtle, curvilinear lines define the dominant architectural interior forms such as the stair, loft, and built-in furniture. These lines are further integrated into the interior details of moldings, trim, and hardware.

However, in order to establish contrast and relief within the space, the windows and freestanding furniture are given a low, horizontal orientation, echoing the coastal horizon. Materials are chosen for their appropriateness, incorporating a variety of texture and color that reflects the coastal environment.

As specific as this concept statement is about the source and application of the forms and finishes, it describes only the qualities of the relevant elements and principles, not the shape, size, color, or material with which they are realized. The concept statement as "big picture" thus allows the designer—and client—a range of options that can achieve the qualities presented.

The catalog and project descriptions we looked at earlier focus on things and places themselves, not on the people who created them. The Outer Banks concept statement, too, on the face of it, may seem to leave out human agency. The designer is not present as "I,' "he," or "she," nor is there a "we" or "they" here. Yet the designer is present in the analogies that represent the imaginative leaps typical of the design. These analogies connect what a client already knows—the character of the outer-bank dunes of a beloved beach that is the site for a house—and what he or she cannot have known before looking at drawings and swatches and reading the concept statement: how his or her wishes and needs can be joined with the designer's creativity to generate something fresh, valuable, functional, and eloquent.

We have seen throughout this chapter how interpretative description imparts meaning that enhances the perception of value. We might say of such language what artist Paul Klee is supposed to have said of art itself, that it "makes us see."[24] For the designer, description is not an act of mapping a passive world, but the record of an interactive process in which the world is written into the design process, which then interprets the world to itself in a creative and transformational way.

Thick Description: An Investigative Tool

Description is a means by which designers, their clients, and other users become active and creative co-participants from the very beginning of their relationship. Long before designers articulate concepts or describe a completed project, they need to perform the data gathering known as *thick description*. This kind of description is a form of pre-writing rather than writing. It is a tool of cultural investigation, and thus a tool in the early stages of the design process, pre-programming, and programming.

Thick description may be defined as a means of observing, recording, and understanding a culture not one's own. Cultural anthropologist Clifford Geertz, the father of thick description, has pegged his ground-breaking conception to a putative analysis of the "wink of any eye." When a man in a culture not your own winks at another member of that culture, Geertz asks, is he merely "contracting his right eyelid" or is he faking a conspiratorial wink to deceive a bystander into "thinking conspiracy is in motion"?[25] Geertz believes that humans live "suspended in webs of significance." The goal of thick description is to dig into nested patterns of meaning so as to understand what people's cultural practices mean *to them.*

Like an anthropologist, an interior designer embarking on a project needs to understand the meaning of people's cultural practices *to them.* In the words of Sue Ballard de Ruiz, who teaches Introduction to Interior Design at Tennessee State University, "the designer needs to learn 'the ins and outs of [the client's] problem,' to discover what the world of the problem looks like."[26] To perform thick description effectively, the writing designer needs to listen as well as to look and, indeed, to engage all the other senses, for "thick" and other descriptions are always multisensory. Crucially for the interior design process, thick description creates mental pictures of human behavior as well as of physical objects. To use it as a tool for discovering what the world of a client's problem looks like, a "thick describer" might investigate the following:

- *Setting*   What are the physical characteristics of the site that are the focus of design activity? What environmental issues are raised?
- *Activities*   What goes on at the site? (Include both typical and atypical activities.)
- *Users/participants*   Who takes part in the activities? Who is excluded? What different roles do participants and non-participants play?
- *Rules* (norms and policies)   What are the formal or informal rules for engaging in the activities and using the space?
- *Goals*   What do the participants seek to accomplish through the activities?
- *Significance or symbolic factor*   What do the activities and goals say about the participants?
- *Critical activities*   Which activities are deemed most important by the client and by various participants? What do these activities consist of?

To find out the answers to all these questions, your observation must be complex, and it must be patient. It may range from the unstructured—looking around and taking notes—to the focused—asking questions of various individuals with whom you need to develop relationships of trust and confidence so as to elicit accurate information. In general, thick description is evoked by questions that have no specific "right" answers. It resists any pull to early abstraction—the teasing out of concepts—but remains in a data-collecting mode until a sense of sufficiency is attained. It requires a well-developed set of listening skills.

The Role of Listening

Unlike hearing, which is involuntary, listening is a learned skill that can be practiced and mastered. You need to concentrate on what the other person is saying and exert conscious mental effort to overcome the barriers that prevent effective listening. These barriers include:

Taking notes helps you listen!

- Reactions to the speaker, such as dislike or contempt.
- Physical reactions, such as fatigue or hunger.
- Contextual distractions, such as a noisy air conditioner.

To overcome these barriers to effective listening, it helps to prepare yourself in advance for any meeting in which you intend to collect information. Allow yourself time to think about your expectations of the meeting and the various topics about which you are collecting information. It also helps to take notes during the meeting. Note taking not only helps with later reconstruction of what has been said, but it actually helps you to focus on what is being said. It is important, however, not to be so involved in the note taking that you ignore the person who is talking to you. Listening is interactive!

A good listener often responds in a manner that both reflects and claims what has been said by *summarizing*—summing up—and *paraphrasing*—putting what the speaker has said into the listener's own words. Good listeners use any lag time between the speaker's halting, searching presentation and their own rapid conclusory leaps to think about what the speaker is saying, rather than letting their minds wander or preparing a reply in their minds while the other person is talking.

As the interviewee is talking, you as listener might want to evaluate the evidence used to substantiate various issues. It is also important to "listen between the lines" for meanings that may not have been directly expressed. What was the interviewee doing while she talked? What was she looking at?

What expressions were on her face? What was the interview setting? What sounds were in the background?[27] These techniques will help you remember what has been said; they will also help you "probe its meaning" (Figure 2.9).[28] When you move beyond spatial description to the description of people and processes, listening becomes as important as looking!

Pre-programming

Thick description techniques, such as listening, are important to the pre-programming phase of the design process, in which the designer investigates contextual factors. Franklin Becker and Fritz Steele name the pre-programming phase "Phase Zero" to establish a way of billing for it. They define it as a "series of direction-setting steps." During Phase Zero, or pre-programming, designers work with clients to "review the core values," "identify key requirements or 'themes' for the project," and "develop a set of behavioral objectives."[29]

Because you accumulate pre-programming information through in-depth interviews, it is very important to allow sufficient time for it to take place. The marriage of detailed observation and fertile, open questions will yield its riches only in an unhurried, non-judgmental setting that fosters both designers' *and* clients' faith in their own creativity—their intuition, will, joy, strength, and compassion.[30] In a work space setting, designers may encounter

Figure 2.9
The designer must be a good listener to probe the client's meaning.

management resistance to a process that avoids the early narrowing of focus. Yet by defining problems too quickly, clients may lose the opportunity to solve them in the most transformative and generative manner.

In *Workplace by Design*, Franklin Becker and Fritz Steele[31] show how "a high-tech company in California" jumped to a narrow solution too quickly:

> The senior managers . . . had realized that their existing approach to space planning, more or less a standard open-plan layout with all the systems people tucked into a rabbit warren–like maze, had become dysfunctional. . . . They quickly decided that furniture was the key issue, and then proceeded to commission a thorough analysis of the wrong thing: which furniture system to buy. . . . [The problem might have been] policies and norms governing how the existing space could be used. Or the problem might have been the basic configuration of the building, or the nature of available information technology, or the question of where different groups were located in the building. Or, more than likely, the problem stemmed from the interaction of several of these factors. . . . Why would managers move so quickly from awareness that some aspect of the workspace is dysfunctional to choosing a new furniture system? One reason may be that furniture . . . can be treated as . . . a procurement problem, for which there are already accepted methods and procedures. If more fundamental questions were being asked about organizational vision, direction, and culture . . . the nature of the conclusion [might be] less certain, possibly more threatening. Jumping to furniture as the solution avoids these bigger questions that don't have easy answers.

During pre-programming, it is important for designers and their clients to "carefully describe the situation and what doesn't work about it," and then look at what they would like to have happening instead. For example, a play school in a windowless basement room might be dark and chilly. The children might be huddling in corners or fighting with each other rather than playing together constructively. An early, too-narrow solution might be to install brighter lighting and a heater. Yet sticking to the problems and elucidating fully behavioral objectives such as "playing together constructively" might yield a broader range of alternatives: lease a warmer space with more windows; schedule more play time outside or more field trips; purchase a faux fireplace and cozy rugs; rearrange furniture and fixtures to encourage group games; install a sound system that creates appealing acoustical environments; create murals of the children's own drawings on the walls; or use the darkness to create a series of caves that encourage adventure and exploration games such as hunts for buried treasure.

Sometimes pre-programming, in the designer's sense, is part of a visionary corporate development strategy that is speculative and projective. For example, interior designer Amy Treff and her client Xavier Lopez, an entertainment entrepreneur, conceived a 100,000-square-foot entertainment center focused on the needs and customs of children. To create the initial formulation of the Kid's City project, Treff interviewed her client for two full days before begining "a seven-week writing effort to thoroughly create and document [the client] company's" vision. In addition to interviewing her client, she worked from a proposed master plan for the project. The completed pre-programming document was to be used by architects and interior designers as "direction for interpreting the [entertainment] concept." Treff enjoyed the opportunity the project afforded "to create environments with words."[32] Here is an excerpt from the introduction to Treff's three-volume document:[33]

> Kid's City is a first-of-its-kind indoor family entertainment concept. The focus of Kid's City is, of course, on kids, but parents and other adults also have the opportunity to participate and interact with the kids. The core philosophy of Kid's City is based on one of the most popular and instinctive games played by all children at one time or another, role-playing. By pretending to be doctors, firefighters, journalists, bakers, and other real-life characters, the kids will imitate adults, a natural part of their development.... Kid's City by its organization strives to package that "instinct" into a challenging, safe, and educational environment where kids can be kids and express themselves through a series of constructive and fun activities.

Later in this book, in Chapter 9, we look at some ways to structure a massive report such as Treff's documentation of the Kid's City entertainment concept. For now, it is sufficient to understand its place within the descriptive spectrum. Note that it developed from listening to a client for two full days—the "thick description" technique of active listening. Note, too, that the reporting style is dry and denotative—no promotional adjectives and no figures of speech—despite the creativity of the entertainment concept and its theatrical aspect.

Kid's City is being presented to the professionals who can bring the concept to fruition—to interior designers and architects, first, but it may also be read by contractors, fabricators, vendors, scenic designers, prop specialists, costume designers, lighting specialists, and so on. As planning proceeds, the document may be read by investors, city planners, and state regulators. Within the emerging Kid's City organization, it may be read by facilities managers, publicists, purchasing agents, and marketing specialists. For all these audiences, the denotative clarity of Treff's description is both appropriate and necessary.

Programming

The preprogramming phase of a project segues naturally into the programming phase, an intensive and comprehensive study of the client's needs. Like preprogramming, programming is based on thick description, though the programming phase is *function-oriented*, rather than context-oriented. Programming is also *solution-oriented*—that is, it is intended to generate the requirements a design will meet. In Chapter 3, we look more closely at the analytic aspects of programming. For now, let us expand upon its thickly descriptive aspect—the role of research, or data collection.

As in preprogramming, *interviews* are a crucial part of the research process, though contract designers may need to work within a clients *standards program*. Highly relevant before, during, and after the programming phase are research activities such as *counting and measuring, literature research*, and *color and materials research*.

INTERVIEWS

As a designer, your programming interviews are a way of gathering specific, accurate pieces of information. If you do a good job, the program you create will be easy to write and interesting to read.

THE ROLE OF QUESTIONS During programming interviews, the designer asks questions, the answers to which will ultimately make a space functional for those who live in it, work in it, own it, or otherwise have an interest in its successful use. If the designer needs to pin down details, he or she asks a *closed question*: "How many times a day do you walk from your desk to the archives?" To gather "whys," "hows," and explanations, the designer asks an *open-ended question*: "What effect does the open office-plan have on your work style?" The questions the designer asks condition the nature of the clients' response. The questions asked of a corporate client are different from those asked of a residential client.

For a *commercial* or *corporate project*,[34] the designers may collect data about:

- How many people need to be accommodated in the space
- How much space each person needs

- What people will be doing in their space
- What technology they require
- How the company or other client is expected to grow and change
- How people communicate and interact with each other
- What groups or individuals need to be near each other (adjacency requirements)
- What services need to be shared and where they need to be located

For a *residential project*, different questions may be relevant. When Frank Lloyd Wright was collecting data about his clients the Hannas before designing a house for them, he and Mrs. Wright lived with the Hannas for several weeks so as to facilitate observation and interviewing. According to the Hannas' later recollection, the Wrights played with their daughter Jovanna and observed her play patterns. They inquired into the Hannas' "habits of housekeeping, family cooperation, [and] recreation." They learned what they could of the adult Hannas' "research, writing, and teaching." The Wrights' thorough program interviewing made it possible for Frank Lloyd Wright to design a home that was fully compatible with the Hannas' "likes, philosophies, and idiosyncrasies."[35]

For the design process, it is usually necessary to have input from everyone who uses a space, although some people's views may be more influential than others. For instance, you can imagine that Mrs. Hanna's thoughts about kitchen layout were more significant to Frank Lloyd Wright than those of her young daughter.

INTERVIEWING TECHNIQUES Your interviews will be more productive if you prepare for them in advance. Before each interview, learn all you can about the person being interviewed. From first contact, it is best to be very clear about who you are, why you wish to speak to the interviewee, and what topics you will be discussing. It is common courtesy to schedule interviews at the convenience of the interviewees and to allow them to review the interviews before making them available to others.

Prepare for each interview in advance.

Here are some additional tips for successful program and other interviewing:

- Prepare a list of specific questions to ask each interviewee. (It saves time.)
- Use your listening skills.
- Ask the easy questions first and save the hard ones for later.
- Remember, you are interviewing for a purpose. Be pleasant but

stay on track. If the interviewee wanders from the subject, ask a clear, direct question to get back on track.

- Let the interviewee do the talking.
- Be objective. Do not offer opinions or argue with the interviewee.
- Ask follow-up questions as they arise. Don't wait till later, as you may forget to ask them.
- Learn or invent a shorthand or learn how to write in your notebook without having to look. (Practice while listening to the news on TV or the radio.)

Above all, don't ask interviewees to slow down or stop speaking while you take elaborate notes. They may lose the trail of their meaning. It is better to take only memory-jogging notes and to record the full thrust of each interview in detailed notes when you are back in your office. If you plan to use a tape recorder, use it only to record your own notes and impressions directly after the interview. Do not record interviewees directly. Tape recorders make people uncomfortable, and direct recording of an interview can be time-consuming to transcribe. Try not to let too much time elapse before fleshing out the skeletal notes you took during the interview. Even people with excellent memories forget the content of an interview and the full meaning of their notes as time goes by.[36] Transcribing interview notes is not about invention; it is about what people actually said.

> Transcribe interview notes promptly, before you forget the details.

THE STANDARDS PROGRAM

For budgetary reasons, contract and other interior designers sometimes replace in-depth interviews with questionnaires composed of the kinds of questions they would have asked in a face-to-face meeting, but without the opportunity to ask follow-up questions. Or designers at individual facilities may need to work within a *standards program* that expresses an overall strategy for similar projects within a corporate, governmental, or institutional framework. You need only compare the multiple outlets of a fast-food franchiser to see how corporate design standards create a consistent and recognizable image with built-in quality control across many sites.

A standards program saves time and streamlines decision making. It helps a large institution plan, implement, and manage efficiently and cost-effectively. Criteria may be established that address items ranging from building selection to programming to purchasing. If written flexibly, the standards can respond to regional conditions, specific building characteristics, and particular needs of individual projects.

Figure 2.10 shows an excerpt from a fictitious document entitled *American General Merchandise District Sales Office Planning Standards*. You can see that the stated standards simplify not only programming in individual instances, but also subsequent design and project-management phases. You can also see that much of the data collection that characterizes programming has already been done by the time the planning standards are disseminated to those entrusted with individual facilities within the larger corporate system. Yet there is still programming work to be done for an individual facility.

The writing for the American General standards program, like other program writing, is presented in a dry, factual, and denotative manner that facilitates understanding by all professionals who must interpret it. Note the manner in which formatting—the table—facilitates access to the information that is being presented. Note, too, how the use of different verb tenses—present and future—economically reinforces the allocation of design tasks within the corporate hierarchy.

From research that has clearly covered many facilities, the American General standards program sets forth abstract concepts to guide the design process. The single most important factor determining all design in AGM sales offices—the *parti*, or master concept, or the design mission, if you will—is stated clearly in this excerpt:

> The color material palette for the AGM Sales Offices is dominated by the fact that there will be a mix of reuse furniture and new purchase. In all scenarios, an existing color and material palette will govern subsequent choices.

From this concept of frugal responsiveness to existing conditions is derived the standards program's "neutral envelope" and its notion of flexible accents within that envelope. Presumably, the standards program, applied at each sales office, will help to generate further concepts relevant to program-research findings at each particular site.

As readers of the parti and other concepts, we can "see" back through them to the individual sales offices with their existing furniture of different colors. We can "read" the desire of the corporation to exercise thrift while projecting a dignified image.

COUNTING AND MEASURING

Not all of a designer's program data are derived from interviews. Many crucial data are the result of task-based research such as counting and

DESIGN ELEMENTS: COLORS, MATERIALS, AND FINISHES

DESIGN GUIDELINES: COLORS, MATERIALS, FINISHES	DESIGN ELEMENTS
The color material palette for the AGM Sales Offices is dominated by the fact that there will be a mix of re-use furniture and new purchase. In all scenarios, an existing color and material palette will govern subsequent choices. This constraint supports the creation of a consistent, neutral envelope and allows flexibility within this context.	*Neutral Envelope* Color choices among warm, neutral, and cool are unpredictable across the range of scenarios. The choice at a given office is made when the existing conditions are set. The neutral envelope entails dark value carpeting, light value walls, white ceiling, and, in most cases, a light wood choice. *Accents: Color, Material Detail* Once this neutral palette is in place, accents may be added within the context of the particular site, taking the following factors into account: 1. Existing architectural finishes 2. Existing furniture 3. Regional conditions 4. Functional conditions of the plan as it relates to the placement of design elements

Figure 2.10
Design elements: colors, materials, and finishes. Excerpt from fictional *General Merchandise District Sales Office Planning Standards.*

measuring. If an interior designer is unable to rely on existing plan documents, the designer will need to measure the rooms of a project site. It may also be necessary to inventory—that is, count and describe—existing furniture and decorative objects, often using tables and spreadsheets to organize and present the information gathered. Without analytic strategies such as division and classification, an extensive inventory would soon sprawl out of control. This all-important analytic aspect of an inventory is discussed in more detail in Chapter 3. From a "thick description" perspective, the principal characteristic of an inventory is thoroughness. The designer must note all relevant aspects of the items that are inventoried.

The perseverance required is the visual equivalent of good listening and requires the same patience.

LITERATURE AND RELATED RESEARCH

During the programming phase, a designer may research code restrictions; perform precedent studies to ascertain the history of a site, a building, and a client's activities; and investigate colors, materials, and project types. Or a designer may research the literature of interior design to see how peers and historic designers have solved problems similar to the current client's. Sometimes the literature research that contributes to a descriptive basis for design programming takes place in a firm's own library of printed matter, swatches, and material samples; sometimes it takes place in a public or institutional library, and sometimes it is accomplished online, using a search engine to find relevant material. Several relevant research strategies are discussed in greater detail in Chapter 9.

Presenting Preprogramming and Programming Data

Before you are ready to present your combined "thick description" data to a client or to others in your firm, you will need to organize your notes, an activity you may find easier if you have developed a project template that provides electronic "boxes" into which you can sort the various pieces of information you have gathered. (Sorting in this manner is an analytic process and is discussed in more detail in Chapter 3.) One good program for data sorting is Eastgate's Tinderbox, visually based note organization and planning software. For those who think visually, who are "wired," or who think in more than two dimensions, as most designers do, Tinderbox can help to gather, understand, preserve, and share notes. (In a more linear fashion, you can use a word-processing or spreadsheet program to perform sorting functions.)

When your notes have been organized in a manner that facilitates an orderly presentation, you need to choose a report *genre*, or type, to present your findings. Chapter 9 discusses some report genres that are widely used in business and professional writing. Some genres that are particularly relevant to programming presentation are discussed in the paragraphs that follow. They are:

- The brief.
- The project-orientation session.
- The observation study.
- The client-user profile.

The Brief

Design program material is frequently presented in the form that the British call a *brief*, a document stating the facts and issues that characterize a client's "case." This writing genre—widely used by attorneys—is highly condensed. It goes from point to point, almost like an outline, without dwelling on detail. It may bear a title like "General Notes from Programming Interviews" (see Figure 2.11.) The observations on which the "Notes" are based may involve interviewing, listening, counting, measuring, and researching. Particularly if a large quantity of information has been gathered—as it would be for a corporate or institutional project—the notes are formatted for clarity and access, using indentation, bulleted lists, and tabulation as appropriate. The excerpt from a compendious set of "General Notes" that you see in Figure 2.11 is richly formatted, denotative, fact-based, and impersonal. It is mostly composed of nouns—such as "workstation"—and numbers—such as "64."

The information presented in a document like "General Notes" may be highly specific to the client and to the nature of the client's business. For instance, The First National Bank of Thruwood, like many other financial institutions, stores information on *microfiche*, sheets of microfilm on which many pages have been photographed in miniature; a magnification system is used to read the pages. Research on this method of storing information is not included in "General Notes" because those notes will be shared with the client, who needs to confirm the veracity and relevance of the data collected. The client already knows what microfiche is.

The Project Orientation Session

Sometimes organized program notes are presented orally, in a group meeting that has been called to acquaint all relevant members of a design firm with a project. For an effective oral presentation, the information items that are presented in Figure 2.11 might be written on separate, individual cards. A Power Point or easel presentation might accompany the oral presentation, highlighting important points. Concept drawings scribbled on an easel pad are often accompanied by written notes with arrows pointing to features that may not be immediately apparent. These "captions" are written directly on the conceptual sketches to enhance their meaning. Material samples and color research might be passed around so as to encourage interaction. There would typically be a question-and-answer period after the orientation proper. (For more on oral presentations, see Chapter 9.)

The Observation Study

Sometimes program notes are entered on an "activity map" in obvious proximity to the location in which each activity takes place. This is a graphic and

Figure 2.11   Excerpt from *"General Notes from Programming Interviews" First National Bank of Thruwood Two South Pemberton—12th Floor Relocation*

CORPORATE TRUST INVESTOR RELATIONS UNIT
COORDINATOR: SUSAN PARKER 212-555-1212

Item	Sq. Ft.	Size	Qty— Existing	Total Sq. Ft.— Existing	Qty— Future	Total Sq. Ft.— Future
Work stations						
E	64	8 × 8	1	64	2	128
F	48	6 × 8	3	144	5	240
G (shared)	36	6 × 6	8	288	12	432
Files						
(See Corporate Trust Account summary)						
Subtotal				496		
Ancillary space						
Fiche Room	192	12 × 16	1	192		

NOTES

1. Access to full-size copier required. Study nearby central copier locations.
2. Acoustical control concerns because of high degree of phone contact.
3. A freestanding work table is recommended in microfiche room.
4. Visual access required to fiche room to control unauthorized visitor use.
5. Existing storage in fiche room consists of Herman Miller panel hung units:

   a. 14" deep open shelving for fiche boxes
      (1) 2'w x 6 to a shelf
      (2) 4'w x 3 to a shelf
      (2) 4'w x 6 to a shelf

      (Storage boxes approximately 6"w x 2'd)

   b. Flipper storage for binders
      (2) 4'w
      (1) 2'w

      Mount over work surface.

   c. Additional shelving for boxes and supplies

      (2) 4'w adjustable steel shelf units

nonlinear way of showing existing usages within the project environment. It works best in design situations in which copious amounts of data need not be presented. Note that summary observations about client activities must be presented with economy—no unnecessary words—in order to fit onto the map. These observations may be understood as a form of caption.

The Client-User Profile

A *profile* explains people and organizations. It focuses on clients and/or users themselves. An example is the writing about Kid's City discussed earlier. A profile is based on interviews or questionnaires and may be written not only as an activity, need, interest, and value description, but also as a *narrative*, or story, an event-based account in which the story illustrates important concepts arising from the client or user's manner of living and/or working. In Chapter 3, we have more to say about stories as we look at so-called strategic stories—case studies with a strong analytic component. For now, let us stick to the basics of descriptive storytelling in the service of program reporting.

What is a story? You know it when you see or read it.

A. *Not a story*:   The man died. Then the woman died.

B. *A story*:   The man died. Then the woman died of grief.

Version A presents two disconnected events, whereas Version B presents two events knitted together by a thread of meaning. Whatever else it does, a story promises that life is coherent, possessed of pattern and meaning. Of course, a story is necessarily told from someone's point of view: we don't all see the meaning of events in the same way. When you as a designer tell a story about your client, you present your version, retelling your client's story in light of a more satisfying ending provided by your design services.

You can structure a profile as a classic story, with a rising action, a climax, and a falling action. Or you can structure it as a journalist's feature story—as an hourglass, with an important introduction, a middle full of detail, and an important conclusion. Whatever structure you choose, bear in mind what Ernie Pyle once wrote: "If you want to tell the story of a war, tell the story of one soldier." Let a person or a group of people or an event stand for the larger story.[37] For instance, if you are writing a corporate profile, you might tell the story of one representative department.

Show the company's engineers walking all the way around the atrium to a fax machine. They can stand for all the other departments negatively affected by poor space planning.

Pay particular attention to the beginnings and ends of your profiles. Your profile can begin with an abstract summarizing statement, but an anecdote usually makes a more engaging "lead."

> *OK:*   After many years of solid business growth, Jones Fine Furniture was outgrowing the premises where it had done business since the company's founding in 1953.

> *Better:*   On February 17, 2004, Gloria Jones of Jones Fine Furniture was on the phone with Ralph Furey, an important customer. She could hardly hear Furey for the noise from the stockroom, where Orlando Perez and Mary Cold Mountain were nailing shut crates for an important express shipment. After five minutes of frustration, Furey hung up on Jones! She had lost an important sale, and she realized it was time to create adequate physical and acoustical separation between departments at JFF.

Whatever the structure of your story, your ending can take its cue from journalistic stories, which "have *conclusions* without having *summaries* . . . Use the conclusion to bring a story into a circle—for example, by referring again to a character from your lead—or to open up a new perspective or synthesis. Often a good quote can do the job: look . . . for someone who has something relatively unexpected and insightful to say about the 'big picture'"[38] that is being presented by your profile.

Here are some additional tips for making your client profiles come alive:

- Your profile should reveal and embody the issues that characterize the client's problem(s) and should also point to your solution(s).
- Use sense impressions to create characters that your readers will see, feel, and care about.
- Slow down to create a sense that action is happening fast. This is nonintuitive, but it works. More detail makes action happen faster, so don't skimp.
- Remember, your job as writer is to *show*, not tell. Stick to verbs and nouns and leave out adjectives like *lovely* and *terrible* that characterize attributes.

In the most rudimentary sense, a profile can speak to issues like the client's budget, the square footage of the project premises, the number of people who will be living or working on the premises, and the desired color scheme. As a more subtle and profound instrument, however, a profile based on thick description can illustrate your clients' lifestyle and philosophy in a dramatic and compelling way. It can reveal their lives, their thoughts, their motivations, and their values. It can impart the sense of immediacy and reality that makes it clear that you as designer are responsive to your client, deeply respectful of her joys and dilemmas, and profoundly engaged in the transformation she seeks.

Sometimes storytelling is *performative*—that is, it consists of oral presentation with theatrical elements. Designers can even sell themselves and their own ideas about design in this way. Consider the storytelling performance of industrial designer Jim Couch, revealed in excerpts from his article "The Persian Riverdance,"[39] which was presented to an audience of designers:

> *As the lights dimmed and the music cued, a Middle Eastern chant filled the room, hauntingly dramatic. Midway through the musical score, a man wearing a kilt, turban, tap shoes and football jersey, his face painted like a Maori warrior, bursts onto the stage. He engages in a series of wild, weird undulations—a Riverdance of sorts. It's a cacophony of cultural icons. A collision of ideas. He ends his dance center stage, with a kick of his heels, his hands in the air. He pulls up a chair and hooks up his microphone. Jim Couch has the full attention of the audience.*
>
> So what'd you think? . . . Did you like it? You think I got something here? Huh? Come on give it up! . . . **It was fun, wasn't it!** . . . It was fun . . . I still have a few bugs to work out, but I'm close. Aren't I? . . . Did I offend anyone? Please tell me. Did I offend you? . . . Yes? Good . . . No? Too bad. I'm disappointed.
>
> I always judge the success of my presentations and my designs on my ability to offend at least one person. If I don't . . . , then I haven't pushed the envelope far enough . . . it was . . . too safe, too clean . . . We [designers] should never be content staying on the road, let alone right down the middle. . . . When it comes to matters of conceptual thinking, matters of creativity, matters of discovering something new, we need to constantly be willing to drive off the side of the road . . . Even at the

risk of failure! . . . We need to give ourselves permission to explore with wild abandonment. . . . We will not change the world by . . . staying within lines that other people painted, by taking the road frequently traveled . . . **we have to continually open ourselves up to new experiences. This will create new dreams, new beliefs, and new hopes.**

And do you know where to start? . . . COLLISIONS! Collisions are great ways to stimulate and provoke radical, alternative thinking . . . We need to force existing paradigms to collide . . . Let's

Ram together technology.
Ram together cultures.
Ram together religions.
Ram together races.
Ram together sexes.
Ram together ideas.
Ram together values.
Ram together beliefs.

You know what this revolutionary action is going to produce, don't you? . . . **Mutants** . . . Some scary, some ugly, some deviant and some beautiful. . . . This is what we seek. This is what we must advocate. This is our mandate. . . . **Collisions are a natural process. The world . . . has been [colliding] since the beginning of time . . . Stop trying to . . . control it. Accept it. Embrace it. Contribute to it. Learn and benefit from it . . .**

It's a small world, becoming smaller every day. We need to tear down the walls that separate us . . . Stop seeing differences as "differences." See [them] as subtle nuances to be understood . . . Embrace diversity. . . . Experiment with it, and integrate [it] into . . . life . . .

[Whenever] you find yourself in the midst of a design assignment . . . take inventory . . . assess the situation and take one thing (just one thing) and do the complete opposite of what you normally would do. I guarantee, this will force an alternative point of view . . . push and transcend boundaries. Reject the norm. . . . Don't be found guilty of following the masses.

In this act of storytelling, Jim Couch makes himself a fictional character, a collision-embracing wild man dancing on the brink of chaos and social failure. He embodies the ideas he promotes. His story is of a "lunatic" with a seemingly disordered mind who is revealed as a "mutant," his mind a work in progress, reordered again and again in the service of creativity. You can read this story as a variant on the ancient tale of the frog who turns out to be a prince. Its freshness and its boldness are in powerful tension with the traditional elements of the tale. You might say that Couch's story profiles the designer's mind at work, as seen from the inside, by the designer and for the designer.

Discussion Questions

1. Discuss the ways in which an interior designer uses descriptive strategies to create meaning for several audiences: the commissioning client, contractors and fabricators, users, and future clients. Which of these communication tasks is the most important and why? Divide your class into four oral-presentation groups, each making the case for the paramount importance of one of these audiences and strategies.

2. Why are observation and listening so important to the writing of description?

3. How can a designer use writing, and particularly descriptive writing, to aid with the actual work of design?

Excercises

1. With reference to drawings, swatches, presentation boards, and other work products, write a walk-through description of a design project that you completed for one of your studio classes. If you have not completed a design project, then use a prominent local interior such as that of the public library as the basis for your presentation.

2. Write a concept statement for the project for which you did a walk-through.

3. The ASID booklet *Workplace Values* cites Fritz Steele,* who, in an article called "Looking for the Center," indicates that "the best way to test whether a center exists in an office setting is to ask workers where they go to find out who's around and what's currently happening in the organization." According to Steele, "when the center area is a good magnet, informal contacts will be greatly increased, a good deal of communication will occur quickly and often without having to make formal

appointments or send formal messages over the internal network. A well-used center enhances employees' awareness and identification with each other and the company." Bonding and so-called energy contagion take place that multiply the total energy.

Drawing on what you have read about thick description in this chapter, interview ten students, teachers, and administrative workers at your school to find out whether a center exists, and if it exists, what it consists of. Present your findings in a three-page brief that details your results.

4. Let each student in your class bring in a small, manual, kitchen implement such as a potato parer, a ginger grater, or a whisk. (Coordinate in advance, so that no two people bring in the same implement.) Prepare captions for an online catalog of all the implements geared to clients who do not have time to cook but wish to have kitchens that project cooking as a fantasy of old-fashioned domestic life.

5. Conduct round-robin pre-program and programming interviews with your teacher and members of your class about their experiences of classrooms throughout their educational histories.

a. Create a client profile based on five of these interviews.

b. Write a program report based on the same five interviews.

*Fritz Steele, "Looking for the Center," *The Journal for Quality and Participation* (Winter 2000) cited in *Workplace Values: How Employees Want to Work* (Washington, DC: American Society of Interior Designers, n.d.g., www.asid.org).

Analysis: A Tool for Understanding

3

The word *analysis* means breaking a subject down into parts and then putting the parts back together to provide a clearer view of the whole. It is a principal tool not only of writing about design, but of design itself, for it promotes understanding at any given stage of the process and aids in solving problems. Indeed, analysis is a useful tool for examining any complicated phenomenon, particularly one with interrelated parts. By breaking the subject down, analysis can discover and explain reasons, causes, and effects[1] while projecting a professional's expertise and objectivity.

"Even when the subject is not simply explanatory," say English professors Alan Danzig and Edith Schor, "emphasis on logical connections can assure an objective tone in an analysis."[2] Because it relies not only on logic[3] but on the organization of evidence, analysis seems to be objective even when it is driven by a strong argumentative thesis, that is, when the writer has an agenda. The appearance of objectivity is crucial for imparting to a designer's written communications an aura of professional gravity.

> Yet . . . in a larger sense [the true nature of] analysis lies beyond the objective and the impersonal . . . What you, the writer, see as logical connections, what you take for natural causes, are in fact chosen by you for inclusion in your analysis. Your insight not only recognizes them but in a sense actually creates them.

This last point is critical to an understanding of the power and significance of analysis in interior design writing. During every phase of the project, the designing writer chooses the best "route" through the evidence in the same way that a downhill ski racer chooses the best route down a hill. Skiers do not simply close their eyes, tuck their poles under their arms, and take off. Through careful scrutiny, assessment, and choice, they *create* the path that enable them to perform well on that particular hill, with its bumps, bare spots, thickets, rocks, ice patches, deep snow pockets, and perfect glides. The skiers' skill in negotiating the terrain establishes the authority of their rides. Likewise, writing designers must analyze the terrain they are to traverse during their rides. This is an active process; the writing designer who is passive will appear to be overwhelmed by the "hill" that is the project.

The Complex Roles of Analysis for the Writing Designer

Analysis is part of the design process itself, and analysis translates a designer's vision into arguments that move others to take action. As a design strategy, analysis provides a "placeholder for specific pieces of a problem as it is being solved."[4] Analysis serves to organize data collected from interviews and literature and other research (see Chapters 2 and 9). It functions as a crucial tool in such documents as scope statements and specifications. It provides a framework for reporting problems encountered during a project's execution and can play a notable role in the post-occupancy phase, for instance, in organizing and reporting survey data.

As a writing strategy, analysis ranges from relatively simple forms such as division and classification and process analysis through complex forms of critical analysis, including the analysis of narrative research. Any and all of these writing strategies can support the design process.

Because analysis is both a *design* strategy and a *writing* strategy, a meaningful discussion of it must distinguish between these two roles even while acknowledging their complex interaction.

Analysis as a Design Strategy

An early analytic gesture a designer may perform on a given project is the teasing forth of issues from the mass of descriptive data collected from pre-programming and programming interviews (see Chapter 2).

Donna P. Duerk defines an *issue* as "any matter, concern, question, topic, proposition, or situation that demands a design response" in order for a project to be successful for clients and users.[5] Duerk's issue and sub-issue checklist[6] covers most of the myriad concerns involved in any design project and can be the basis for a well-made program document. An excerpt from the issue checklist is presented in Figure 3.1. A checklist like this can function as a template, but like all templates, it needs to be customized to the particular job at hand.

You can use writing techniques to assist you in developing a customized issue "template" for a specific project. For instance, you can use the outliner's technique of *clustering* to note and group the issues emerging from interview data. To cluster effectively, you need to indicate which ideas or issues belong together, based on your scrutiny of data. ("Three people in this family mention a problem finding quiet, private space for reading and study. That's an issue.") You can use symbols to mark your data for clustering: stars for one issue, squares for another. You can then list the emergent issues in a separate document, where they form an *outline*—a

Cluster related
issues to organize
interview data.

ISSUE AND SUB-ISSUE CHECKLIST

MOOD/AMBIENCE
Attitude
Emotional response
Spirit of the place

PERSONALIZATION
Group
Individual

PRIVACY
Group
Individual

SAFETY
Accidents
Hazards

Figure 3.1
Issue and sub-issue checklist.
Adapted from Donna P. Duerk, Architectural Programming: Information Management for Design *(New York: Van Nostrand Reinhold, 1993), 24.*

writer's discovery and planning device—that can be compared against the checklist presented in Figure 3.1. As you work, you can move your issues around, check for redundancy, make sure you've covered everything, and so on, clustering and re-clustering until the best shape for your presentation emerges. (You can also cluster through drawing, using visual factors such as vector of inscription and placement on the page to show the dynamic outline that is emerging. Your document might look something like the one shown in Figure 3.2.)

Note how the following discussion from a technical writing book[7] sheds light on outlining as a technique for the development of issue-based programming, helping a writing designer see the relationship between ideas (or issues):

Let the outlining capabilities of word-processing software help you develop issue-based programming.

> [Outlining] progresses in stages. In the early stages, you must move, merge, expand, and eliminate ideas [or issues]. Your goal is to discover basic topics, logical principles of organization, and an effective approach. . . . Theoretically, if you have thought through all the ideas [or issues] well enough, you should be able to write your [programming] document from your final outline. In practice, however, writing is a process of continuing discovery, and outlines frequently change. Many word-processing programs such as WordPerfect and Microsoft Word include outliners, features that allow you to construct an outline on screen and then expand it into a document.

Figure 3.2
A cluster diagram indicating which ideas or issues belong together. Visual factors such as vector of inscription and placement on the page show the dynamic relationship between issues. *Courtesy of Dan Beert and Gail Cummins's "Space and Multiple Intelligences: Finding the Multidisciplinary Process," an oral presentation given at the Writing Across the Curriculum Conference at Cornell University, Ithaca, NY, 1999.*

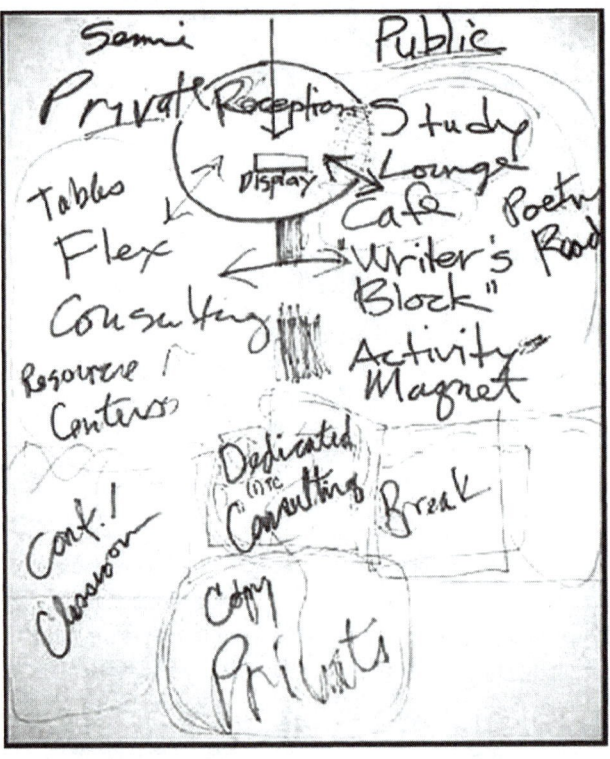

You might try saving Duerk's issues checklist as an outline in your word-processing program, thus creating an electronic template for issue-based programming. You need to understand, though, that Duerk's checklist consists of *generic* items. It shows you the *kinds* of issues you should be considering. Particularly for a residential client, your customized outline for issues presentation relating to a given project may not have headings such as the following:

MOOD/AMBIENCE
Attitude
Emotional response
Spirit of the place

Rather, your outline for a particular residential project may designate issues in a manner that reflects the nature of a client's world. You may supplement or replace Duerk's generic language with particulars drawn from your project. In the following example, it is replaced.

CONSTANT CRISIS: A TWO-CAREER HOUSEHOLD WITH
SIX CHILDREN IN SCHOOL (mood or ambience)
Striving to stay on top (*attitude*)
The Hansens' desire for calm (*emotional response*)
The soothing effect of the Hansen home's riverside setting (*spirit of the place*)

Issue presentation for a business client might proceed in a similar manner, but you would be more likely to keep Duerk's generic issue and sub-issue labels as "handles" that make the various items easy to retrieve and talk about. This is particularly important for a complicated project, be it residential or commercial. The more issues and sub-issues there are, the more value to keeping intact the generic "handles" that function as place markers and help to create a shared language that facilitates discussion.

Suppose you were designing an office setting for an insurance company. If you had information about individual employees' expectations for personalizing their cubicles, you might let these expectations generate an item in your customized issue outline. It would correspond to Duerk's checklist item "Personalization: Individual." If your research showed that employees function more effectively when the identities of their departments, based on different floors, are well established, then that fact might generate another item in your issue outline. It would correspond to Duerk's checklist item "Personalization: Group."

For the insurance-company client, you might present these two issues with the generic handle followed by particulars drawn from the client's world. Your items might read "Personalization: Individual—The Cubicle" and "Personalization: Group—The Floor." The handles "speak" a short-hand language, businesslike but easily shared. They give the client confidence that the basics are being covered and design standards are being met. The client-derived designations, on the other hand, show how your design would help this particular client's employees express identity.

Note that each issue identified by Duerk and contained in her checklist represents a "continuum of qualities from one extreme to the other."[8] Thus, "personalization" ranges from a *low* to a *high* degree of personalization. Personalization might have a low value in a sales-office setting that serves mostly transients—sales reps coming in at different times of day to use the same spaces for only a few hours apiece. Personalization might have a high value for a nursery school in which teachers wish to customize their classrooms. In practical terms, these continuums suggest another way to customize the checklist for particular clients. If personalization has a low value in the sales-office setting, it might not even figure in your program document for a project relating to the sales office. If personalization has a high value in the nursery-school setting, then this issue will figure prominently in your program document.

Goal Statements

Identification of project issues helps the designer and the client to generate goals, or statements about what the design should do for the client (see Figure 3.3). Goal statements speak of the future conditions that you wish to achieve. As they are articulated, project discussion shifts to the *prescriptive* realm—the realm of how things ought to be—providing remedies for problems. "Goals," says Duerk, "should be developed for each design issue that has been uncovered . . . and for each issue that is subsequently uncovered as the design process unfolds."[9] These goal statements, says Duerk, should be "short and to the point." Following are other important characteristics:

- For each project, there should be a meta-goal or mission statement that characterizes the project as a whole. You might think of this as your initial concept statement (see Chapter 2), though it may change over the life of your design.

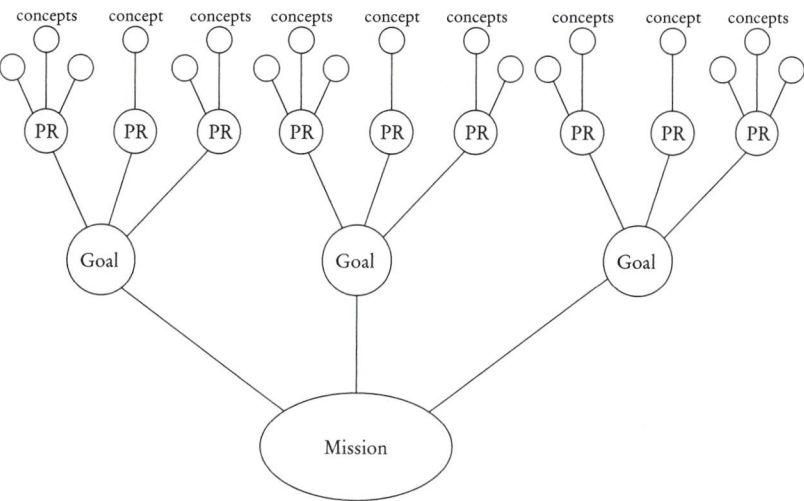

PR = performance requirement

Figure 3.3
The Programming Tree
Analysis provides a framework for data collected from interviews and other research and helps a designer solve problems and realize a vision while remaining responsive to the client.
Adapted from Donna P. Duerk, Architectural Programming: Information Management for Design *(New York: Van Nostrand Reinhold, 1993),* 20.

- Statements should be relatively abstract in order to remain useful throughout the project with *minimal* changes as the project evolves.

- Each goal should focus on the *quality* to be achieved for the issue that the goal is delineating—for example, *warmly welcoming*.

- Goals need to be based on adjectives and adverbs, carefully chosen—*nurturing, stimulating, joyous, serene,* and the like. You may boil a list of numerous adjectives and adverbs down to the few that seem most essential. (See Exercise 1 at the end of this chapter.)

- Each goal statement must contain *should* or a closely related verb, to express its prescriptive nature. Note that *prescriptive* does not mean regulatory. It describes a norm or quality standard.

- Goals should be positive and proactive. Avoid words like *not, no,* and *never*. Also "avoid negative descriptions of existing conditions," advises Dan Beert, lest you offend the client. "Yes, the interior might be 'boring,'" but "avoid words that can be interpreted in a derogatory or derisive manner."[10]

- All goal statements for a given project should be written at the same level of abstraction, cover an equivalent scope, and indicate the same level of importance. (This is an important instance of the need for parallel construction in writing, discussed in Chapter 1.)

- A goal statement should be as simple as possible; yet all relevant performance requirements should fall within its scope. (A discussion of performance requirements follows shortly.)
- Goals should not telegraph particular solutions to the problems that have been expressed as issues. If the goal is a warm, welcoming ambience, it is premature to suggest yellow paint.[11]

Goal statement ->
Performance
Requirement ->
Design Concept

Bearing all these points in mind, a goal statement about personalization for the nursery school project might read: "The classrooms should be comfortable, nurturing venues for the creative expression of students in art, music, theater, poetry, and dance."

Performance Requirements

In Duerk's system, the goal statements are *operationalized*—that is, made measurable—as "performance requirements" before being interpreted as design concepts. *Performance requirements* are statements about the level of function that an interior setting must meet in order to satisfy a goal.

The three relevant types of measurement are:

- *Binary* (yes or no)
  - Each classroom should provide three distinct means to display students' artwork. (Either there are three distinct means or there are not—two would not suffice. Whatever the designated number, be it 2, 14, or 5,213, one less than that number would mean "no.")
- *Scalar* (measures a range of values)
  - Each office floor should be illuminated by a mixture of direct and indirect ambient lighting, with 40 percent being indirect.[12]
- *Judgmental* (measures by cognitive assessment)
  - The home will provide family members with a rich variety of privacy options. (How much variety is *rich*? It's a judgment call.)

Duerk suggests that performance requirements be created by imagining that a project is doing things for its users—*creating*, *supporting*, *maintaining*, and so on. Such verbs focus the writer's mind on action. This is resonant with the performance requirement's embrace of *function*. In addition to its focus on function, a performance requirement, or PR, must be suited to a clear and particular purpose. Yet it does not have the physical specificity of a concept (discussed shortly). The PR's emphasis on function serves as a bridge between the generality of a goal and the physical specificity of the concept.

Donna Duerk offers these tips for writing excellent performance requirements:

- A good PR tells how a goal is to be implemented.
- Adjectives and adverbs should describe a level of function.
- The dominant verb should indicate function.
- The word *should* expresses the prescriptive element of the PR's statement of ideal function. (If the PR must be implemented 100 percent, then *should* is replaced with *shall*.)
- A PR should have the power to exclude concepts that are inappropriate for the purpose or inadequate to the task—that is, it should be subject to testing. Yet it should allow for all relevant concepts to emerge.

Note also the need to cover each major aspect of the functional requirements for each goal. Several performance requirements must be met in order to generate the quality expressed in each goal statement. For example, the goal of supporting children's creative expression would yield performance requirements having to do with art, music, dance, theater, and poetry. For each variety of creative expression mentioned in a goal statement, a separate performance requirement must express a measurable level of function, as in the following guidelines for a fictional dance institute:

- To facilitate theatrical study and performance, each classroom should be easily convertible to two types of presentation
- To facilitate dance study and performance, each classroom should conform to the "healthy dancer" guidelines of the Dance in Education Institute

Concepts

Because performance requirements ensure the quality of an interior setting without dictating how to achieve the desired result, they should stimulate design development by suggesting a variety of solutions, or *concepts*. Concepts define relationships between physical elements under an interior designer's control. Duerk offers the following guidelines for developing design concepts:

- A group of concepts supports the level of function measured in a single performance requirement, expressing its various aspects.
- Each concept is an idea expressed as a simple diagram with a concise caption.
- A concept may be an analogy or a metaphor. (See Chapter 2.)

Concepts are "the most specific elements in the programming hierarchy,"[13] yet a concept expresses a generic relationship capable of a wide range of implementation. Thus, the PR for conforming to "healthy-dancer" guidelines may be supported by the concept of the sprung floor (along with, for example, glare-free mirrors, pads for some floor work, barres at the appropriate height). Simply put, a sprung floor (Figure 3.4) is one with *spring* (give, or elasticity) built into it; the running, leaping dancer bounces upon impact and thus avoids the shin, ankle, and back injuries that come from slamming down on concrete slabs or other hard, nonresilient surfaces.

Figure 3.4
A sprung floor gives dancers bounce, preventing rigid impacts that may cause injury.

The sprung-floor concept[14] can be implemented in a variety of ways, for instance:

- *Basket weave*   One-by-threes are woven together beneath a plywood top that is then covered with linoleum.
- *Foam rubber*   A layered floor is built up from a Masonite bottom, with a filling of foam-rubber squares, topped by plywood.
- *False floor*   Modules of four-by-eight plywood are each supported by an inch-and-a-half frame with a crossbar at the four-foot mark. Rotolocks snap the modules together.
- *Multiple impact baffles*   A hardwood floor rests on a layer of felt and acoustical paper. The felt and paper are installed over a subfloor of pine that floats above support beams on strips of cork.

These implementations range in cost from the false floor to the multiple-baffle floor. A designer would work with a client to select the dance flooring that presented best value within the budget. Note that the concept does not dictate a specific solution to the client's problem, but points to a number of solutions.

Within the programming hierarchy, then, successful concepts fulfill performance requirements and point to a range of physical expressions for the physical relationships they define. "[Concepts] are the ideas that guide the outcome of the whole project and solve the important problems raised by each issue."[15] Yet the term *concept* can apply to ideas expressed at varying levels of abstraction. The building-block concepts that support performance requirements are collectively subsumed under the overall theme statement, or *parti*, the "super-organizing" concept corresponding to the *meta-goal*, or mission statement (see Chapter 2), for the entire project. Indeed, concepts, are defined as follows in Duerk's eloquent words[16]:

> A concept can be the solution to a particular problem, the implementation of an ideal, or the manifestation of the spirit or essence of a building or building aspect.

As a design project continues to unfold, and even after it is finished, the concepts informing it continue to be refined in writing. Some designers create proposal documents based on the analytic strategies and categories set forth by Duerk. These documents serve as a springboard for action, promoting the client's mission and offering concrete ideas on how that vision might be realized. Such documents may be discussed with and used by another designer or an architect who has been hired to create the actual design, giving a collaborator valuable insight into the client's priorities. The client, who at the beginning of the programming process may have been able to express a vision for a new facility only in general terms, now shares with the design team a language that translates vague or abstract ideas into concrete, architectural form. On your CD-ROM are proposal documents for a Japanese garden interpretive center in Seattle, WA, created by students of design professor Dan Beert (Bellevue Community College, Bellevue, WA). Highly visual in nature, they combine thoughtful Duerkian analysis of issues and concepts using a variety of written and graphic formats.

Analysis as a Writing Strategy

In addition to its use in Duerkian proposal documents, analysis as a writing strategy continues to play a great many other roles in support of an evolving design project. Sometimes a writing designer uses analysis simply to organize data for clear presentation, as with *division-and-classification* or *process analysis*. Specifications, arguably one of the most important kinds of writing a designer is called upon to perform, are organized through both classification *and* process analysis. Complex in a different way is the *critical analysis* that examines causes, effects, reasons, and interrelationships, "[informing] a reader fully about differences, or about options and their drawbacks so that [she or he] can make [a sound] decision."[17] The writing interior designer may be called upon to generate several different types of critical analysis, among them *problem-and-solution analysis, comparative analysis, summary analysis*, and *evaluation*.

Any of these kinds of analysis may form the *body*, or core, of an essay or report that customarily requires an *introduction*, or opening statement, explaining the purpose and *context*, or frame of reference, of the presentation, as well as the main idea you want to put across. The body of the analysis should be followed by a *conclusion*, or closing statement, telling readers what they are to make of the information they have been given. If the analyzed data speak for themselves, as they sometimes do if tabulated, for instance, then the introduction and conclusion may be omitted.

Division and Classification
From childhood you have doubtless been familiar with the thought process that lies behind the writing strategies of division and classification. In your everyday life, you encounter it when you perform such taken-for-granted operations as sorting laundry. From the tangled mass of clothing that you pull

from the dryer, you create a separate pile for clothing for each member of your family, with other piles for household linens such as sheets and towels. By creating these piles, or categories, you perform an act of *division*—separating a whole into parts in a useful manner by creating various categories. By actually sorting the laundry and placing each item in the appropriate pile, or category, you perform an act of *classification*—grouping individual items within the appropriate categories. These simple acts are emblems for the infinitely more sophisticated mental processes that underlie a writing designer's use of division and classification for purposes such as inventory, space-planning reports, and the presentation of survey data.

Division and classification make it possible to arrange space-programming data in a way that is easily accessible to all readers, as you can see from the sample shown in Figure 3.5, an "excerpt" from a fictional space-programming report. The unclassified data would be very hard to present coherently, let alone to manage, access, and interpret.

It is important to note that the division categories for any given classification are related to the designer writer's purpose. For instance, if your purpose is to display a client's inventory of chairs by function—task chairs, executive chairs, conference chairs, and so on—the categories would be different than if you need to show which chairs your client needs to purchase when—in which case a function-based classification might be less useful, because all the categories might contain items that the client needs to purchase at each particular juncture.

Once you have established the basis for division and classification, "apply it consistently, putting each item in only one category."[18] For instance, if the executive office chairs are sometimes used during conferences but are mostly used by managers working at their desks, then you would not classify these chairs within the conference-chair category, but rather as executive chairs. When the inventory has been fully classified, you can use it as the basis for summary or interpretative conclusions, recommendations, or the presentation of meaningful alternatives. (If you have inserted your data into a fully relational database, then you can cross-reference to create reports using various classification systems.)

Process Analysis

The genre known as process analysis is a subgenre of division and classification. It breaks a process down according to *sequence*—the steps that need to be executed in order for a process to be correctly performed. Any subject that can be broken down into distinct steps lends itself to process analysis, including sets of directions and instructions. One basic guideline applies to all analysis of this

A SPACE PROGRAMMING REPORT

FM: SPACE MANAGEMENT   12/15/88
DEMONSTRATION PROJECT   PAGE 1
SPACE-PROGRAMING REPORT   PROJECT CODE: DEMO

Comp   Compensation
Manager: Martin Proctor
Contact: Edna St. John

Job-Code Space Std Description	Space Std Area (SF)	Qty 01/88	Rqd Area (SF) 01/88
2000 A2 10 x 12 Office	120	1	120
DE1: 30 x 60 Desk			
CH1: Desk Chair w/arms			
Ch2: 2-Guest Chairs			
CR1: Credenza			
EL3: Cable to System 5			
2100 A2 10 x 12 Office	120	4	480
DE1: 30 x 60 Desk			
CH1: Desk Chair w/arms			
Ch2: 2-Guest Chairs			
CR1: Credenza			

Needs special cable connection to stock quote systems.
Talk to telecomunications department.

4410 B1 8 x 10 Workstation	80	3	240
FILE1 File Room	120	1	120
F11: 10-36" 2 Drawer Lateral File			

Check Floor Loading

Subtotal		4	440
Subtotal Assignable Area			440
Circulation		35%	154
Core Factor		12%	71
Total Rentable Area			665

type. Whatever is required for the completion of the process belongs in the analysis. Organization of the analysis is clear if underlying observation has been keen. The analyzed process is broken down into steps in order to clarify and reveal its nature, and these steps are presented in the order in which they normally occur. You can see this very clearly in "The Residential Interior Design Process: What Happens Next?" by Adrianne Dale, FASID (Figure 3.6), a purely informative document written for Dale's clients. List-like presentation

Figure 3.6
A process analysis document.
Courtesy of
P. Adrianne Dale,
FASID; Whardale
International,
Sumner, WA.

THE RESIDENTIAL INTERIOR DESIGN PROCESS

what happens next?

- Interview a series of potential interior designers with good credentials.
    Discuss fee options.
    Discuss availability for your schedule.
    Discuss office/ordering procedures.
    Discuss budget for project.
- Sign a Letter of Agreement with the designer outlining scope of service and fees plus responsibilities of each party.
- Designer will prepare for an initial presentation.
    Conduct space and needs analysis.
    Review building plans.
    Collect sample materials—fabrics, carpets, tile, wall coverings etc.
    Meet with any other professionals or trades involved (architect, contractor)
- Initial presentation meeting to discuss information gathered to date.
    Review results of needs analysis.
    Elimination of non-acceptable materials.
    Discuss next stage.
- The client may request visits to vendor showrooms for quality review at any time.
- Information gathering and consultation meetings may continue to fine tune design requirements of space.
    Frequency may depend on client decisiveness and communication skills of designer.
- Site visits may be required frequently for remodeling or new construction.
- When decisions have been reached, designer may prepare specification lists for builders and for products that the designer will sell to the client.
    Price estimates will be prepared at this time to confirm purchases before transacted.
- Client will sign authorization-to-purchase agreement with designer before purchase orders are prepared.
    A deposit is required at this time, usually a minimum of 50 percent.
    Orders are not usually returnable or cancelable.
- Designer will monitor progress of product orders. It may be a good idea for client to call occasionally for status checks.
    Balance of payments is usually due on receipt of product or earlier if manufacturer requires before shipping.

gives it a sense of chronological sequence that closely resembles a set of instructions. Except at the beginning. Dale does not use the *command*, or *imperative*, mode that is characteristic of instructions, nor should she; it is not an appropriate manner in which to address clients consistently. Most of her analysis is written in the *indicative* mode that is used to say what is objectively true. Here are some other notable characteristics of Dale's process analysis:

- She has not wasted any time in speaking to her clients' need to know. The title "The Residential Interior Design Process: What Happens Next?" clearly and completely indicates the nature and purpose of the process writing that follows. It functions as the introduction to the piece.
- The steps of the process and the sub-steps are set forth clearly.
- Essential details—and only essential details—are presented in an economical manner. (Note the sparing use of articles and other words that do not advance understanding. This is characteristic of sets of instructions, though it is not a style rule for all process analyses.)
- Dale fully and implicitly addresses the questions: Why undertake this process? Who would need to know how to do it?

Dale's design process analysis serves a function similar to a *scope-of-services statement,* setting forth the range of services offered by a design firm. Such a statement typically combines classification and process analyses, breaking down the design process into a sequence of phases such as "programming," then classifying within each phase the activities that are characteristic of it—for instance, for programming, to "identify and analyze the client's needs and goals."[19] In combining classification and process analysis, the scope-of-services statement is similar to the all-important scope-of-work statements and specifications that detail the construction and renovation work to be performed for a client.

SCOPE-OF-WORK STATEMENTS

Customarily part of a designer's agreement with his client, the *scope-of-work* statement outlines and forecasts construction work to be performed. It becomes the basis for *specifications*, or design criteria for the work to be performed. We look further at these two genres in relation to other construction contract documents in Chapter 7. We also look at the role of specifications for purchasing in Chapter 8. For now, our focus is on the analytic aspect of scope-of-work statements and specifications.

A *scope-of-work statement* divides the work of a proposed renovation project into its component parts in a clear and comprehensible manner. For example, work may be classified by trade or by room. Thus the scope-of-work statement is an example of division and classification. In addition to its classification element, the scope-of-work statement in Figure 3.7 is written as a set of instructions, in the imperative mode. Scope-of-work statements are not always written as instructions. Many work-scope statements are written to express future necessity, using "shall" or "will." Even if the scope statement is not written as a set of instructions, a work process is implicit and will become explicit in the specifications that follow from and are based on the scope statement. Because specifications are closely linked to the scope-of-work statement—which is generated earlier in the design process than the specifications— it is important that the designer write the scope statement carefully, based on painstaking observation.

SPECIFICATIONS

Like scope-of-work statements, specification sets for construction and renovation combine elements of division-and-classification and process analysis. As you will see in greater detail in Chapter 7, construction specifications set forth the correct "ingredients" for each part of a project, classified by trade or room or another relevant set of criteria. For instance, Benjamin

---

INTERIOR FINISH

A. ELECTRICAL
    i. Set & wire panel unless installed at plant, then terminate wires in panel.
    ii. Install any glass fixture globes; all other lighting pre-installed.
    iii. Pull phone & TV wires to the electrical panel for outside connection.

B. FLOORING
    i. Install carpet & vinyl if shipped loose or omitted.
    ii. Seam installed carpet & vinyl at the mate wall & between 1st and 2nd floors.

C. PAINT
    i. Touch up paint where drywall and trim are field installed.
    ii. Perform any custom painting required.

Figure 3.7
Excerpt from Generic Scope-of-Work Statement for a Modular Home.
Adapted from "Scope of Work after House Is Set," Modular Homes & Plans. *http://www.modular-homes-plans.com/modulars/scope_of_work.html.*

Moore eggshell dulamel in Cloud White may be specified for painting custom-milled crown molding (Figure 3.8). It would likely be classified in the section of the specification set dealing with paint type and color. This listing of ingredients is crucial for the control of quality.

Figure 3.8
A residential paint
specification.

> **Custom-milled crown molding**: Furnished by Chip Block, Inc. Prime with Benjamin Moore Latex Quick Dry Prime Seal. Finish with two coats Benjamin Moore Eggshell Dulamel in "Cloud." Provide color SAMPLE on molding stock as required.

The manner in which the paint is to be applied will also be specified—for instance, a certain number of coats over a certain primer. This aspect of the specifications is akin to process analysis, which, as we have seen, includes directions and instructions. The "directions" contained in specifications are as crucial for the control of quality as the ingredients.

Because they contain both ingredients and directions, specifications resemble recipes for cooking. After listing what must go into the particular dish to be cooked, recipes use numbered steps and the command voice, saying "do this," (imperative mode) rather than "The cook does this" (indicative mode). So it is with specification sets.

Specifications for purchasing are *not* linked to scope-of-work statements. They are a less hybrid analytic genre, as they do not necessarily involve instructions or other process analysis but only division and classification. They are discussed in more detail in Chapter 8.

The Problem-Cause-Solution Pattern

Division-and-classification and process analyses are strategies for data organization and presentation. Although a strong element of quality control may be implicit or explicit, they are not primarily interpretative or argumentative. The problem-cause-solution pattern of analysis, however, is more interpretive, even argumentative, than the analytic strategies previously discussed—*interpretive* in that it is an individual response that assesses meaning and *argumentative* in that it advocates an alternative or option.

Components of Problem-Cause-Solution Analysis
- Contextual introduction, if needed
- Problem section

- Cause section—chronological or inventory presentation
- Solution section

After a brief contextual introduction providing a frame of reference, problem-cause-solution analysis begins with a problem-presentation section; it ends with a solution-presentation section. The middle or "cause" section presents an analysis conceived as a *chronological* sequence or as an *inventory* of causes. In both cases, effect is examined along with cause. The ultimate "effect" is the designer's solution of the client's problem. The problem-cause-solution pattern, as we shall see, is particularly useful for troubleshooting and for the presentation of case studies, including narrative case studies.

CAUSE AND EFFECT: CHRONOLOGICAL

Sometimes, the cause of a problem can be usefully presented as a sequence of events in time—for example, when a chain of events explains a problem. The temporal component is well represented in the proverbial saying, "For want of a nail, a shoe was lost, for want of a shoe a horse was lost, for want of a horse a rider was lost," which follows the cause-and-effect chain to the net result: loss of a war.

Similarly, an interior designer might examine the chain of events leading to a vendor's failure to ship the client's chair in a timely manner. Perhaps the shipping clerk labeled the crate improperly. The chair was shipped to a different client, who refused to accept delivery of the chair, which was returned to the vendor's shipping department, where a new clerk, unfamiliar with the chair, consigned it to the warehouse, where it was stored in the wrong unit because it had once again been mislabeled . . . and so on. These causes are a chain of events. One thing leads to another to create the problem: the client's chair has not been delivered.

In this context, it needs to be noted, the chronological presentation is process analysis with a difference. A true process analysis presents a sequence that always has the same result if the steps of the process are executed correctly, whereas cause-and-effect is best conceived as a story, or *narrative*, presenting events as they happened once but need not happen again. In the "cause" section of a problem-solution analysis, the supposition is not only that things could have been different; indeed, they *should* have been different. The desired difference is presented in the "solution" part of the analysis.

The careful writer about cause and effect will be very careful about transition. Danzig and Schor have noted the following[20]:

Only when a cause-and-effect relationship has in fact been established can you use a word or phrase indicating causality. *For this reason, therefore, thus we have seen*—such words and phrases sum up a carefully reasoned discussion. They are not just official-sounding ways to move into a final paragraph. Remember, too, that the fact that one event happens before another is not evidence that the first caused the second. . . . You must show the connecting links in a chain of logic, or else be certain the reader will understand the steps you take for granted.

CAUSE AND EFFECT: INVENTORY

Sometimes, the *etiology*, or origin and growth, of a problem can be usefully presented as an inventory of causes—for example, when multiple factors come together to create a problem. The shipment of the client's chair may have been delayed because a fire broke out in the manufacturing plant, the upholstery fabric delivered by the vendor's supplier was defective, the clerk labeled the chair crate improperly when it was finally shipped, and no one was present at the project premises to receive the delivery, which was returned to the factory. These causes are not a chain of events: except in the last case, one thing did not cause another. Yet all these causes contributed to the problem: the client's chair was not delivered.

> When writing a cause inventory, build to a climax by moving from the least to the most important causes.

When writing an inventory of causes, make sure the sections and subsections of your analysis flow logically and smoothly from one to the next. Try to build on what has gone before so that the analysis moves toward a climax. This means discussing the least important causes first, and the most important last.

How you decide upon the boundaries of causal analysis depends on the nature of the problem, your purpose in writing, and what you have to say. Similarly, the "solution" part of your analysis depends on the same set of factors. If you are writing about the chair problem for a grieved client, the solution may lie in your willingness to find an alternate means of delivering the client's chair. If you are writing about this problem for your designer employer, the solution you propose may involve dealing with a different chair manufacturer or complaining about the vendor's shipping department. Be sure that your solution is in line with the analysis you have presented, so that your writing flows smoothly. For the chair examples just discussed, it would *not* do to propose a solution like "Encourage future clients to sit on sofas rather than chairs."

THE PROBLEM-CAUSE-SOLUTION PATTERN IN CASE STUDY

The problem-cause-solution pattern may prove useful not only in troubleshooting, but also in proposals and case studies. Proposals are covered in

Chapter 5. We will look here at the *case study*, a genre that typically focuses on one design project or a small group of them. As we shall see, the writing designer may be called upon to write three types of case studies: *promotional*, *investigative*, and *narrative*.

PROMOTIONAL CASE STUDIES   Many interior designers publish brief promotional case studies of challenging or interesting projects that showcase their firms' capabilities. These may be illustrated, one-page print flyers suitable for inclusion in customized capability packets (see Chapter 4), or they may be posted on design firms' Web sites. Typically, each promotional case study focuses on a single project. The "problem" section of the study encapsulates the issues that were presented in the design program, while the "solution" section explains how the design firm solved the client's problem. The discussion of "cause" is usually an inventory rather than a chronology; often it is folded into the "problem" section. Much of the story may be told with photographs, sometimes before-and-after photos. Points are simplified and are often made by means of bulleted lists.[21]

Especially if your case study is of a successfully completed commercial, corporate, or institutional design project, it is important to discuss your solution to the client's problem in a manner that will speak to the values of similar clients who are considering future projects. You can do this by evoking the themes of business-oriented analysis to generate a design-based study that is also client-centered. It is prudent to convey the impression that you and your case-study client arrived at a solution that met the following criteria[22]:

> In a promotional case study, much of the story is told through photos.

- Cost less
- Was effective
- Was minimally disruptive
- Is consistent with the client's organizational culture
- Is consistent with the client's ethics—for instance, green design
- Enables flexibility in shifting to alternative paths
- Maintains the client's strengths
- Supports the client's mission
- Furthers the client's goals

Your case study should reveal what implications your design solution has on the operation of your client's organization in the short and long term, and what benefits the client realizes from your design solution.

A case study must reveal the benefits your design brings to the client.

INVESTIGATIVE CASE STUDIES   A promotional case study draws part of its power from the in-depth analysis and authoritative objectivity that are associated with true investigative case studies, not only in interior design and related fields, but in fields such as business, law, and medicine. These case studies focus on multiple sources of evidence within their topic areas, yet they do not attempt to survey a whole field. For instance, suggests Donna P. Duerk,[23] "you might do case studies of several innovative schools as preparation for" renovating the interior of a school. You would look very closely at the *empirical*, or observation-based, evidence yielded by a small number of examples. Although your study might elicit copious data, you would not expect to generate any statistical predictions based on quantitative data from a variety of schools that function in different circumstances.

It needs to be noted that the "solution" section of an investigative case study of this type may yield a set of recommendations or questions rather than a clear-cut solution. Alternatively, the "solution" section may evaluate the ways in which, say, particular schoolroom designs do or do not address the issues and solve the problems that the interior designer is studying. In the instance cited, the designer's investigation is part of programming research. An investigative case study may also be undertaken as an in-depth analysis of a completed project or ongoing designer-client relationship. In general, in-depth case study in the design field is suitable for investigation in a real-life context. Within a complex setting, case studies can "yield a much richer picture of who the typical clients are than any survey could yield."[24]

NARRATIVE CASE STUDY   A case study that presents a *narrative*, or story, is called a *narrative case study*. This hybrid methodology combines case-study analysis in the problem-cause-solution pattern with elements of *narrative inquiry*, a "research methodology that captures narratives from specific populations and analyzes [their] language and content."[25] This excerpt from "Narrative Research in Design Practice" further explains the role of narrative inquiry:

> [Narrative inquiry is] utilized by many disciplines including sociology, psychology, anthropology, law, history, literary criticism, psychotherapy, and organizational research. . . . [It] is typically used to uncover social phenomena, social drivers, and collective beliefs both within and between populations. . . . [It] captures information difficult to attain by traditional means of data collection such as . . . questionnaires . . . and observation."

Classic investigative case studies, according to Margaret Portillo and Joy H. Dohr, "often require time-consuming data collection efforts and produce voluminous data sets. Working with a narrative structure has an inherent focus that helps allay this concern,"[26] but narrative inquiry has even more compelling virtues for writing designers.

Like the classic case study, narrative inquiry presents multiple sources of evidence. "However ... the narrative structure reveals a particular unfolding of events emphasizing the subjective experience ... [expressing] not only the cognitive but the emotional."[27] The power to communicate subjective experience—to relate "personally meaningful" experience of "physical interior space"[28] makes narrative a compelling vehicle to convey "the intangible qualities of design."[29]

As Katie Sosnowchik points out,[30] we have all listened to and read stories since childhood:

> [We] eagerly awaited the introductory words, "once upon a time ..." We knew that what followed would ... [set] our imaginations in motion ... in the course of the storytelling we made a personal connection to the characters involved and the situations they found themselves in. We imagined ourselves into the stories, and came away learning a valuable life lesson or two.

Because readers identify with the characters in stories, or narratives, they are able to convey the power of design to transform, not just spaces, but people's lives. Stories are especially useful for the study of themes such as creativity. For instance, the strength of the narrative mode in the cognitive, emotional, and structural realms guided a study of "creativity and narrative that had some of the following research objectives[31]:

- To articulate a many-voiced narrative of a design project, independently recounted by designer and client/end-users
- To communicate through narrative that design is an important strategy for the design client
- To create a well-structured narrative demonstrating creativity in practice

Portillo and Dohr's study of Eileen Jones of Eva Maddox Associates and client Dupont Antron is part of the larger Strategic Stories™ project sponsored by the Foundation of Interior Design Education and Research (FIDER). The Strategic Stories project collects real-life stories "told through the voices of actual clients and designers" illustrating "how design impacts lives in a contextually rich and imaginative narrative."[32] In the stories, says Sosnowchik, "voices from the business community speak about the role of design in maximizing intellectual capital, recruiting and retaining the best talent, facilitating knowledge transfer within the organization, shifting organizational cultures to accept change, and creating agile organizations. The designer's voice tells of the impact of technology on communications, the changing nature of design services, and provides tangible examples of creative problem solving."[33]

We read a story of an organization shifting cultures to accept change in Christopher Budd's "Narrative Research in Design Practice: Capturing Mental Models of Work Environments." Budd, an associate principal of STUDIOS Architecture, demonstrates how narratives, or "voices within the organization," uncover "mental models of how people perceive work and what belief system affects their actions and perceptions." Narrative inquiry is a means for STUDIOS to understand "the greater context into which the physical environment is introduced."[34]

> As an example, narrators often relate stories of how they see themselves working in the future, particularly in a different physical environment. These stories of work often involve behaviors such as listening to loud music, retreating into isolated spaces, and "allowing" people to enter their environment. Each of these behaviors, embedded into a story, suggests that the person's mental model is one where he or she works alone and maintains complete control of his or her environment. None of these behaviors appears to be based on an assumption of a group environment where behaviors such as listening to loud music may be inappropriate, where isolating oneself is unlikely to occur, and where other individuals come and go from one's space without having to have permission. If teaming behaviors and continuous collaboration are goals of the organization to be supported in the new environment, a mental model that does not reflect the necessary assumptions for a collaborative environment signals conflict and an inability of population to embrace that new environment.

Segments of narratives elicited by STUDIOS are tabulated in Figure 3.9. In the first column, Figure 3.9 displays the segments themselves, which have been analyzed for assumptions (the middle column) that will not support the concept set forth by the design team in support of corporate business objectives. The third column, "Model Implication," points to the nature of training required for a successful transition to the proposed new environment.

Figure 3.9   EXAMPLE OF CRITICAL SEGMENTS OF NARRATIVE

Narrative Segment	Assumptions	Model Implication
"I've always had an office and I've always listened to music. I expect to be able to do this in the new space because this is how I work. I need to have an office."	Individual behaviors are more important than group behaviors; alternatives such as headphones are not considered.	Transition individuals from a personal focus to a group and enterprise focus. Expand the range of alternatives for personal work habits.
"Things tend to go wrong. Staplers break and I have to go find a man to fix them. I don't get a lot of support."	Gender specific expectations; passive approach to simple problem solving."	Create the expectation of active participation in the environment. Increase personal problem solving.
"I don't care about those others getting natural light, they haven't had it before and aren't used to it. You just can't take something like offices away from people who have come to expect them."	Natural light is an entitlement; low level employees don't need what they have never had; entitled employees cannot have entitlements removed.	Determine the degree to which human needs and entitlements can be manipulated. Make explicit what is being allocated as rewards and what is being allocated as basic needs.
"I am just getting to the point where I should be moving to the window. I don't want to change the system midstream."	Change will be personally detrimental; personal entitlements are more important than group entitlements.	Benefits of any change must be made explicit.
"I don't need to interact with other groups. Not that I personally have anything against them, but they have nothing of value to offer me."	Relevant information has specific domains; nonspecific conversations cannot yield valuable results; all relative is currently known.	Teaming and social facilities may need to be linked to benefit; experiential realization of this as a benefit should be emphasized.
"I should not have to default to a quiet room to get some heads-down time. I should be able to do that at my desk."	One should be able to perform all functions in his or her assigned work areas; geographic relocation for specific task is not an option.	Illustrate the degree to which activities are compromised by making one space accommodate too many of them.
Concept of Physical Model	Multitask/activity user-defined work areas: focus on organizational learning through collocation of disparate groups; emphasize enterprise needs before personal needs; create greater range of options for individuals to actively seek out and utilize; allow for user-definition of space with an emphasis on no-hassle modification by the individual or small group; expand the possibilities by removing time, activity and geography dependencies.	

Adapted from Christopher Budd, "Narrative Research in Design Practice," Journal of Interior Design, 26, No. 2 (2000): 64.

Note that the three columns present problem-cause-solution analysis—elements of classic investigative case study. At the same time, the study is based on methods of narrative inquiry: employees have been asked to tell their stories. The study as a whole tells a many-voiced strategic story about the way in which a designer-client relationship can be the agent for transformation in the service of client business strategies. It is worth reiterating that this complex analytic genre is typically used with large clients in the contract sector of the interior design field rather than with small clients in the residential sector.

The STUDIOS research team is "composed of six individuals. . . . [each] . . . trained in the collection and analysis of narratives." In the course of a typical narrative-based consulting project, "50 narratives [are] collected in a six-week period for a corporate organization of 1,000 to 1,500 employees." Prior to data collection, *domains*, or categories, have been developed so that clients can see that the information collected will be relevant to their concerns. After the raw data are recorded and transcribed, narratives are "gleaned" from interviews and are analyzed "for overarching themes of the existing work model and potential complications. . . . Often . . . perspectives emerge that cross several or all domains. Typically themes such as the degree of active or passive communication, individualism versus collectivism, etc. become indicators of the overall organizational culture."[35]

During the analysis phase the researcher asks questions such as the following:

- What are the explicit and implicit values exhibited in the narrative?
- To what degree is each motive, behavior, or belief presented positively or negatively?
- How potent is the motive, behavior, or belief to the narrator?
- What demographic group is most likely to express the motive, behavior, or belief?
- To what degree is the narrator actively or passively involved in the issue?
- And most important, which of these motives, behaviors, and beliefs are in conflict?[36]

Postproject interviews indicate that clients find the STUDIOS approach "extremely beneficial in early identification of potential problems and . . . in developing a tailored approach" to the cultural-transformation issues evoked by provocative and robust design.

The stories in the FIDER collection are not simply a group of anecdotes or "a prescriptive or best-practices collection."[37] Rather they "provide the means to both teach and learn through systematic analysis, rigorous qualitative research methods, and multiple interpretations of the same case study."[38] In the words of STUDIOS's, Christopher Budd, narrative research as part of interior design allows "new behaviors and ways of thinking about the working environment to develop." This kind of inquiry permits "new models [to] emerge when there is a new reality to be explained."[39]

Comparative Analysis

Complex as the STUDIOS research is, it examines the multiple aspects of *one* event—a proposed change to a new physical office model that will entail a new way of working. Comparative analysis compares and contrasts *two* events or items—two solutions to the client's problems, two kinds of carpet, the influence of two historically important interior designers. Comparative analysis may stand alone, or it may be used in conjunction with another kind of analysis: for instance, if two schools are being investigated as part of a case study, data from the schools would need to be subjected to comparative analysis.

According to writing specialist Kerry Walk of Harvard University, there are two kinds of comparative analysis; *classic* comparison; and *lens*, or keyhole, comparison.[40]

CLASSIC COMPARISON

If comparative analysis is "classic," it weights equally the two items or events that are being discussed. For instance, two similar things may have crucial differences (two nylon carpets may deteriorate at different rates in a landfill). Alternatively, two similar things with crucial differences may have interesting commonalities. (An expensive computer desk with many features and an inexpensive desk with fewer features may both be ergonomically sound.)

LENS COMPARISON

If comparative analysis is of the "lens" type, it uses one item or event as a lens through which to view another. "Just as looking through a pair of glasses changes the way you see an object, using A as a framework for understanding B changes the way you see B."[41] Lens comparisons are useful for challenging our sense of what, before the analysis, we thought we understood. "Often," Kerry Walk explains, "lens comparisons take time into account."[42] For example, an examination of computer-assisted drafting and design (CAD) technology may usefully illuminate the strengths and weaknesses of hand drawing, or vice versa.

Organization of the Comparative Analysis

Whichever type of comparative analysis you are writing, you will need to find a way to make your raw data—the similarities and differences you've observed—cohere into a meaningful argument. You can't achieve that goal simply by stating all the ways that two items or events are similar, then stating all the ways they are different. To achieve coherence and meaning, you need to compose an effective introduction and structure the body of your essay in a consistent, orderly, and appropriate manner.

Structure a comparative analysis carefully to achieve coherence and meaning.

INTRODUCTION

The introduction focuses and provides context for the comparison that follows. It is crucial in this form of analysis that the introduction be clear. It should contain the following:

- *Frame of reference*   This is the umbrella under which the compared items or events are assembled. The simplest frame of reference is a group of similar things from which you choose two for special attention. Other frames of reference might include biographical or historical perspectives. Or you might discuss two design projects in terms of a well-known design theory such as Postmodernism.
- *Grounds for Ccomparison*   This is the rationale for your choice of the two items or events you are discussing—for example, "the two best-selling kitchen ranges." Here, the two ranges being compared were presumably selected from a larger group of ranges on the grounds that these two are the best-sellers. This part of your introduction explains why and how your choice is deliberate, not random. It anticipates the comparative nature of your main idea.
- *Main idea*   The gist of your argument should follow naturally from your frame of reference. In comparative analysis, the main idea, or *thesis*, states how the two items or events chosen for comparison actually relate to each other. The verb of the thesis statement is important. Do the two things compared contradict, complicate, or complement each other? Many relationships are possible, and your main idea should state precisely which one prevails in your comparison-contrast. (Try composing your thesis sentence last, after you have drafted the body of your comparative analysis.)

Compose the thesis sentence of a comparative analysis after you have drafted the body.

BODY

There are two principal ways of organizing the body of a comparative analysis. In *whole-to-whole* comparison, you discuss all of A, and then you discuss all of B. In *point-to-point* comparison, you present a series of points and discuss both A and B in terms of each point. If B extends your sense of A, then you may choose a whole-to-whole comparison. If B and A seem to be engaged in a debate, then a point-to-point organizational scheme may better capture the tension of conflict. You can organize a classic comparison by either means, but a lens comparison is usually organized whole-to-whole. That is because the "lens" is merely a tool to help the reader understand the true, focal subject of the comparison.

Point-to-point comparison can have a very distracting jumpy quality, like a fast Ping-Pong game. You can sometimes avoid this by grouping points together so that you jump less frequently from A to B and back again.

To prevent jumpiness in point-to-point comparison, group points together.

Whether you choose whole-to-whole or point-to-point comparison, you need not discuss similarities and differences in an even-handed manner. If you wish to point out that carpet A is greatly superior to carpet B despite some superficial resemblances, then you will spend more time explaining the differences between the carpets. If you wish to point out that carpet A and carpet B are similar in several important respects despite a significant price difference, then you will segue quickly to the similarities. For the writing designer, a good rule of thumb is the one offered to Harvard students by Kerry Walk: "Get to the heart of your argument quickly."[43] Early in his article "Curtain Wars,"[44] Joel Sanders illustrates the efficacy of Walk's advice:

> Curtains, that element of the domestic interior on which the hands of the [interior designer] and of the architect come directly into contact, embody many of the tensions and prejudices that have divided interior designers and architects since the emergence of the professional decorator in the late 19th century. Here the hard walls designed by the architect meet the soft fabric that is the [interior designer's] trademark, in a juxtaposition that confirms the common perception that architects work conceptually, using durable materials to shape space, while [interior designers] work intuitively, adorning rooms with ephemeral materials and movable objects.

Without undue focus on the mechanics of his comparison, Sanders clearly sets up its terms:

In writing comparison, make your main argument early.

- Interior designer versus architect
- Soft and ephemeral versus hard and durable materials
- Intuitive versus conceptual work modes

As he examines the "tensions and prejudices" inherent in the "common perception" of the differences between interior designers and architects (Figure 3.10 a & b), Sanders prepares for a conclusion that points to their similarities, always staying close to the terms established early in his essay.

Figure 3.10a The architect's term for a hard exterior wall of glass is "curtain wall." This refers to the way the glass extends from and hangs across a whole structure like a curtain. *Reprinted with permission of Corbis/G.E Kidder Smith.*

As you write your own comparative analysis, remember that you need to link each point of argument to the thesis, or main idea. You can do this by making judicious and appropriate use of the transitional expressions that signal comparison and contrast:

Similarly
Moreover
Likewise
On the contrary
Conversely
On the other hand

Figure 3.10b
In his essay
"Curtain Wars,"
Joel Sanders uses
the distinction
between a soft
curtain of fabric
and a hard wall of
glass as an entry
into a discussion of
the similarities and
differences
between the pro-
fessions of archi-
tecture and interior
design.
*Reprinted with
permission of
Corbis/Farrell
Grehan.*

You can also use an explicitly contrasting vocabulary, as in the following excerpt[45]:

> The Czech color researcher Ewald Hering distinguished between the catabolic (tearing-down) effect of the warm colors red, yellow, and white and the anabolic (building-up) effect of the cool colors green, blue, and black on receptors in the human brain.

In this example, *catabolic* and *anabolic* are in clear contrast, as are *warm colors* and *cool colors*.

Summary Analysis

The previous observation on a color psychologist's views might also be considered an example of summary—a brief account that presents in a concise form the main points of someone's thinking. "In a world awash in information," note technical-writing specialists Daniel G. Riordan and Steven E. Pauley, "the ability to construct and present concise, short versions of long documents is not only helpful but essential,"[46] whether for interior designers or for professionals in any other field. Also important in today's data-flooded world is the ability to *synthesize* information from a variety of sources, then to integrate it with direct observation and your own opinion, combining different ideas into a complex whole. By means of synthesis, a *summary analysis* compares the ideas and information from several sources in a series of brief summaries. In this way, documents and other items and events can be *evaluated*, or judged for value relative to each other.

Such an analysis might be used by an interior designer who has been asked by a client to evaluate several studies of computer technology in workplace design or several different books on green design. Overall, as you will see, summary analysis is useful any time a writing designer must report on a body of research in a professional situation. Although a single summary of a single work may be presented in some situations, the genre of summary analysis is at heart a comparative one in which summaries of several works are judged for relative worth and for the cumulative wisdom that emerges from the group of works.

An effective summary analysis contains a *summary* component and a *synthesis-and-evaluation* component.

THE SUMMARY COMPONENT

If you have ever given a friend a brief account of a missed episode of a television serial, you were *summarizing*, giving your friend a succinct substitute for actual viewing. In a business or professional setting, summaries enable busy people—particularly managers—to "discover the gist"[47] of a report, article, book, or other document without reading the whole thing. A summary restates the major findings, conclusions, or recommendations presented in a document. It also conveys the major facts on which the conclusions are based. *Indicative summaries*, or abstracts,[48] start with the main idea. They list a document's topics with pertinent supporting details. *Informative summaries* present the document in miniature, giving emphasis to each section in proportion to that given in the original, with brief versions of its principal qualitative and quantitative data.

Although the *executive summary* that appears at the head of a 250-page report (see Chapter 9) might need two to five pages to clearly convey all that is in the report, the individual summaries within a summary analysis are typically much shorter—no more than 500 words, and typically about 250–300. These individual summaries are usually structured as inverted pyramids, with the most important points presented first. They should not contain terms that need to be defined. (Note: although many people use the term *executive summary* loosely, to mean a single freestanding summary of an article, say, or a book, the term *executive summary* historically refers to a summary that is attached to a long formal report. The techniques described here for summary analysis may of course be used for executive summaries.)

To summarize documents effectively, you must learn to read with two separate goals in mind simultaneously:

- *Finding the main terms and concepts*   Read as if you were outlining. Look for the principal divisions in the documents and key statements. Ask yourself which sentence expresses the overall purpose of the document and which sentences express the main ideas in each paragraph. Look for the key terms that are repeated or emphasized. Ask yourself which details most effectively support the main ideas.
- *Deciding how much detail to include* Take into account the needs of your audience. Do they want an overview? Are they trying to keep up with the latest writings in interior design and related fields? Will they read the summary in place of the full document? What decisions will they make on the basis of its contents?

As you read, mark all the key words and phrases. Arrange them into clusters based on their similarities until you begin to see an overall pattern. Write a sentence stating the main point you want to convey. List the clusters in the order in which you plan to present them. Then draft your summary.

THE SYNTHESIS-AND-EVALUATION COMPONENT

The content of each individual summary is partially dictated by the requirement for *synthesis*, or the combining of ideas, and evaluation. The synthesis-and-evaluation component of a summary analysis finds patterns in how information fits together. It organizes this information in relation to an overview. It shows the relationship between the thoughts and research of different people. To accomplish these aims, you must select *criteria*, reference points against which you can evaluate each document summarized, drawing conclusions about whether it meets the criteria.

You would use the same process to evaluate furnaces, bids from single-trade contractors, interior designers' Web sites, or the occupants' response to an office setting that your firm had designed (post-occupancy evaluation). Here are the steps involved in the process of *evaluation*[49]:

1. Establish the evaluation criteria.
2. Select the projects to which you will apply the criteria.
3. Evaluate in terms of the criteria.
4. Present your results in support of your *premise*, or main idea.

You will find many examples of evaluation throughout this book, for instance, in Chapter 10, where post-occupancy services are discussed. Whether you are evaluating clients' satisfaction with a medical office or a group of articles on kitchen renovation found in different design journals, your evaluation must be accomplished within the framework of criteria that permit the discussion of similarities and differences.

Literature Review

A very common type of summary analysis is the literature review—a critical look at existing research that bears on the current or pending work of a design firm. For instance, in connection with a particular project, a designer working for Weber Design may report on books about the vintage residential designs of Billy Baldwin, "Sister" Parrish, and Eileen Gray. Writing a literature review can help designers find and understand relationships between their own thought and work and that of others.

The literature review is *not* like *TV Guide*, which simply summarizes various programs without establishing purpose or context. Your literature review should be written for a clear purpose within the clear context of *your* design work or the work of your firm. Within that context, here are some of the questions[50] your review should answer:

- What do we already know in the immediate area we have chosen to cover?
- What are the key concepts or main factors?
- What are the existing theories?
- What are the inconsistencies or other shortcomings in our knowledge and understanding?
- What ways of looking at the issues seem satisfactory or unsatisfactory?

A literature review supports your own work or the work of your firm.

You need to highlight the controversies between different thinkers on a similar subject. You need to convey what is known and is not known on a given topic. Finally, you need to develop questions for further research. For instance, Weber Design may decide to do more research into the ways that Eileen Gray solved problems analogous to their clients'.

But what is the "literature" that a literature review examines? Obviously, it is impossible to read all the literature that might be relevant in a large field of knowledge such as interior design. You must limit the scope to a manageable number of excellent information sources. The sifting process—deciding what to read and report on—is a key strategy of design and other research, which is also discussed in Chapter 9. A literature review usually begins with a statement setting forth the terms of your sifting, defining the area you have chosen to cover and the types of works to be discussed. For example, your review might be limited to books and might not include articles in magazines and journals, or vice versa.)

The value of your review depends not simply on how many sources you find, but on the quality of your sources, their relevance to your subject, and their currency. The value of your review will also depend on your awareness of how the different perspectives of the reviewed authors (and in some cases editors) affect the nature of their evidence and the way in which it is presented.

In order to write an effective literature review, bear in mind that your purpose as a writing designer is always to support a design objective, for example, to find an inexpensive wine-colored drapery fabric that resists deterioration in strong sunlight. You may be writing to support a recommendation or to clarify a set of alternatives. You are not writing the literature review simply to demonstrate your knowledge of what various people have thought and said about the topic you are researching. In general, your aim should be to shore up the value of your design concepts or those of your firm.

To this end, you need to summarize the documents you read, but you must also decide which ideas or information are important for your purposes so that you can emphasize them. Ideas and information that are less important can be covered briefly or even left out. If you are looking for curtain fabrics that do not deteriorate in strong sunlight for your corporate client's reception area, you may choose to ignore findings that suggest, say, military applications for these fabrics in tropical settings.

Always look for the major concepts, conclusions, theories, or arguments that *underlie* the work you are writing about. Look for similarities and differences within closely related documents. (This will become easier

In writing a
literature review,
look for the
concepts and
theories that
underlie the work
you are discussing.

the longer you read within a given area.) In order to show such relationships clearly, you will find that it is necessary to carefully plan the organization of your literature review. Not all forms of organization work
equally well.

- *Chronological* Sometimes it matters in what order different
  documents were written. It is a good idea to indicate the position of a reviewed work in the research area's history. However,
  a chronological order is not usually an effective way in which to
  organize a literature review.
- *Classification by theme or by trend* It is usually more effective
  to discuss the various pieces of literature in a manner that supports a subtle elucidation of similarities and differences. Try to
  organize your review into "useful, informative sections that
  present themes or identify trends."[51]
- *General to specific* It often makes sense to move from a brief
  general discussion of the research to the more specific area that
  you yourself are researching.

Keep track of
bibliographical
data as you
research.

Whichever form of organization you choose, the literature review (see
Figure 3.11) is written in standard paragraph form, with the names of the
works and authors mentioned in the ordinary sentences of the paragraph—
sometimes in parentheses. The references cited within the report are keyed
to a standard reference list at the end, listing the works in alphabetical order
by the last name of the first author. Many interior designers use APA style
for reference citations. You can read more about this in Chapter 9. (Be sure
to keep track of the bibliographical data as you do your research. It can be
tedious and frustrating to track it down later.)

Annotated Bibliography

A report form closely related to the literature review is the annotated bibliography (see Figure 3.12), which also gives readers information about
printed and electronic research material. The annotated bibliography combines the *bibliography*, or reference list, and the summary report. The discussion of each item goes directly under the bibliographed note. The
annotated bibliography is usually organized in alphabetical order by the last
names of reviewed authors. This arrangement does not permit you to discuss the relationships between documents in a fluid and logical manner. The
summaries are discrete and self-contained, like those of a catalog. However,

The Elements of Style (Strunk & White) is an elegantly concise guide to writing well. It sets forth basic guidelines in fourteen pages. Another hundred pages cover topics like commonly misused words. The engagingly clear introduction by E. B. White is a sterling example of the book's approach.

Those who need more step-by-step guidance in negotiating the tricky shoals of English usage may require a usage guide that is richer in detail. Theodore Bernstein's *The Careful Writer* addresses diction, style, clarity, and grammar issues in 2,000 high-quality entries. The explanations are clear and lively. The formatting is user friendly: the pages have only a single, full column with bold heads and plenty of white space. This standard reference work for professional writers and editors will also be a frequently consulted reference work in most design offices.

Wensberg/Follett's *Modern American Usage* has a convenient alphabetical format that allows the reader to zero in on troubling words and phrases without having to know whether the problem is one of grammar, style, or syntax. Hundreds of cross-references make it easy to browse context. Modeled on Fowler's *Modern English Usage*, Wensberg/Follett is geared to standards of current American English and conveys the full flavor of contemporary idiom.

REFERENCE LIST

Bernstein, Theodore M. *The Careful Writer: A Modern Guide to English Usage.* New York: Athenaeum, 1977.

Follett, Wilson, and Erik Wensberg. *Modern American Usage: A Guide.* Rev. Ed. New York: Hill & Wang, 1998.

Fowler, Henry W. Introduction by Simon Winchester (London and New York: *Fowler's Modern English Usage,* (Oxford Language Classics Series). Oxford University Press, 2003.

Strunk, William, Jr., and E. B. White. *The Elements of Style*, 4th Ed. Boston: Pearson Allyn & Bacon, 2000.

Figure 3.11 Excerpt from a literature review of reference books for writing designers. *Book selections and many descriptions adapted from those of Martin Kohl,* The Freelancer's Bookshelf. *(New York: Editorial Freelancers Association, 1994.) Based on resource list discussed in Chapter 1.*

an annotated bibliography can be focused by evaluative criteria and a writing designer's disciplined sense of scope.

Writing an annotated bibliography or a literature review in support of your work as a designer will call on many of the same analytic capabilities as the work of design itself. Indeed, analytic writing of all kinds is a crucial support of the design process, which has its own strong analytic component. Writing, like

As you compose an analysis, accept the transformation of changing ideas.

design, repays patient engagement over a period of time, and this is particularly true of analytic writing, for which the data under discussion may yield new interpretations and new insights with every revision. For writing designers, "writing is a way of thinking"[52]—*about design*. As you compose an analysis, allow yourself as many drafts as you need. Accept the transformation of ideas as you learn more about your own perspective and the subject you are exploring.

You have a good model at hand in the design process itself for the kind of creative spiral that is involved in developing an analysis or any other piece of writing. As shown in Figure 3.13, your writing can provide you with feedback on the process of design. From the pre-programming to the post occupancy phase, design, like writing, is a constant flux of analysis, synthesis, and reevaluation—a spiral, like the shell of the chambered nautilus that houses life and growth and continuous transformation.

Figure 3.12
Excerpt from an
annotated bibliography of reference
books for writing
designers.
*Adapted from the
literature review
excerpted in Figure
3.11.*

BERNSTEIN, THEODORE M. *THE CAREFUL WRITER: A MODERN GUIDE TO ENGLISH USAGE.* NEW YORK: ATHENAEUM, 1977.

This richly detailed manual offers step-by-step guidance in negotiating the tricky shoals of English usage. Bernstein addresses issues of diction, style, clarity, and grammar in 2,000 high-quality entries. The explanations are clear and lively. The formatting is user friendly: the pages have only a single, full column, with bold heads and plenty of white space.

FOLLETT, WILSON, AND ERIK WENSBERG. *MODERN AMERICAN USAGE: A GUIDE.* REV. ED. NEW YORK: HILL & WANG, 1998.

A convenient alphabetical format allows the reader to zero in on troubling words and phrases without having to know whether the problem is one of grammar, style, or syntax. Hundreds of cross-references make it easy to browse context. Follet and Wensberg is geared to standards of current American English and conveys the full flavor of contemporary idiom.

STRUNK, WILLIAM, JR., AND E. B. WHITE. *THE ELEMENTS OF STYLE,* 4TH ED. BOSTON: PEARSON ALLYN & BACON, 2000.

This elegantly concise guide to writing well sets forth basic guidelines in fourteen pages. Another hundred pages cover topics like commonly misused words. The engagingly clear introduction by E. B. White is a sterling example of the book's approach.

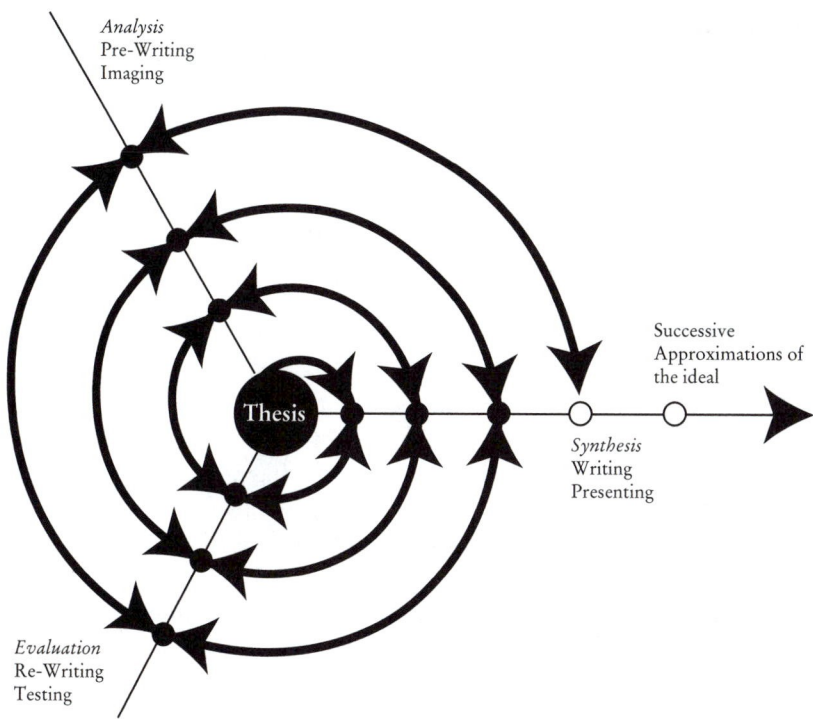

Figure 3.13
The cycle of analysis, synthesis, and evaluation enables the writing designer to achieve successive approximations of the ideal in writing and design. It also assists writing designers by making what they do explicit to themselves, their clients, and their collaborators. *Courtesy of Dan Beert.*

Discussion Questions

1. In a whole-class discussion, identify three to five areas of improvement that might be addressed in a renovation of your writing classroom. Assign each area of discussion to a small group of three to five students. (If necessary, create more discussion areas, but all groups must focus on different aspects of the same redesign "project.") Let each group then develop a program analysis of the work that needs to be done in that group's area. Identify issues and develop goals, PRs, concepts, and possible implementations. Let each group give a brief oral report on its findings, with your teacher making a bulleted list on the blackboard of each group's presentation points. What work needs to be done to create a programming report for your client, the facilities manager of your school?

2. Divide your class into four groups, one each for theater, dance, poetry, and the visual arts. Let each group create binary, scalar, and judgmental performance criteria for fostering children's creative expression in the assigned art

form. As a whole class, discuss the ways in which each group's criteria do or do not conform to the definitions of binary, scalar, and judgmental performance criteria set forth in Chapter 3.

3. Figure 3.9 contains a number of words that many people may not know. Discuss how you might rewrite some sentences to make them clearer to ordinary readers. What is the audience for the original language, and what is the audience for your revised language?

Exercises

1. From a shelter magazine or professional interior design periodical, select an article from each of five issues. Make a list of the adjectives and adverbs in each article that are used to describe a successful interior setting. Compile a master list of adjectives for use in generating goal statements, classifying the adjectives and adverbs in relevant categories for easy retrieval.

2. Go to the Web sites of three paint companies that display online swatches. For instance, you might go to the following sites:

Farrow & Ball: www.farrow-ball.com
Fine Paints of Europe: (distributes Schreuder) www.finepaints.com
Benjamin Moore: www.benjaminmoore.com

Find six red whites, six blue whites, six yellow whites, six green whites, six gray whites, and six beige whites. At least one white in each category should come from each of your three sites. Take careful notes on each color, including its name, its number, the name of the vendor, and the category the white belongs in—for example, blue white.

When you have collected your data, classify it according to color category—green white, gray white, and the like.

3. Create a classified inventory of the furniture in the cafeteria or library of your school. Your classification should organize the following information:

Item: (chair, table, lamp, and so on)
Color and finish: (material)
Number (units of each item)
Manufacturer
Size

In addition, your inventory should contain comments about information not anticipated when the categories were created, such as function, context, relationship to other elements, and the like. You may also comment on the suitability of the categories. Note: parenthetical information is for illustration and reference only.

4. Interview a successful solo practitioner in the residential interior design field about a successful design project. Write a promotional case study that is suitable for use as a promotional flyer or on a Web site.

5. The ASID booklet *Workplace Values: How Employees Want to Work** contains discussion of what makes a workplace effective. It provides guidance for interior designers in tailoring the workplace to the ways people actually work. Obtain a copy of this booklet through ASID. Read it, taking notes on what you read. How might the insights presented in this publication apply to an analysis of the effectiveness, as workplace, of the ID studio at your school? Develop four criteria that an interior designer might use in evaluating the usefulness of this book for the redesign of ID studio classrooms. Write a three-page evaluation applying the criteria to *Workplace Values.*

6. Divide your class into several groups, each to prepare a summary analysis. Let each group choose a current design topic, based on your teacher's recommendations. Each member of each group must find and summarize a *different* design-magazine article treating the topic the group has selected, following the guidelines in Chapter 3. Working together, group members will then draft the synthesis and evaluation component of the summary analysis. Your teacher will guide you in editing the various summary drafts and the group's evaluation draft into one cogent summary analysis.

*Washington, D.C.: American Society of Interior Designers, www.asid.org.

4 Professional Identity and Capability Presentation

Wouldn't it be wonderful to have someone on duty 24 hours a day, telling your design story in words and pictures when you are not available to do it yourself? Few people can afford to hire marketing specialists whose job is to get out the word. Most designers entrust much of that task to printed and electronic emissaries. The words and pictures that tell your story to prospective clients without your being present to talk them through it are called, collectively, the *capability presentation*. Such a presentation often centers on a printed folder, booklet, or kit—the *capability brochure*. The term *brochure* may also apply to capability materials presented on a CD-ROM or a Web site.

To suppose that capability presentation begins and ends with a brochure suggests that it is a one-time event. Yet experts in marketing and sales agree that single exposure to a capability message does not yield reliable results. The best results follow from multiple exposures to a message. Accordingly, capability presentation should be viewed as an ongoing process. It may begin with a casual meeting and the exchange of business cards. If prospects express interest, capability presentation continues with a folder, booklet, or kit. The process culminates in your presentation of a

Multiple exposure to your marketing message yields better results than a single exposure.

personalized design proposal (Chapter 5) followed by a letter of agreement (Chapter 6).

After contracted work has been completed, the message about design capabilities continues to be projected in a follow-through phase that reaches out not only to former clients, but to new prospects, directly and through the media. (This follow-through phase is covered in Chapter 11, which focuses on marketing through promotion and publicity.) Meanwhile the design message is, in Vilma Barr's useful phrase, "translated [for residential designers] into three-dimensional space" through show houses, rooms in model homes, or marketing suites.[1] Commercial interior design is visible in three-dimensional form in public spaces.

Continue marketing after project completion.

Professional Identity

Before you begin thinking about capability presentation for your design practice—or, if you are job hunting, before you put together your portfolio (see Chapter 12)—you need to give some thought to the overall image of your practice and to the graphic identity that presents your image to prospects. The difference between *image* and *identity* is subtle. *Image*, according to Crane & Company, the fine paper maker, is "what people perceive the personality of the company to be," while *graphic identity* "is a visual reality that enhances the image. Identity is the accumulation of all visual elements of a company's presentation or communication to the outside world. . . . It can answer basic questions like who or what you are, the values you hold, the quality of [what] you sell, or your personality. It can even communicate something about your strategic goal. "[2]

Think about how your practice will be perceived.

Some aspects of graphic identity that relate closely to capability presentation are firm name, stationery package, logo and customized design elements, and choice of paper for the package.

Firm Name

An article on the American Society of Interior Designers (ASID) Web site[3] recounts the story of one design firm's name change:

> Terry Maurer, FASID [Fellow of the American Society of Interior Designers], a sole proprietor in Akron, Ohio, recently changed her firm's moniker to Maurer Design Group from T. L. Maurer Design/ Associates. Its non-specific nature leaves open the possibility of a variety of design services; the lack of a first name sounds more businesslike; and the use of the word "group" implies a staff of some size. Maurer,

a commercial designer who specializes in offices, nursing homes, and small health-care facilities, says "clients don't always ask how large we are, and if they don't ask, I don't volunteer."

Let your firm's name project dignity and significance.

Maurer's name change is part of a survival strategy for small design businesses that Buehl summarizes as, "Look big, sound big, and act big." Other aspects of this strategy include team building with peer professionals such as engineers and lighting designers; answering the telephone in a professional manner; using state-of-the-art technology; being courteous to all; getting thoroughly organized; and engaging in sound financial practices.

A good firm name evokes a rich complex of reactions and associations in diverse groups of people. The branding company Lexicon identifies two important elements in the process by which brand names "carry" ideas and images. "*Intrinsic values*," or connotations, are the images or ideas conveyed by a name that go way beyond any narrow definition of the products or services that are for sale. "*Expansiveness* represents the ability of a name to support multiple messages and to grow and adapt" as your design practice grows and adapts.[4] The name "Maurer Design Group" is rich in both these elements. It carries the strong *intrinsic values* of "bigness" and business seriousness; the name's *expansiveness* lies in its adaptability to new design contexts.

Experts in name development use concepts adapted from the field of linguistics to aid them in choosing appropriate and powerful names. They pay special attention to three crucial attributes of words as they apply to American language: *speech stream visibility*, *notational visibility*, and *phonetic transparency*.[5]

- *Speech stream visibility* is the probability that a word will be recognized in a normal spoken stream of English—that is, American—speech.
- *Notational visibility* is the probability that a word will be deciphered from words that appear on paper pages or monitor screens.
- *Phonetic transparency* means that a word is spoken as it is spelled.

In accordance with these principles, an Anglo-American designer whose family name is *Cholmondeley* (pronounced "Chumley") might choose a firm name that is easier for most Americans to read ("notational visibility") and that has greater phonetic transparency.

Any design-firm name that is chosen for use in today's multicultural society will have broader viability if it can easily be pronounced by members of all the significant groups in the region in which a design firm practices. Thus, with an eye to broadening practice opportunities, a Vietnamese-

American designer whose family name is *Ngu* might choose a firm name that is easier for Americans who are not Vietnamese to pronounce.

Not all design-firm names are based on family names, of course. Some designers name their firms with *neologisms*, or new words, that are rich in intrinsic value and wide in expansiveness. Examples include Dezignaré (Austin, Texas), istudio (Washington D.C.), and Workstage (Grand Rapids, Michigan). A true neologism may be easier to copyright and to reserve as a corporate name in whatever state than a firm name based on a family name. Whatever its basis, "a great name," in the words of Lexicon, "speaks for you. It leads the way, breaking down old perceptions and creating new ones."[6] Be sure to test the names you are considering on peers, relatives, and friends to ascertain whether the perceptions created by the name you choose are in line with your intentions.

Stationery Package

Whatever name a design firm chooses, its professional identity needs to be consistently projected through what Vilma Barr has called the "stationery package."[7] The letterhead stationery, transmittal memos, fax forms, folders, labels, brochures, CD-ROM case liners, and all other stationery-package components "should belong to the same family of colors, typefaces and images, if any." This kind of visual coherence is what Crane & Company means when it speaks of graphic identity as "the accumulation of all visual elements of a company's presentation." To see some stationery packages created by a leading graphic designer, go to the corporate-identity part of the graphic-design section of www.davidcurrydesign.com, where a number of logos are also on display. Check out high-quality generic stationery packages such as "Ambassador" and "Acropolis" at www.paperdirect.com.

Project professionalism in all aspects of your practice.

Logo

A *logo* is an emblem that compresses corporate or professional identity into a unique graphic device. The consistent use of it projects a clear identity in every part of a stationery package. A successful logo is rich in symbolic associations and meanings, but is easy to read. (Fussy or gimmicky logos proclaim cheapness.) For example, the logo of interior designer Jessica Helgerson (www.jhinteriordesign.com), a graceful stylized tree branch, economically conveys a trove of associations that illuminates the concept "green design." To see other successful logos created by graphic designers, browse through the portfolios at www.creativehotlist.com.

Color selection is an important part of a graphic designer's work on the logo and other elements of a graphic identity. For instance, a graphic designer might assist you in choosing black for font or text, another color with black for artwork, and an accent color for certain areas. Well-trained graphic designers can create custom colors. They also assist with decisions about paper color, weight, and texture when the logo is imprinted onto stationery items. Above all, they search for ways to project their clients' business and professional identities through their logos and by other graphic means.

The design firm Workstage LLC has on its capability Web site[8] and in its print brochure an effective logo that changes to express the four design principles that undergird the firm's design philosophy. These principles are people, flexibility, environment, and speed/cost. For each of the four logo permutations, an abstract human figure (with a body that combines angular, spiky elements and curvilinear forms) is represented in an appropriately evocative posture. The figure is always seen on a richly shadowed and shaded "stage," a square that seems to be floating, almost like a magic carpet in motion. Although this four-image logo is not an animation, it reads as four "frames" of an ongoing film in which the logo figure is in a state of flux, adapting to new and different situations. Thus the logo conveys a sense of change in response to needs that arise—which is very much what Workstage is "about."

The creation of a complex logo like that of Workstage requires a graphic designer's participation in a long-term identity development process. This can be an expensive proposition. Marketing and public relations consultants Ursula and Bob Garrett emphasize that a logo is not merely an attractive visual element unifying a firm's presentational materials. It is an expression of a firm's clearly articulated sense of vision. The graphic or marketing designer does not and cannot provide that vision. Interior designers need to do the conceptual homework, answering for themselves such questions as:

- What is my special niche, or position, in the marketplace?
- What are the principal benefits that I am offering my clients?
- How do my services differ from those of other designers?

Define your business and goals before investing in designer graphics.

If you are a student or novice interior designer, refine your sense of what you wish to offer before making an expensive investment in professionally executed graphics. Such an investment will be most productive if it expresses your already well-defined and tempered vision.

An alternative to professional graphic design is the purchase of desktop publishing (DTP) software that permits you to create and manipulate images and layouts. Both Microsoft Publisher and Adobe Pagemaker[9] offer extensive identity and layout templates, some customized with paper selections in colors that coordinate with the layout to create handsome capability materials. Unfortunately, MS Publisher, the most popular choice for small design firms, is not bundled with the standard version of MS Office.[10] It is available only with the Small Business and Professional versions, which are considerably more expensive. MS Publisheris widely acknowledged to offer excellent value, with significant advantages for graphic design over MS Word. However, we focus our discussion on the no-frills approach, seeing what can be achieved in graphic design with MS Word, as bundled in the standard version of MS Office.

Figure 4.1 shows a simple, no-frills fake logo in the Trebuchet font created by a non-graphic designer in MS Word in three sizes. (Trebuchet was selected for its simplicity and its readability.) Around the letters in each of the three boxes is an outside border created through Word's format menu. Within each of the boxes is a gray "fill," also created through the format menu of the standard Word toolbar.

Of course, the "logo" in Figure 4.1 lacks some significant attributes of a logo created by a graphic designer. The range of meaning it carries is limited, for instance. It also lacks the stability of a true logo image created with special software such as Quark or PhotoShop. You can test the instability of the no-frills fake logo yourself, even while making it your own. On your CD-ROM is a digital copy of it. Open the Word file and practice manipulating the logo.

A false logo like the one in Figure 4.1 is inserted into a document as styled text. A true logo, once set as an image, would be inserted into documents as

If your budget is limited, create your own logo.

Figure 4.1
Fake logo created with Microsoft Word.
The lettering in the larger box is Trebuchet 72—the largest font size offered by MS Word. The lettering in the medium and small boxes, respectively, are Trebuchet 48 and Trebuchet 12—the latter is a standard-sized font used in many word-processed documents.

art, using Insert -> Picture, and could not be as easily manipulated by anyone opening the document. False or true, once a logo has been created, it can then be used with digital *templates*, or patterns, to publish a stationery package that is visually coherent. For instance, in Figures 4.2 and 4.3, the fake logo has been inserted into templates from the gallery at office.update.microsoft.com to create shipping labels and a CD-ROM face label. (These figures are also featured on the CD-ROM.)

Figure 4.2
Shipping label with fake logo created from a template.

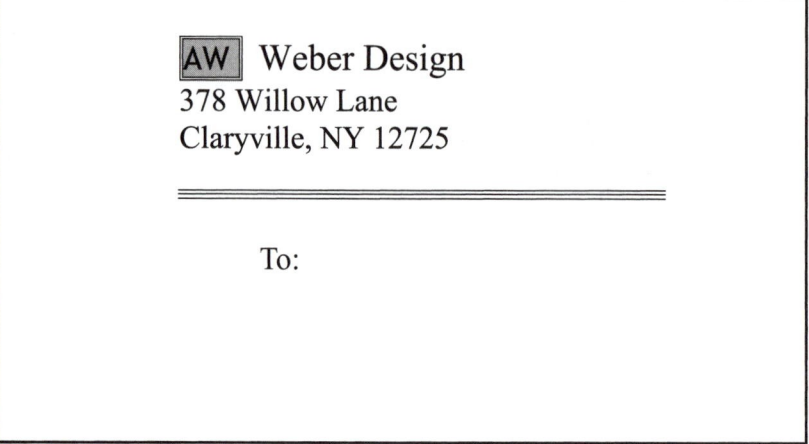

There are many other simple ways to use the features of word-processing software to create a customized stationery package that suggests a professional identity. For the most part—as in the examples in Figures 4.2 and 4.3—they involve the customizing of standard templates.

Figure 4.3
CD-ROM face label with fake logo created from a template.

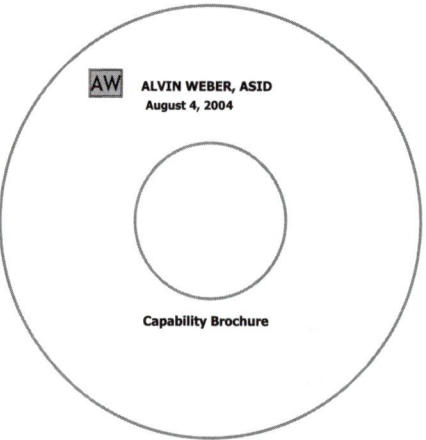

Customizing with Fonts

The manipulation of font is one easy way to customize a stationery package created in Microsoft Word. Choose a typeface to create a logo-like iteration of your professional name. Use it on your letterhead, business cards, labels, capability brochure, and any other materials you create to tell the story of your design business. You can change font style, size, family, color, or effect to create a customization that will express your personality, design philosophy, and special skills. Remember, your fonts will be seen at sizes as small as 7 points on business cards. As you customize your stationery package, be sure your font is legible in every size you need to use.

CHANGING FONT STYLE AND SIZE

You are probably already familiar with the three buttons on the formatting toolbar that allow you to control bold, italics, and underlining. These can be used with a change in font size to create many different visual expressions of your firm's name. The sample below shows an experiment with the name "Alvin Weber." Here is the Weber name in the same font used for this sentence but in a much larger size, italicized and bold:

ALVIN WEBER

Your word-processing software also permits you to underline, but it is best not to use that feature in the customization of your firm's name. Sometimes the underline obscures the letter form and the *descenders*, or parts of lower-case letters such as g and q extending below the baseline on which most of the letters stand. Instead of underlining, create a ruled line by using the bottom border choice on the bordering pull-down menu found on the formatting toolbar:

ALVIN WEBER

By changing the line spacing in the paragraph window of the Formatting menu, you can place the ruled line nearer or farther away from the underlined letters. Of course, you can change not just the style and size of your font, but the font itself.

CHANGING FONT FAMILY

Even without using any of the special fonts that are available online (for instance, check out the hundreds on display at www.getty.com) or as packaged software, you can choose from a considerable variety of standard fonts that are part of your word-processing program, although you should limit yourself to two fonts for each piece, one for the headings and one for the body. Without changing the size or styling of the customization created for the previous paragraph, we create a font variation on the name *Alvin Weber*, by clicking *Castellar* in the list on the font-formatting window:

ALVIN WEBER

Note that the firm name is now in caps and is no longer bold and italic. That is because the Castellar font in Microsoft Word has only capital letters and no bold or italic.

Are other changes in order in this thought experiment? In the spirit of "looking big," a change from the firm name *Alvin Weber* to the name *Weber Design* might be profitable.

WEBER DESIGN

By means of just such experiments, the patient trial-and-error work of customization accumulates in the expression of a graphic identity. The words *Weber Design* can be transformed into a logolike iteration of a firm's name, then put to work. For example, in Figure 4.4 a different customized name iteration has been entered into the Microsoft Elegant Letter template, which is packaged with MS Office. (Later in this chapter, we talk more about the templates available for other components of the stationery package.)

Explore your firm's names in multiple fonts.

You can experiment with font variations for your name or firm name by typing it into a document, then using the sample box on the font-formatting window to see how your evolving professional identity will express itself in different fonts. A good font-selection guideline comes from marketing author Carol Davitt, who advises that simplicity be the watchword of those choosing fonts; ornate lettering, she points out, is hard to read.[11] If you want to appeal to high-end clients, take a tip from "marketing doctor" Janet Wagner, who advises that "tailored" typefaces—which are simple in line and design, with an appearance of clarity—are appealing to this market segment.[12]

Choose **Georgia** rather than **Forte**.

Some fonts are more efficient than others, that is, they take up less space for the same number of letters. Condensed or compressed fonts usually take up less space, for instance, than expanded fonts.

FONT SELECTION TIPS   The *Computer Tips*[13] newsletter offers other, more technical font-selection tips. First, if you've found a font that is almost right, there is a quick way to pull from the listing all fonts similar to your almost-right one. Click on the Start button, then on Settings→Control Panel. Open the Fonts folder. (If you are a Windows ME user and you don't see this folder, click on "View all control panel options" on the left side of the control panel.) From the View menu, select "List fonts by similarity," then use the drop-down box to select the font that is close to being right. You will see a list in descending order of similarity. For samples, double-click on the various fonts.

Second, use a font other than the popular **Arial** or Times New Roman for documents that you intend to print. According to graphic designer and writer Tom Dalton,[14] these fonts were designed to look good on a computer monitor rather than on paper. As Dalton points out, "there is a whole world of subtlety on fonts that just cannot be expressed in the 72 dots per inch of a monitor." Dalton recommends **Georgia** or a font like Book Antiqua with the word *book* in its name. The result, he claims, will be more professional-looking print documents. In general, some experts claim, fonts with *serifs* (short lines at the ends of the main strokes of letter characters) are easier to read on print pages, while fonts like **Verdana** without serifs (*sans serif*) are easier to read online.

EMBEDDING FONTS   If you decide to use in your stationery package or elsewhere a font downloaded from the Web, your font may not show up as itself if you send the document via e-mail to someone else's computer. That's because the other computer's user hasn't downloaded the font you have. The other computer's Word program will substitute a close match for missing fonts, and its idea of matching may not be yours. You can specify the substitutions to be made, but if you want to make sure that your font shows up in the document when it opens on any computer, you need to include the font with the document—that is, you need to *embed* the font in the document. This is actually quite a simple process. From the Tools menu select Options to bring up the Options dialog box. Click the Save tab and click the option Embed TrueType fonts. You also have the option of embedding only the characters that are in use in your documents. This helps to keep the file size down but could mean that a recipient of your document could not make a change or correct a spelling error. Of course, the safest procedure is to limit yourself to the fonts that come with Word. (Bear in mind that fonts occupy a lot of file space. If you decide to download alternative fonts from the Web, store them on CD-ROMs or Zip disks if there is any chance that they might take

> Embed fonts if you e-mail a document.

up too much room on your hard drive. If you purchase sets of fonts, they will usually come to you stored on CD-ROMs from which you can then access them, uploading only those you actually intend to use.)

It is prudent to stick with TrueType fonts, which look the same both on-screen and in print. Not all fonts advertised online or sold in stores are TrueType. On a recent visit to www.getty.com, for instance, of more than 500 fonts offered for sale, only 200 plus were TrueType. To see only TrueType fonts in the programs on your computer, go to Control Panel -> Fonts -> Tools -> Folder Options;-> the TrueType tab. Check "Show only TrueType Fonts."

CHANGING FONT COLOR

The choice of font colors opens up another area for creative expression of your firm's identity. If you have your stationery printed commercially, you can, to be sure, have one or more colors in, say, your letterhead. You can then load the preprinted stationery into your own printer's paper tray and print out the bodies of individual letters—most likely in standard black. Even with the highest quality commercial printing of your letterhead, it is a good idea to choose letterhead font colors such as red or a bright blue or green, which contrast crisply with the black of a laser printer's work product. Or choose shades of gray and black itself—rather than choosing, say, dark brown, dark green, or dark blue—any of which might appear muddy next to the laser printing commonly used for the body of letters, which is very dark, bright, and black. Likewise, a letterhead in a pale color may look washed out next to laser-printed body text.

A graphic designer or marketing specialist will be aware of distinct trends and fashions in colors suitable for letterhead and other parts of the stationery package. In the September 2002 issue of *Remodeling*, for instance, marketing expert Janet Wagner critiques the blue and rust scheme of one stationery item as "dated," while praising the red and black of another as "contemporary."[15] Collecting examples of good, recent, stationery-package items should help you to see what looks fresh and contemporary in the graphics realm.

If you are creating your own stationery package by means of desktop publishing, you need to take into account the attributes of the printer you will be using even as you select the colors for your letterhead. An ink-jet printer will print several colors at once. That is, you can simultaneously print a letterhead in color while printing in black the body of a letter, pro-posal, or report. If you are using a printer that prints only in black, to simul-taneously print a letterhead and a letter body, you will need to stick with black and shades of gray as letterhead colors.

In the digital version of Figure 4.4 on your CD-ROM, you can see how the "Weber Design Elegant" template looks with a red letterhead. You can copy it from the CD-ROM and experiment with font colors by selecting the customized name; clicking Font Color on the Formatting toolbar; and clicking on different colors, including black. You can also select the text *Weber Design* and type in your own firm name, which will then appear in the existing customization.

Figure 4.4
Customized letter-head stationery created from a standard Microsoft template.

Weber Design

January 5, 2004

[Click **here** and type recipient's address]

Dear Sir or Madam:

Type your letter here. For more details on modifying this letter template, double click ✉. To return to this letter, use the Windows menu.

Sincerely,

Alvin Weber, ASID, IIDA
Principal Designer

378 WILLOW LANE • CLARYVILLE, NY • 12725
PHONE AND FAX: 845-555-6789 • E-MAIL: ALVIN@WEBDESIGN.COM

LEADING, KERNING, AND TRACKING

You can use your word-processing program to adjust the *leading*, or amount of space between lines of text. "Most applications automatically apply standard leading based on the point size of the font. Closer leading fits more text [in] . . . but decreases legibility. Looser leading spreads text out. . . . and makes the document easier to read."[16]

A word-processing program like MS Word enables you to adjust *kerning*, the space between individual letters. Go to Format -> Font -> Character Spacing tab. You can kern characters that are above a particular point size—thus adjusting certain pairs of letters—or expand or condense selected type. "Adjustments in kerning are especially important in large display and headline text lines," explains desktop-publishing teacher Jonathan Lang. "Without kerning adjustments, many letter combinations can look awkward. The objective of kerning is to create visually equal spaces between all letters so that the eye can move smoothly along the text."[17]

MS Word will permit you to adjust, not only kerning, but *tracking*, the "average space between characters in a block of text, also referred to as letter spacing."[18] This can improve legibility or can allow you to fit more or less text into a given space. "[Tracking or] letter spacing is applied to a block of text as a whole . . . [and] is sometimes referred to as *track kerning*."[19] In MS Word, go again to Format -> Font -> Character Spacing tab. Choose the option to expand or condense space evenly among all the selected characters. This can adjust the tracking for a selected block of text. Of course, a desktop-publishing (DTP) program will permit even finer adjustments in tracking and kerning than are possible with a word-processing program, but you can do quite a bit with MS Word.

If you look at the various examples given for *Alvin Weber* and *Weber Design*, you can see that, while the setting of *Weber Design* looks "visually equal," the setting for *Alvin Weber* in Castellar does not. The *l* and the *v* of *Alvin* as set in Castellar are too far apart.

Not Kerned: ALVIN

Kerned: ALVIN

Further Customization

Your word-processing software makes it possible to customize templates even further with the use of its other capabilities. For instance, you can activate the WordArt functions in MS Word, incorporate clip art using the

Drawing toolbar, or insert *Wingdings* (typeface symbols or characters from picture fonts) from the symbol menu. (You can also incorporate photos and other images, an option that is discussed later in this chapter and in Chapter 12.)

WORDART

The *WordArt* function permits you to insert decorative text into a document by clicking "Insert WordArt" on the Drawing toolbar. You can create shadowed, skewed, rotated, and stretched text, as well as text that has been fitted to predefined shapes. (You can also use other buttons on the Drawing toolbar to change the effect.) In Figure 4.5 there are two variations on the firm names *Alvin Weber* and *Weber Design*, projecting different professional identities.

In Figure 4.6, the first of the WordArt customizations in Figure 4.5, "shadowed wavy letters," has been inserted into the Microsoft Elegant Fax template. You can copy the figure from your CD-ROM to experiment with the WordArt customization, inserting your name or firm name, for instance. Or you can customize from scratch, beginning with a template of your choice. Where the template reads [Click **here** and type company name], for instance, you could insert your name or the name of your design firm—in a variety of fonts, in different sizes of type, and in various shapes from the WordArt Gallery. (Alternately, you could insert a logo image created with a program like PhotoShop, using insert –> picture.)

Figure 4.5
WordArt
customizations
of a firm name.

Shadowed wavy letters

3-D silver letters

Figure 4.6
Fax-transmission
cover document
customized with
WordArt, created
from a standard
Microsoft template.

Alvin Weber

FACSIMILE TRANSMITTAL SHEET

TO:	FROM:
[CLICK **HERE** AND TYPE NAME]	[CLICK **HERE** AND TYPE NAME]
COMPANY:	DATE:
[CLICK **HERE** AND TYPE COMPANY NAME]	7/9/04
FAX NUMBER:	TOTAL NO. OF PAGES INCLUDING COVER:
[CLICK **HERE** AND TYPE FAX NUMBER]	[CLICK **HERE** AND TYPE NUMBER OF PAGES]
PHONE NUMBER:	SENDER'S REFERENCE NUMBER:
[CLICK **HERE** AND TYPE PHONE NUMBER]	[CLICK **HERE** AND TYPE REFERENCE NUMBER]
RE:	YOUR REFERENCE NUMBER:
[CLICK **HERE** AND TYPE SUBJECT OF FAX]	[CLICK **HERE** AND TYPE REFERENCE NUMBER]

☐ URGENT   ☐ FOR REVIEW   ☐ PLEASE COMMENT   ☐ PLEASE REPLY   ☐ PLEASE RECYCLE

NOTES/COMMENTS

Select this text and delete it or replace it with your own. To save changes to this template for future use, choose Save As from the File menu. In the Save As Type box, choose Document Template. Next time you want to use it, choose New from the File menu, and then double click your template

[CLICK HERE AND TYPE RETURN ADDRESS]

CLIP ART

Artwork that is available free of charge for anyone's use in illustrating documents is known as *clip art*. Microsoft Office XP comes with a sizeable clip-art gallery on a CD-ROM. In addition, Microsoft makes free clip art available online at office.microsoft.com, as does Avery-Dennison at www.avery.com. These companies are by no means the only providers. If you research clip art online, links to a mind-boggling number of possibilities will display themselves. Clip art is also available in printed form, such as the many collections from Dover Books, which can be scanned to produce a digital image. Figure 4.7 shows a piece of clip art from the basic Microsoft library inserted into the template for Elegant Report. Through the colors-and-lines tab of the WordArt formatting window, the colors of the "Alvin Weber" wave-letter customization (Figure 4.5) have been changed to make them harmonize better with the colors of the clip art.

In Figure 4.8, a different piece of clip art has been copied into the Company Name box of the Elegant Report template. The source of the clip art is the "Buildings" folder in the MS Office collection found on the MS Office Media Content CD-ROM that is bundled with many computers. The 3-D Silver Letters customization from Figure 4.5 has also been inserted into the Company Name box. (All these insertions were handled through the Insert Menu. Choose "Picture" and then WordArt or Clip Art, as appropriate.) The same clip art is used in Figure 4.14, a folder brochure. Figures 4.7 to 4.11 are featured on the CD-ROM.

PICTURE FONTS

One of the simplest ways to customize your stationery package is through the use of so-called picture fonts such as Wingdings, which is bundled in Microsoft Word. Wingdings and its sister fonts are accessible through the font windows or the Insert menu. Here are Character Codes 208 and 209 from Wingdings, inserted in the same typeface as this book's text: ✌☞. Figure 4.9 shows these same two Wingdings, enlarged in font size. The contact information has then been added in smaller-sized Georgia font, though the telephone number is in Times New Roman to avoid the "saggy" appearance that the telephone number's three fives would have in Georgia. (It is sometimes necessary to substitute characters from an additional font in a situation where legibility has been compromised—but use a similar font.) The Wingding pair and the contact information have been put into a text box (created through the Insert menu) so that they can be freely moved on the document page. The Windings and contact information have then been bordered by means of the borders-and-shading option; the area in the box has been filled with 25 percent gray.

On page 160 you will see a different Wingding in a designer's brochure created with the standard brochure template that is packaged with Word. (Figure 4.14) The small, stylized column above the name and address in the middle panel of the first page is Character 51 from the Wingdings 2 font.

Create a unified stationery package.

Alvin Weber

.·. *A S I D , I I D A* .·.

PROPOSAL FOR REDESIGN OF THE RODERICK MURPHY RESIDENCE AT

329 HURLEY DRIVE

Weber Design

378 WILLOW LANE • CLARYVILLE, NY • 12725
PHONE AND FAX: 845-555-6789 • E-MAIL: ALVIN@WEBDESIGN.COM

Desktop Publishing: The Stationery Package

Whatever customizations you decide on to create a professional identity, use them not only on your letterhead but on labels, envelopes, business cards, and throughout your stationery package. For no-frills desktop publishers, templates for reports, memos, faxes, brochures, and other documents are accessible through word-processing software. Other choices are available at officeupdate.microsoft.com. The Avery Company, which produces labels, has cooperated with Microsoft to produce label and business-card templates,

Weber Design

378 WILLOW LANE, CLARYVILLE, NY 12725
845-555-6789

PROPOSAL FOR REDESIGN OF THE OFFICES OF OLMSTEAD, HARPER, GIDEON & YATES

PRINCIPAL DESIGNER: ALVIN WEBER, ASID, IIDA
∴ *RESIDENTIAL AND COMMERCIAL INTERIORS* ∴

Figure 4.8
Report cover for a contract project customized with WordArt and clip art, and created from a Microsoft template.

some available on officeupdate.microsoft.com and some at www.avery.com. Between the template resources packaged with your word-processing and business software, those on the Office and Avery Web sites, and other templates available online (for example, through PaperDirect™), you should be able to customize and publish every component of your stationery package.

Again, you need to bear in mind that this simplified form of desktop publishing will not yield the level of quality, complexity, and subtlety that can be achieved through high-end commercial printing. Nor will you

Figure 4.9
Letterhead created
without a
template, using
Wingdings.

AlvinWeber, ASID, IIDA
378 Willow Lane
Claryville, NY 12725

845-555-6789

achieve with pre-designed templates the sophisticated and individualized results that a highly trained graphic designer can achieve with special layout and image-manipulation software.

Some examples of superb stationery design are in the gallery of Crane, the fine paper manufacturer, at http://www.crane.com. When you consider the beautiful examples of meticulous and sensitive graphic design showcased there and study any samples you collect when you do Exercise 4, it will doubtless cross your mind that a customized stationery package created with a word-processing program is at best a compromise. Yet, for many novice interior designers, it is both a workable compromise and an affordable one. Until your budget permits you to buy a DTP program like MS Publisher or to retain a graphic designer, you can create a working stationery package that will help project your evolving professional identity, particularly if you choose with care the paper suite for your package.

Paper

Paper is manufactured in a delicious variety of colors, textures, weights, and finishes. When choosing special paper for items like letterhead stationery and business cards, you need to keep the entire stationery package in mind. For instance, a color and texture may not be available in business-card stock that is available for letter paper. Double-pocket folders, frequently used for capability packets or kits—see below—are available in a more limited range of colors than letter paper and business-card stock. Whatever papers you choose, it is prudent to select from *open stock*, which is always offered for sale, rather than relying on the odd lots of appealing paper that may be available through discount paper stores on a one-time-only basis. Odd-lot papers, however, can represent significant value—beautiful paper at surprisingly low cost—for your one-time-only or limited-run printing jobs. For the most part, paper falls into one of three categories: bond paper, book paper, or cover paper.

BOND PAPER

Bond paper is the pre-cut paper that has been traditionally used for correspondence. It is most frequently purchased in the $8^1/_2$"-by-11" "letter" size that is standard for business letters. It is also available in the $8^1/_2$"-by-14" "legal" size and in so-called "full sheets"–big sheets from which smaller ones are cut. Bond and other paper are sold according to "basis weight"–the weight of 500 sheets of that kind of paper at its full size–which indicates thickness. The weight that is customarily sold for general workaday use is 20 pound. This is the weight of the so-called copier paper, plainly finished and low in brightness, that is the workhorse of the business and professional world. Paper sold for good-quality ink-jet printing is 24 pound, while paper for good-quality laser printing is 24 pound, 28 pound, or 32 pound. In general, the heavier the paper, the more distinguished the appearance of the printed product, although a 17-pound translucent paper may lend an interesting aura in some situations and may even be used for business cards.

At any given weight, there will be a variety of quality choices, varying from a very cheap sulphite grade up to fine sheets made of 100 percent cotton fiber.[20] You will find that finishes vary in accordance with weight and quality. The cheaper grades are smooth and plain. Better grades are finished with ripples or fine "laid" lines. Hold fine papers up to the light to see the watermarks bearing a proud manufacturer's imprint.

In addition to whites, creams, tans, and grays, bond colors include the inexpensive but lackluster pastels that are used for run-of-the-mill commercial flyers and rich or brilliant shades that are more costly. If you choose colored paper for your stationery package or print brochure stick with black ink, you can project the cheer of color in your professional identity while keeping costs down.

BOOK AND TEXT PAPER

According to Clifford Burke, author of *Printing It*, "middle-grade book paper is of a little higher quality than good sulphite bond and is bulkier and softer." A typical weight for this type of paper is 60 pound. Many commercially printed brochures and annual reports and even some magazines are printed on this grade of paper. Higher in quality and heavier is so-called text paper, with 70 pound as an average weight for one of the less expensive papers in the category. Burke explains that "most [paper] mills have a prime grade text paper in several weights, including covers . . . with an extensive range of colors" and finishes and with rough "deckle" edges "for fancy jobs." The papers in the book-and-text category are considerably more expensive than the bonds, partly because they are generally not pre-cut. You may choose a stock for business cards from this paper category—or you may choose harder-finished cover paper. It is not a good idea, says the Manhattan paper dealer JAM, to choose stock any heavier than 65 pound for printing your own business cards.[21] Heavier paper may get stuck in a desktop printer. Read your printer's manual before shopping for card stock (or any other paper), so as to brief yourself on its capacities. Always try one sheet before committing to a full print run.

COVER PAPER

Cover stocks start at 65 pound, with the average weight being 80 to 100 pound—roughly that of a paperback book cover. These sturdy stocks are available in as wide a variety of colors and finishes as book and text paper and are frequently coordinated with them. If you are planning a booklet-style brochure, you may select cover stock—or then again, you may choose to save money by using the same paper for your booklet's outer and inner pages. The purpose of using tougher stock for a cover is to protect the content pages, but often the risk of damage to unprotected pages is not that great.[22]

You can get a rudimentary sense of the range of paper products on the market by comparing the elegant fine-quality papers offered through the Crane & Company Web site (www.crane.com) or the specialty envelopes and papers at JAM (www.jampaper.com) with the user-friendly and templated product lines offered at PaperDirect™ (www.paperdirect.com) and at the Avery Web site (www.avery.com). To fully appreciate the differences among papers, visit an actual store where you can see and feel the differences among products. Choose papers that are laser- or ink-jet–friendly (as appropriate), of adequate weight, and with good toner and ink adhesion. (If your printer is ink-jet, choose paper that will resist unsightly bleed-throughs.)

Components of Capability Presentation

Once you have begun to evolve a working professional identity for your firm, you are ready to project that identity with full-fledged capability presentation. The two most characteristic components of capability presentation are the business card and the capability brochure. As you develop your sense of how your professional identity might be represented in these presentation vehicles, your sense of your firm's vision and image will continue to evolve.

Business Cards

A business card helps to create a prospective client's first impression of you, as it is handed out or exchanged upon casual meeting on business or social occasions. It may also be clipped to a capability brochure or kit that is mailed to a prospective client. Because it conveys first impressions, it is important that the card present you in a manner that is compatible with the professional identity that you have been developing for yourself.

If you have used a logo or a logo-like customization in your letterhead, it should be repeated (though probably in a different size) on your business card, along with the names of the professional organizations through which you are accredited. Above all, the business card delivers contact information, including your street address, postal address if different, phone number, fax number, e-mail address, and the address of a capability Web site if you have one. Although the nature of your business may seem to be apparent from your professional designation—"Alvin Weber, ASID, IIDA"—you may still need to indicate the nature of your services: "Alvin Weber, ASID, IIDA. Corporate and commercial design." There may also be room for a *tag line*, or business slogan (for example, "Better spaces by design"). However, it is a mistake to cram in so much information that the card becomes difficult to read. Any typeface smaller than 7 points is too small for most people to see. For aging eyes, type needs to be 8 points or larger.

BUSINESS-CARD FORMAT

You may think of a business card as a simple rectangle of white or colored cardboard with some text and perhaps an image printed on it. This is the traditional and still most typical format, and there are many advantages associated with its use. It fits the slots in the two-pocket folder that is frequently used for capability kits. It also fits the business-card files that some prospective clients may maintain. However, there are other format possibilities, among them a standard-sized card in *portrait orientation* (vertical format) rather than *landscape orientation* (horizontal format). Such a card may convey a sense of individuality, although vertical format requires shorter lines of print, which may make it difficult to convey your message clearly. Information that takes one line in horizontal format may need to be broken into two or more lines in vertical. Thus, it makes sense to place fewer information items on a vertical card, so as to avoid the crowded feeling that is generated by insufficient space between lines.

Another useful business-card format is the so-called brochure card, discussed at greater length in Chapter 11. This card is twice the size of an ordinary card and is folded in two. The outside holds the contact information, while the inside panel holds a brief capability message such as a tag line.

Still another useful card format is a larger unfolded card with room for a message—perhaps twice the size of an ordinary card but unfolded. The contact information is usually at the top, with a blank space below. The layout of the card should be such that it looks complete even if the blank space is not used, although the virtue of this format lies in the uses to which the blank space can be put. Most notably, the space can be used for a very brief cover note when sent with a brochure, or you can customize it on the spot when giving your card to a new contact. For example, a card imprinted with a firm's name and contact information and the words "Interior design—commercial and residential" could be customized for a particular prospect with the handwritten words "Extensive experience in the design of medical facilities" if the designer possessed such experience and were about to hand the card to a hospital administrator.

Some business cards are created in so-called "novelty" formats. For instance, a business card can be shaped with notches at the bottom to fit the holding rods in the rotary-flip files in which many people store telephone numbers. Alternately, an interior designer who had designed a line of furniture might have a card that was shaped like a sofa, table, or chair. Some interior designers believe that novelty cards lack the dignity associated with professional stature. Shaped cards are also relatively expensive, since they generally involve tricky custom paper cutting that does not utilize the full sheet of card stock. In addition, nonstandard card formats cannot be stored in a business-card file or desktop-published from templates.

SELF-PUBLISHED BUSINESS CARDS   If you decide to produce your own business cards, you have two basic choices: either you can work with templates or you can design your own card from scratch, which is easier than you might think, though the simplest way to publish a business card is with the assistance of a template. Figure 4.10 shows a simple business card created for Alvin Weber from the "Business Cards for a Small Business Owner" template found in the MS Office Template Gallery online. Like other business-card templates, this one is created as a table with the same business-card text and layout in every cell. It is designed to print perfectly onto Avery card stock (#5371, #8371, or #8871) that is perforated for easy separation into individual cards.

The template was downloaded by clicking on "Edit with Microsoft Word" and customized as follows: In the print view, after Selecting All

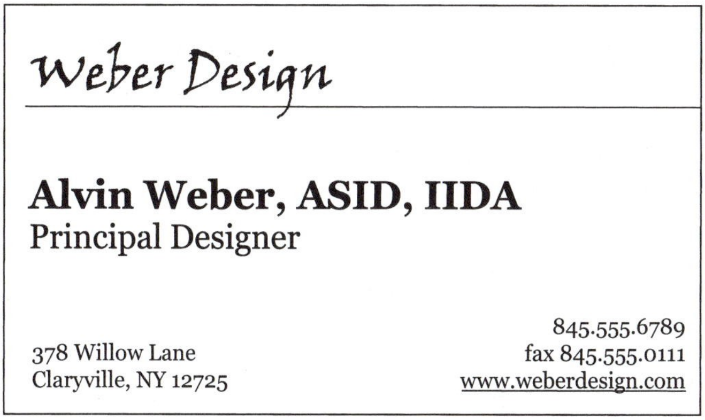

Weber Design

Alvin Weber, ASID, IIDA
Principal Designer

378 Willow Lane
Claryville, NY 12725

845.555.6789
fax 845.555.0111
www.weberdesign.com

Figure 4.10
Business card
created with
template from
Microsoft Office
Web site.

(Control A), the Tahoma font was replaced with the Georgia through the font-family selection procedure previously described. The business information for Alvin Weber was then inserted into one cell of the table, copied, and pasted into the others. You can download the template from the Office Web site and customize it for yourself, making similar changes.

You can also create your own business-card templates through the Envelopes-and-Labels feature in Word, which is accessed through Tools→Letters and Mailings→Envelopes and Labels. Figure 4.11 shows a business card created in this manner. An article available at http://office.microsoft.com/assistance/2002/articles/wd/MakeBusiness Cards.aspx[23] tells you how to create it, explaining that you enter the business-card text in the window in the Envelopes-and-Labels dialogue box. You then right-click on the text and select Font and Paragraph to format it. However, this procedure does not permit you to choose styling options such as shading. To get around this difficulty, leave the window in the dialogue box blank, with the "Full page of the same label" option checked. Go to options and choose a business-card stock. Now click on "New Document" and save to your hard drive as "Yourname Business Card," or whatever file name you prefer. Then choose "Show Gridlines" from the Table menu. A grid will appear on your document that corresponds to the pre-sized business cards on a sheet of the Avery stock you have chosen. You can then proceed to create and customize a business card in one of the cells on the tabular layout, being careful to maintain congruence between the tabulation and the business card.

In Figure 4.11, the words *Weber Design* are in the font Viner Hand ITC, in keeping with customization of this professional name previously used for

Figure 4.11
Business card
created without
a template through
Microsoft Word's
Envelopes-and-
Labels window.

Weber Design

Alvin Weber, ASID, IIDA
Residential and Commercial Interiors

378 Willow Lane
Claryville, NY 12725

ph: 845-555-6789
e-mail: Alvin@weberdesign.com
Web site: www.weberdesign.com

letterhead stationery. The rest of the card is Garamond, a light, graceful type-face that also happens to be the body font of the Elegant Letter template from which letterhead was created for Weber Design (see Figure 4.4). After creating the card in the first cell of the tabular layout, the prototype cell was selected and copied into all other cells of the layout. Further customization is, of course, possible. On your CD-ROM, you can see Figure 4.11 with the 25 percent gray fills changed to red fills. The completed business-card layout can be saved as a template or as a document. In either case, your self-published card would be ready to print onto the card stock you have selected.

CD BUSINESS CARDS   A few years ago, so-called CD Business Cards were considered a tricky novelty, not, perhaps, fully suitable for a professional. These versatile little CD-ROMs have now become mainstream, and they are an excellent way to introduce your prospective clients to the full range of your skills and services. Even if you have a CD burner on your computer, you will probably need to consult with a computer-design specialist to create a CD business card. Accordingly, a CD-ROM may not be the first business card that you choose to represent yourself as a novice designer. Still, this is an option worth bearing in mind, particularly for interior designers with graphic-design capabilities. If you can create a simple capability Web site, then you may be able to burn a capability CD after changing your Web site's links to local ones.

A typical calling-card CD (Figure 4.12) is about the same size as a credit card; yet it plays in the CD-ROM drive of any computer and can hold between 30 and 50 Mb of data. As with paper business cards, novelty or shaped CD cards are available. Although their appropriateness to ordinary professional purposes is debatable, shaped CD cards may serve some interior designers well as an expression of professional identity. Of course, a CD card of any shape can be

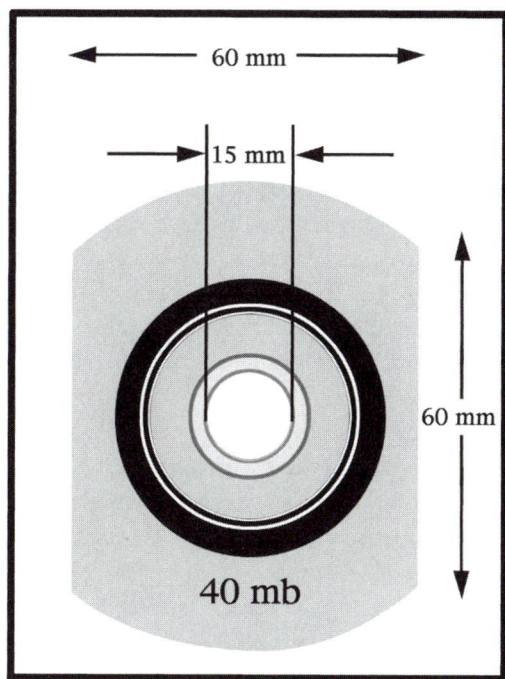

Figure 4.12
A card-sized
CD-ROM holds a
library's worth
of information.

imprinted with artwork that expresses the image you want to project and is consistent with your stationery package. Most CD replicators will create artwork for you or provide you with a template that permits you to create your own artwork.

Although they are not much larger or bulkier than pasteboard business cards, CD cards function as multimedia marketing pieces or electronic portfolios and provide an alternative or a supplement not only to printed business cards, but to printed capability brochures and kits.

The Capability Brochure

The primary purpose of the capability brochure is to get the attention of prospective clients. By speaking to the as-yet-uncommitted and convincing them of your capability, the brochure frees you to concentrate your attention on the design work itself and on your serious prospects—those who invite you to demonstrate your skills and experience with respect to a particular project idea. A print or CD brochure can be sent to prospects in response to requests for information about your firm—or these prospects can be directed to a capability Web site. A print brochure or a CD-ROM can be also be used as a *leave-behind*, distributed as part of the closing remarks at a design presentation. (The concept of the leave-behind is discussed at greater length in Chapter 12, as is the portfolio—which is to the individual interior designer what the capability brochure is to a firm.)

The most elaborate print or electronic brochures are usually developed in conjunction with a graphic designer, an expert in layout and image manipulation. However, many novice interior designers do not have large budgets for creating brochures and other marketing materials that tell their firms' stories. As with stationery packages, you can produce your own print brochure with desktop-publishing software, or you can use the rudimentary tools that are packaged with Microsoft Word. Of course, if you are interested in working with large corporate clients, you may find that you need an elaborate, expensive brochure that presents you as a well-established designer with prestige that answers the corporation's own. If you are interested in working with, say, young married couples or savvy singles, you may get good marketing results with a brochure that suggests an economical approach to interior design.

ELEMENTS OF THE CAPABILITY BROCHURE

A good brochure is a marriage of text and image. Most graphic designers would prefer to create the graphics first, situating the images, or illustrations, within the initial layout and creating boxes or blank areas to be filled with text blocks limited to a given size. Yet many marketing experts believe that the text should be created first, and the layout created and illustrations chosen to enhance the text. If you are using a template, that decision has been made for you, although you can change the line spacing and font size of text to make it occupy more or less space. Whatever format priorities prevail, most capability brochures cover some or all of the following ground:

- The firm's mission, or design philosophy
- The principals and staff
- The work of the firm
- A list of principal projects
- A list of references
- Special inserts
- Illustrations (figures, charts, and photographs)
- Captions, titles, and other "signposts"

The amount of information presented in a brochure partly depends on the format selected for it. A brochure in simple folder format may have room only for a discussion of the firm's mission, brief professional biographies of the principals, and a brief overview of the services provided by the firm—ideally presented in conjunction with carefully chosen photographs. In addition to these crucial elements, a brochure in kit form may contain case studies and lists of clients and references as well as a number of special inserts, all customized for a particular client or client category. A brochure on a Web site or CD-ROM may contain the principals' full résumés as well as larger sets of photos and drawings.

THE FIRM'S MISSION STATEMENT   This part of the brochure puts a designer's design philosophy into words. The mission statement should be clearly expressed, though it may be implicit rather than explicit. It is important to establish the proper professional tone, but it is a mistake to focus the mission statement on the procedures you and other designers follow to achieve results. Instead, create a bridge between your particular firm and the target client. Remember, a client buys not your design capability but the prospect of pleasure and pride in living or working in a beautiful, functional interior.

> Concise mission statements are most effective.

While there are mission statements that go on for pages and pages—as in some corporate mission statements that you may have seen—for the purpose of your folder, kit, or online capability brochure, your mission statement should not be longer than 50 words. Online readers notoriously lack patience, and you simply won't have room for more words in, say, a simple folder. In fact, you may need to boil your folder mission statement down to 25 words or fewer. A booklet brochure affords more space. Still, it is best to avoid statements that take up more than a booklet page. A capability kit easily permits an $8^{1}/_{2}$-by-11-inch page for a mission statement—about 500 words single-line spaced. Again, though, you'd be better off with fewer words that are bulleted.

You may think it is easier to describe your mission in few words than in many, but the shorter the mission statement, the more difficult the writing task is for most people.

To write a brief but dense mission statement, begin by brainstorming all the benefits you can provide for your client. These should not be a list of the standard services that define the profession of interior design and that any firm would provide. It should be a list of the benefits that only you can provide to your target clientele. For instance, Jane Maxon, a designer with a fine-arts background, might write: "my knowledge of painting and sculpture enables me to choose investment-grade art that expresses my clients' lifestyle values." Begin by free-writing without any worry about grammar, punctuation, quality, or relevance. There will be time and opportunity to edit later. After you have written 20 or more benefits, cluster them by similarity, then write a smaller group of more abstract benefits that encompass whole clusters. Jane Maxon might subsume her fine-arts capabilities under "Maxon Design creates civilized interiors." Repeat this process until you have boiled your mission-statement draft down to an essence of what you have to offer: "Civilized, cost-effective designs for discerning clients."

A mission statement providing a clear bridge to clients' needs is found in the print brochure of Workstage LLC (www.workstage.com). It has a compelling blue-and-silver striped cover with the words "Rewrite the Rules" written backwards. Below these words is the question "How is it possible to create turnkey work environments that inspire the people who work in them and delight the people who pay for them?" Even before opening this large booklet-style brochure, a prospective client knows what the firm *does* (create turnkey work environments that are ready to use on completion of the design project); knows its *goal* (to satisfy two target audiences—office workers and business owners); and knows its *design philosophy* (rewrite the rules). On the first page of the brochure, the phrase "Rewrite the Rules" is repeated in large type, this time not reversed, accompanied by the simple but compelling graphic device of two arrows:

This device suggests the commitment to reciprocity between:

- Client and designer.
- A building's occupants and passers-by.
- Workers and management.
- Humans and the environment.
- Tenants and landlords.

The emblem of reciprocity carries a powerful message of creative cooperation that is visible throughout the firm's capability brochure.

Sometimes a firm's mission is conveyed through a simple *tag line*, or business slogan, that succinctly expresses the company's philosophy or professional specialty. Tag lines may be as short as two to three words or as long as nine or ten words, which is all that most people can *chunk*, or recall verbatum.[24]

You can see the power and economy of evocative, short business slogans by considering two tag lines from interior designers' online capability brochures. Jo Tilghman Interior Design, a firm that specializes in the design of office space, uses the tag line "Changing the way your workspace functions," while Bauer Interior Design, which specializes in quirky, bright residential interiors uses the tag line "It's always different."[25] Each of these two tag lines succinctly conveys a sense of the designer's specialty and philosophy. Prospects who experience a resonance with these simple but rich statements will read on. They will be interested in finding out more about the designers in question.

THE PRINCIPALS AND STAFF   The brief biographies that are typically contained in brochures are a distillation of the résumés of a firm's principals. This section of the brochure speaks to the questions, "Who are they?" and "What are their credentials?" Very much to the point are a designer's affiliations with ASID, IIDA, and other organizations in which membership is based on merit, experience, skill, and knowledge. (You will find an extensive list of interior design professional organizations in Chapter 12.) Also to the point are certifications, academic degrees, previous work experience, publications, and professional honors.

If a print brochure is expensively produced, then it is prudent to limit the "who" section to a firm's principals, who probably won't change, although the staff list might. Or you can present fuller biographies for the firm's principals but list the names of associates and staffers only with their professional affiliations. Even in the more capacious brochure formats, such as the online or CD brochure, it is best to limit biographies to 25–75 words. Readers simply will not have patience for more! Boil the biographies down using the method suggested for the mission statement. If your credentials are extensive, select the best or most recent to represent others of their kind. For any brochure format, the "bio" section should be designed, presented, and written in such a way that it can be easily updated, avoiding the use of columns and other hard-to-handle formatting options.

This boilerplate section of the brochure need not be boring and can contribute importantly to the brochure's expression of a particular designer's mission. At her Web site www.bauerdesign.com, for instance, Lou-Ann Bauer has an appealing biographical and contact page that combines a personal note with a savvy presentation of important credentials. The page itself is a statement about Bauer's eclectic yet unified style, since it combines disparate elements into a resonant whole and is itself a demonstration of Bauer's "home rule" No. 2: "Mix it all up."

The page begins with testimony: "I got the chance of a lifetime to start my own business twelve years ago and now I'm doing what I want to do: artful and whimsical interiors." This statement has the charm of the personal, but it delivers important information in an economical way, conveying experience, passion, and an aesthetic that embraces both art and whimsy. Since most testimony on a business or professional Web site is from satisfied customers, Bauer is humorously tweaking the conventions of capability presentation and, by implication, those of interior design.

The testimony segues into a brief biographical narrative that touches on Bauer's experience, her aesthetic, her firm's range of services, and the particulars of her education in art and interior design. There is a link to Bauer's awards and publications, which are extensive enough to be featured on their own page. There is also a link to Bauerware, where visitors may order "whimsical cabinet knobs and pulls." The page concludes with contact information and an electronic "leave-behind" consisting of "Lou-Ann's Home Rules," an eclectic, entertaining, and thought-provoking set of guidelines such as "Color—select ones where no one dares to go" that express this designer's bold style while leaving the site visitor with a memorable and valuable gift of insight.

THE WORK OF THE FIRM   Even if a design firm is not marketing itself as highly individualistic and quirky, like Bauer Interior Design, it is important that the overview of the services provided by the firm in its brochure not sound too generic. The "work" section should describe the firm's specialties with reference to its target customers. To help avoid the generic, it may be useful to compare a description of interior design services on a regulatory agency's Web site with a particular design firm's client-oriented description of its services.

The Office of the Professions of the Education Department of the State of New York makes available at its Web site[26] a brochure for prospective interior design "consumers" that details what they should know about designers' services. The following criteria were established by the Department of Education, the agency certifying interior designers in New York State:

A Certified Interior Designer (CID) licensed in New York plans, designs, supervises, and/or consults on various aspects of interior spaces including:

* Layouts and planning of interior construction
* Furnishings and fixtures
* Cabinetry, lighting, and finishes
* Other aspects of interior construction not materially related to the main structural building components or systems

To safeguard people and property, certified interior designers incorporate construction, fire, safety, and accessibility codes and data into their design services.

While this statement adequately defines a New York State–certified interior designer's work, it does not convey a sense of the benefits to the prospect of using a particular designer's services.

By comparison, the work of the Chicago-based Environments Group[27] is described as follows:

> The Environments Group is a full-service design firm that specializes in the creation of effective workspace. We provide strategic planning, interior design, and facility-management support to corporate and professional organizations.
>
> Based in Chicago, we partner with clients nationwide to deliver effective business solutions. Our mission—Design in Service to Business—guides all of our work.

Note the importance of the target client in this brief description of the Environment Group's work. All the services contained in the New York State description of a designer's work are encompassed by the expression "full-service design firm." The rest of the Environments Group's statement provides an overview of the firm's specialties with reference to the target clients: business and professional organizations.

PRINCIPAL PROJECTS   Depending on format considerations, a brochure will contain a list of principal projects and may also contain case studies of a selected group of projects. The list of principal projects should be grouped by categories, most typically residential design and contract design. You may need to break these large categories down into subcategories: for example, Jo Tilghman Interior Design (www.jtidworx.com) presents its all-contract work under the headings educational, corporate, health care, and retail. Like the biographies of principals and staff, the principal-projects list should be designed and written for easy updating, without the use of columns or other hard-to-handle formatting options.

The emphasis in this section, as in other parts of the brochure, should be on benefits to the client, not on design procedure. If your brochure includes case studies (see Chapter 3), explain clearly what problems were posed by the job under discussion, and then state the firm's solution to the problems and spell out the positive results for the client. The benefits may be quantifiable—80 percent fewer work days lost to illness—or qualitative—a warmer, cozier environment for a newborn—or both. If quotations (testimonials) will make your point, don't hesitate to use them.

REFERENCES   It is probably better not to put references into a folder, booklet, or electronic brochure, as most designers prefer to customize references to client or client category. A prospective residential client who is about to undertake an expensive and lengthy renovation of a historic Victorian house will not be interested in a designer's stunningly contemporary work for Fortune 500 corporations and vice versa. Remember to ask for permission before citing references. That way the individuals who provide references are prepared; you can be confident that they are happy to tell your story in a manner that will burnish your reputation. If your brochure is kit-style, it will, of course, accommodate a list of references tailored to each particular client.

SPECIAL INSERTS   These might be reprints of articles about your firm or written by your firm's principals; speeches by principals; a large firm's latest annual report; or any other materials that will help prospective clients understand the firm, including press releases and other materials that have been prepared for promotion and publicity purposes. At www.workstage.com, for instance, you can find a reading room that provides important and useful links on current and projected developments in the field of office design. The firm istudio provides a link to a radio panel by one of its principals on the subject of green design.[28] Among print-brochure formats, a kit brochure permits the selection of special inserts customized to each client prospect.

High-quality photos are an essential promotional tool.

ILLUSTRATIONS   Capability brochures may be illustrated with drawings, clip art, charts, tables, cartoons, diagrams, Wingdings, and, indeed, figures of all kinds. Needless to say, the images most crucial for the brochures of interior designers are photographs of completed projects. Good photographs are arguably the part of the presentation for which it makes the most sense to hire professional help, if you can possibly afford it. Professional photographers who specialize in interiors and in other architectural subjects work with highly specialized equipment (see Chapter 11), so it is not easy to duplicate their results with ordinary equipment such as a 35-millimeter or digital camera. If your budget for a project will cover the cost of professional photography, which is usually sustained by the designer rather than the client or the contractor, the photographs can be used to make an eloquent statement about your design capabilities for years to come, particularly if you have purchased the photos on a "publicity" or "all rights" basis (see Chapter 11). However, the budgets of many novice designers do not permit the hiring of a professional photographer on any basis whatsoever. In order to achieve adequate results, these designers find it advantageous to learn all they can about what techniques to employ with a 35-millimeter or digital camera.

In the 60-plus-year-old *How to Make Good Pictures: A Handbook for the Everyday Photographer*,[29] the Eastman Kodak Company offers a collection of simple techniques for taking effective black-and-white photographs of interiors that remain useful and also apply to color photography. They are slightly adapted here:

- Because the photo will necessarily contain both near and far objects, the photographer must employ a small lens opening to obtain "sufficient depth of field, or range of sharpness." This means that f-stops must be set at the larger-number end of the scale, and the interior you are photographing must be brightly lit.
- If you don't have a wide-angle lens, it is better to photograph a room from two or more viewpoints than to cram all its furnishings into a small physical space so you can show everything in one shot.
- There needs to be enough clear space between the lens and the nearest piece of furniture so that only the floor can be seen in the immediate foreground, particularly in the middle. Any object that is closer than that to the camera will appear disproportionately large in relation to more distant objects.
- The camera should be high enough that more of the ceiling than the floor appears in the viewfinder; otherwise, the picture will look top-heavy.
- Avoid reflections from glass-covered pictures. You may need to draw a window shade or curtain or tilt a picture slightly away from a wall.
- Particularly if you are making a time exposure, place your camera on a table or tripod or other firm support.
- Even out the light in the room by raising or lowering window shades and by opening or closing doors. The aim is to reduce or eliminate dark pockets and to reduce the contrast between, say, strong light entering through a window or doorway and adjacent darker areas. You can also even out lighting with floodlights or with flash—although lighting that is too even lacks dimension and does not appear natural. (With a digital camera, you can take the same picture at several exposures that selectively reveal dark and light areas. Then you can digitally combine them into one evenly lit photo.)
- If need be, use simple reflectors such as sheets of white cloth or paper (about the size of ordinary window shades) to increase the illumination in corners.

If your photographs are taken with a digital camera, you can easily download them onto your hard drive. If they are taken with a 35-millimeter camera, then you will need to scan them or have them scanned. If you do not have a scanner, then check out the services of professional copy and imaging centers. For a reasonable price, you can have your pictures scanned onto a CD-ROM in several different sizes for flexibility of use. You can then use Insert -> Picture to insert them into a document with your word-processing program.

CAPTIONS, TITLES, AND OTHER "SIGNPOSTS"   Throughout your brochure, the various parts need to be identified and, where necessary, explained by titles, labels, captions, and descriptive statements. Chapter 2 contains guidelines for creating these important elements of your brochure. It is important to remember that a caption can do much more than identify a photograph or other figure. Consider the captions on the home page of www.InteriorEdge.com, the capability Web site of the design firm The Interior Edge, for which the principal designer is Joanne Riley, ASID. On the home page, a series of very simple captions under photographs comprise a mission statement for the designer: "Eclectic," "Sleek Sophistication," "Subtle Classicism," "Integrity," "Restrained Opulence," and "Color Symphony." (Note that the photographs are bordered as photographs and appear to be strewn on the page as photographs might be strewn on a table during a work session between a client and a designer.)

Linked project pages on Riley's site engage the interest of prospects with conceptually rich captions such as the following:

> The Foyer . . . is large and airy with an inlaid hardwood floor and custom designed balustrades. . . . The room is accented by an antique newel post and antique prints going up the stairs. The mirror is an Eighteenth Century replica. The style embodies ornament of earlier periods. A lovely urn and spray of bluebell flowers make up the top crest. These details make a welcoming space for guests.

Like the styling of all other text in your brochure, the styling of signpost elements should be resonant with that of your stationery package.

Capability Writing Style

Though an interior designer's capability brochure is a marketing tool, it should not be written in an overtly promotional manner.

Some overly conclusive adjectives to avoid are:

- Significant
- Exciting
- Successful
- Elegant
- Beautiful

You want the prospects who are reading your brochure to decide for themselves that your firm's work is significant and exciting. This will put them in charge of their own perceptions and will encourage their sense of involvement with your firm.

The writing that supports visual representations of your work should be richly observant yet concise and clear, accumulating carefully selected details within a framework of careful organization. Use the following checklist[30] to help you plan and write your brochure, asking yourself:

- Who are my readers?
- What do I want them to do?
- What is the single most important benefit I am offering to target clients?
- What additional benefits am I offering?
- Does my brochure address the concern "What's in it for a prospect"?
- Why should readers trust my design firm?
- What makes my firm special?
- How can readers of the brochure respond?

    - Phone number
    - Business location
    - Hours of operation
    - E-mail address or Web site

According to arts marketing consultant Cindy Ballaro,[31] "people won't read a solid page of text," even in a print brochure. "On a Web site, text has got to be very concise . . . Have a picture with bullet points—aspects and highlights—rather than a bunch of text." Don't be afraid of white space, in print or online. The most effective strategy is often to display a relatively small number of carefully chosen words on a page, with a lot of space around them. If need be, use heads and subheads to organize your points.

Capability writing style is:
- richly observed
- concise, clear
- selectively detailed
- carefully organized

In brochure text, be focused, brief, creative, subtle, well targeted, expert, empathic.

When items are bulleted or otherwise listed, they need to be in parallel construction, which means that similar concepts are presented in similar grammatical forms. Apples, oranges, and ducks do not constitute a list that is satisfying to read. Nor do the following items:

- Kitchens
- Bathrooms
- I am available for one-time consultations.

Unless you are selling products, there is no need for obvious *action words* that drive readers to purchase options. However, as Cindy Ballaro points out, interior designers do "definitely want someone to take an action. You don't want to sound pushy, so you need to find a creative and subtle way to encourage action. 'Affordable pricing'—little lines like that get people. (A lot of people think they can't afford things, so they won't look into them.) Designers need to identify their audience. Who is your target? What will be of value to them? It is important that designers relay their expertise—why someone would utilize their services when they have a lot of choices." Above all, says Ballaro, "put yourself in the customer's shoes" as you are writing.

To make sure you understand what your clients value about you, interview them. It's a good way to cultivate your empathy, advises Ballaro. "Even your descriptions should be targeted to your clients, so get testimonials from those for whom you have done work. Ask the customer, 'What is the greatest value of what I did for you?' . . . An important part of marketing is analyzing what you have done in the past."

Interview your clients to see why they value you.

SURVEYS

Surveys are frequently used to identify the common characteristics and interests of a target market. By asking clients to complete a brief survey, you can learn how they perceive your practice. You can quote favorable comments from your marketing materials. The following tips will help you create successful surveys[32]:

- *Offer an incentive* You'll get better results if you offer your respondents something in return for the information they provide. One cost-effective strategy, for example, is to enter all survey respondents in a drawing for a book or a gift certificate. You might also give respondents a small gift that bears your company's logo. You can research logo gift ideas at www.thinkideas.com.

- *Keep the survey short* Focus on what you need to know.
- *Get advance feedback from your friends* To make sure your questions are clear and will generate answers that are helpful, ask a small group of family, friends, and colleagues to test-take the survey and to provide feedback. Some members of your test group should be relatively unfamiliar with your business.
- *Don't take it personally* Don't react defensively to criticisms or feel disappointed if your survey respondents fail to comment on what you consider your strengths. You can learn from these comments and can use them constructively. Be prepared for surprises both pleasant and unpleasant. For instance, you may have thought that your greatest strength was the quality of your design. If your survey reveals that an equal strength is the quality of your attention to clients, then your capability presentation should take that into account.

Formal surveys that need to be statistically significant are carefully designed and are much more complicated than an informal survey of your clients based on five simple questions. Still, an informal survey should help you learn more about your audience so as to better target your brochure by what you talk about and how you talk about it.

WRITING FOR RESIDENTIAL CLIENT PROSPECTS

The Web sites for Lou Ann Bauer's design firm and Joanne Riley's The Interior Edge indicate the considerable range of tone and style that is appropriate when writing for residential prospects. Bauer's site (www.bauerdesign.com) addresses reader-viewers directly and personally, sometimes speaking in the first person, as if she were talking about herself to a friend. Her tag line, "It's always different," uses the contraction *it's,* which is a distinctly informal usage: this is the way people talk in their homes and to their friends.

Bauer's use of personal testimony further reinforces the sense of intimacy, while the richly hybrid nature of her site—its use of rhetorical strategies ranging from storytelling to establishing rules—embodies her maxim, "Mix it up."

It needs to be stressed that the informality of this site is an artful creation. The marriage of intimate, hybrid writing and colorful, quirky graphics—themselves hybrid, including comical clip art and serious photos—perfectly embodies the design philosophy that Bauer espouses. She speaks very directly to a target audience of discerning residential clients who want something different and whose lifestyle might be characterized as sophisticated, intelligent, and casual.

The site of Joanne Riley's The Interior Edge (www.InteriorEdge.com) seems to be targeting a much more traditional clientele. The text of her site is written in the third-person, in a tone that is reminiscent of a friendly, knowledgeable guide giving a house tour. The vocabulary evokes luxury, grace, and "good taste." The pace of the writing is even and unhurried, as if each carefully selected detail were worth dwelling on.

Both Bauer and Riley stress the creation of special places, dwelling on such qualities as comfort and opulence rather than on the more stringent and programmatic requirements of businesses.

WRITING FOR CONTRACT-DESIGN CLIENT PROSPECTS

The tag line of Jo Tilghman Interior Design, "Changing the way your work-space functions," clearly encourages corporate, institutional, and commercial clients. Not only is the diction formal—no contractions here—but the vocabulary is functional, drawn from the realm of brisk efficiency that characterizes the business world[33]:

> This project exhibits a masterful renovation of an existing warehouse space into the social hub of a large and growing southeastern college campus. It houses the Human Resources Department, postal functions and Student Union, providing meeting, office, game room and concert/lecture facilities for the student population as well as the community.

Writing for a business audience should be plain-spoken and concrete. Like the project description just cited, it should sound not as if one business were talking to another, but as if someone were giving a presentation in a business meeting, speaking in a low-key, matter-of-fact, informative manner—always in complete sentences. Clarity and brevity are important attributes of capability presentation targeted to this group, though a designer should be able to back with relevant supporting information any capability statement.

WRITING BASICS

Whether you are writing brochure copy for residential or commercial client prospects, in print or on the Web, the following tips will stand you in good stead:

- Create a *platform* before you write, identifying your target audience and the principal concepts you need to convey, as well as your focus and approach.
- Write as one human being talking to another, in order to inform and persuade. Read what you have written out loud to check it on the humanity scale.

- Get to the point quickly. Don't waste words.
- Organize your ideas carefully.
- Keep sentences and paragraphs short.
- Avoid clichés.
- Use the present tense and the active voice.
- Use double spacing between paragraphs, even if you are indenting, so as to avoid a cluttered look.
- Let the messages of print and picture complement each other.
- Punctuate correctly to help the reader.
- Don't put testimonials on a separate page—they won't be read.
- Proofread, proofread, proofread. (Use the spellchecker, but proofread manually as well.)

If you are writing for the Web, here are some additional tips:

- Identify the site and its purpose clearly on the home page.
- Avoid setting light text on a dark ground. It's hard to read. Use a dark font color on a light background, and strive for sharp contrast.
- Don't underline for emphasis. To avoid confusion, let underlining be reserved for clickable links in the standard "traffic-sign" colors— blue for pages not yet seen, purple or red for pages previously seen.
- Organize your material so that it is easy to understand no matter what the point of entry to your site. "Web writing," according to the marketing guidelines of Purdue University, "is not linear; it is circular."[34]
- Outline and subordinate, advises Inkwell Editorial. "Use links to take readers into deeper levels of a topic. Think of upper-level pages as summaries or abstracts to whet the reader's appetite. Use links as a map of where they can go from there."[35]
- Cluster information in easy-to-understand bits—perhaps four or five sentences to a Web page. Purdue cites research determining that people read from the Web 25 percent more slowly than from paper, and recommends that "Web site pages contain 50 percent of the copy a traditional printed page would include."[36]
- Avoid lengthy scrolling pages. If a page is more than two or three screens long, break it down into shorter pages. Use subheads in bold when text is more than a screen in length.
- Because the Web is perceived as a more intimate medium than print, write in as informal a manner as suits your purpose and your audience. If appropriate, address readers directly.

Choose the best
media for your
capability
message.

Capability-Presentation Vehicles

Providing the information your audience will respond to, in a manner that will motivate favorable action, is not only a matter of carefully scripting your message and choosing the right pictures. You need to determine the most effective vehicle to convey your message. As you know, capability is presented in several print formats as well as online or on CD-ROMs. The print brochure formats range from folder to booklet to hard- or soft-cover book to kit, or packet. The choice of a print or electronic vehicle to convey your message need not rule out your later choice of other vehicles, though you probably won't need all of them. Choose vehicles with complementary strengths and uses. The more ways you have of getting your message out, the better.

FOLDERS

A compact and typical capability-presentation vehicle is the *folder*—made from a single folded sheet of paper. This type of brochure is very well suited to pique the curiosity of a prospect who is attracted to your work but does not have a particular design project in mind. Folders are also useful as leave-behinds, handouts, or take-ones. (Read more on those uses in Chapter 11.) They convey basic capability information that is not particularized to specific clients. They can be a very economical choice if printed a dozen or a hundred at a time on your own computer. However, this format does have limitations.

Many folder brochures are laid out in six columns, in landscape orientation, on each of the two sides of an $8^1/_2$-by-11-inch sheet, which is then folded in thirds. This is a good format for an all-text brochure, fitting easily into business-letter envelopes to help you respond to casual inquiries, but it is not particularly friendly to images. A simple variation is exemplified in a recent brochure produced by IDEC (the Interior Design Educators Council). It was laid out in eight columns on each of two sides of an 11-by-14-inch sheet. The use of larger paper permitted the presentation of more information, although, again, the narrow columns are not particularly well suited to the presentation of images.

Many variations are possible. One of the simplest has to do with the way the brochures are folded. Figure 4.13 shows two ways to fold a three-panel folder: accordion fold and standard letter fold. Other variations have to do with paper and printing. For instance, folders may be printed on stiff, glossy, coated papers; they may have elaborate die-cuts or *embossed* (raised) lettering.

Those who produce their own folders usually choose pre-cut bond paper. (PaperDirect™ recommends 38 pound for many folders.) DTPers need to be alert to a characteristic of paper known as *grain direction* that is created by the movement of the paper's fibers in one direction through the paper-

making machine. As Clifford Burke explains, "grain affects folding properties."[37] You want folds to lie "along the grain, to assure ease of opening" and
to help your brochure lie flat when opened. Pre-cut bond stock usually has
the grain running the long way. If you are folding the short way, the grain
will be wrong. This may or may not pose a difficulty that you cannot live
with. If you purchase larger sheets and have the paper custom-cut, you will
be able to avoid the problem.

If you are having your brochures custom-cut, you can save money by
choosing a size and shape that can be cut from supply sheets without scrap.
Be sure the result will fit into a mailing envelope available through ordinary
retail channels.

You can easily make your own folder brochures. A template for a folder
brochure is bundled with MS Office and can be accessed through MS
Word. Figure 4.14 on your CD-ROM shows an in-progress customization
of this brochure template, which MS Word users can access through File ->
New. The template permits you to customize a brochure by inserting your
words and illustrations in place of the instructions. The folder is laid out on
two 8$\frac{1}{2}$-by-11 inches pages that are printed back-to-back onto sturdy
paper. Each printed sheet is then folded twice to create a letter-fold
brochure.

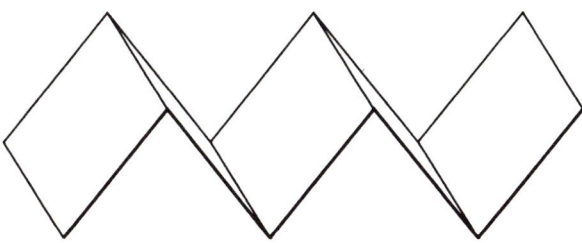

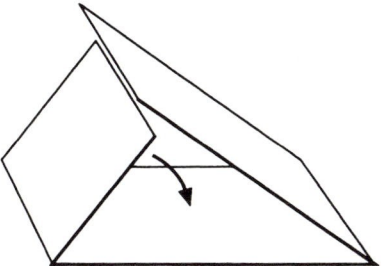

Figure 4.13
A folder can be
created by creasing
the paper in one of
two ways: the
accordian fold
(top) or the letter
fold (bottom).

Figure 4.14   Brochure created from an MS Word template.

WEBER DESIGN

RESIDENTIAL AND
COMMERCIAL INTERIORS

Better Spaces by Design

Weber Design
378 Willow Lane
Claryville, NY 12725
845-555-6789

Weber Design

Better . . .

Residential Spaces

- Houses
- Apartments
- Lofts
- Kitchens
- Bathrooms

Commercial Spaces

- Offices
- Studios
- Factories
- Stores
- Restaurants

Institutional Spaces

- Schools
- Libraries
- Arts Centers

. . . By Design

WHO WE ARE

Alvin Weber, ASID, IIDA

Andrew Weber, IIDA

WHAT WE BELIEVE

The focus of our design work is comfort and elegance in a contemporary setting. Artful simplicity, rich color, and good craftsmanship are central concepts for Weber Design. Our interiors are distinguished by an inspired blend of new and old. We offer practical, yet innovative design services for residential, commercial and institutional environments.

WHAT WE DO

OUR SERVICES

- Houses
- Space planning
- Design concept
- Image coordination
- Budget development
- Ergonomics
- Furnishings specification
- Sustainable design
- Color, finishes, tile, carpets

OUR PARTNERS

- Mimi Parsons, AIA
- Concept Lighting Design
- PGM Contracting
- Jeff Lawrence Landscape Design

PROJECTS

RESIDENTIAL

- Condo, Ossining, NY
- Townhouse, Brooklyn, NY
- Model Home, Bend River, NJ

COMMERCIAL

- The Mirror Café, Brooklyn, NY
- Jean-Louis Salons (fifteen branches in major American cities)
- Think Thin! Ramapo, NJ

INSTITUTIONAL

- Jackson-Jefferson Library, Milbrook, NY.
- Student Center, Packard College, Hartwell, NY
- Steiner YMHA, Brooklyn, NY
- Easton Community Adult Center, Easton, PA

WEBER DESIGN
BETTER SPACES BY DESIGN
845-555-6789

Microsoft recommends that you use the Styles and Formatting window to change the style of any paragraph in the sample on the template. It is also possible to select the text you want to change, then customize it through the Format menu, clicking Font, Paragraph, Borders and Shading, and other menu items in turn.

BOOKLETS

Serving most of the same functions as folders are brochures laid out as thin, paper-covered mini-books, usually stapled along the center fold. Booklets, like folders, present capability in the same manner to each client prospect—they are not customized to particular clients. A booklet like a folder speaks to the curiosity of a client prospect who is attracted to your work but may or may not have a design project in mind. It is good for getting the word out.

Some booklets are unusually shaped or very large in size, like the brochure of Workstage ($8^1/2$"-by-14"). A typical booklet size is $8^1/2$"-by-$5^1/2$". This size is created by folding $8^1/2$"-by-11" sheets in half. Such a brochure is laid out in landscape orientation, two book pages to each side of an $8^1/2$"-by-11" sheet of paper. The resulting booklets will fit a standard-sized envelope that is readily available in office-supply stores, although they do not fit a business-letter envelope without folding that may put a crease in them and make them harder to read. Because the column is less narrow than that of a standard-sized folder, a booklet of this type is more accommodating to images.

Booklet publishers must be "four-sighted." When any piece of paper is folded in two, four pages are created. Thus, the planner of a typical booklet-style brochure must think of four-page modules, printed *two-up* (two on each side of a sheet of paper). Many booklet brochures are 8 or 12 pages; some are as long as 24. Of course, the more pages in a booklet, the more information it can contain.

Long ago, when type was set by hand, layout on two-up or four-up or more sheets, printed back to back, was worked out with the aid of a *dummy*, or preprinting mock-up—and still is—although Word will negotiate the complexities of layout for you, as will dedicated publishing software. (Look, too, for the Click Book software available at www.paper-direct.com, which permits you to "automatically [create] double-side, scalable booklet pages . . . in . . . more than 20 layouts.")

To create a brochure booklet on a virtual dummy in Word, open a blank document. On the margins tab of the page-preview window accessed through the file menu, select multiple pages and "book fold." Then select the number of pages for your brochure in the sheets-per-booklet box. (If you create more pages than the number you selected, they will print as additional booklets.) Working in the document, enter hard pages (Control plus Enter) until you can see that you have created the number of pages you want (it helps to be in print view).

When you have thus created the virtual dummy, enter text and insert pictures into the pages, formatting as you would any other document. (You may need to be patient if you attempt headers and footers in booklet layout.) When you print, choose the "manual duplex" option on your print screen. (You may need to adjust the "gutter" option on the margins tab.) After printing, the next step is folding.

You need to exercise special care in folding the pages of a booklet, to make sure that the page edges are aligned with each other. A commercial printer would have a folding machine that folds each sheet exactly the same way. If you are manually creasing your pages, you may wish to invest in a *folding bone*, a 6-inch bar of plastic, bone, or ivory, slightly curved, with rounded edges. A big soup spoon will also do the job of smoothing and pressing your folds.

To create a fold manually, make sure that the outer edges of each sheet of paper line up with each other and that the top edge lines up with itself all the way across. Then, as Clifford Burke instructs, "Hold the sheet down firmly at the point where the two outside corners meet and with the other hand run the bone [from the edges] back toward the fold to avoid wrinkling."[38] Only then do you run the bone along the fold, which must be properly executed the first time, since it cannot be redone. Even if you refold it properly, the mark of the wrong fold remains.

BOOKS

Comprised of many glued-together booklets called signatures, a *hard- or soft-cover book* is typically hundreds of pages long. Although some books are self-published, a book that is intended to supplement a designer's capability presentation is usually released under a publisher's imprint. The cost of book production—particularly with numerous pictures—represents a significant speculative investment on the part of the publisher. This investment will most likely be made in a designer who already enjoys a substantial reputation that can be predicted to sell a great many books. Having a book published is generally not a viable option for a designer who is just beginning a career.

Among the designer authors who have recently written or contributed to books on interior design are Clodagh, Lady Henrietta Spencer-Churchill, Phillipe Starck, and Roderick N. Shade.[39] These celebrity designers join highly successful individuals in other businesses and professions who elect to share their collected wisdom with the world through books. In general, a well-received book can win its author increased respect and added credibility. It can also win the author what Amy Zipkin, writing in *The New York Times*, has referred to as "modest fame, if not fortune." Zipkin explains that "publishing often leads to speaking engagements, increased visibility . . . and . . . additional income from electronic publishing rights."[40]

While it is a great advantage to have published a book, the actual writing of it can divert time needed for actual design work. There is also the risk that a book will link its author with fads that have an all-too-brief currency. Finally, as Amy Zipkin points out, "bad reviews—if the book is reviewed at all—can cause . . . pain."

Writing about your practice may help you understand it.

The downside notwithstanding, business and professional authors in general report that writing their books has helped them to think more clearly. Through books, an author may come to be viewed as a thought leader. Certainly Clodagh's book *Total Design* positions her as the principal spokesperson for a deeply prescriptive and utopian vision of interior design, as asserted in the book's subtitle, with its direct address of readers: *Contemplate, Cleanse, Clarify, and Create Your Personal Spaces.* A book like this one arguably escapes the market-based realm of the folder or booklet. It is not a capability presentation targeted to prospects, but rather speaks to a much wider audience. Yet the already celebrated Clodagh gains even greater stature from having articulated her design philosophy reflecting a spiritual approach. A high-minded how-to book like hers claims for its author an endowment of creativity so great that she can afford to give generously even to those who do not become clients but simply purchase her book. Of course, increased stature may very well yield increased (and more lucrative) commissions. Yet even celebrity designers need to market themselves and their vision in a manner that is targeted to actual client prospects.

PACKETS

For bread-and-butter capability presentation, there may be no more versatile vehicle than the *packet*, or kit—a collection of print documents that is tailored to individual recipients. Often the capability packet is a collection of unbound pages in a two-pocket folder, though it could be a collection of pages in a ring or other binder. (Many of the binders suitable for an individual designer's presentation described in Chapter 12 would also work well for a firm's capability presentation.)

The principal advantage of packet presentation is its flexibility. While such formats as the folder, the booklet, and the Web site are fixed presentations, geared to a general audience of client prospects, the kit can be tailored to each individual prospect. To be sure, any configuration of the kit would need to contain such basic elements of capability presentation as the firm's mission statement, a listing of principals and staff, and an overview of the firm's work. However, if each of the firm's principal projects is pictured and discussed on its own sheet of paper, then only those project pages that are appropriate to a particular client need be selected. A customized list of references can be inserted along with special inserts, such as article reprints, that are appropriate to the particular client prospect's needs, interests, and projects. (Special inserts could include any of the materials suggested in Chapter 12 for the portfolio, or any of the materials suggested in Chapter 11 for the press kit.)

The principal disadvantage of the kit format is its appearance of impermanence. The provisional aspect of kit presentation can be mitigated by the use of a customized, printed folder or binder (an expensive proposition) or, more modestly, by the creation and use of a logo label on the front of the folder or binder.

A *logo label* carries the graphic elements that identify a firm and provides space for a title for a particular presentation. Such a label can be designed and printed commercially, created from a template, or generated through MS Word's Labels-and-Envelopes-option as described earlier in the chapter for the creation of self-published business cards. A logo label created by the third of these options might use the letterhead pictured in Figure 4.9.

You can unify unbound kit materials—which readers, after all, can arrange in any order they wish—through the use of a *header* on all pages except the cover letter, which is presented on letterhead stationery. Headers also ensure that your brochure's contents will not be confused with anyone else's if client prospects are comparing the capability materials of several firms.

A header typically appears at the top margin of each page in a printed document. Apart from the name of the document, for example, "Mission Statement," you can repeat the same elements in all document headers. Your header can include not only text, but graphics, although these should be small. Typical header items are a company logo, the date, a document title, and page numbers. Remember that the page numbers, like the document title, are document-specific and should not be copied to other documents.

Be sure to create a table of contents for your capability kit, and to format items such as titles, heads, and subheads in a similar manner from document to document. Items not created by you or your office (for instance, tear sheets of reviews of your work) can be scanned into documents that contain your characteristic header in order to maximize the desired impression of unity.

A CD business
card is a versatile
presentation tool.

THE CD BROCHURE   A surprisingly large capacity (30–50 Mb) means that you could store on a CD business card an entire capability brochure's (or portfolio's) worth of information, as well as the résumés of a firm's principals, all with links to photographs. You would still have room for full-scale project profiles complete with drawings and photos, scans of articles published about your firm, reports or papers written by a firm's principals, transcripts of speeches, product information, and much, much more. (Of course, you would need to edit your content rigorously so as not to overwhelm your prospects. The portfolio-editing guidelines presented in Chapter 12 are also useful for electronic brochure publishers.)

As capability presentation pieces, CD-cards have two great advantages. One is their relatively low cost, compared to commercially printed brochures created with the assistance of a graphic designer (though they are nowhere near as economical as a simple desktop-published folder or booklet). The other is the small size their huge content is packed into (they can be passed out as cards or enclosed with a cover letter in a standard business envelope). It is hard to conceive of a capability presentation for which 30–50 Mb are insufficient space. Certainly this amount of space is likely to suffice for a novice designer or a small firm. However, a designer may wish to present capability on a standard-sized CD-ROM, which holds some 650 Mb. With a full-sized CD-ROM, you would lose the advantage of card size, although you would gain cost advantage from the use of a widely standard product and would present clients with an easily archived brochure.

Full-sized or card-sized, CD-ROMs can hold MacroMedia Flash introductions, PowerPoint presentations, full-motion video, animation, graphics, and photos with a voice-over recorded on a background audio stream, though these gimmicks may alienate more people than they entice. If you have a Web site, you can probably store all of it on the business-card–sized CD-ROM, with local links. (A CD-ROM of any size can also contain links to a Web site and/or online product catalog.)

THE CAPABILITY WEB SITE

One of the greatest advantages of an online brochure is the ease with which it can be updated or modified one page at a time, though you need to be sure that your layout has not shifted or a rogue code sneaked in. Cindy Ballaro of Marketing Matters, an arts-marketing firm in Charlotte, North Carolina (www.marketingmatters.org), puts it succinctly: "A Web site is an ongoing brochure."[41] Since capability presentation itself is an ongoing process, you might say that a capability Web site is the quintessential brochure. Although it is not particularized to individual client prospects, the nature of online browsing encourages client prospects to self-select what they are interested in seeing or knowing.

Many interior designers engage a Web designer to help with online brochures in order to ensure a rich visual coherence. However, as Ballaro explains, "If there's someone computer-savvy enough at your firm, there are some really easy Web design packages" that will help you set up a simple site that is an effective promotional tool. Ballaro recommends the software programs DreamWeaver and Front Page, while others recommend Adobe-Go-Live. These are *WYSIWYG* programs—What You See Is What You Get. They simplify site-building, but they tend to produce excess code, which can make a site slow to load. In order to clean out the excess, you would need to learn some HTML (hypertext markup language) even if you were letting your WYSIWYG software do most of the coding that permits online display in the format and layout you choose. There are even simpler do-it-yourself routes.

Many Internet service providers make available online Web-page construction templates that permit clients with very little computer savvy to build rudimentary sites through back-door access. Some design-directory sites offer similar services; the directory format makes it easy for client prospects to find you. A heads-up: the templates at some design "malls" are product- rather than service-based. If you choose a virtual mall that functions as an incubator for start-up sites, look for a host that permits you to strike a balance between hiring a Web designer and doing it yourself. Ballaro recommends www.commercemarketplace.com, which she describes as "very user-friendly." There are charges, she says, for setup and site design, and there is a small hosting fee. Users can make changes in their own sites from a back door on the host's server.

Although you may not be able to post keywords in a mall situation, it is important for an independent site to be picked up by *search engines*—sites that compile information on other sites and then classify and post that information, which may be searched, like a library's catalog, by single or multiple search criteria, then clicked for instant referral to the listed sites. To be noticed by engines, you need to write the so-called key words that are part of your site's metalanguage very carefully. Research is crucial. Before you write the keywords—about thirty to fifty of them—go to the sites of other interior designers. On the View menu of your browser, choose Source. Then see at a glance the keywords that your competition is using. Yours should probably be similar, though they should accurately reflect the content of your site; the "spiders" that search engines use to gather data from the Web are on the lookout for deceptive keywords that do not echo the language used on a site's content pages.

> By browsing, prospects automatically customize a capability Web site.

In fact, there are two kinds of keywords, *visible* and *invisible*. The invisible ones are those you can see by looking at source code. The visible ones are found in three places:

- *Title*   Use keywords in the title of a page that appears at the top of the browser window.
- *Headlines*   Use keywords in headlines and subheads on your pages.
- *Site description*   Use keywords in the 25–word site description placed near the top of the home page to introduce visitors to the site.

By writing keywords, you create the categories under which you will be found on the Web. You can place yourself under any rubric you like, but keywords will not be effective if there is no match between the categories you choose and the categories that many or most people use to find services like those you are offering. If you call yourself an "interior designer," many people will find you. If you call yourself an "interior space articulator," it is unlikely that anyone will find you.

As you are compiling your list of keywords, try out the words on major search engines to see what comes up. The term *Interior Design* will yield a daunting number of results. The terms *Interior Design* and *Yourtown Yourstate*, used together, will yield a more manageable number. It is smart to include "Yourtown Yourstate" when writing your key terms because it is likely that anyone narrowing the vast category "Interior Design" on a search engine will think of doing so geographically. If you are a proponent of a well-known design school such as green design or minimalist design it would be a good idea to include those terms among your keywords, too. Since not all your keywords need to be present as search terms when someone is looking for you on the Web, you can include, say, "residential design" and "retail design." Anyone entering either of those terms in a search box might then find you.

Be sure to proofread the invisible key words. Because the browsing public does not see them, a site creator may be tempted to proofread them less carefully than the visible text of content pages. Search engines are not imaginative about spelling, however. They cannot figure out what you really meant; they respond only to the exact configuration of letters in your keywords.

Any creator of a site that is image- rather than text-based needs to be especially careful about load time. If photographs and other images on your site are large and high-resolution—that is, if they contain a lot of detailed visual information—they can be very slow to load into peoples' computers. Web users lose patience with slow-loading sites; they simply go elsewhere. It makes sense to post smaller, lower-resolution images containing less visual information. The rule of thumb is: post images at the smallest size and lowest resolution that is adequately readable for your purposes. (You can save the high-resolution versions of your images for print applications.) You can also post tiny "thumbnail" images. Users can elect to view larger resolution images by clicking on these. (It is even better if they appear in a separate browser window.)

A load-time caveat applies as well to fancy features such as video and animation—including those MacroMedia Flash introductions that are dear to the hearts of graphic designers. A Flash introduction, like any other introductory, or *splash*, page that appears before the home page, can be intensely annoying to repeat visitors—the online equivalent of having to go through a telephone tree to talk to your mother. Prospects who are part of families in which all adult householders work often shop for products and services on their office computers during lunch hours or breaks. These harried researchers—increasingly typical client prospects—have little or no patience with flashy, balky sites, nor will they respond well to pop-up windows, blinking and scrolling text, sound that can be heard in the next office, or even frames, which cannot be bookmarked, are difficult to exit, and are increasingly seen as a poor substitute for properly organized navigation aids such as button bars, an on-site search engine, and a table of contents or site map.

You do not need to exhibit a play chest of techno-toys in order to project a distinctive identity. For example, www.HCD3.com, the Web site of Heiberg Cummings Design (a firm with offices in New York City and Oslo, Norway) presents a strong and appealing identity without bells and whistles. The home page presents simple, minimalist elements on a white background. When you move your mouse over each section link (alternate text in Norwegian) a photo-collage shifts in an elegant, revealing, and unobtrusive manner. Simple instructions that aid in site use appear below open windows. Navigation is utterly transparent. A well-designed capability site like this invites repeat visits, which means repeated exposure to the designer's message and eventual work for the firm—what capability presentation is all about. Web sites are virtual environments, after all, and clients should expect no less care to be taken regarding their experience in virtual space than with regard to their experience in the built space created by the interior designer.

Discussion Questions

1. Suppose you had hired a graphic designer to create a stationery package for your firm. What instructions would you give her? If your budget were limited and you could not create all components of the package at the same time, how would you prioritize the importance of the various pieces of stationery within the package?

2. How is brochure writing different for residential clients and for contract-design clients? What strategies might a firm employ in order to address both kinds of clients?

3. How does Web-based brochure copy different from print copy? What are the strengths of each kind of presentation?

4. Would you rather have a capability CD or a print-based capability kit? Why?

5. If you have a capability folder, do you need a more elaborate capability presentation? Why or why not?

Exercises

1. In a small group, based on self-interviewing, create a firm name for an imaginary firm of which the members of your group are the principals. Your firm's name should "carry" the idea of your firm by means of intrinsic values and expansiveness. It should have good notational and speech-stream visibility and high phonetic transparency. Working as a team, use a computer's word-processing program to create a logolike professional-identity graphic for your firm.

2. Working with other members of your group, create brochure copy for your firm containing the elements of the capability brochure discussed in this chapter. See if you can fit your copy into the MS Office brochure template. If you cannot, change the format and/or edit the copy to fit. Your goal is a professional-looking brochure that is eye-catching and informative.

3. By Googling interior designers' Web sites, find four captioned photos of principal projects. Prepare a brief oral report (no more than two minutes) on the strengths of the two you like best and the weaknesses of the two you like least.

4. With other members of your class, create a reference library of interior designers' print, online, and CD brochures. (The online brochures can be represented by partial print outs.) Using the summary analysis techniques discussed in Chapter 3, prepare as a class a written report evaluating these capability materials in a literature review or an annotated bibliography.

5. Extend your class reference library to logos and identity packages, with particular reference to business cards (include CD cards if possible). Your evaluation reporting should take into account color, font, kerning, and layout.

5

Writing to Win Business

Once you have created capability materials that display your message in a fetching way, you will no doubt welcome the opportunity to put that message out into the world (more on that in Chapter 11). Yet you are not the only interior designer whose message may reach a prospect. How can you improve the odds that your firm will be selected from a group of competitors?

Not all designers are aware of the role that *correspondence*—good old-fashioned letter writing—can play in turning a prospect into a client. For residential and smaller contract-design projects, a series of letters is often crucial. Letters are not, of course, the only business-development route. More familiar to interior designers who deal with large projects, particularly governmental ones, may be the process whereby response to an RFQ (Request for Qualifications) leads to an RFP (Request for Proposal), and ultimately to the awarding of a design contract. Along both these business-development routes, writing has an important role to play in winning clients for the designer.

Effective Business-Development Style

Although business-development writing should impress readers as dignified and professional, it should not be puffed up with grandiose phrases or swirled with obvious "spin." For all prospects, write in solid, plain English, carefully covering each relevant point. Here are some other tips that will stand you in good stead:

Good, plain English helps win business.

- When possible, convert elaborate prepositional phrases following nouns to simple adjectives preceding them.

Ineffective
- The bedrooms of the children need to be furnished with materials of high durability and brilliant color.

More effective
- The children's bedrooms need to be furnished with durable, colorful materials.

- Pay particular attention to parallel construction in lists and sublists.

Ineffective
Weber Design provides consultation with prospective purchasers
- For space planning
- To discuss remodeling concepts
- Relocation move-in planning

More effective
Weber Design provides consultation with prospective purchasers
- For space planning
- For discussion of remodeling concepts
- For relocation move-in planning

- Use the client's name and the design firm's name whenever possible, avoiding abstractions and the passive voice. Choose instead concrete nouns that refer to people or places in the active voice.

<u>Ineffective</u>

With the requirement for durable, flexible window treatments, withstanding sustained public use, an opportunity is created for the use of translucent Venetian blinds that present a favorable cost profile compared to conventional blinds.

<u>More effective</u>

The Mario Richetti Library and its patrons need durable, flexible window treatments. Weber Design proposes translucent Venetian blinds that compare favorably in price with conventional blinds.

If you are dealing with high-end residential clients, government agencies, or prestigious corporations, you may be tempted to use fancy phrases or archaic business diction to present your firm as well established. Remember, reading is a solitary act. No matter how many people read what you write or how important they are, each of them reads alone. Write simply, as an individual speaking to an individual, however formal the business situation and however much is at stake. This principle is at the heart of all good writing.

Marketing Correspondence

According to Jay Conrad Levinson, "the writing of personal letters—not direct mailings of large quantities of letters and brochures, but simple, personal letters—is one of the most effective, easy, inexpensive, and overlooked methods of marketing. . . . If you can write clear English, spell properly, and keep your message short enough, you ought to be able to develop enough business through this mode of marketing so that you need not employ many other methods."[1] The first step in writing effective business-development letters is learning the business-letter format.

Simple, personal letters are an easy, effective method of marketing.

Business Letter Format

Before the advent of word processing, professional people did not prepare their own correspondence for readers. In the days when typewriters ruled, well-trained office assistants, proficient in seven different business-letter layouts,[2] prepared correspondence from *dictation*, a spoken version to be reproduced in print. Many designers and other professionals had their own assistants, who were familiar with their tastes in formatting. Nowadays, several individuals may share an assistant who is too pressed to indulge individual preferences. Many professionals do their own word processing, composing and formatting as they go.

In our fluid electronic era, business-letter layouts are less rigorously differentiated than they were in the more rigid typewriter, or mechanical, era. In fact, as long as the basic elements are in place, you can create your own rules, letting your eye be your guide. Even if you are using pre-printed letterhead, you can use the letterhead templates provided with MS Word as layout patterns, saving the ones you like for reference as you prepare your marketing letters. You can save any layout as a template, reopening it as a document each time you write a new letter, replacing the various template elements with current, relevant versions as appropriate. If your correspondence is to be professional in appearance, however, you need to be faithful to the layout standards you adopt, and you need to keep the basic business letter guidelines in mind as you work on each new letter.

- For the most part, business letters are single spaced, with an extra line between the paragraphs of the body.
- The paragraph format is block, with standard margins—an inch on either side and an inch and a half at top and bottom.
- The letter is topped by an eye-catching letterhead created by a graphic designer, with desktop publishing software, or from a template in your word-processing program (see Chapter 4).
- The letter paper and envelopes are matched in size, weight, and color, which should be a light neutral such as white, off-white, pale gray, or pale tan.
- The paper is of standard size, 8½″ by 11″, to make filing easy in the folders ordinarily used in offices and at home.
- Plain paper of the same color and quality as the letterhead is used for second and succeeding pages. (Do not use the letterhead itself.)

Components of a Business Letter

Your letters will be better received and more effective if they contain the components that are standard for business correspondence and that help to define it. In addition to a letterhead containing contact data and a letter body prepared according to your layout pattern, the standard business

Write business letters that look like business letters.

letter components include the *date line*, the *inside address*, the *salutation*, and the *complimentary closing*, followed by the *signature* and *copies* or *enclosure* lines. Highly effective in marketing correspondence, although not necessarily a part of routine business letters, is *the postscript*, or P.S.

THE DATE LINE

The date line is frequently placed flush at the left margin but may also be aligned with the right margin, situated at the center of the page, or placed in another position to complement the letterhead design. Write the name of the month in full. It is never abbreviated, and it should not be represented by figures. The year is written in full as well: February 22, 2005, not 2/22/05. The European style of day, month, and year—22 February 2005—is also acceptable.

THE INSIDE ADDRESS

Usually set about five lines below the date line, the inside address contains the following information:

- The name of the person to whom you are writing
- And/or the company, agency, institution, or other organization
- The street address
- The city, state, and zip code

The name of the person is typed on one line, the organization on a second line, the street address on a third, and the city, state, and zip code all together on a fourth line. Sometimes the inside address also contains the letter recipient's position (entered on the same line as the name) and the name of a department within the organization (entered on a separate, additional line).

Professor Herman Marx, Chair
Department of Interior Design
Atlantic Coast University
329 Pelican Drive
Angel Bay, FL 32000

Note that there is no punctuation at the end of each line, and no punctuation between the name of the state (abbreviated in the manner prescribed by the U.S. Postal Service) and the zip code.

Although tradition once dictated the use of a title before the name of the person addressed, contemporary usage sometimes eliminates this nicety, unless the title is special. We may address a letter to Jane Bryant, President, The Farmington Group (no Miss, Mrs., or Ms.), but we would say The Honorable Arthur Doyle, Mayor, City of Brighton. Of course, it would be more courteous to say: Ms. Jane Bryant, President, The Farmington Group.

THE SALUTATION

Usually consisting of the word *Dear* followed by a title and a name, the salutation is typed flush at the left margin, about two lines down from the last line of the inside address, followed by a colon unless the letter is business-social (like a thank-you note), in which case, the salutation is followed by a comma. It is customary to capitalize the first word as well as the names and titles in the salutation:

Dear Mr. Smith:
Dear Ms. Jones and Mr. Rogers:
Dear Mr. and Mrs. Laera:

If you can't discern the gender of the intended recipient, use the full name—also acceptable with a clearly gendered recipient's name.

Dear Leslie Marmotan:

Very formal business salutations sometimes leave out the name of the individual and replace it with "Sir" or "Madam," as in "Dear Sir," or somewhat peremptorily, "Madam." However, a marketing letter is more effective if it is addressed to an individual or individuals.

Some business letters have an attention line rather than a salutation:

Attention: Henry Winton

You would not generally use an *attention line* in marketing correspondence, for it creates an impersonal impression. However, you might use a subject line, which may either replace the salutation or be used in addition to it, in which case it is placed above it, below the inside address. In a letter, as in a memo or e-mail, a subject line helps the reader figure out where to file a document; it can also serve as a marketing tool.

Subject: Saving Time and Money through Design

THE COMPLIMENTARY CLOSE AND SIGNATURE

Two lines below the last line of the body is a closing phrase. It may be formal, business-personal, or informal, depending on the situation and on your relationship with the person to whom the letter is addressed.

The closings in the business-personal column of Table 5.1 (the shaded area) will probably be your most effective options for marketing correspondence, as they strike a balance between the stuffy and the chummy. Complimentary closings are usually followed by a comma. (A word to the wise: if you begin to use informal closings with a client with whom you have formed a relationship, it is inadvisable to shift suddenly to a more formal closing. The client may wonder whether something has gone wrong.)

Four lines below the closing is the signature line—your name in print. Above the printed version of your name is the handwritten version, always in ink rather than pencil. Sometimes a job-title line appears beneath the printed name line, but only the name line is duplicated in handwriting.

Mariella George

Mariella George

Director, George & Partners

Be sure that all the lines in the closing and signature section of the letter begin at the same tab setting. For utilitarian business letters, such as those inquiring about the accuracy of a bill, it is customary to put the complimentary closing and the signature flush left, along with all other elements of the letter. This is the most time-saving format, but hardly the most elegant. If you have placed the date line of your letter to the right, for a more graceful appearance, then your closing and signature sections may be

TABLE 5.1 COMPLIMENTARY CLOSINGS

Formal	Business-Personal	Informal
Yours truly,	Sincerely,	Best wishes,
Yours very truly,	Cordially,	Kindest regards,
Very truly yours,	Sincerely yours,	Best regards,
Very sincerely yours,	Cordially yours,	Best,
Very cordially yours,		

placed in a corresponding position, with, again, all the lines beginning at the same tab setting.

Sometimes a business letter that is not a marketing letter is copied to people other than the recipient named in the inside address and the salutation. It is customary to let the recipient know who else has been sent the letter. The other readers are indicated in a copies line following the signature and a few lines beneath it, placed flush at the left margin even if the complimentary closing and the signature are placed further to the right for the sake of visual balance. Because marketing correspondence is designed to seem personal, there is usually no copies line in a business-development letter. If you need one for a different kind of business correspondence, it would look like this:

> *CC:* Jeremiah Hodgkins
> Marcy Green
> Samuel Jones

Two lowercase *c*'s are also correct, and the colon may be omitted. The names should be listed according to the rank of the persons, or, if rank is not important, alphabetically. Use a separate line for each name, and align all names at the same interior margin.

Why two *c*s? That usage is a holdover from the days when copies were made mechanically, with a typewriter, by using carbon paper under the recipient's letter to imprint additional sheets of paper with the text of the letter. *Cc* stood for "carbon copy(ies)." It now stands for "courtesy copies."

Beneath the "CC" line, if there is one, several line spaces down from the signature and always flush at the left margin, place the "enclosure" line, which indicates what you have sent along with the letter. Since most marketing letters do contain enclosures, this will likely be a part of all your business-development correspondence. The very idea of an enclosure, of course, is linked to physical pieces of mail; with an e-mail you send an attachment, not an enclosure, a fact that is indicated in the header of the e-mail, beneath the subject line, so need not be noted beneath your signature. An enclosure line usually looks like this:

> Enc. (1)

Enc. is an abbreviation for enclosure. It is also correct to spell out *enclosure* or *enclosures*, and the enclosures may be itemized.

Enclosures:
1. Brochure
2. Case Study

THE POSTSCRIPT

You may think of the P.S. as an afterthought to the letter where you tell the reader what you forgot to say in the body. This is certainly an acceptable use of the *postscript*, which follows the signature and any copies or enclosure lines several line spaces further down. Afterthought postscripts date from a time when educated people spoke Latin and wrote slowly and laboriously on expensive parchment or vellum with quill pens. Writers hesitated to mar beautiful calligraphy (artistic handwriting) with emendations or marginal notes to add something that had been forgotten or had not been known when a text was written. The new information was added at the end. Postscript, in fact, means "after" (*post*) "the writing" (*script*).

Nowadays, our word-processing capability makes it easy to emend a text so as to include what had previously been forgotten, although we still use postscripts when we are in a rush or for effect. Appended to a rigorously edited and carefully formatted electronic text from which most traces of process have vanished, postscripts project the charm of spontaneity and engage readers with their informality, their directness, and their air of improvisation.

According to Jay Conrad Levinson, when people read letters—even printed letters—they read the salutation first and the postscript next. Levinson suggests that you reserve for the postscript your most important marketing point, or an invitation to action, or "anything that inspires a feeling of urgency."[3] He further suggests that you handwrite the postscript, thus suggesting that you "have created a one-of-a-kind letter" rather than a form letter that was mailed to dozens, hundreds, or even thousands of people. (Ironically, in an effort to seem "big," novice designers sometimes style marketing letters to read as if they were form letters created for a mass mailing, when in fact no more than a few were sent.)

How to Market through Correspondence

Five types of marketing letter are typically a part of the business-development process for interior designers who market through correspondence, although not all designers use all letter types. You are apt to find yourself writing the *prospecting letter*, the *letter of interest*, the *letter proposal*, the *preliminary-agreement proposal,* and the *letter of thanks or regret* after an agreement has or has not been signed.

The Prospecting Letter

The prospecting letter has three major objectives:

- To create favorable interest on the part of a stranger
- To provide context for capability materials enclosed with the letter
- To pave the way for further contact

Writing a letter to a stranger who may or may not be interested in you and your services is humiliating on the face of it. Most contemporary design professionals accept the need for business development, yet some balk at writing to people with whom they have had no prior social or business contact. This type of letter is the paper equivalent of the *canvassing* or "cold" *phone call*; like its telephone equivalent, it can be a highly effective business-development strategy, but it should be directed only to likely prospects targeted by means of careful research.

PROSPECT IDENTIFICATION

To figure out who your best prospects are, you first need to have a clear idea of your core strengths as a designer. Next, ask yourself who your clients should be and how you can help them. Then ask yourself how you can best approach them—whether you already know someone who can help you put your message across, whether you know someone who knows someone, or whether you will have to reach out to a stranger.

THE ROLE OF BUSINESS INTELLIGENCE

Prospect identification is partly based on *business intelligence*, the gathering of data to further your objectives. If you are a residential designer, make a practice of regularly perusing the real estate sections of newspapers serving your area, which list homes that have recently been sold to new owners who may require design services. Real estate agencies may also be willing to share information about recently sold homes. In addition, the Chamber of Commerce or another business group in your area can provide information about newcomers to town.

Business intelligence helps you identify likely client prospects

If you are a contract designer, you may get valuable information from the business section of the newspaper and from business magazines and newsletters. You may also be able to get valuable *leads*, or tips about potential opportunities, from government publications such as municipal or state records or from government Web sites.

But doesn't all this take time? Alas, it does. If you create capability materials that do not have to be rewritten for each prospect, you save time that would otherwise have been spent describing your business. Yet prospect research is an ongoing responsibility for those who pursue business development. The 20 percent rule is a good rule of thumb for independent professionals. Twenty percent of your time—two hours a day or one day a week—needs to be spent on business development.[4]

ELEMENTS OF A PROSPECTING LETTER

When you have done your business intelligence, you are ready to write a prospecting letter, the body of which has three parts: the contact paragraph, the presentation paragraphs, and the close.

- The *contact paragraph* states the reason for writing. If this part of the letter is not clear, convincing, and credible, the prospect will not read on. State simply and politely what prompted you to write to someone you have not met. In 25 words or less, tell prospects what you can do for them. Your opening paragraph, like those in Figures 5.1 and 5.2, must ask a simple question that is very important: *Do you need design services?* The process of asking this question and obtaining an answer is known as *qualifying* the prospect.

Qualify the prospect by asking whether he or she needs your services.

- *The presentation paragraphs* highlight the capability materials that are enclosed with the letter, drawing on them without duplicating them. This is the part of the letter that lists one by one the benefits of doing business with you. Here you clarify what you can offer a particular client that other interior designers cannot. Since most people do not like to be the first to hire you for a particular kind of project, stress your track record in the appropriate area.

Stress your track record.

- The *closing paragraph* looks toward your follow-up. It should be short, positive, assertive (though not aggressive), crisp, and courteous, without pleading. It need not ask for a reply or a phone call, though it may. If your purpose is to whet the prospects' appetites, simply let them know that you will be calling soon. This effective tactic leaves your reader hanging, waiting for the promised follow-up. It also prepares the reader for your call, so you will no longer be a stranger when you make it. In addition, the closing paragraph often restates the qualifying question: *Do you need design services?*

THE "YOU" ATTITUDE

A prospecting letter usually functions as a *letter of transmittal*, or cover letter, for capability materials in which your skills and experience have been made clear and visible. In the prospecting letter, you need to make a connection between your skills and experience and the person reading the letter. This means putting yourself in the letter recipient's shoes, or displaying the "you" attitude.

Because the reader of the prospecting letter is not yet personally known to the designer and vice versa, the "you" that needs to be kept in mind is a *generic*, or Brand X, *you*—a member of a group of individuals who can reasonably be conceived to require design services and who have a good record of opting for them. For instance, new homeowners, especially those relocating to an area, are likely to welcome the information that is contained in the letter shown in Figure 5.1. In contrast, the letter displayed in Figure 5.2 is written for a very different category of prospect, the real estate agent. Remember, although the "you" it addresses may be generic, a letter will be more effective if it does not read like a form letter.

THE MASTER PROSPECTING LETTER

Of course, it would be impossible to write an altogether different letter to each prospect, so you will need to construct a master letter that is the basis for all the prospecting letters you write in a given category. It is not a *form letter* because it is not printed in multiple copies and mailed to your list of recipients. A *master letter* contains some *boilerplate*, or standard formulation, but it is carefully constructed to provide a bridge between design services and the needs of a particular set of prospects. The master letter is typically customized, or rewritten, for each particular prospect. For example, the texts in Figures 5.1 and 5.2 are based on master letters customized to particular recipients. They could not be printed and sent as multiples, not even with the mail-merge feature of a word-processing program, because the customization is based on more than the insertion of a different inside address and a different name in the salutation line.

Well-customized letters "sound" as if one person is addressing another person at key points throughout the letter. Even when writing a commercial prospecting letter (business to business), it is better not to speak as a category addressing a category. It is better to say "Weber Design can help Max Harper Realty increase sales" than to say "interior design firms can help real estate agencies increase sales." If you cannot find time to customize more fully, then you may need to settle for "Weber Design can help your realty firm increase sales," but this construction smacks of boilerplate and is thus less convincing.

Always display the "you" attitude.

A customized letter addresses an individual at key points.

Figure 5.1
Prospecting letter
to a new
homeowner.
*Letter adapted from
a sample provided
by Adrianne Dale,
FASID*

Weber Design

Ms. Linda Evans
9696 Signet Drive
North Adams, ME 04000

July 16, 2004

Dear Ms. Evans:

As I was looking over *The Claryville Courier* last Sunday, I discovered that you have recently purchased the splendid Hamblee house on Morningside Drive in the Bluff Woods historic district. Although I've never seen the interior, I have long admired the turrets and porches of the Victorian exterior.

I am a *professional interior designer* in the Claryville area and would like to introduce my services in the event that you may require design assistance with the transition to this marvelous old house. A move from Maine to New York can be dauntingly complex, particularly for families with school-age children in which both parents have demanding, high-powered jobs. I have helped many new home owners with relocation move-in planning and have found that I can significantly decrease the confusion associated with transition, particularly when it is combined with renovation.

As you will see from the materials I'm sending along, I have enjoyed the opportunity to work on a number of homes of similar vintage, and it is an era that I particularly enjoy. I have become something of an expert in translating Victorian taste into a style that is both authentic and suited to today's lifestyle. Clients can take pride in a period home while enjoying contemporary comfort and convenience.

378 WILLOW LANE • CLARYVILLE, NY • 12725
PHONE AND FAX: 845-555-6789 • E-MAIL: ALVIN@WEBDESIGN.COM

When customizing a master prospecting letter, careful proofreading is crucial to eliminate all traces of earlier versions of the letter. You need to look over every element of your carefully customized letter, including the date, inside address, and all body paragraphs, to make sure that the customization is smooth, consistent, and accurate for the particular letter's addressee.

PERSONALIZED VERSUS PERSONAL   Depending on the category of client you are addressing and the amount of time at your disposal for business development,

Figure 5.1
(continued)

Page 2

My work has been published locally, and a project was filmed by Hannah Jones for her program a few years ago. The show provides an excellent overview of the interior design process and of how I work with clients and their families. It was a popular show and has aired frequently. I can make a video cassette available for viewing if you would like.

For now, I'm sending a variety of materials that will give you a more detailed view of my expertise—particularly with Victorians. I would be delighted to discuss any interior design needs you may have for this new home.

Sincerely,

Alvin Weber

Alvin Weber, ASID, IIDA
Principal Designer

you can customize your prospecting letters to a greater or lesser extent. You want them to sound personal, but how personal? It is helpful to understand the difference between a *personalized* letter and a *personal* letter.[5] A personalized letter has an individual's name in the inside address, in the salutation, and (see the second paragraph of Figure 5.2) in the body of the letter, although much of the letter could be sent to everyone in the recipient's marketing category—in the case of Figure 5.2, real estate agents.

Figure 5.2
Prospecting letter
to a real estate
agent.
*Letter adapted
from a sample
provided by
Adrianne Dale,
FASID*

Weber Design

Rodney Sparks, Office Manager
Max Harper Realty
3945 Rose Mountain Road
Sparta, NY 12000

March 23, 2004

Dear Mr. Sparks:

Have you and your colleagues considered the use of a professional interior designer to assist with your home sales?

Here are a number of ways that Weber Design could work with Max Harper Realty for our mutual benefit:

- Staging of properties currently on the market
    - Effective for slow-moving listings that could benefit from improved visual impact by addition of furnishings to empty rooms or by "editing" of possessions for occupied residences

- Consultation with prospective purchasers
    - For overcoming difficulties with space planning
    - For discussion of remodeling concepts
    - For relocation move-in planning

- Customer appreciation awards
    - For completed purchases—a gift certificate of a complimentary interior design consultation to help personalize the new residence

378 WILLOW LANE • CLARYVILLE, NY • 12725
PHONE AND FAX: 845-555-6789 • E-MAIL: ALVIN@WEBDESIGN.COM

A personal letter is clearly directed to one person and contains many references to the person's situation garnered from such sources as the local Chamber of Commerce. "Personal," in this context, does not mean that you refer to a stranger by the person's first name. In the salutation, you need to greet a person you haven't met as "Dear Mr. Smith," rather than as "Dear Jack." The business-personal tone that is appropriate for talking to strangers is considerate and circumspect. What makes it "personal" is not intrusive chumminess, but rather your tactful understanding of another person's situa-

Figure 5.2
(continued)

WD Page 2

- Consultation with contractors
    - For custom home-building specification and detailing

Please consider how your sales team may be able to make use of these concepts. Please feel free to call me if you have any immediate needs, or await my follow-up call.

Sincerely,

Alvin Weber

Alvin Weber, ASID, IIDA
Principal Designer

tion. In Figure 5.1, the designer has made discreet references (based on business intelligence) to the location of the prospect's home and to its style and era, as well as to the prospect's marital status, employment situation, and children's age range. Anyone reading this letter would understand that the interior designer who wrote it had taken the time to find out who the prospect is.

A letter this personal may seem well suited only to a residential client, but it is also possible to add an appealing and appropriate personal touch to a letter for a contract-design prospect. For instance, the writer of the letter

Business-personal is tactful, not chummy.

in Figure 5.2 could add a personal touch to the opening paragraph by congratulating all at Max Harper Realty on the award recently received from the Max Harper national office for record sales figures in the Northwest Region. Such a personal touch (based on a careful reading of the business section of the local newspaper or the Max Harper newsletter) might segue smoothly into the designer's pitch. For instance, the designer might say: "A record like this often goes hand-in-hand with an eye for opportunities to maximize client profits. Have you and your colleagues considered the use of a professional interior designer to assist with your home sales?"

FEATURES AND BENEFITS   As noted in Chapter 2, one of the best ways to make a connection to a potential client is to translate the *features*, or attributes, of your design service into *benefits*, or advantages, for your prospect. The letters in Figures 5.1 and 5.2 both translate features of interior design service into tangible benefits for the groups of clients to which they are targeted. In Figure 5.1, the feature-benefit statements are highly individualized to the prospect. A feature—such as, in Figure 5.1, experience with historic houses—is turned into a *benefit*—pride in an authentic interior plus contemporary comfort and convenience. In the letter in Figure 5.2, the feature-benefit statements are more generic—less individualized—but still very well thought out and highly appropriate. For instance, real estate agents are offered the benefit of moving slow listings, a benefit derived from improved visual impact that is in turn derived from furnishing empty rooms and editing possessions in occupied ones.

Be sure to translate features into benefits.

FOLLOW-UP

A prospecting letter is more effective if it is followed up within two weeks by a second, or follow-up, letter, or by a follow-up telephone call, or by both. Follow-up letters or phone calls should be brief; they are mainly a reminder of your original letter. Following up on the letter in Figure 5.2, the designer might ask whether the real estate agent has had the opportunity to read the original letter and might then briefly restate its salient points.

It is a good idea to offer new information in a follow-up letter or phone call—new reasons to do business with you. For instance, a follow-up to the letter in Figure 5.2 might state that a display house that the designer had recently completed for a local developer had already improved sales figures by a substantial margin.

Follow-up builds relationships that yield business.

Follow-up helps you create a relationship with a prospect. The stronger the relationship, the likelier the person is to do business with you. According to Chris Engel, vice president for sales at Plumb Design (www.plumbdesign.com), you are looking to create a dialogue with your prospects. You may be building the relationship for a year or more, checking in now and then, or sending along articles on subjects of interest to the prospect.[6]

MULTIPLE MAILINGS   People in the position of Linda Evans, the new homeowner in Figure 5.1, receive myriad letters and brochures from people trying to sell them something. The first letter from each mailer may go into the wastebasket with no more than a cursory reading. Many of those sending letters, particularly corporations targeting mass markets, are sending mail-merged form letters. Most will not undertake the trouble and expense of sending more than one letter—a practice known as *multiple mailing*. A small business is at an advantage in this respect: it is truly feasible for an entrepreneurial design business with a carefully targeted market to follow up on the relatively small number of carefully written prospecting letters that it sends out.

THE PROSPECTING FILE   One way to schedule follow-up is with a so-called prospecting file—a box in which 3″ × 5″ cards are filed behind tab cards according to when the next contact must be made, with appropriate intervals between each contact. On each contact card might be noted not only data such as the name, address, telephone number, fax number, and e-mail address of the prospect, but the letters sent and phone calls previously made to that individual.

You can create an electronic prospecting file within a database program such as Filemaker by creating a notes section on your basic record form and entering there the history of letters sent and calls previously made. You can also create date buttons corresponding to the "next contact" tabs of a physical card filing system. Then you can click a button in the Find mode to call up all the records for contacts to be refreshed during the current week, let us say, and do your follow-up mailings and phone calls accordingly. You could also create your prospecting file within a dedicated program such as ACT that assists in contact management; you could use the basic contact-management software provided with MS Office; or you could keep your prospecting file in your personal digital assistant. What matters is not how your prospecting file was created, but the fact that you created it and regularly use it to stay in touch with client prospects. (Avoid mailing just before tax time and during the summer. Fall and spring tend to work best for many, but the timing of your mailings needs to be carefully calibrated to your own prospect base.)

Conrad Jay Levinson[7] has this to say about the effectiveness of multiple contacts, and particularly of multiple mailings:

Study after study confirms that people patronize businesses with which they are *familiar*. When asked in a study what factors influenced a buyer's purchase decision, 5000 respondents indicated that *confidence* ranked first, *quality* second, *selection* third, *service* fourth, and *price* fifth. . . . By engaging in multiple mailings of personal letters, you are building up . . . customer confidence through familiarity, paving your way to a relationship [and a design contract].

FORMAT OF THE PROSPECTING LETTER

Although prospecting letters need to be written for eager readers, not everyone pays close attention to letters from strangers. Many people skim. The letters you write need to be formatted with this in mind. That is, they must work as well when skimmed as when carefully read. Genuine personal letters rarely contain underlined phrases, italics, bulleted lists, subheads, and layers of indentation, but "personal" prospecting letters do contain them. That is because readers' attention is drawn to these devices, which make it easy for them to get the gist. Both skimmers and close readers will appreciate fair-sized margins, an easy-to-read type size (no smaller than 10 points), and ample white space between paragraphs.

Format prospecting letters for skimmers as well as close readers.

Resist the temptation to send prospecting letters via e-mail. Although the appeal of this inexpensive, easy medium is huge on the face of it, e-mail contains none of the context information provided in telephone calls by diction, accent, tonality, and other speech markers. Nor does it provide the contextual information that is supplied in hard copy by good-quality stationery or careful formatting.

Multiple e-mailings to strangers may have an adverse effect, for there is little more irritating than an in-box clogged with marketing letters from strangers whose credentials the recipient has no easy way to evaluate. Worse for an interior designer, you have no control over the look of a message as it opens in someone's in-box, nor can you count on providing visual support for your message. From fear of viruses, many people set their mailers to accept text only and will not open attachments from people they do not know. This means that you cannot send images as you could to accompany a marketing letter snail-mailed with an attractive brochure.

Do not e-mail prospecting letters.

The best way to enlarge your client base through e-mail is to build a mailing list, perhaps through a Web site, then to snail- or e-mail newsletters and periodic news releases to those on your list. See Chapter 11 for more on these marketing strategies. Meanwhile, your business-development correspondence is best conducted through snail mail.

The Letter of Interest

While a prospecting letter is sent to a carefully targeted stranger, a letter of interest responds to a feeler on the part of a prospect. It may be written in response to a mailing that invites designers' interest in a particular project, or it may be written as a follow-up to a contact with the client in which the designer has learned something about a project—though not enough interest has been expressed in the designer's services to indicate that a design-services agreement is imminent. Usually the designer does not know enough at this early stage to provide a preliminary scope-of-work statement. A letter of interest speaks directly to client concerns, but it does not propose solutions to problems that have not yet been clearly formulated.

In its purest form, a letter of interest resembles the cover letter that is sent with a résumé (see Chapter 12). It provides the opportunity to discuss your expertise as it relates to the prospect's project type. If there has been a written invitation to submit a letter of interest, you, as the designer, pick up on specific points, paraphrase them, and respond to them in order to demonstrate a careful reading of the invitation. In relation to these points, you assert the relevance of your qualifications in terms of specific and tangible accomplishments, addressing, insofar as you ascertain them, the needs that are driving the project.

If the letter of interest follows up on a social contact, then continue the dialogue that has begun. As in responding to a written invitation, highlight the manner in which your accomplishments prepare you for the challenges posed by the project. (If you have had an opportunity to display your presentation book, then express your gratitude for this opportunity in a simple and dignified manner.)

The letter of interest usually serves as a transmittal letter for capability material, which it should highlight *only* in terms of the project at hand (Figure 5.3). It should not restate the entire content of a capability brochure with sections describing, say, the work of the firm.

> Highlight your brochure contents in your letter of interest.

ELEMENTS OF A LETTER OF INTEREST

The letter of interest typically contains the following:

- An appropriate salutation
- A statement of the reason for writing
- A discussion of staffing, qualifications, and likely collaborators
- A preliminary schedule projection
- A statement about the relationship structure

Figure 5.3
Letter of interest.

Weber Design

Mr. Hiram Garland, President
The Garland Company, Inc.
35179 Veterans' Highway
Blackman's Corner, NY 12000

Salutation → Dear Mr Garland:

Statement of the → Thank you for calling Weber Design this morning regarding the office expansion
Reason for Writing   and renovation you are planning. I have been thinking about the interesting
design ideas you expressed and your desire to implement them for the Garland
Company's centennial. This looks to be an exciting and feasible project; we at
Weber Design would welcome the opportunity to participate.

Staffing, → As senior design partner, I would be the principal designer on this project,
Qualifications, and   while my partner, Ned Jones, would function as project manager. To deal with
Collaborators   any changes in the load-bearing structures of the Garland Building, we would
collaborate with Lucy Chin, AIA, who has recently been involved in the
successful renovation of the Hartman Company's headquarters in Monksville.
Both Lucy and I have worked on a number of successful office renovations with
Jack Soames, a general contractor with a fine reputation for efficiency, honesty,
and sound workmanship who has expressed an interest in submitting a bid for
the renovation of the Garland Building.

Preliminary → Although it is early in our discussion to project a time frame, I believe that the
Schedule   scope of work you propose can be completed in a timely manner. However, the
Projection   suppliers of the Italian office furniture that we both admire have been slow to
deliver on past projects. This could forestall full and timely completion.

Statement about → In accordance with our standard practice on successful past projects, including
Relationship   the new Manning town hall and the Mountainview Plaza Medical Center, we
Structure   would work with you to enhance the beauty of your historic building, rather

378 WILLOW LANE • CLARYVILLE, NY • 12725
PHONE AND FAX: 845-555-6789 • E-MAIL: ALVIN@WEBDESIGN.COM

- A preliminary discussion of the financial basis for the project
- A marketing close

SALUTATION   It is important that the letter of interest begin with an appropriate salutation. Often the letter of interest is written to someone the designer knows quite well. If so, the salutation will be informal—for example, "Dear Jack." Less informally, it may read "Dear Jack Smith." Or it may be fully formal: "Dear Mr. Smith."

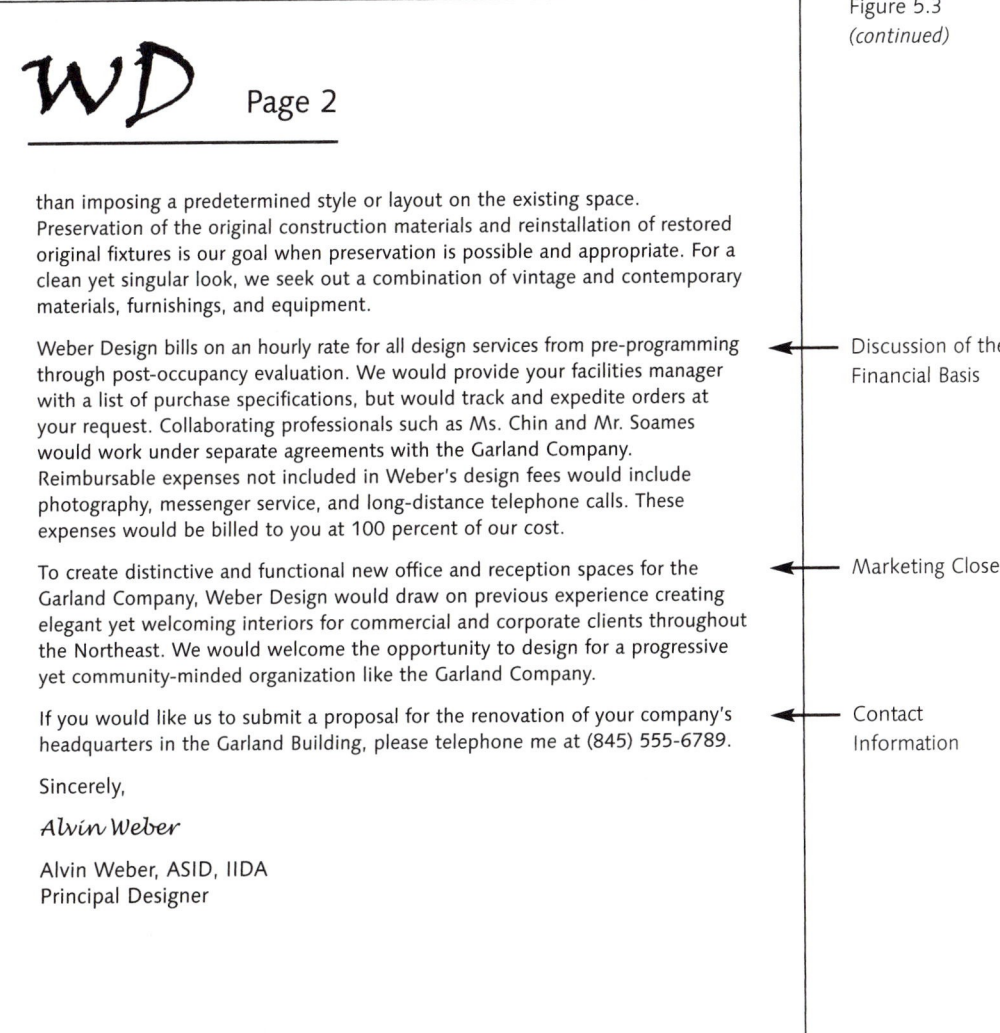

Figure 5.3
(continued)

WD Page 2

than imposing a predetermined style or layout on the existing space. Preservation of the original construction materials and reinstallation of restored original fixtures is our goal when preservation is possible and appropriate. For a clean yet singular look, we seek out a combination of vintage and contemporary materials, furnishings, and equipment.

Weber Design bills on an hourly rate for all design services from pre-programming through post-occupancy evaluation. We would provide your facilities manager with a list of purchase specifications, but would track and expedite orders at your request. Collaborating professionals such as Ms. Chin and Mr. Soames would work under separate agreements with the Garland Company. Reimbursable expenses not included in Weber's design fees would include photography, messenger service, and long-distance telephone calls. These expenses would be billed to you at 100 percent of our cost. — Discussion of the Financial Basis

To create distinctive and functional new office and reception spaces for the Garland Company, Weber Design would draw on previous experience creating elegant yet welcoming interiors for commercial and corporate clients throughout the Northeast. We would welcome the opportunity to design for a progressive yet community-minded organization like the Garland Company. — Marketing Close

If you would like us to submit a proposal for the renovation of your company's headquarters in the Garland Building, please telephone me at (845) 555-6789. — Contact Information

Sincerely,

Alvin Weber

Alvin Weber, ASID, IIDA
Principal Designer

STATEMENT OF THE REASON FOR WRITING Like most other business letters, the body of the letter of interest begins with a statement of the reason for writing, including an initial expression of interest in the project.

It was a pleasure to meet you at the Carters' open house last week. It was good to hear about the office expansion and renovation you are planning. I have been thinking about the interesting design ideas you expressed and your desire to implement them for the Garland

Company's centennial. This looks to be an exciting but feasible project; we at Weber Design would welcome the opportunity to participate.

After the reason for writing has been clearly stated, the body of the letter continues with those elements that characterize the letter of interest.

STAFFING, QUALIFICATIONS, AND COLLABORATORS   This section—a crucial part of your letter of interest—contains brief summaries of the qualifications of people within your firm who are likely to be deployed on the project. It may also discuss the qualifications of likely collaborators outside your firm. For instance, you might say

> I would be the principal designer on the project, while my partner, Ned Jones, would function as project manager. To deal with any changes in the load-bearing structures of the Garland Building, we would collaborate with Lucy Chin, AIA, who has recently been involved in the successful renovation of the Hartman Company's headquarters in Monksville. Both Lucy and I have worked on a number of office renovations with Jack Soames, a general contractor with a fine reputation for efficiency, honesty, and sound workmanship who has expressed an interest in submitting a bid for the renovation of the Garland Building.

To sell qualifications, give the argument for selecting you rather than competitors.

Note that the example mentions the interior design firm's success with similar projects and also points out the qualifications of likely collaborating professionals. When selling qualifications, give the argument for selecting your team from among other teams with similar capabilities. Do not provide a laundry list of generic services. Focus instead on the intersection of your team's qualifications with the prospective client's project. Highlight *only* relevant aspects of the participating professionals' histories. (If you send along a printed brochure or provide the URL of a Web site, the prospect can look at a broader slice of your history.)

To help you make the best argument for your qualifications, prepare a qualification/benefit table (see Table 5.2) where qualifications responding to the client's problems are described as benefits for the client.

This analysis would be undertaken as an important part of your pre-writing and would not be inserted into the letter. Still, it should help you present your skills and experience and those of your associates in a persuasive and economical manner.

TABLE 5.2 A QUALIFICATION/BENEFIT TABLE

Client's Problem	Responsive Qualification	Benefit to Client
Researchers and executives do not use the conference rooms near their desks but confer informally after large meetings. Their social pattern requires support.	I trained in a university with a social-behavior research component as part of ID training. I have since specialized in social-behavior-based interior design.	I already know how to research the problem and am familiar with solutions for similar problems. I should be able to solve this client's problems more quickly and efficiently than other designers.
Employees are more productive if they eat lunches near their desks, though there is no room to install kitchens.	I have experience creating kitchens in cramped quarters, such as small apartments.	My experience in designing cost-effective small kitchens and kitchen substitutes will contribute to a creative solution to the client's problem.

PRELIMINARY SCHEDULE PROJECTION   This section typically comments on the time frame proposed by the prospect and states any obstacles the designer foresees. "The suppliers of the Italian office furniture that we both admire have been slow to deliver on past projects. This could forestall timely and full completion." In some cases the schedule projects a start date and a finish date. In other cases, the designer indicates the total amount of time the job is expected to take but does not project start and finish dates.

STATEMENT ABOUT RELATIONSHIP STRUCTURE   Often the relationship section of the interest letter reminds prospects of the importance of their own involvement. If you are to renovate the offices of a group of busy physicians and it would be helpful for them to designate someone from their office to expedite decision making, you would say so in this part of the letter, particularly if that is the condition under which you could ensure that the renovation went forward with minimal disruption of each physician's practice. It is also customary to mention reporting relationships among participating design professionals in this section—who reports to whom.

DISCUSSION OF THE FINANCIAL BASIS   In this section of the letter, you would furnish preliminary information, brief and generic, about the financial relationships that would ensue should you become the prospect's designer. As explained with admirable economy by Laura Mankin in "Basic Contract Law for Interior Designers,"[8] residential designers' fees are generally calculated in one of two ways. "The designer may charge his clients the retail price of the items used in the project" that the designer has purchased wholesale, "plus a design fee . . . or the designer may use a smaller markup on the items used . . . and then charge a larger design fee." Mankin suggests that an actively involved client may be a better candidate for the first fee structure, while a less involved client, who "places a greater premium on the designer's services may wish to pay a larger design fee and smaller markup on each item."

The fees for contract-design services may also be handled in a third way. A designer who has billed on an hourly rate or charged a fixed fee provides the client's facilities manager with a list of specifications, or the specifications for purchase are handled through the client's purchasing agent. The designer may then track the orders and act as expediter.

Savvy designers carefully tailor their fee structures, which are discussed in further detail in Chapter 6. For instance, if a residential client requires all new furnishings and purchasing is handled by the interior designer, the designer may stipulate that he or she be paid on a retail basis. If all purchasing is to be handled through a corporate client's purchasing agent, then the designer may charge an appropriately higher design fee than if products are also being provided.

Whatever basis you use for computing your own fees, your letter of interest must indicate the manner in which your collaborators would be paid. For instance, if you were working with a general contractor on a kitchen, you might state that the client would come to a separate agreement with the contractor, who would submit a fixed-price bid, although you would supply materials.

The financial-basis section of the letter of interest often contains a statement about how expenses would be charged. The designer includes a stock list of reimbursable expenses. For example:

> Reimbursable expenses not included in the fee include photography, messenger service, and long-distance telephone calls. These reimbursable expenses will be billed to you at 100 percent of our cost.

MARKETING CLOSE   The typical letter of interest concludes with a two-part marketing close that comprises: (1) a you-oriented statement of design and business philosophy and (2) a restatement of interest in the project.

- *You-oriented statement of design and business philosophy* End a letter of interest on a note of earnest belief that you are the person who can solve the prospect's problems. Do so by summarizing in the next-to-the-last paragraph of the letter the aspects of your experience that are most relevant:

To create a distinctive and charming ambience for Riverside Inn, I would draw on my previous experience in creating unique yet functional interiors for small hotels throughout the Southeast. I would be delighted to help you re-enact in a fresh, contemporary manner the historic role of the Riverside Inn in the life of Shadyville. I welcome the challenge of configuring the inn as a regional and national travel destination, serving both tourists and business travelers, including their need for banquet and convention facilities.

- *Restatement of interest in the project:* The last paragraph of the letter of interest usually expresses the hope that the designer will be invited to work on the project.

If you would like me to submit a proposal for the renovation of the inn, please telephone me at (845) 555-6789.

The Letter Proposal

Short, informal business-development propositions written as correspondence are known as *letter proposals*. A letter proposal might follow a letter of interest in the typical progression by means of which an interior designer secures work. Or it might replace the letter of interest. A letter proposal contains many of the same elements as a letter of interest, but there are some important differences. Usually a letter proposal is based on a greater familiarity with the client and the project. The designer who writes a proposal, however informal, has usually been encouraged to do so, for the proposal commences in preliminary fashion the design process.

COMPONENTS OF A LETTER PROPOSAL

Like a letter of interest, a letter proposal typically contains the following elements:

- An appropriate salutation
- A statement of the reason for writing
- A discussion of staffing, qualifications, and likely collaborators

- A preliminary schedule projection
- A discussion of the financial basis for the project
- A marketing close

These sections may be more detailed than they would be in a letter of interest. In addition, the letter proposal also contains:

- A preliminary scope-of-work analysis and a preliminary design proposal
- A preliminary breakdown into phases, listing trades involved and the principal items to be ordered
- A preliminary cost estimate

The letter proposal is often accompanied by a set of *references*—a list of the designer's previous clients who are willing to discuss the designer's qualifications in a favorable light—often by telephone.

THE SCOPE DESCRIPTION AND PRELIMINARY DESIGN PROGRAM   The outline of major scope elements and the summary design program of a letter proposal are based on pre-proposal discussions, program criteria provided by the client, and a preliminary visit to the project site. It needs to be stressed that this is a preliminary outline that is subject to modification as the discovery phase of the project continues. (The writing of scope descriptions and preliminary design programs is covered in Chapter 3.) If the discovery phase is pre-agreement rather than Phase Zero—an agreed-upon and billable part of the design work—the designer's approach will be more rudimentary.

BREAKDOWN INTO PHASES   Even if you are charging a fixed fee for your design services, you would be prudent to break the work (and thus the fee) into phases. According to Tad Crawford, it will be "easier to collect the appropriate fee for completed work phases" in the event the project is cancelled.[9] You might break the project down into such categories as program development; schematic design; design development; the creation of contract documents for contractors, fabricators, and vendors; purchasing; implementation (fabrication, construction, and installation); *punch-listing*, or tweaking of the substantially completed job; and continuing services such as post-occupancy evaluation.

If design work is on a fixed-fee basis, be sure that the amount of time allotted is roughly comparable to the cost of the time it will take to complete the job. To avoid unpleasant surprises for the client, allot time to complete all scope elements and be sure that each segment of the work can be completed within its portion of calendar time. Leave ample time to solve unforeseen problems and to correct any flaws that emerge in the design. It may be necessary to project a deadline for each phase, but it should be emphasized that the projections are preliminary.

PRELIMINARY COST ESTIMATE   The designer needs to state clearly that the preliminary cost estimate is subject to revision. It is *not* a fixed bid. When talking about financial matters in a preliminary proposal, don't present too much detail. A too-precise breakdown gives the client unnecessary entry into possible arguments during the negotiations that will ensue if your proposal is accepted. However, you must provide enough information that your figures will appear to be credible. Think of your estimate as an outline broken down no further than is necessary to provide a clear picture. To prepare what you will present to the prospective client, create a much more detailed estimate, then simplify, retaining the detailed breakdown for your own reference later as you negotiate your way toward a letter of agreement or a contract. You need to prepare for every contingency, but there is no need to share worst-case scenarios with the prospect. You also need to consider how you are going to charge for your *overhead*, or the portion of your regular business expenses allotted to the project. Overhead might be figured into design fees or might be a consideration in determining a cost-plus markup. It is not usually presented as a line item.

Note that the estimate of construction cost can be tricky for inexperienced designers who cannot rely on in-house estimators. If you are procuring estimates from contractors or fabricators in order to supply a client with a preliminary estimate, be aware that the contractor or fabricator is likely to have the same aversion that you would to unpaid pre-agreement work. This aversion will turn to rancor if you repeatedly ask for pre-agreement estimates, falsely implying that a contractor or fabricator has already been selected or has an inside track, only to put the project out for competitive bids after you have signed a designer-client agreement. It is best to be honest with contractors and fabricators, to deal only with those whom you truly respect, to be up-front about asking for favors such as free preliminary estimates, and to find a way to return the favors later—such as recommending the contractors or fabricators for work with other clients if projects for which estimates have been prepared are not ultimately awarded.

The Preliminary Agreement
Professionals of all stripes agree on the difficulty of distinguishing between business development and billable investigation, or *discovery*. This difficulty

can be especially acute for interior designers who cater to the residential and small-business markets. Corporations and institutions are more likely to undertake a detailed discovery phase on their own, providing the designer with elaborate programming criteria. Budget is clearly defined and understood in this market, while smaller residential clients may not even know what their budgets are.

It can be expensive for a designer in the pre-agreement phase to deal with questions like, "Can you give me some sense of what I would get for $25,000, what for $50,000, and what for $75,000?" A question of this type would call for unpaid consultation or would elicit a multilevel proposal. Such a proposal is so complicated that it is properly considered a subject for billable Phase-Zero study—akin to a *feasibility study*, the goal of which is to create a budget for a defined project.

On the one hand, early partnering with an anxious, uncertain, or demanding client often wins the interior designer the job, without extensive shopping on the client's part. On the other hand, the cost of spending too many unpaid hours on business development can be high, particularly if you must deal with a difficult client after agreement has been reached. (You may wish to do more unpaid consultation with a returning client of proven value than with a previously unknown prospect who may be shopping.)

THE ROLE OF PRELIMINARY AGREEMENT

A *preliminary agreement* enables the designer to be paid for work that might otherwise have been classified as pre-agreement and therefore have been unpaid. Written as an interim contract, the preliminary agreement elicits a retainer as a non-refundable binder, to be applied against the fees and other remuneration that will be set forth in the full agreement. (Ideally, the retainer will be applied to the final payment.) The goal of a preliminary agreement is very limited in comparison with the goal of a full letter of agreement (see Chapter 6), which seeks the client's authorization for an entire design project. The preliminary agreement seeks the client's authorization only for the investigative or pre-agreement phase. It is stated and understood that the rest of the project will be clarified as investigation proceeds. *A preliminary agreement in no way substitutes for the full letter of agreement.*

It is not always easy to discern when a preliminary agreement would be appropriate. Most designers will go directly to full agreement when they can, and rightly so. The preliminary proposal is useful when pre-agreement consultation looks to be a protracted give-away—often because the budget has not been sufficiently narrowed down. This is an important issue in an era when "Clients increasingly expect more with less, and [more] up front work."[10] A preliminary agreement for the discovery phase also reduces price concern by presenting prospects with successive smaller budgets rather than with one larger one.

A preliminary agreement makes it easier to bill for discovery.

COMPONENTS OF A PRELIMINARY AGREEMENT

Preliminary agreements, documents of no more than three pages, are basically letter proposals with a contract close. They not only cover the pre-agreement phase of the standard design-service contract but also enhance Phase Zero with value-added services that extend the range of what designers have traditionally offered their clients.

THE CONTRACT CLOSE   The preliminary agreement does not have a marketing close that invites more discussion of a business proposal. Rather it closes with a brief contract statement, followed by spaces for appropriate signatures. A typical contract close might read something like the following, offered as a suggestion and in no way intended as a substitute for consultation with your attorney:

> In signing this preliminary design agreement, you and we are establishing our mutual intent to work together in a relationship of Interior Designer and Client, subject to the terms and conditions of the enclosed standard contract, until the completion of the project, although we mutually recognize that circumstances may arise to require terminating the project after the discovery or investigative phase of the design work. We can begin work based upon your authorization, which you may signify by returning the enclosed copy of this letter with your signature and a retainer payment of $1,000. We will notify you when $750 in fee-hours have been expended and will credit applicable portions of the fees received during Phase Zero against fees due on whatever basis for subsequent phases. Please indicate your concurrence by signing your acceptance below.

BLANK COPY OF THE FULL-PROJECT CONTRACT   A blank copy of the designer's full contract or agreement is frequently enclosed with the preliminary agreement proposal and is referenced as the framework for it, as in the example above. (Presumably the designer's standard contract has been reviewed by a lawyer. A standard ASID contract form might serve as an appropriate enclosure.) The inclusion of a blank standard contract protects designers from any ills that might befall them if clients sign preliminary agreements. The designer is saved the time and trouble of crafting a comprehensive and fully protective agreement with a client whose commitment has not yet been made completely evident.

VALUE-ADDED PRELIMINARY SERVICES   Writing in 1973, design marketing expert Gerre L. Jones stated his belief that clients are frequently unwilling to sign preliminary agreements. The value Jones assigns to these agreements is largely presentational. He notes that they call attention to designers' seriousness about their projects and their convictions about the value of their time.[11]

In the years since Jones wrote, interior designers have enhanced their offerings in the pre-design (and post-design) phases of project relationships. Firms such as that of Arthur M. Gensler (FAIA, FIIDA)[12] market themselves to clients as advisers and strategic planners:

> "There was a time when our clients did a head count, predicted their growth and handed us the information so we could design accordingly," explains Gensler. "That era is gone. Now our clients look differently at their facilities. Before it was just a place to house their organization. Today it is a line on their financial statement." To this end Gensler helps clients analyze facility needs and develop a real estate strategy. Developing this strategy usually requires analyzing sites, buildings, and communities. There is also cost to consider, as well as the number of people who will use the facility. Gensler is helping clients make critical decisions, such as whether or not to build new, where to lease and whether to locate employees in one facility or more. Only then does the firm continue with architectural or interior design services.

Gensler's example suggests a rule of thumb that may be useful for residential as well as contract designers: offer enough services to justify payment for Phase Zero and the presentation of a preliminary contract. If at all possible, establish a relationship with a client early, before a new house or office space has been purchased or leased. This may take some creative marketing. For instance, a residential designer might market to executive search firms, convincing them to offer space-needs analysis and real-estate strategy planning to *their* clients as a value-added service.

The Thank-You or Regret Letter

It is customary to send a brief thank-you or regret letter to the client or the client's contact person after a designer has been chosen (or not been chosen) for a project. Unlike a thank-you note for a social occasion or a personal gift, the business thank-you (or regret) letter is not handwritten. Although e-mail is acceptable in some situations, this type of letter is usually a short, printed document sent via snail mail on your letterhead. The thank-you or regret letter is usually dated, yet it does not contain an inside address. After the salutation, one or two short paragraphs convey the pleasure of dealing with the prospect.

If you are writing a thank-you note, express your delight in the ongoing relationship (see Figure 5.4). If you are writing a regret letter, express your hope

Both thank-you and regret letters help build business relationships.

Figure 5.4
A thank-you letter.

Weber Design

Dear Dr. Hernandez,

What a delight it was to hear this morning that you have selected Weber Design to renovate the offices of the Spartan Heights Medical Center! We welcome the opportunity to design a state-of-the-art facility that provides a warm and supportive environment for your diverse clientele.

We will be calling you early next week to schedule programming interviews. We look forward to a cordial and productive relationship with you and your physician partners in Spartan Heights Medical Center. We are confident that we can create a facility that will serve your practice well for many years to come.

Sincerely,

Alvin Weber

Alvin Weber, ASID, IIDA
Principal Designer

378 WILLOW LANE • CLARYVILLE, NY • 12725
PHONE AND FAX: 845-555-6789 • E-MAIL: ALVIN@WEBDESIGN.COM

that you will be considered for a future design opportunity (see Figure 5.5). The thank-you or regret letter ends in a traditional manner, with a closing such as "Sincerely yours" followed by a handwritten signature over a printed signature line.

If you have worked hard to prepare a proposal but were unable to come to agreement, you may find that writing a polite regret letter taxes your powers of courtesy. Remember that the prospect—even the residential prospect—has made a business decision in choosing another designer.

Figure 5.5
A regret letter.

Weber Design

Dear Dr. Hernandez,

We enjoyed our meetings with you and were disappointed to hear that you have selected another design firm to renovate the offices of the Spartan Heights Medical Center. As you know, we specialize in providing interior design services to medium-sized group medical practices such as yours. We would welcome the opportunity to work with you on future projects. Meanwhile, we wish you the best of luck with the WHMC renovation.

Yours sincerely,

Alvin Weber

Alvin Weber, ASID, IIDA
Principal Designer

378 WILLOW LANE • CLARYVILLE, NY • 12725
PHONE AND FAX: 845-555-6789 • E-MAIL: ALVIN@WEBDESIGN.COM

Assume that the decision was impersonal. A polite note of regret may lead to future consideration for a project that is perceived as better suited to your skills and experience. It may also lead to referrals. You have everything to gain and little to lose from swallowing your pride and "making nice." By all means, keep your near misses in your prospecting file; send them follow-up mailings on a regular basis as appropriate.

Marketing in Response to RFQs and RFPs

Designers who cater to residential and smaller contract clients may move toward agreement by means of informal meetings, phone calls, e-mails, and letters. For corporations; government agencies at the federal, state, and local levels; educational institutions; arts organizations; and nonprofit service agencies, the selection of a designer is a more formal process. Government procurement rules for proper expenditure of public funds require an open public process, with agencies advertising for qualifications as appropriate and soliciting competitive technical and fee proposals.

Government agencies and other organizations requiring an open process may begin by putting out public RFQs (requests for qualifications). Vendors who wish to market goods or services to agencies at any level of government may be asked to pursue certification or a related process in order to qualify as providers. For example, in order to do business with New York City, a designer or other vendor must fill out Vendex questionnaires (available for inspection at http://www.nyc.gov/html/selltonyc/pdf). The city uses the questionnaires to determine that the prospective vendor has no unpaid taxes at any level and no pending charges of fraud or other wrongdoing. After a government agency or other organization has designated a vendor as being qualified, based on an evaluation of the response to an RFQ, approval via Vendex or a similar process, or federal or other quality certification, the vendor may then respond to RFPs (requests for proposals) from that organization.

RFQs

An RFQ elicits capability materials from designers along specific lines. The packet you send as your response may include a breakdown of your technical and/or administrative qualifications as well as—for government work—a price list for specific services. The CD-ROM shows some pages from an RFQ. It also shows the Experience Profile Code numbers used in responding to the RFQ. For governments at various levels, there may be many boilerplate clauses, and they may swell your qualifications packet to a hundred pages or more! Fortunately, help is available from counselors in PTACs (procurement technical assistance centers) or similar facilities at all levels of government.

In general, the designer's proper response to an RFQ is to custom-assemble capability—that is, qualification—materials so as to create an elaborate dossier highlighting the firm's expertise in relevant projects. Often the designer submits these materials as a book held together by a spiral or other binding. The response to an RFQ is, in essence, a much-expanded version of the capability brochure described in Chapter 4.

Brief letters of recommendation usually attest to the design team's qualifications and are an important part of the RFQ response. They should confirm the designer's design and project management skills and affirm the letter writer's personal pleasure in the work relationship.

The response to an RFQ typically mentions any awards or other honors a design firm has received, as well as any publications on or by the principals. Honors and publications burnish a designer's reputation with a glow of authentic prestige that will be favorably noted by, say, the procurement officer of a government agency who must justify dispersal of taxpayers' money to a particular firm. In interior design and related fields, qualifications can and do sell large institutional design jobs.

THE LETTER OF TRANSMITTAL

The response to an RFQ is generally accompanied by a letter of transmittal, or cover letter. This short letter highlights in a single presentation paragraph what you and your firm have to offer and puts a positive spin on your submission. The presentation paragraph is sandwiched between an opening paragraph stating the reason for writing and a closing paragraph restating your interest in the project. (See discussion of the cover letter in Chapter 12.) The transmittal letter may or may not be bound with the RFQ.

WEIGHING THE COST OF RESPONSE

The responses to an RFQ may be widely read within the prospect organization. As many as 50 copies may be requested from each respondent! Of course, the copying expenses will seem negligible if the projected fees are large and the designer has a good chance of being selected. Clearly, however, it can be time-consuming and expensive to respond to RFQs and RFPs. Designers need to ask themselves probing questions about business-development work this intensive. As always, they need to figure out in advance whether it makes sense to pursue a particular opportunity. According to Kate Hartnick, president of Hartnick Consulting (www.hartnickconsulting.com),[13] it is wise to consider such questions as:

- How important is this project to you?
- What expenses will you sustain in getting to agreement?
- What is the *opportunity* cost of getting and doing the project? That is, what other work would you have to give up?
- Will it cost you more to do the project than the project will bring in?
- How likely is it that you will be chosen?
- Could this project lead to a long-term relationship?
- Is this an area in which you have experience and expertise?
- How much pleasure will you get from this project?

Government procurement of goods and services is a precise process that scrupulously avoids the appearance of favoritism. In responding to questions or completing forms, mirror the language of the procuring agency in order to demonstrate a good fit with its needs and objectives. Be sure your answers are accurate, succinct, and fully responsive to questions.

> To win government business, mirror the procuring agency's language to demonstrate a good fit.

ACHIEVING QUALITY CERTIFICATION

Sometimes the qualification process is handled not through RFQs, but through advance quality certification or a *term contract* awarded to cover work orders for a period of time up to an annual maximum. Advance qualification procedures such as these save time for agencies seeking to procure services and goods, as well as for those seeking to provide them. Quality certification or a term contract is often arranged through an agency or branch of government different from the agencies likely to purchase services and goods. Designers who have achieved quality certification with, say, the General Services Administration (GSA) of the federal government are issued a number, which the designer then uses throughout a period of, say, five years, in responding to requests for proposals (RFPs) from various federal government agencies.

New York State has excellent term contracts for all kinds of furniture and equipment, which New York City and other municipal agencies and quasi-municipal agencies like a public library can "buy off."[14] Most other states have similar methods of qualifying vendors and making goods and services available for purchase by local government agencies.

At the federal level, the GSA places qualified providers on "supply schedules" for various categories of goods and services. Of interest to a business-oriented interior designer in a recent Federal Supply Schedules Listing might be Schedule 71 II K[15]:

COMPREHENSIVE FURNITURE MANAGEMENT SERVICES
Project Management, Assets Management, Reconfiguration/ Relocation Management, and Packaged Environments (all Furniture/Furniture Related; Furniture Design/Layout; etc.)

Once scheduled or otherwise qualified, design professionals and other providers of services and goods need not wait for an RFP. They can canvas for clients among the various agencies that might need their services. This prospecting frequently involves selling themselves over the telephone. Below a certain threshold (sometimes called the "micro-purchase threshold," though it may be as high as $50,000 and thus might not seem very "micro" to a novice designer), the contract officers responsible for purchasing goods and services in governmental agencies can hire from their individual short lists of certified professionals without putting out an RFP that would open the work-procurement process to the public. If you are a designer looking for government work, you want to be on as many of these short lists as possible. Walter Maxwell, a procurement outreach specialist employed by the Department of Small Business Services of the City of New York, suggests that you overcome whatever "call-reluctance" may be holding you back from calling prospective agency clients and letting them know of your interest and availability.[16] People with job titles similar to his are ready to help you market your services at all levels of government.

Overcome "call-reluctance" to place yourself on the short lists of government agencies.

QUALIFYING AS A SMALL OR MINORITY- OR WOMAN-OWNED BUSINESS

There may be particular advantages in doing business with the government if your design firm is small, is minority-owned, or is owned by a woman. For instance, New York City has an explicit policy of favoring small, local firms. It is called LBE, or Local Business Enterprise. To qualify, firms must have gross annual receipts below the specified threshold.[17] Small design firms doing business in other locations may find that they can benefit from similar policies.

At the federal level, the U.S. Small Businesses Administration (SBA) maintains the Procurement Marketing and Access Network, or PRO-Net, an "online, interactive, electronic gateway of procurement information—for and about small businesses. It is a search engine for contracting officers, a marketing tool for small firms, and a link to procurement opportunities and important information."[18] The PRO-Net database contains profiles of more than 250,000 firms, which can be searched according to key words, location, quality certifications, business type, the race and gender of owners, and other relevant search terms.

According to the GSA Procurement Directory, the electronic profile of each firm registered in the database includes the following:

> . . . the identification of the business (including world-wide-web and e-mail addresses, if available), organization and/or ownership, products and services, and performance history. . . . Profiles provide vendors an opportunity to put a controlled "marketing spin" on their businesses. Companies with "homepages" can link their web site to their PRO-Net profile, creating a very powerful marketing tool. . . . As an electronic gateway, PRO-Net provides access and is linked to the Commerce Business Daily (CBD), agency homepages, and other sources of procurement opportunities.

Although laws mandating that a certain portion of government work be contracted to minority- or women-owned businesses have, by and large, expired or been "sunsetted," many agencies continue to respect the guidelines developed under those laws. From 5 to 8 percent of government supply contracts are with minority- or women-owned businesses. If appropriate for you and your firm, you may acquire Minority- and Woman-Owned Business Enterprise (MWBE) certification at whatever level of government. To be certified, your firm typically needs to be 51 percent owned by women or by members of minority groups and needs to have been in business at least a year. The results of this certification—separate from the qualification processes described earlier—may be published in a frequently updated directory that is used by procurement specialists within government agencies to maintain diversity. (Veteran status and disability are also taken into account.)

While certification as a small or minority- or women-owned business is not in itself a ticket to success in finding clients among government agencies, it can be a useful adjunct to quality certification and may be taken into account by agencies hiring beneath their micro-procurement thresholds or through RFPs.

RFPs

A typical RFP for design services includes a description of the project result, a description of relevant contextual factors, a projected delivery schedule, and a detailed description of design services needed to complete the project.

A preliminary budget may also be requested. In the RFP, respondents are issued instructions about the proper format for response submission.

Current governmental RFPs are publicized in such venues as the municipal or state record publications for a given locality. They are also publicized on Web sites for city, state, and federal governments. A good portal for the federal government is the GSA's site, www.fedbizopps.gov. (Do not go to any sites bearing the acronym *GSA* or the domain name *fedbizopps* followed by a domain extension other than *gov*, as these sites, which abound, are apt to be shady dealers selling services that are available for free on the government's own Web site.) Interior designers can register at www.fedbizopps.gov to receive e-mail notification of solicitations and awards in their areas of interest.

Designers may be particularly interested in RFPs put out through the GSA's Public Buildings Service (PBS), which is "responsible for planning, designing, building, restoring, renovating, decorating, providing landscaping for, and leasing (civilian-occupied) Government owned buildings and other facilities. It is also responsible for the operation, maintenance, and security of its buildings."[19]

PROPOSAL ORGANIZATION AND FORMAT

Some RFPs dictate the organization and format of solicited proposals; they are said to be eliciting a "closed" response. An "open" response is elicited by a proposal that dictates no set response format. However, even if response is open, brevity is appreciated by those who must evaluate numerous proposals. (The soliciting organization will ask for more information if it is needed.) Busy proposal readers will also appreciate your use of bullet points, headers, italics, and other features that make skimming easy.

Cater to busy readers by making your proposal easy to skim.

THE CRITERION-BASED RESPONSE

Whether it calls for a closed or an open response, an RFP not only explains a project but establishes *criteria*—detailed and comprehensive specifications governed by precise standards. Christine M. Erikson, a senior consultant with CTGi (www.ctgusa.com), who works with public-sector clients to improve their RFP processes, suggests that a respondent copy the RFP and use it as a template, for decision makers will expect a response to each criterion. To ensure that your responses are thorough and convincing, compile a criterion response table (see Table 5.3). You will be able to see at a glance how well you are meeting the needs set forth in the RFP. Such a table would not be submitted as part of your proposal but would serve as part of your pre-writing, which should also include extensive research.

TABLE 5.3 CRITERION RESPONSE TABLE

CRITERION	RESPONSE	BENEFIT TO CLIENT
Researchers and executives do not use the conference rooms near their desks but confer informally after large meetings. Their social pattern requires support.	"Soft" conference rooms placed near all exits from meeting rooms and auditoriums.	Employees can confer spontaneously as projects require. Soft conference rooms can also function as booths at trade shows.
Employees are more productive if they eat lunches near their desks, though there is no room to install kitchens.	Kitchens-on-carts are rolled out at lunch time and docked in conference rooms when not in use. Conference rooms may be used as mini-lunchrooms.	Client retains control of employee's time before and after lunch. Kitchens-on-carts are inexpensive and easily replaced or upgraded. Use is made of currently unused conference rooms.

RESEARCHING BEYOND THE CRITERIA

According to Erikson, it is a mistake to address *only* the criteria set forth in the RFP. She suggests that you learn to look at the needs behind the criteria. To ascertain what these needs are, a respondent obtains business intelligence from all appropriate and relevant sources, including but not limited to the group conferences that may be set up for all those who are responding to an RFP. According to Chris Engel, vice president for sales at Plumb Design (www.plumbdesign.com), "The written [proposal] should contain no surprises"[20] if the proposer has previously obtained adequate business intelligence. Here are some questions[21] that you should consider asking as you persue publicly available resources such as Web sites and agency publications:

Research beyond the announced RFP criteria.

*   What are the prospect's organizational objectives?
*   How would success at achieving these objectives be measured?
*   Who will benefit from the interior-design project?
*   How can you help the client organization excel in its field?

It is always useful to know the prospective client's budget. Even if none has been announced in the RFP, it may still be possible to ascertain the numbers by looking at publicly available materials of a government agency or any other entity that must practice financial transparency. It is sometimes a pleasant surprise to see what an online search will turn up!

ELEMENTS OF A RESPONSIVE PROPOSAL

An RFP may be defined as a request for a solution to a problem. A responding proposal needs to explain in detail how the problem would be solved, and the resulting project developed, by a particular design firm. The proposal should state an approach and then present an outline of *scope* (extent-of-work) elements and a design program based on the criteria provided in the RFP. Feeding into the proposal, of course, will be business intelligence and any visits to the site where the design work will be executed and/or installed.

A proposal responding to an RFP can be as short as four or five pages or longer than a hundred. (Lengthier proposals are sometimes commissioned and may involve a large firm in months of work by a sizeable team of collaborators.) While some responses to RFPs are written as informal proposals, many are written as *formal proposals*. Like a formal report (see Chapter 9), a formal proposal has a title page and, for longer proposals, a table of contents. It may also have headers, a list of figures, and other book-like elements.

A proposal responding to an RFP is usually preceded by a summary, sometimes called *the executive summary*, which succinctly presents the main ideas developed in the sections that follow. (The summary is usually written last and should be proportionate to the length of the proposal itself. It is geared to the busy executive reader whose specialty is management, not any particular facilities usage.) In addition to a summary, the responding proposal typically contains a statement of how the client's problem is to be solved, a statement of the designer's approach, and a scope outline as well as the following:

- a schedule
- a phase breakdown
- a relationship section
- a fiscal section
- a staffing section, which may contain a full *vita*, or professional life history—an expanded résumé—for each of the collaborators proposed for the project (For senior designers, these vitas may be as long as 10 pages each, and they are often very detailed.)

The response to an RFP is accompanied by appropriate letters of recommendation and often by supporting materials such as project description sheets, slide sleeves, reprints, CD-ROMs, and diskettes. It is also accompanied by a letter of transmittal that may be bound in.

FISCAL RESPONSIBILITY

The fiscal sections of a response to a government RFP must be very carefully conceived. Government work is billed by a fixed-fee or project rate, *not* by the hour. A response to an RFP put out by a government agency or other large public or quasi-public organization is no mere business pitch. The fixed-price aspect means that you are making a formal *bid* for the design work that will not be subject to upward negotiation unless new conditions are discovered. Then again, you may be asked to negotiate your best price downward! Although a proposal is not a contract document, the fee basis and the cost estimate will be taken seriously and must be carefully calculated.

To protect yourself, you would be well advised to spell out precisely the terms and *conditions*, or set of assumptions, under which your price is valid. These conditions must be as detailed and specific as those of the contract you wish to elicit with your bid.

THE SUBMISSION DEADLINE

Be certain that your proposal arrives at its destination before the deadline for submissions. Do not skimp on postage. If you need to use Express Mail or FedEx to be confident of meeting a deadline, then do not risk a cheaper and slower means of delivery. Because the RFP process is public and transparent, deadlines are serious. No exceptions can be made for late proposals.

EVALUATION OF PROPOSALS

When an organization that put out an RFP has received all proposals, an evaluation team—including some members who have developed the RFP—begins to rank the proposals according to how well they have fulfilled the criteria. Often the responses are ranked along a point scale, with hundreds or even thousands of points awarded for clear, cost-effective concepts; appropriate design experience; and a credible delivery schedule.

THE PROPOSAL AUDIENCE

Savvy proposal writers try to speak to all the presumed readers of a proposal:

> Write for all readers of a proposal.

- Some readers have control of the purse strings and the *power to make decisions*. It is to these readers that the executive summary is pitched. They do not usually have time to read the entire proposal and may not have a grasp of technical terminology. They need to have the big picture clearly laid out for them.

- Some readers function in an *advisory capacity*; although they have no decision-making power, their opinions weigh heavily. These are the "technical" readers. For instance, if a proposal is for the interior design of a municipal library, then librarians will read the entire proposal very closely. Their opinions may be all but determinative, though the mayor, the members of the town council, and the library's board of directors may make the final decision. The technical readers are often people who would have to work in the environment that you design. They will read each proposal to see that their needs and problems would be met and solved.
- Some readers may function as *screeners* who make sure that all criteria are addressed. These administrative readers have the power to veto a proposal but not to adopt it. To do their jobs properly, they must cultivate a checklist mentality: *yes/no; criterion met/not met*. It is for these readers that you must be meticulous in clearly responding to criteria.

When pitching your proposal to the likely evaluation process, note that government agencies may not look at the fiscal section until they have evaluated a proposal on its merits. If the RFP did not make this clear, inquire whether the fiscal section should be submitted separately. After all proposals have been evaluated, the client will usually establish a short list of design firms to call in for interviews. It is to members of this small group that the work will ultimately be awarded. (See recommendation of the Finance and Administrative Committee of the Town of Markham on your CD-ROM.) To improve your chances of being "shortlisted" and ultimately selected as the designer for a project, write your response to an RFP with careful attention to all relevant instructions and guidelines. Proofread, proofread, proofread!

Discussion Questions

1. If you were to contact the Chamber of Commerce in your town, what information might you gain about newcomers in your area? How would you use this business intelligence to approach prospective clients? How might you supplement it with other business intelligence?

2. Would you prefer to keep a manual or an electronic prospecting file? Why?

3. What are the differences between a prospecting letter, a letter of interest, and a preliminary agreement letter? What situations are appropriate for the use of each of these letter types?

Exercises

1. Adapt the master letter that is presumably the basis of Figure 5.1, and pitch your firm's services to a single client, a professional woman with no children who has just moved into a condo in a luxury high-rise building constructed in 1980. Her unit is a one-bedroom apartment with a living-dining room, a small kitchen, and a balcony.

2. Interview another student about the changes he or she would like to see in his or her family's home. Then write a letter of interest proposing your firm's interior design services to the student. Be sure that your letter contains each of the elements that are characteristic of a letter of interest.

3. Prepare a qualification/benefit table (see Table 5.2) in which your qualifications in responding to an imaginary client's problems are described as benefits for the client. Transform these data into a paragraph suitable for a letter of interest.

4. Go to www.fedbizopps.gov. What opportunities can you find for an interior design firm? Where would you look for future opportunities? Prepare a brief oral report for your class.

5. Use the experience code profile numbers located on the CD-ROM to fill in the project-example chart excerpted below, describing your own school design projects in a manner that would be suitable for Form 254. (An expanded chart is on the CD-ROM.)

Profile Code	Project name and Location	Owner Name and Address	Completion Date (Actual)

Writing for Agreement

When a prospect has responded favorably to a proposal or a letter of interest, and the pre-agreement phase of the design process has been completed—on most residential projects, after the first interview—the designer and the client need to come to terms about the scope of work in the agreement phase of the design project. The agreement they reach may or may not be called a contract, but it has the force of a contract if it involves an *exchange of considerations*. In general legal terminology, this means that something of value—*consideration*—is exchanged for something else of value. Typically, when a designer comes to agreement with a client, the consideration offered by the designer is professional services, while the consideration offered by the client is appropriate payment and performance of a client's duties.

Oral Agreements

For small projects lasting less than one year (or for the sale of goods costing less than $500), oral agreements may be tempting. Even large projects have been executed on the strength of a handshake. Adrianne Dale, FASID, tells the story of an elderly couple—let us call them Mr. and Mrs. Goodheart—who refused to sign a contract with their designer for an expensive vacation home on the grounds that they never signed contracts, not even for construction. When asked how they resolved the typical problems that arise over issues of payment or schedule, the Goodhearts replied, "we discuss them."[1] While the couple's civilized approach to problem solving can only be praised, Dale hesitates to recommend the old-fashioned oral-contract model—relying on an individual's word and honor—to students in her professional-practices classes. Nor can it be recommended here.

In our *litigious*, or lawsuit-prone, society an oral contract between designers and their clients is decidedly risky. It is subject to misunderstanding and reimbursement failure and can lead to disputes with clients less civilized than the Goodhearts. Designers are well advised by their lawyers (and their mentors) to confirm an oral contract in a written agreement providing clear evidence of both parties' intentions.

In theory, an agreement scrawled on "a napkin from a restaurant . . . [if] signed by the . . . [client could] serve as a legal contract."[2] In practice, written contracts between designers and their clients are typically presented in one of two ways. Sometimes they are composed and negotiated as *letter contracts*—a relatively informal mode that is appropriate for residential clients with small or simple projects—and sometimes they are negotiated from *form contracts*—appropriate for commercial or corporate clients or any large or complex projects.

Core Contract Elements

In order to be legally enforceable, all contracts contain at a minimum the following core elements:

- The date
- The names and addresses of the parties to the contract
- An adequately detailed description of the services to be provided
- A statement of how fees are to be charged and payments made

These elements delineate the exchange of considerations and so constitute the core of an agreement. Of course, the contract must be signed to be valid—most particularly by the party being charged, which is, of course, the client. It is best if both parties in a marriage or other domestic partnership sign a residential design contract, so that the designer can be paid in the event of death or failure of the relationship. It may need to be stipulated

Confirm an oral contract in a written agreement.

All contracts contain core elements that state the nature of an exchange.

what relationship the actual signer of the contract has to the client (for instance, if the contract is being signed by the agent for an absentee owner). A commercial contract should be signed by someone legally qualified to represent the commercial enterprise.

Although letter contracts and form-based contracts differ in important ways, each contains the core elements. Additionally, so as to protect designers and their relationships with clients, both types of agreement set forth the *conditions* under which the core agreement is valid. In the letter contract as well as the form-based one, it is crucial that the language used to articulate the core agreement and the conditions be clear, unequivocal, and precise.

Conditions say when and how the agreement is valid.

The Letter Contract

Recent statistics suggest that 60 percent of the designers now in practice are independent practitioners who offer customized services to their clients. Rather than deriving their income from a markup on furnishings, these designers work on a fee basis. Although their clients may insist on a clear advance agreement setting forth the design services to be performed, the clients shy away from preprinted formal contracts. For these situations, a letter contract, more personal in tone, is the appropriate type of agreement.[3]

Usually written on a designer's letterhead, a letter contract—also called a letter of agreement—begins like any other business letter with a date line, an inside address (usually the home office of a business with branch offices), and a salutation. There is typically a brief first paragraph expressing the designer's delight in having been selected for the project and stating the purpose of the letter that follows—to establish the terms under which designer and client will work together. Because it has the appearance of a custom-tailored communication, a letter contract is less intimidating than a form contract with filled-in blanks. The letter of agreement conveys a sense of responding to the individual needs of a client. Yet, typically, it is composed for the most part of a set of standard clauses adapted from a master letter contract.

A letter contract seems more personal than a form-based contract.

Components of a Letter Contract

For legal purposes, all sections of any contract are equally important, since each defines an aspect of the designer-client relationship or guards against a potential problem. Some of the requisite sections in the letter contract— such as the project description and scope statement—are particular to the agreement at hand. Others set forth the *conditions*, or assumptions, under which the agreement for the project work is valid. The sample letter contract presented by lawyer Tad Crawford and Eva Doman Bruck in *Business and Legal Forms for Interior Designers*[4] comprises 17 numbered paragraphs, corresponding to those excerpted in Table 6.1. (Numbered paragraphs underscore the contractual nature of the letter and make it easy for readers to find and refer to its component parts.) While it may seem that a letter contract could be shorter—limited, for instance, to the core agreement elements—in truth it needs to contain the full range of components represented in Table 6.1 to afford adequate protection.

All sections of a contract are equally important.

The items presented in Table 6.1 function as a checklist that you can use to make sure your letter contracts contain all the necessary components. An electronic version of the checklist is on your CD-ROM and may be copied and printed out as needed. (Crawford and Bruck's actual letter contract, from which the list was adapted, is printed in *Business and Legal Forms for Interior Designers*[5] and is also available in electronic form on a CD-ROM that may be purchased with that book.) A checklist is not a sufficient precaution, of course. You also need to be alert to the more detailed considerations in the paragraphs that follow.

TABLE 6.1   ELEMENTS OF A LETTER OF AGREEMENT

1. Description	9. Payment
2. Schedule	10. Term and Termination
3. Purchases, Fabrication, and Construction	11. Ownership of Design
4. Approvals	12. Consultants
5. Client Responsibilities	13. Publicity
6. Remuneration	14. Relationship of Parties
7. Changes	15. Assignment
8. Expenses	16. Arbitration
	17. Miscellany

Adapted and modified from Tad Crawford and Eva Doman Bruck, Business and Legal Forms for Interior Designers *(New York: Allworth, 2001), 137–142.*

Project Description and Scope of Services

Letter contracts, like other contracts, begin with a description of the project that is being undertaken. As discussed in Chapter 2, the proper basis for a

A project
description
is based on
observation,
interviewing,
and note taking.

project description—and, for that matter, the linked scope statement—is careful observation, adept interviewing, and accurate note taking. The project description focuses on the project premises, while the scope statement focuses on the design work to be accomplished.

Some parts of the project description are obvious and basic but are nonetheless important. Among the most basic passages are those describing the date when the agreement commences, the location of the project premises, and the square footage. The designer must precisely stipulate which parts of the premises are to be worked on, so that it will be clear if additions to the scope of work are requested later.

The scope of the services offered must be set forth with painstaking accuracy, so that the designer's duties are crystal clear to the client. In the words of Mary V. Knackstedt, FASID, FIIDA: "Declare exactly what you will do," and then, of course, "live up to your contract."[6]

If the project is residential, as a project governed by a contract letter typically would be, then the scope statement might delineate designer responsibility in areas such as the following:

- Programming and initial study
- Preparation of plans and other drawings
- Presentation of design concepts, including thematic statements and color work-ups
- Layout for and selection of fixtures, furnishings, and equipment
- Presentation of swatches and samples for floor surfaces, wall finishes, and window treatments
- Lighting design and electrical plan, if relevant
- Design of storage areas, including cupboards, cabinets, shelves, and closets
- Collaboration with consultants
- Preparation of purchase orders and, in many cases, purchase of furniture, furnishings, and equipment
- Preparation of contracts between the client and fabricators or construction contractors

In your scope
statement, divide
the work into
phases.

Often, a detailed scope statement (see Chapter 3) is attached to the letter contract as an *appendix*, or supplement, rather than inserted into the agreement proper.

In your scope statement, divide the work into phases: five are the accepted standard. Most services offered by interior designers fall into the categories of:

- Programming
- Schematics
- Design development
- Contract documentation
- Contract administration

You can use the phases to help you organize your interview notes and to present the specific services you will be offering on this project as an orderly series of steps necessary to implement the project. As the job progresses, your scope statement will provide a reference for discussing job progress. It will aid with "time-frame planning"[7] in meetings and assist with the scheduling of design work. A clear division into phases also simplifies billing—particularly if the project is terminated.

Scope statements and project descriptions, like other parts of the letter of agreement, should be reviewed more than once and revised as necessary before the agreement is presented for signature.

Review and revise your contract more than once before presenting it for signature.

Schedule

While every designer, residential or contract, wants to meet a client's schedule expectations, there are many *contingencies*, or possible events, that the designer cannot control. A construction contractor may take on too many jobs at the same time and be unable to complete projects in a timely manner. A client may decide against the carpet previously selected. A key fabricator with a sick child may fall behind and be unable to deliver custom cabinets or frosted-glass partitions in a timely manner. A civil war may break out or a volcano erupt in the country in which the client's dining-room chairs are being custom-manufactured. Designers can help to keep projects smoothly on track, and an occupancy date may be projected; but designers must never guarantee move-in dates, whatever expectations their clients may harbor.

Never guarantee a move-in date.

PURCHASES, FABRICATION, AND CONSTRUCTION

In general, designers need to spell out their responsibility with regard to all means of implementing their work. If a cost estimate for implementation of the project is to be submitted with the concept presentation, it should be specified in advance—in the letter of agreement—how the estimate will be calculated. It must be clearly stated that the cost estimate is indeed an *estimate*, not binding and not a promise.

Although part of a designer's remuneration may be based on the total purchase prices of goods acquired to realize a project, the designer may not wish to serve as financial intermediary unless a showroom will sell only to designers. Otherwise, to reduce financial exposure and liability, it is safer for the designer to have a residential client purchase directly,[8] as is customary in any case for corporate and commercial clients.

Spell out your responsibilities with regard to purchase, fabrication, and construction.

If a designer *is* submitting bills for reimbursement, the client has a right to clear, accurate accounting, though the designer is not customarily required to reveal the prices paid for merchandise subjected to a markup.

The agreement between client and designer should clearly state whether the designer is responsible for preparing purchase orders. A clear policy also needs to be stated regarding deposits on merchandise ordered through the designer. In addition, it should be stated whether substitutions by the designer (which of course should be individually approved in advance) are acceptable to the client when specified items turn out to be unavailable or have risen in price. Indeed, it needs to be stated whether the client is allowed to make substitutions (subject to the designer's approval and based on the integrity of the design).

It is important to clarify whether you are being paid to review the ongoing progress of any fabrication or construction work. The letter contract should stipulate the basis of your compensation for the review as well as the nature of the review. Are you to be paid on an hourly basis or paid a percentage of a contractor's fees? Does "review" mean a visit to a job site or shop once a week, or will you merely be available on a consultant basis once design documents have been prepared? Certainly, "review" must never mean the direct supervision of construction or fabrication, which remains the responsibility of the relevant contractors. (Be sure that you have not taken on any responsibilities that are assigned by law in your state to architects or other peer professionals or to general contractors.)

As discussed in more detail in Chapter 7, the designer does not usually take financial responsibility for construction or fabrication, but assists the client in establishing appropriate relationships. Although designers naturally try to work with trusted vendors whose high-quality work is well known to them, it is nonetheless inadvisable for designers to guarantee the quality of construction or custom fabrication, or, for that matter, merchandise. The designer communicates the level of quality desired; it is the vendor's responsibility to meet that standard.

If the residential client passionately believes that the chintz on the sofa should not have faded as quickly as it did in the harsh light of a southern exposure; if the commercial client believes that the coir matting laid down in the entryway of a store should have withstood more traffic; if a university's administration believes that latent defects in the glass walls of librarians' offices have generated a greater number of cracks than could have been predicted—you as a designer are not responsible. In fact, you would be well advised to assign to your clients any rights you might have been conceived to hold in such matters. This means that if your client sues, you will not be a party in the lawsuit and will not enjoy any financial benefit from a favorable settlement. As a courtesy, you may assist a client in rectifying problems caused by merchant, fabricator, or contractor error or omission, but, again, it is unwise to guarantee the work of others.

Do not guarentee the work of others

Approvals

If a designer is functioning as a financial intermediary, making purchases for which reimbursement is forthcoming from the client, it is crucial that the purchase orders prepared by the designer be approved by the client prior to the actual purchase. (A substantial deposit may also be required.) Even if the designer is not a financial intermediary, the client's approval at every step of the way is the best guarantee against dissatisfaction with the final product.

The agreement between designer and client must clearly state that the designer is not responsible for any changes in the price of merchandise, fabrication, or construction presented post-approval. For instance, if a previously unrevealed steel beam in a ceiling complicates the insertion of a custom *coffer* (ornamental sunken panel in a ceiling), the designer is not responsible if the contractor raises the price on the grounds of a discovered condition.

In general, approvals create a "paper trail" that may be helpful in resolving any disputes that arise. In the words of Tad Crawford and Eva Doman Bruck, "Every document that the client reviews and approves should be initialed or signed to reflect that approval, including purchase orders, plans, drawings, and renderings."[9] (There is more on the subject of approvals in Chapter 7.)

Let client approvals at each step create a paper trail.

Client Responsibilities

It is sound practice to impress upon your clients their own role in the design process. To make selections and approve work and purchases, clients need to be available throughout the course of the project. Unless they have delegated the authority to make selections and decisions, they cannot leave town for an extended period while the design work is executed in their absence, nor will decisions pertaining to work-in-progress wait until clients are less busy at their jobs or have replaced a babysitter who suddenly quit. Be sure your client commits to the approval schedule and understands his or her time-related responsibilities.

Remuneration

A design agreement stipulates the basis for computing forms of payment such as the following:

- Full retail markup on items used in the project
- Percentage of the total cost of executing the project
- Cost plus (across-the-board agreed-upon markup on all aspects of the project)
- Square-footage-based fee
- Fixed design fee
- Hourly design fee
- Time and materials (may be relevant for some aspects of design-build projects)
- Fixed-price bid (may be required for government work)

Choose the right compensation structure for the job.

The range of ASID agreement documents summarized in Table 6.2 on page 231 (and discussed in more detail later in the chapter) provides language for a variety of compensation structures.

If all or part of the designer's remuneration is based on purchases, then it should be made clear what is included and what is *excluded*, or left out. For instance, if some of the client's own furnishings are to be incorporated into the design, then these items may be specified as *s.b.o.*, "supplied by owner," and excluded; their value will be ignored for purposes of computing the designer's fee.

Similarly, a policy needs to be stated for the handling of purchases made by the client or by other collaborating professionals that would ordinarily be made by the designer. Frequently, the clients' own project-related purchases are "treated as purchases by the designer for purposes of computing the designer's fees."[10] In addition, purchases of custom plumbing fixtures, painting and wallpaper, or custom cabinets may be made on the client's behalf by an architect or general contractor, either of whom may expect a full or partial markup on items that would ordinarily be marked up by the interior designer. Potential purchase-related disputes need to be handled in the letter of agreement with the client and will, of course, affect contracts for construction and fabrication and agreements regarding the services of collaborating professionals.

It is important that the agreement state who is responsible for shipping, handling, and tax on all purchased items. (These costs will not appear on the designer's purchase orders when they are approved by the client.) In addition, particularly if all or part of the designer's remuneration is based on purchases, the contract letter must state that copies of any purchase orders *not* prepared by the designer be forwarded to the designer.

When working on a fee basis, states Diane B. Worth, "it is imperative that the client understand that product sales are by separate purchasing or procurement contracts and are not part of the design fee. Nor are they interrelated contractually except by special arrangement; i.e., fees are stated as a percentage of product sales, or square footage."[11]

The interior design profession is moving away from what H. Don Bowden, president of ASID as of 2002, has called "the old model of [compensation] through the sale of materials and furnishing. . . . Certainly within contract design," he asserts, "and to a growing degree within residential design, the trend is to move toward a consultative model, whether that involves charging a flat per-project fee or an hourly rate for services rendered."[12] According to Bowden, this development is in keeping with the ongoing professionalization of the interior design field, since it makes clear that the designer-client relationship is based on consideration for services rendered, not a markup on furniture sold.

Changes in the Design

How many times for no additional fee are your clients allowed to change their minds about selections they have made? When does the revision of design work that has previously been approved become "new work" for which additional payment is forthcoming? How are additions or deletions to the scope of the work to be approved and billed? These important issues must be covered in any letter of agreement. The handling of design changes is much more difficult to negotiate after the design work has begun. For example, a contract might state that revisions requested after approvals are subject to billing at an hourly rate.

Knackstedt suggests that you "disclaim responsibility for changes made by anyone but yourself. . . . Even if the change the client makes is small," she points out, "[it] can affect the quality and safety of the design."[13] Whether or not you agree with her, it is important to express a clear policy on design changes.

> Express a clear policy on design changes.

Expenses

As discussed in Chapter 5, it is important to clarify for the client which expenses, if any, are to be billed separately from the designer's remuneration and which, if any, markup applies to some or all categories of expense. A typical expense category involves transportation to another city, state, or country to monitor a fabricator's work-in-progress; this transportation expense is usually not covered by the designer's basic fee. Also billed separately may be communication expenses such as those for messenger service, long-distance phone calls, and *expedited* (or express) delivery. It is not customary to bill separately for expenses associated with *overhead*, the ongoing expense of maintaining an office, although overhead should certainly be taken into account when structuring compensation.

State when expenses are billed separately.

Payment

How soon after billing is payment due, and what penalties will be charged for late payment? Some agreements state that work will cease if a designer is not paid in the appropriate manner. Penalties can include interest, and even the requirement that the client must pay the designer's legal expenses if the designer must sue for payment! Note, however, that clients may balk at paying interest on "their own" money, although, strictly speaking, it is the designer's overdue compensation on which interest would be charged and on which the designer could be earning interest if remuneration had been prompt. Moreover, suing for payment is a worthless option if the client declares bankruptcy and has other creditors, or if the client's assets cannot be tapped for some other reason.

LIENS

In some states, designers are entitled to place so-called mechanics' liens if they are not paid in a timely manner. A *lien* confers the right to another's property if monies owed have not been paid. *Mechanics'* liens originated as a way of ensuring that general construction and single-trade contractors would receive the money owed to them.[14] If a designer has placed such a lien—typically through a lawyer—then a client who sells the property where unpaid design work has been executed would have to pay the designer before realizing benefit from the sale. A lien may not have much immediate effect on a home or *condominium* owner who is not planning a sale. (Like a home owner, the owner of a condominium apartment holds title to the actual, physical premises.) Even if no sale is pending, however, a lien can bring a delinquent client who owns *co-operative* apartment shares to the attention of the co-op's board and thus create embarrassment and pressure. (Co-op owners do not own the physical premises of their apartments but rather own shares in the co-operative that entitle them to occupy and use a particular set of premises.) A designer should be leery of any client who requests a *waiver*, or formal relinquishment in writing, of the right to place a lien. (There is more discussion of liens in Chapter 7.)

RETAINERS

To help avoid disputes over payment, a savvy designer will require a nonre- *Require a retainer.*
fundable *retainer*, or fee charged in advance for services to be rendered. This
will help to ensure that the designer is remunerated for all work performed
if the agreement is cancelled. It is best for the designer if the retainer is
applied to the final payment, but this is not always possible. (See Chapter 5
for a discussion of the preliminary agreement proposal, which solicits a non-
refundable retainer as fee for a preliminary design phase.)

Term and Termination

Under the best of conditions, it is wise to set time boundaries for the exe- *Specify the term*
cution of a designer's work—the *term* of the project. It needs to be clearly *of the project.*
stated, too, that the term will be extended if delays not caused by the
designer hinder the progress of the project, whether these delays be caused
by suppliers; contractors; events beyond the designer's control, like hurri-
canes or war; or by client indecision or overcommitment elsewhere.

What about the worst-case scenario in which the relationship between
the designer and client fails? How can designers extricate themselves from
agreements they have come to regret? The simplest way to handle this issue
grants both the designer and the client the right to *terminate*, or end, their
relationship upon proper *notice*—that is, advance, written announcement to
the other party at the address contained in the letterhead or the inside
address of the letter contract or at any other address selected for receiving
notices. (Delivery of notices should be traceable.) It needs to be stated that
the client must pay for all design and other work executed up to the point
of termination and must also pay for related expenses and for all purchase
orders approved before termination.

Ownership of Design

If you are a novice designer, it may not seem to matter much who owns the
work you do on behalf of a client. That illuminated Lucite-and-glass-block shelf
unit you designed looks spectacular in the Smiths' apartment. Its photographs
on your Web site have helped you get other work, and one of your new clients
wants an identical shelf unit. You decide to have it made by the same fabricator,
who has been storing the models, samples, and other production materials, but
when you phone the fabricator, you discover that the Smiths' lawyer has asked
for these materials on the grounds that the shelf unit and the design for it
belong to the Smiths, who cherish the assurance that the shelf unit is unique.
If the agreement between you and the Smiths has adequately spelled out the
ownership of the design-work product, this phone conversation will offer no

surprises. In general, it is in a designer's best interest to copyright drawings and specifications. The designer may then *license* them, permitting each client the use of them for a particular project only. The designer "should be free to adapt the details to other projects, publish them or use them in any way."[15] (As reflected in Chapter 7, the paragraph in the designer-client agreement regarding ownership of design must harmonize with the language of any contract that your clients may make with fabricators or construction contractors.)

Spell out ownership of the design work product.

Consultants

It is important to clarify relationships with other professionals with whom an interior designer may collaborate—for instance, a landscape designer, a structural engineer, a lighting designer, an architect, or an audio-system designer. It is usually best for the interior designer to have the agreement state that these consultants are retained and paid by the client. However, designers need documentation of their consultants' adequate performance and may require support documents prepared and provided by them. For instance, designers may require relevant architectural drawings and specifications provided by a consulting architect before they can complete their own work. Timely delivery of required documents by client-retained consultants should be part of the interior designer's agreement with the client. A designer should never appear to be offering the services of other professionals if not licensed to do so and certainly should not take responsibility for code compliance in any of the consultants' areas of expertise.

Clarify relationships with other professionals who consult on the project.

Publicity

Suppose a design magazine wants to publish pictures of your client's house, now under occupancy. Is that permitted? The publicity section of the agreement details the handling of such contingencies. It is important that relevant policy be established in advance of any publicity opportunities and that it cover both progress photos and photos of the completed project. That way, there will be no unpleasant surprises for anyone. Most clients—residential, corporate, or institutional—enjoy public recognition of their well-designed and well-executed interiors. If privacy is an issue or if residential or other premises contain valuable artwork or antiques to which the owners do not wish to call attention for fear of attracting thieves, it may be stipulated that publicity for the interior design disguise the location of the premises and that no photographs be published of the most valuable objects. (Very high-profile clients may even request complete nondisclosure for the duration of a lengthy project and thereafter, to help prevent worst-case contingencies like kidnapping.)[16]

Establish a publicity policy in advance of any opportunity.

It is customary for designers to pay for the high-quality photographs that are used to publicize interior design. Will the client permit these photographs to be taken? If so, who will own the negatives? What rights will the photographer retain? How many sets of prints will the client and other interested parties receive? The designer-client agreement needs to reflect the understanding between the designer and any photographer retained for the project. The designer-client agreement can also stipulate that the client will buy rights and order additional prints directly from the photographer and must credit the photographer appropriately for all public uses of the work. (See Chapter 11 for more on publicity photographs of interior design work.)

Of course, the designer should receive appropriate credit in any and all publicity. So, for that matter, should the photographer. The agreement should clarify how the client, the project, and the photographer will be identified, not only for publicity purposes, but in promotional materials such as print and online brochures.

Relationship of Parties

In your letter of agreement with any client, you need to state explicitly that you are an *independent contractor*, someone who practices a profession, offers services to the public on a regular basis, and is not employed by the client—who is also, for purposes of your mutual agreement, an independent contractor. Most pointedly, you are not the client's employee, and there is no partnership or *joint venture*—co-business relationship in which you mutually profit—between you and the client. This is important for tax purposes: your clients don't want to handle the taxes on the portion of your income that they have generated. It also serves to underscore your professional impartiality in any disputes that you are called on to *mediate*, or broker, between your clients and merchants, fabricators, or construction contractors. You have agreed to provide the client with certain design and review services; you have not agreed to acquiesce to your client's wishes in all matters, as might more reasonably be expected of an employee.

> Spell out your independent-contractor status.

Assignment

What if your excellent client, a rapid decision maker, an individual of superb taste, open to new ideas and willing and able to purchase the finest, succumbs to an illness and dies, leaving all affairs in the hands of a dithering, tasteless, tight-fisted heir? The structure of your compensation may not have prepared you to deal with the heir in a manner that ensures a profit on the project. Do you have any recourse? Alas, your best recourse would have been before the fact. If you were prudent, your contract letter would contain an assignment clause stating that the rights conferred by the contract cannot be transferred or delegated to another person without advance written notice and consent. Your client would probably want reciprocal language in this clause that requires advance notice and consent if you choose to assign the design work to a different designer whom the client has not selected and might not like or respect. Negotiated in this way, an assignment clause can protect both you and your client, although it should be written in a way that permits you to assign payment to other parties, for example, those from whom you have purchased furnishings on the client's behalf.

Protect yourself
and your client
with an
assignment
clause.

Arbitration

In the majority of designer-client relationships, the interaction is smooth and harmonious; it is possible to work through any disagreements that arise. However, if a serious dispute does emerge, it will be resolved more quickly if advance provision has been made for handling it. Many design contracts call for the submission of serious disputes to the American Arbitration Association (www.adr.org). If the dispute cannot be resolved in a nonbinding negotiation phase, or *mediation*, it is subjected to the *arbitration* phase, which, like the mediation phase, is conducted by an impartial and authoritative go-between. Unlike the mediation phase, however, the arbitration phase is *binding*—that is, once an arbitrator has worked out a solution, all parties to the dispute are obligated to accept it. The use of this two-part process—nonbinding mediation followed by binding arbitration—can help prevent costly *litigation* (a proceeding before a judge in a court of law) and is usually acceptable to both designer and client as a means of dispute resolution.

Provide for
arbitration as
a means of
dispute resolution.

The nonbinding mediation phase is a relatively recent addition to the arbitration process. It has solved a shortcoming of arbitration that had been previously noted by lawyers who described arbitration as "litigation without discovery." As a legal term, *discovery* refers to compulsory pre-trial disclosure of documents relevant to a case. It enables one side in a litigation to elicit information from the other side concerning the facts. In effect, the mediation phase of the arbitration process provides a discovery stage and ensures that no party to a dispute will be unpleasantly surprised later on.

Arbitrators tend to be broadly experienced individuals who bring to the table not only a general knowledge of business law but a well-developed sense of fairness. This inexpensive, common-sense method of dispute resolution is not popular with people who habitually engage in sharp or manipulative business practices, relying on high-powered, expensive lawyers to extricate them from any litigation that may result. Designers should be wary of affluent clients who reject arbitration as a means of resolving disputes. To go directly to litigation puts a high price tag on dispute resolution and may put it beyond most designers' reach.

This is not to say that arbitration is without cost. The arbitrator must be paid appropriate fees. In addition, many parties to an arbitrated dispute hire lawyers to help them prepare and present their cases. Yet arbitration is less costly than litigation, which is why it is specified in so many design and construction contracts as a means of dispute resolution. (Indeed, construction and design are so important an area of focus for the American Arbitration Association that it has a special publication, *Punch List*, to deal with the many issues raised. You can find out more about it at www.adr.org.)

The arbitration process is usually *global*—that is, well rounded and not limited in scope. Of course, you should come to any arbitration well prepared with the facts as you see them, and you need to have kept meticulous records—the paper trail that is discussed in greater detail in Chapter 10. A well-written agreement will also contribute to the success of arbitration. (As Knackstedt observes, "when a contract document . . . is ambiguous or incomplete . . . , the ruling is generally against the author of the document."[17]) The arbitrator may not study the detailed records closely but is more apt to glance through them to see that documentation is orderly, clear, and thorough. He or she will ask questions designed to penetrate to the heart of the disputed matter, understanding that gaps in the paper trail may result from stress and schedule pressure rather than malice, incompetence, or fraud.[18]

Arbitrated dispute resolution often results in neither party's walking away from the table empty-handed. If the arbitration is over an issue of nonpayment, as it typically is, you may get some, rather than all, of what you believe you are owed. In cases of malicious default, full payment is more likely to be granted, of course, but these cases are less frequent than run-of-the-mill disputes involving alleged error and omission or, above all, simple misunderstanding based on faulty or inadequate communication.

Arbitration invokes the honor of parties who have agreed to be bound by it. Though it is binding, the process is not linked to any enforcement mechanism. Only litigation is linked to enforcement procedures, and, as noted earlier, even a litigated judgment may not result in payment from a client who does not have assets that can be reached. The best way to handle disputes is to avoid having them in the first place.

Miscellany

Gathered into the miscellany section of a letter or other contract is a variety of *boilerplate* (standard legal concern) not covered elsewhere. For instance, somewhere in the contract it needs to be stated that the agreement currently presented for signature is the only agreement and supersedes all earlier agreements. You also need to insert the name of the state of which the laws govern the contract.

The Master Letter Contract

Although the letter contract with each client may differ in important particulars such as the project description and the compensation structure, the designer had best not attempt preparation of any given agreement from scratch. As stated earlier, it is best to use a master letter contract as a template and to customize it for each client, proofreading carefully before presenting it for signing. Your master may be based on a sample master letter, such as the one provided by Crawford and Bruck[19]; or it may draw on a contract form provided by a professional association such as ASID. (See Table 6.2 for ASID forms suitable for various types of jobs and compensation structures.) Once a master letter is in your computer, you can print it as needed, nicely formatted, with your letterhead as the first page.

Use a master letter contract as a template and customize it for each client.

Before adapting your master contract letter to any actual business situation, however, it is sound practice to have it reviewed by a lawyer who is expert in the laws affecting design, fabrication, and construction. Comparing your letter to other existing design contracts will help guard against error or omission, but it is not a sufficient precaution, nor, again, is it sufficient to read your letter against a checklist of necessary components. Likewise, your reading of the discussion presented in this (or any) book is an inadequate legal safeguard, since discussion is presented to educate, in a general sense; cannot be considered legal advice; and can only hint at the full complexity of the considerations that go into the creation of a solid master agreement. The eye of a trained lawyer will best ensure that the language of your master agreement satisfies state and local requirements and protects you and your relationships with clients. When your lawyer has completed the review of your master letter, you can customize it for each client as needed, though it is prudent to run each customization by your lawyer as well. The cost of doing this should be counted as part of the cost of doing a given project and will probably be relatively low once you have established a working relationship with a particular lawyer. (The initial consultations will be more expensive.)

Protect yourself with legal review of your master letter.

The Form Contract

In circumstances that call for a conventional contract—most especially for any large or complex project—many interior designers avail themselves of the standard agreement forms prepared by professional organizations. Contracts prepared by the ASID,[20] for instance, cover many different kinds of residential projects. In addition, the AIA publishes B171 ID-2003 and other contracts suitable for non-residential—that is, commercial or institutional—interior projects. (You will find an excerpt from B171 on the CD-ROM.) You can purchase ASID contracts through the ASID Web site, www.asid.org, or by telephoning 202-546-3480. AIA contracts may be purchased at www.aia.org/documents.

Use a form contract for commercial or institutional work or any large, complex job.

A respected organization's imprimatur on a contract carries a message of professional seriousness and dedication to your clients. You may be confident that contracts generated by professional organizations have been carefully reviewed by lawyers, which saves you the expense of legal review. The sheer conventionality of a form contract suggests that standard practice is invoked throughout the agreement process. Table 6.2 sets forth the range of interiors documents made available through ASID (at a lower price to members). You can study the range of interiors contracts available through the AIA at www.aia.org/documents.

Among the ways in which the form contracts differ, two are notable: (1) the manner in which the project work is divided into phases; and (2) the treatment and presentation of general conditions. These document differences proceed from differences within the range of interior design projects, from simple to complex and from residential to commercial, corporate, or institutional.

Breakdown into Phases

A complex or large project is usually broken down into many more phases than is a simple project. For example, a relatively complicated commercial project might be divided into the following phases:

- Programming
- Schematic design
- Design development
- Preparation of drawings associated with fabrication and moveable items
- Preparation of contract documents for renovation and construction

TABLE 6.2 ASID INTERIORS AGREEMENT

ID300-1994 **Standard Form of Agreement Between Owner and Contractor for Furniture, Furnishings and Equipment**

Intended for use on projects where the basis of payment is a fixed fee arrived at in advance by bid or by negotiation. Four pages. For use with ID320.

ID320-1994 **General Conditions of the Contract for Furniture, Furnishings and Equipment**

For use between an owner and an interiors contractor who is engaged in providing and installing furniture, furnishing, and equipment. Twenty-one page general-conditions form incorporated into the ID300 and ID100 agreements. Considered the keystone document coordinating the many parties involved in the process.

ID310-1994 **Abbreviated Owner-Contractor Agreement for Furniture, Furnishings and Equipment**

For fixed-fee projects that are not of a complexity to require the combined ID300 and ID320 forms. Eleven pages.

ID325-1994 **Guide for Interiors Supplementary Conditions**

A guide to assist with the preparation of supplementary conditions intended for use with ID320 and ID330. Notes the information most frequently required to accommodate variations in project requirements. Thirty-two pages.

ID330-1994 **Instructions to Interiors Bidders**

For use with ID320. Comprehensive considerations regarding bidding, including definitions, procedures, and specifications. Five pages.

ID100-1994 **Standard Form of Agreement for Interior Design Services**

An 11-page agreement for use on interiors projects where services are divided into five phases: programming, schematic design, design development, contract documents, and contract administration. For use with ID320 (General Conditions).

ID110-1994 **Abbreviated Form of Agreement for Interior Design Services**

Intended for projects of limited scope where the more complex and detailed

---

TABLE 6.2   (*continued*)

ID120-1996 **Residential Interior Design Services Agreement (Short Form)**

Contains no printed description of design services or compensation structure. For those who wish to set forth their own description of services and method of compensation.

ID121-1996 **Residential Interior Design Services Agreement with Compensation Basis Consisting of:**

- **Hourly Fees with a Fixed Initial Design Fee**
- **No Fee Charged on Purchases (alternate language for fee on purchases)**

ID122-1996 **Residential Interior Design Services Agreement with Fixed Fee Compensation Basis**

ID123-1996 **Residential Interior Design Services Agreement with Compensation Basis Consisting of:**

- **Cost Plus on Purchases**
- **Fixed Initial Design Fee for Design Concept Services (alternate language for hourly fees for design concept services after initial fixed fee)**
- **Percentage of Contractor's Fees for Project Review**

ID124-1996 **Residential Interior Design Services Agreement with Compensation Basis Consisting of:**

- **Cost Plus on Purchases**
- **Fixed Initial Design Fee for Design Concept Services (alternate language for hourly fees for design concept services after initial design fee)**
- **Hourly Fees for Project Review Services**

ID125-1996 **Residential Interior Design Services Agreement with Compensation Basis Consisting of:**

- **Presented Price for Purchases**
- **Fixed Initial Design Fee for Design Concept Services (alternate language for hourly fees for design concept services after initial design fee)**
- **Percentage of Contractor's Fees for Project Review Services**

Instruction sheets included with most documents.

Adapted from ASID Web site.

- Administration and implementation
- Post-occupancy services (such as the preparation of a user manual, post-occupancy evaluation, etc.)

As with the more elementary phasing for a simple project, the phasing for a complex project needs to be closely coordinated with the project description and the scope statement.

General Conditions

As in a letter contract, the work covered by a form contract has been priced and will be executed under a set of *conditions*, or assumptions on which the validity of an agreement rests. In the short contract forms suitable for smaller projects, a limited number of general conditions are stated within an agreement, as in a letter contract, and are not offered as a separate, linked document.

The agreement forms suitable for larger, more complex projects are often used in conjunction with a separate document that sets forth the conditions for the agreement between designer and client while laying down guidelines for all other agreements relevant to a particular project—such as those between the client and fabricators or contractors. The conditions document is sometimes called a *keystone* document. Like the central building block at the top of an arch or vault, it holds together the entire structure of contractual agreement that may be needed to execute a complex design project. In it, you will find language that speaks to the types of issues set forth in Table 6.1 but in greater detail, as is appropriate for projects of greater complexity.

Supplemental Conditions

The forms supplied by designers' professional organizations are written from a designer's point of view, as will be any letter contract that you present for signature. For instance, a designer-drafted contract may state that the designer has the right to have photos taken and to publicize the project in an appropriate manner. As previously discussed, there are circumstances in which and clients for whom this may be problematic. In such circumstances, clients (and their lawyers) may insert *supplemental*, or additional, conditions. Likewise, supplemental conditions may be inserted by a designer (or a designer's lawyer), sometimes in response to a client's supplemental conditions. For instance, a strict Muslim client may stipulate that no photographs of a restaurant be taken or published in which the human figure is represented—in accordance with the Muslim prohibition against figurative representation.

The designer may negotiate an exception for drawings in which a vertical bar representing average human height is used to show scale.

Supplemental conditions are usually prepared as a separate document and folded into the contract, which will thus comprise the core agreement, the general conditions, and any supplemental conditions, all referentially linked. The contract documents may also, of course, include a separate scope statement. Since supplemental conditions are amendments to the standard contract, they must be prepared with care and should be submitted to a qualified lawyer for review before the revised contract documents are presented for signature.

> The contract documents comprise the core agreement, the general conditions, and any supplemental conditions. They may also include a scope document.

Negotiating to Full Agreement

In Frank Stavioski's "Making It Alone" seminars, he suggests that interior designers present their clients with a self-carboning agreement document. On the face of the document is the core agreement, including the scope of the work and the payment terms; and on the back, in light gray print, as on a department-store bill or an airline ticket, are 52 conditions under which the agreement is valid. The presumption is that most clients will not read the fine print and will not ask for changes in the conditions.[21]

Certainly, standard design contracts are not subject to the same intense negotiation as standard construction contracts. Often, as Stavioski suggests, the contract a designer presents is *mirrored*—that is, accepted without changes. Yet you may sometimes find that conditions accepted without question by most of your clients are subject to negotiation by others. The design agreement itself may be subject to negotiation that changes the scope of work. For instance, if no architectural floor plans of the project premises currently exist, it may be necessary to negotiate responsibility for site measurements and creation of an accurate set of as-built drawings. Likewise, responsibility may be negotiated for *shop drawings*, small drawings that display the manner in which a detail or aspect of a construction or fabrication project is to be executed. (These might be billable additions to the work scope, or they might be offered as *value-added services*, that is, additional services based on your expertise and offered to enhance your competitiveness.)

Sometimes an entire contract must be negotiated. This would typically occur when a large corporate, governmental, or institutional client presents a contract of its own devising, numbering as many as 150 pages, and containing all the conditions that the corporation imposes on the wide variety of agreements it makes.[22] For example, a contract written by the U.S. Navy for interior design services may be found on your CD-ROM. An excerpt from it appears in Figure 6.1a. An ASID residential contract, is presented in Figure 6.1b. A designer who is considering whether to accept a lengthy client-generated contract must factor in the cost of extensive legal review, which may exceed the profitability of the project. The lawyer will compare the client's contract to the designer's standard contract and will help the designer negotiate all significant differences.

Negotiation issues that arise in connection with any contract may be related to scheduling, financing, remuneration, client responsibility, or designer responsibility, among other issues.

Scheduling Issues

As stated earlier, it is best for designers that an *occupancy* (move-in) date not be promised for any project, residential or commercial, for many factors can delay occupancy. For example, delays may be caused by contractors, fabricators, suppliers, and collaborating professionals; social upheaval; natural disasters; personal tragedy; illness; or the client's own protracted decision making. If a move-in date is specified, it needs to be clearly stated that it is subject to revision for delays beyond the designer's control—for instance, the circumstance described by one residential designer in which a truck containing the client's custom-made furniture hit an icy patch on an Idaho road and crashed, destroying its cargo.[23]

You will probably be better off negotiating work delivery in phases rather than a project completion date. For instance, you might negotiate a period of six months for ordering and installation. Rather than committing to a completion date, suggests Knackstedt, "it is safer to say that," barring unforeseen circumstances, "your firm will finish the project three months after the completion of the construction program, when the building is available for interior work. If the construction is delayed, your project will then be delayed too."[24]

Avoid committing to a project completion date.

If a schedule of milestones tied to payments is part of the designer-client agreement, then its contents are subject to negotiation. In addition to start-up and move-in, a milestone schedule might include:

- Presentation of initial design concepts based on completed programming.
- Presentation of preliminary plans, drawings, and cost estimate.
- Presentation of the completed design work and revised cost estimate.
- Preparation of any necessary purchase orders.
- Selection of bidders on construction and fabrication projects.
- Preparation of construction and fabrication agreements.
- Commencement of construction and fabrication projects.

Contract Number: _____

1. This contract, made and entered into this _____ day of _____, 20__, by and between the _____ herein after referred to as the Nonappropriated Fund Instrumentality (NAFI), and _____, herein after referred to as the Contractor, is for interior design services at _____ _____ (name of installation) in _____ (city, state).

2. The NAFI agrees to engage the services of the Contractor, and the Contractor accepts the engagement to design and to do the work hereinafter specified by the NAFI in connection with the project. The contractor shall design and specify furniture, fixtures, and equipment (FF&E) as required for the _____ _____ (facility) at _____ (name of installation).

3. With the exception of the inspection and acceptance phase, Contractor shall complete all other phases of the interior design project within _____ days after receipt of contract award (see schedule) below.

  a. Period of Service:

  (1) The contractor shall deliver the Preliminary Interior Design Phase Submittals within _____ calendar days after receipt of the contract award.

  (2) The NAFI will review the Preliminary Interior Design Phase Submittal within _____ calendar days and return it to the Contractor directing any changes, corrections to be incorporated.

  (3) The Contractor shall deliver the Pre-final Interior Design Phase Submittal, with noted changes and corrections incorporated, within _____ calendar days after receipt by the Contractor of written instructions on the Preliminary Submittal.

  (4) The NAFI will review the Pre-Final Interior Design Phase Submittal, with noted changes and corrections identified, within _____ calendar days and return it to the Contractor directing those changes, corrections to be incorporated.

  (5) The Contractor shall deliver the Final Interior Design Phase Submittals within _____ calendar days after receipt by the Contractor of written instructions on the Pre-final Submittal.

  (6) The NAFI will review the Final Interior Design Phase Submittals, within ___ calendar days and return them to the Contractor for corrections if necessary.

  (7) The NAFI shall deliver the corrected Final Interior Design Phase Submittals within _____ calendar days after receipt by the Contractor of written instructions for correction.

  b. Final inspection and acceptance by the Contractor of the furnishings phase of the project will be accomplished as scheduled by the Contracting Officer.

Continued on CD-ROM

Figure 6.1a
Excerpt from U.S. Navy contract for interior design services.
Excerpted from "Interior Design Contract," www.met.nsvy.mil/ mwrprgms/facdocs/ indesign.rtf.

ASID

ASID Document ID120
RESIDENTIAL INTERIOR DESIGN
SERVICES AGREEMENT

This AGREEMENT is
made this _____ day of _____ in the year of Two Thousand and _____,

BETWEEN the CLIENT:
(name and address)

and the DESIGNER:
(name and address)

The Client and the designer agree as follows:
The project pertains to the following areas within Client's residence located at

_____:

(List areas below)

Financial Issues

Many of the issues negotiated by designers and their clients have to do with reimbursement policy. Designers need to be sure they will be reimbursed for any funds they disperse to pay for goods or services for the client. Is the design firm spending its own money to purchase antiques for the client? If so, the designer might require the client to approve each disbursement in advance—in writing—and either put down a large deposit or pay in full when requested to do so. For installed fabrication or on-site construction, the designer might negotiate a requirement for full payment from the client prior to installation or completion. In addition, a significant retainer may be negotiated to provide the designer with adequate funds to draw on for merchandise deposits and for ongoing expenses.

A designer asked to spend money that will be reimbursed later—for instance, paying an upholsterer—can also negotiate a noncancellation clause preventing the client from canceling approved orders the designer has placed.

Remuneration Issues

Each compensation structure potentially raises issues to be negotiated before an agreement is deemed fair and workable by all parties. For instance, a designer who is being paid a flat fee may wish to negotiate time constraints and to ask for additional remuneration if the project takes longer than anticipated. For a designer who is billing on the basis of square footage, it may make sense to charge more for some project areas than for others. The reception area and entrance to a corporate headquarters may require more detailed specification than the employees' lunchroom and so may be billed at a higher rate.

> Each compensation structure raises issues for negotiation.

If there is downward pressure on your fees during negotiation, it may make sense to add more services rather than to lower your fee. For instance, in a contract-design setting, you might agree to offer a post-occupancy manual for no additional charge. (This may make sense only if you have drafted such a manual previously and can adapt it quickly.) Or you might offer a free facilities-management seminar to aid in maintaining the quality of the interior environment. Value-added services like these can help you maintain a long-term relationship with your client and contribute to the desirable impression that you are, in the words of Arthur M. Gensler, not "in the design business [but] in the design service business."[25]

> In response to downward negotiation pressure, add more services rather than lower your fee.

Issues of Client Responsibility

It may seem that clients, residential or commercial, must necessarily be willing to do all they can to facilitate the completion of their projects in a timely and otherwise satisfactory manner. However, clients who are unfamiliar with the demands of the design process or who do not understand the importance of their role in it may not behave in a manner that encourages progress. The following client responsibilities need to be clearly stated and may need to be negotiated:

- The provision of accurate information in a timely manner—including selections and approvals.
- The arrangement of interviews necessary for adequate programming or for other design purposes.
- Adequate access to the project site not only for the designer but for the general construction contractor and key trade contractors. (The provision of keys is often the subject of intense negotiation. How many sets are to be provided and to whom?)
- Designating a surrogate if, say, business calls a key decision maker out of town for a protracted period.
- Facilitating communication among all professionals hired to work simultaneously on a given set of premises; for example, the computer systems consultant who is setting up the LAN (local area network) may need to collaborate with the interior designer, the general contractor, and the electrical contractor.
- Informing the designer promptly (and preferably in writing) of any designer errors or omissions and of any difficulties with suppliers, fabricators, or contractors that might hinder the progress of the project.

A frequent subject of intense discussion—particularly in the residential field in urban areas—is the issue of who will be responsible for receiving, inspecting, and accepting deliveries, as well as for storage of not only deliveries but the client's existing possessions. These are more problematic issues than they may appear to be at first glance if all members of a client's household are working.

RECEIVING, INSPECTING, AND ACCEPTING DELIVERIES

Delivery must be made to a secure location. Inspection must be thorough and accurate, since often, once delivery has been accepted, it is less credible to report defects or other problems. According to the Uniform Commercial Code—the set of laws governing all commercial transactions—receipt, inspection, and acceptance are the responsibilities of the buyer. Accordingly, paragraph 2.6.12 of ASID form ID100 states that the designer's duties shall not include these activities.[26] However, paragraph 3.5.12 of ID100 states that the activities may be undertaken *on behalf of* the client, which may be a necessary—and billable—option if busy clients are unavailable. Although no one likes to wait for deliveries or to painstakingly inspect merchandise, the agreement between designer and client should tackle this issue rather than ignoring it or assuming that these responsibilities can automatically be delegated to renovation contractors who are "there anyway."

Contractors are usually reluctant to take responsibility for accepting and inspecting deliveries that are not related to the direct performance of their work and are outside the range of their own contracts with clients. For instance, a contractor might be reluctant to accept—and certainly to inspect—a delivery of lamps or furniture; you as designer will promote harmony if the contractor is not asked to do so. In the event of project delay, moreover, it is unwise to assume storage of deliveries (or, for that matter, of a client's existing possessions) on the project premises if the storage would impede the progress of workers actively engaged in renovation under a contractor who has made a fixed-price bid.

STORAGE OF DELIVERIES AND CLIENT POSSESSIONS

Paragraph 4.11 of ID100 states that the client must provide suitable space, not only for receipt and inspection, but for storage. There is good reason for this stipulation, particularly with clients who live in apartments and thus cannot store possessions in a garage or a basement. A veteran renovation contractor tells the story of the client whose new mattress, wrapped in plastic, was delivered while work was still in progress. It was carefully moved from room to room of the apartment undergoing renovation, using up considerable amounts of contractor goodwill and thus placing stress on the designer. However, despite careful wrapping and moving, the foam mattress absorbed the smell of sheetrock dust and paint and was thrown out by the angry clients on move-in day.[27] (Of course, more timely delivery would have helped in this instance.)

Clients may resist ferociously, but it is usually better for everyone involved in the implementation of a design project if clients are not permitted to store delivered items and possessions on the project premises while work is in progress. The designer can strive for a head start in this matter, as the agreement between the designer and client will have an impact on the client's later agreements with construction contractors and fabricators. Like all other facets of an agreement, this one needs to be considered in terms of its implications for the project as a whole and over time. The designer's agreement with the client needs to be written—and may need to be negotiated—as the keystone that will affect the content of all subsequent contracts required for implementation of the design.

Issues of Designer Responsibility

The designer's agreement with the client affects all subsequent contracts required for the project.

Is it reasonable for clients to expect their designers' "best efforts" to control quality and ensure "faithful performance"? "Perfection" is clearly unattainable, but what about standards of "excellence"? Best effort, quality, faithful performance, and excellence are obvious norms to advocate, but they are all highly vulnerable to diverse interpretations. (There is more discussion on the issue of quality in Chapter 7.) Designers may wish to negotiate more specific performance-based monitoring criteria, which will be remunerated. For instance, a designer might agree to make project site or shop visits on a weekly basis, based on an hourly fee, and to report any problems.

Institute performance-based monitoring criteria.

Clients may request that designers function as mediators when disputes arise with fabricators, construction contractors, or suppliers. This can be a stressful and time-consuming role. You need to take into account your overall relationship with the client when deciding whether to accede to such a request. You may not wish to take on responsibilities as a mediator with first-time clients. If you do agree to take on these responsibilities, you would be well advised to clearly specify the exact nature of the responsibility and the basis for remuneration. For instance, your flat fee might cover your attendance at meetings between the client and fabricators, contractors, or suppliers, with a cap on the number of meeting hours covered. Above the cap, you might be paid at an hourly rate. In the course of these meetings and of project review, you may "uncover," in Dan Beert's phrase, issues relating to quality and faithful performance[28]; however, this should not make you responsible for fulfilling the client's expectations if they are unrealistic.

Create a value-added service package.

Rather than agreeing to increased responsibility for slippery judgment-based norms, residential designers can provide a value-added service package that includes such items as a willingness to attend meetings on weekends and seven-day availability for spot telephone consultation. A contract designer's value-added service package might be similar to Arthur M. Gensler's, which includes "services in setting real-estate policy, graphics, management services and facilities management." These value-added services, says Gensler, "benefit our client and enhance our position as a full-service organization."[29] Ideally, residential as well as contract designers should conduct negotiations with Gensler's goals clearly in mind at all times.

Legal Language

Because seemingly simple issues can be of great consequence, designers preparing agreements may be tempted to use high-flown archaic language to impart and reflect the dignity and authority they would like their contracts to express. Yet lawyers themselves have become aware of the need to simplify and clarify the arcane formulations that have characterized many contracts and other documents within the English and American common-law traditions.

Although barely intelligible scribbles or the bald statements contained in invoices or purchase orders can be construed as adequately written contracts, good contemporary legal language, as defined by legal-writing experts, is graceful, plain English—ordinary language that differs from everyday speech most significantly in being more accurate and less ambiguous. "The . . . letter [of agreement] should be businesslike but friendly" states Diane B. Worth, "simple enough to . . . talk . . . through with the client, yet firm enough for each party to understand their responsibilities for the project at hand."[30] Above all, good legal writing in letter or form-based contracts communicates the same clear meaning to all readers.

If you are relying on the language of contract forms such as ASID's, you may suppose that you will not be involved in any legal writing and so do not have to be concerned about appropriate language, as you would when creating a master letter contract. Yet in the rapidly changing world we live in, sooner or later you may find yourself drafting supplemental conditions for which there is no adequate guideline in ID325. Even if you are able to cobble together supplemental conditions from bits of pre-written language, you must fit them together in a manner that is easily comprehensible, without undue repetition, and with proper transition.

Use plain English for legal writing.

In his introduction to *Plain English for Lawyers*,[31] a book that is widely used in law schools, Richard C. Wydick criticizes the murky, arcane language that is sometimes known as "legal English":

> . . . lawyers do not write plain English. [They] use eight words to say what could be said in two. [They] use arcane phrases to express commonplace ideas. Seeking to be precise, [they] become redundant. Seeking to be cautious, [they] become verbose. [Their] sentences twist on, phrase within clause within clause, glazing the eyes and numbing the minds of [their] readers. The result is a writing style that has, according to one critic, four outstanding characteristics. It is "(1) wordy, (2) unclear, (3) pompous, and (4) dull."

Designers crafting agreements (and other documents, for that matter) need as much guidance from Wydick's criticisms as lawyers do. Yet, if you are practicing the guidelines for good plain writing set forth in Chapter 1 of *Writing for Interior Design*, you are already on the way to crafting clear agreements. In addition, here are some tips adapted from *Plain English for Lawyers*:

- *Avoid "lawyerisms" such as aforementioned, whereas,* and *hereinafter.* As Wydick explains, "they give writing a legal smell, but they carry little or no legal substance. [Not only do they baffle and annoy,] . . . they give a false sense of precision and sometimes obscure a dangerous gap in analysis . . . [For] example . . . *aforementioned* is . . . useless [in the following example:] "The fifty-acre plot aforementioned shall be divided . . . " If only one fifty-acre plot has been mentioned before, then *aforementioned* is unnecessary, and if more than one fifty-acre plot has been mentioned before, then *aforementioned* is imprecise. When precision is important, use a specific reference: "The fifty-acre plot described in paragraph 2 (f) shall be divided. . . . "[32]
- *Avoid shotgunning.* This is the practice of stating all the synonyms for a word so that no nuance of meaning will go uncovered. It is comparable, says Wydick, to taking rough aim and letting loose a blast of words, hoping that one of them hits its target. Wydick gives the example of the following statute:

Every person who . . . overdrives, overloads, drives when overloaded, overworks, tortures, torments, deprives of necessary sustenance, drink, or shelter, cruelly beats, mutilates, or cruelly kills any animal, or causes or procures any animal to be so overdriven, overloaded, overworked, tortured, tormented, deprived of necessary sustenance, drink or shelter, or to be cruelly beaten, mutilated, or cruelly killed . . . . is guilty of a crime . . . [33]

Wydick suggests that a writer tempted to shotgun prose like this use a dictionary or thesaurus to find one word that expresses the intended meaning—in this case, *abuse.* If *abuse* is too vague, the best composition strategy may be to define it, then to use the term in a manner that is consistent with the definition.

In like manner, the interior designer who is writing a letter contract may insert definitions parenthetically. One who is working with a form contract may insert definitions as supplemental conditions (more on this practice in Chapter 7) if doing so would make the document clearer to readers. For instance, a designer whose compensation structure is based all or in part on the markup of merchandise purchased for the client might insert a definition of *merchandise*.

- *Place preconditions and exceptions where they are easy to read within sentences.* For our purposes here, a *precondition* is an "if" or if-like statement: if A is true, then B follows. An *exception* is an instance that does not conform to a rule. (D is true, except when E). While there are no strict rules in English to govern the placement of preconditions and exceptions, Wydick proposes the following:

  - Put *short* preconditions or exceptions at the beginnings of sentences.

    Except for the bathroom, the entire apartment shall be painted with Benjamin Moore 2012-60 (Creamy Peach).

  - Put preconditions or exceptions that are *longer than the main clause* at the ends of sentences.

  The entire house shall be painted with Benjamin Moore 2012-60 (Creamy Peach), *except for the bathroom, the children's bedrooms, the kitchen, the breakfast nook, the butler's pantry, the foyer, the library, and the artist's studio.*

- *Watch out for "shall."* Designers who are engaged in legal writing need to watch out for what Wydick calls "words of authority"—words like *must, will, may, should* and their opposites: *must not, will not, may not,* and *should not.* The most problematic authority word, according to Wydick, is *shall,* which sounds "legal" because it is not necessarily a part of everyone's ordinary speech—many people use only *will* to express future tense—and so may seem to impart a high-flown archaic dignity. Legal-writing experts are wary of *shall* because lawyers have used it for such a variety of purposes. Among them are the following:

  - *to impose a duty* ("the client shall pay all invoices submitted by the interior designer within 30 days")

- *to express a future action*
- *to express an entitlement* ("the interior designer shall have the right of approval over client substitutions")

In recent years, according to Wydick, many U.S. legal-writing experts have "come around to the British Commonwealth view; don't use *shall* for any purpose—it is simply too unreliable."[34] Wydick suggests dispensing with *shall* altogether, leaving "a fairly well-behaved roster of words to express duty, permission, discretion, entitlement and the like." He further suggests that these words be "used consistently" with the meanings put forward in Table 6.3.

TABLE 6.3   AUTHORITY WORDS

WORD OF AUTHORITY	MEANING
Must	"Is required to"
Must not	"Is required not to; is disallowed"
May	"Has discretion to; is permitted to"
May not	"Is not permitted to; is disallowed from"
Is entitled to	"Has a right to"
Should	"Ought to"
Will	Expresses a future contingency or
	Expresses the strong party's obligations in a contract between unequals or
	Expresses both parties' obligations in a contract between equals

Adapted from Richard Wydick's Plain English for Lawyers, *4th ed. (Durham, NC: Carolina Academic Press, 1998), 67.*

- *Do not use redundant legal phrases.* Have you ever wondered why lawyers say "null and void" when *null* or *void* would seem to do? Even if we have no idea why such coupled synonyms are in common legal use, it is tempting to use them in order to impart a rich, traditional flavor.

While the use of coupled synonyms is often justified on the grounds that they are legal "terms of art," they are not truly so, according to Wydick, who points out that a "term of art is a short expression," like *hearsay*, "that (a) conveys a fairly well-agreed meaning, and (b) saves the many words that would otherwise be needed to convey that meaning."[35]

Wydick suggests that coupled synonyms continue to be prevalent in legal writing because lawyers have reproduced them from forms used in their offices for many years. Presumably these forms were based on older forms, which were based on older forms, and so these coupled synonyms were passed on like hand-me-down clothes in a large, ancient family. Lawyers resort to them from a sense that they have worked in the past, based on long precedent, while newer and simpler constructions may somehow raise questions.[36] Not even all lawyers, it seems, fully understand why coupled synonyms such as *free and clear, full and complete*, and *good and sufficient* continue to be a part of legal documents.

Interestingly, the use of these coupled synonyms stems from the social and cultural turbulence of long-ago eras. Wydick points to several junctures in the history of England when conquest by outsiders meant that two languages were spoken simultaneously, by members of different parts of the population, who couldn't understand each other very well. Early on, the Celts who lived in what is now England were conquered by the English speaking Anglo-Saxons; later, Latin-speaking Romans conquered the English speakers; still later, French-speaking Normans established hegemany. For many years, lawyers who wished to communicate clearly became accustomed to using words in pairs, one from each of the languages spoken within the bipartite culture of their era. (In the pair *free and clear*, for instance, *free* comes from the Old English *freo*, while *clear* comes from the Old French *cler*.)

Our contemporary American culture is hardly bipartite. In fact, despite our multicultural diversity, we share many features of a common culture, including the language that binds us together. Contemporary American English is relied upon not only by Americans (including those who speak it as a second language), but by speakers of many different languages in far-flung parts of the world. American English-speaking interior designers thus have the benefit of composing agreements in a language that is understood by virtually all other citizens, including many recent immigrants.

The ASID contract forms reflect that, as do the contract forms presented by Crawford and Bruck. If you need to draft new language in response to negotiation, your best shot at effective communication is to emulate these models in terms of simplicity and clarity—good, plain English, with no coupled synonyms—always, of course, subject to the review of an experienced lawyer who specializes in laws affecting design and renovation.

Managing Risk

Although well-composed, readily comprehensible agreement deemed workable by both designer and client is your best hedge against risk, it is not a guarantee of success for the designer-client relationship. A contract must be composed and signed in a context that promotes harmony. Knackstedt urges you to protect yourself by carefully determining the services that your firm will offer a client. As you proceed with negotiation, you should continue to "review your contract carefully to be sure that your firm is able—both practically and legally—to provide the services" in question. "It is more prudent," says Knackstedt, "to offer fewer services—but ones that [your firm] can securely perform—than to offer services that may put the firm in jeopardy."[37]

In addition, you can protect yourself with seven important strategies:

- First, if prospective clients are not already well known to you, run a check on their credit before any agreement is signed. Make sure that they are financially qualified, that is, able to pay and have a history of paying.
- Second, strive for full, clear communication throughout the design process, with frequent approvals.
- Third, check and double-check your drawings and specifications for errors and omissions. If you are responsible for measurements, bear in mind the carpenter's maxim: "Measure twice, cut once."
- Fourth, cite your sources for design detailing. If information is based on architectural drawings or on data provided by the client, say so. If an error is based on faulty information provided by others, you are far less likely to be held liable if your documentation is clear and adequate.
- Fifth, have guarantees (such as for appliances) and certifications (such as for flame proofing) sent directly to the client, not through your office. That way the issuing manufacturers and agencies are responsible, rather than you.

- Sixth, maintain good, long-term relationships with contractors, fabricators, and suppliers, so that they will be willing to provide accurate estimates for budget preparation in the pre-agreement phase and to work out small implementation problems before they become larger, with the smallest possible inconvenience to your client and to you.

- Seventh, discuss disagreements with clients in a common-sense manner before any disputes become bitter enough to require arbitration or litigation. Even if you are confident that you are entirely in the right, respond to a client's sense of injury with an understanding that in design projects, as in other business transactions, "the customer is always right," though this should not mean that anyone must unfairly absorb loss.

In one legendary case, the 90-year-old widow of a famous French artist—a celebrated artist in her own right—moved from Paris to New York with a personal museum of priceless artwork. Although the vintage apartment into which she was moving lacked adequate wiring for contemporary living, and, in particular, adequate general lighting in most rooms, the owner asked that no distracting light switches appear on the walls that were to display her artistic legacy. Although the designer, the general contractor, and the electrical contractor remonstrated with her, repeatedly suggesting that she authorize the wiring of switch boxes before the walls were repaired and painted, she refused. Only after the wall finishes had been applied did she change her mind, insisting that—her instructions to the contrary notwithstanding—French designers and contractors would have inserted switches near the entries of the various rooms, rather than forcing her to feel her way through dark rooms to table or floor lamps.

The omissions the designer stood to be charged with were not true omissions, but responses to clear client requests. The contractors likewise had complied with the client's wishes and could not be expected to open the walls, insert the switch boxes, rewire as needed, and repair and repaint the walls at no charge. Even though the paper trail clearly documented the widow's stubbornness and the designers' and contractors' meticulous concern, no one connected with the project thought it appropriate to leave the ancient widow in distress.

The arbitration clause was not invoked, nor did the parties to the dispute go to court. Rather, they sat down and worked out a compromise whereby the penalty bonus clause in the construction agreement between client and general contractor was amended, and the client got her wall switches. The designer charged less than the usual fee for design work associated with the switches, the client paid less than the going rate for the additional electrical work required, and the general contractor charged a lower-than-usual markup. In the abstract realm of logic, the client was entirely in the wrong. However, in the concrete realm of ordinary experience where interior designers must practice, the client is rarely wrong even when wrong.[38] As a designer, you need to pick your battles carefully, understanding that compromise with your clients (and with contractors, fabricators, and merchants) is bound to bring about a more satisfactory resolution than the rocky road through mediation, arbitration, and litigation. Such recourses need to be specified in your otherwise airtight and comprehensive agreements, but truly they are a last resort.

Pick your battles carefully; compromise where possible.

Discussion Questions

1. Which model for the interior design profession do you prefer: the old model of compensation through the sale of materials and furnishings or the new consultative model? Provide a rationale for your choice in terms of your geographic region, your area of specialization within the field of ID, and the client base that you would like to serve.

2. What are the differences between the design business and the design-service business, and how would those differences be reflected in agreements and contracts?

3. As you envision the ideal design practice for your ambitions, talents, and interests, what value-added services do you imagine yourself supplying to clients? Why?

Exercises

1. Interview an interior designer to discover what compensation structures he or she is most likely to use for typical purposes in his or her practice. Prepare a brief oral presentation for your class. Using techniques discussed in Chapter 3, classify the data gathered by your class and present them in a table using the resources of a word-processing or spreadsheet program. If your class has a Web site, post the table (with proper formatting and any appropriate annotation). Invite comment from the interior design community within your university. If relevant, post the best comments.

2. Create a narrative in which you imagine the worst possible set of contingencies resulting in serious disagreement between a designer and client. Read all students' narratives aloud in class and choose the "worst" one—that is, the most horrifying. Let someone write it on the blackboard.

Divide into as many groups of four as possible in which one student takes on the role of the designer, one the role of the client, one the role of the arbitrator, one the role of note taker. (Additional students may be assigned as note takers to various groups.) Let each group role-play the arbitration of the differences presented in the narrative. After a given period of time, the note takers will report on what they observed in their groups. Then the entire class will discuss what took place in the groups.

3. Draft a supplemental condition defining a term in an ASID or other master contract.

4. Divide once again into small groups and compare the Navy contract found in its entirety on your CD-ROM with the sample residential ASID contract also found in its entirety on your CD-ROM. (Let each group be assigned one or more of the elements found in Table 6.1.) Let the work of comparison be guided by the following question: If the ASID contract were your firm's master agreement, how would you react to the contract offered by the Navy?

7

Contracts for Construction and Fabrication

When an agreement with a client has been signed and design intent has been established, designers begin to prepare the documents that provide a footing for all work to be performed to renovate the premises. Based on *specifications*—detailed, itemized descriptions of design criteria—bids will be solicited for any construction or fabrication required to shape and articulate interior space. Of course, much of an interior designer's traditional role involves the purchase of items from manufacturers' regular product lines. (Purchasing is covered in Chapter 8.) This chapter examines the role of the interior designer in helping to negotiate contracts for work by construction contractors and custom fabricators.

Construction Contracts

Historically, construction of walls and other "hard" structures has been the professional realm of architects, while interior designers have occupied themselves with the "soft" applications that transform structures into comfortable, usable, and expressive spaces. Nowadays, the line between architecture and interior design is blurrier than it once was. "Professionals who can integrate . . . [the] supposedly opposite skills [of architecture and interior design] are newly empowered to . . . invent a . . . design vocabulary that will merge the best features of [both professions], thus reinventing domestic space in a manner that expands our sense of its possibilities."[1] Of course, interior designers are not legally permitted to issue drawings for construction; most interior designers are comfortable working with registered architects if significant structural alterations need to be made.

Work with a registered architect if significant structural alterations need to be made.

Collaborating with Architects

Indeed, where structural integrity is affected, interior design firms sometimes employ architects to review designs, or architects may be retained by interior design firms on a freelance basis as needed. After careful perusal and any necessary revision, the architects stamp, or sign off on, the design documents.[2] More typically, clients hire and pay separately the architects needed for construction projects, whether to provide design services or to prepare documents for filing with building departments, which require the stamp of a licensed architect on plans and other pertinent drawings. A licensed architect carries difficult-to-obtain and costly errors-and-omissions insurance and is legally liable for design-based error. In no case should interior designers practice in areas where they are not licensed[3]; yet interior designers are often integrally involved in construction projects and have many roles to perform.

Interior designers should practice only in areas in which they are licensed.

The Multiple Roles of the Interior Designer in Reviewing Construction

Wherever space is being put to work on behalf of clients, interior designers can play a crucial role in cost-estimating, in monitoring the time line to make sure the project stays on schedule, and, above all, in monitoring and maintaining standards of quality. They may play an important role in "helping clients get their spaces to help them."[4] In all these roles, the interior designer must know how to read a construction contract and must be able to decipher its language or languages. The designer's agreement with the client will clearly state the nature of the designer's participation. In some cases, the interior designer will be the consultant for clients in matters relating to the construction project. In other cases, an interior designer may function as a construction coordinator, a surrogate for the owner, or an important witness.

In putting built space to work for clients, interior designers can play an important role.

THE INTERIOR DESIGNER AS THE CLIENT'S CONSULTANT

Even on projects supervised by architects, an interior designer may function as the owner's consultant, providing more detailed assistance in such matters as paint colors and window treatments than an architect may be willing or able to provide. Clients hire and depend on interior designers to make sure the spaces enclosed by built structures will help them with their lives or their businesses. As a consultant, the interior designer may be interpreting, or reinterpreting, a construction contract for the client—providing that extra, disinterested eye that can be so crucial in ensuring quality.

In a contract-design setting, consulting service may include space planning in the final stages of building selection. A developer hires an interior design firm to make a quick study of the client's space needs and to see whether they are a good fit in an available space. Often, the client is deciding between several buildings; the interior designer helps the client estimate potential build-out costs, better negotiate the terms of a lease, and shorten the turnaround time. The interior designer receives a flat fee from the developer or a real estate broker of just pennies per square foot. Because consultive service may lead to a contract for full-service design, many designers accept the low fee and rapid time line. In a contract-design setting, interior designers may also consult on tenant standards development, architectural programming, facility audits, move relocation plans, asset management, identity packaging, and a host of other related—and non-traditional—interior-design roles.

In a residential design setting, some real estate agents, developers, remodeling contractors, and building firms offer as an added service to their clients the assistance of interior designers as construction-related shopping consultants. According to Linda W. Case, president of Remodeling Consulting Services, "One of the most difficult production problems" faced by remodelers and custom builders is getting their clients to make shopping selections "in a timely fashion." Case explains[5] some of the problems home buyers and owners may have:

> Today's [home buyer] is most of all short of time. Yet the [home buyer's shopping] choices may involve long lead times because they must be special ordered. . . . Without any guidance, [home buyers] often go off track and choose materials that will not fit, will not match, or that present technical problems.

Case asserts that builders and others who hire interior designers to assist custom-home buyers usually pay the designer a flat fee for assisting with purchases such as door knobs and lighting fixtures that are necessary for construction to proceed. Although home buyers will take varying amounts of a designer's consulting time to make all the needed selections and purchases, presumably the home buyers who make decisions quickly will balance out with those who make decisions more slowly.[6]

The flat fee to which Case alludes is not the "flat rate" describe by ASID for design services ranging from conceptual development through layouts, specifications, and final installation.[7] Arguably it is not a fee for design services at all, since it is charged for shopping without clear design intent. Although the home buyer is ultimately charged for the designer's services, which are factored into the cost of the home, the designer is in fact employed by the developer, builder, or real estate agent, whose interest is not in *which* faucet or kitchen flooring is purchased, but only in a timely selection that is technically feasible

Paying a designer the same fee for clients who require a lot of shopping consultation as for those who require a little encourages the designer to support not quality choices, but speedy decisions.

Bob Prest, a custom design-builder interviewed by Case, sends clients to an interior designer "as soon as the slab [the foundation for the home] is poured" to help with shopping, "with particular emphasis on those choices (such as the tub or shower) that affect early construction phases. . . . " Typically, reports Prest, home buyers "use 30 to 40 hours to make selections." Prest pays a designer a set fee for each custom-home buyer assisted plus so many cents for each square foot of the home. According to Prest, "Clients don't seem to abuse the number of allotted hours. I think they get tired of the selection process."[8]

As well they might! This speeded-up assembly-line version of an interior designer's role seems to exhaust the potential of a bond with a prospect; yet, according to Linda Case, some designers charge low fees to undercut competition for this type of consulting, using it as a referral mechanism that generates leads for more lucrative business arrangements directly with home buyers. The designers, Case explains, "may be able to sell the client curtains, carpet, furniture, and accessories"[9] that are not part of the construction process, as are shower heads and drawer pulls, and so would be subject to the designer's usual markup.

The merchandise-based model of interior design that Case presents is at odds, of course, with the increasing professionalization of interior design noted by observers such as Don Bowden (see Chapter 6). From the designer's point of view as well as the client's, it is best if the designer is employed by the home buyer, not by the developer or builder. In that way, interior designers fulfil their historic role as intermediary; are able to offer the full range of design services; and position themselves to monitor quality as well as efficiency.

It is best for designer and client if the designer is employed by a home owner, not a developer or builder.

THE INTERIOR DESIGNER AS CONSTRUCTION COORDINATOR

Where the scope of construction work involves repair and renovation of existing interior spaces, with no significant structural changes, an interior designer may advise in the preparation of the construction contract between the client and a multitrade construction contractor, known as a *general contractor*. The interior designer may be asked to verify that the terms outlined in the contractor's general conditions and agreement keep the client's best interest in mind. Most experienced commercial interior designers know how to read a construction contract and are able to anticipate situations where trouble may arise if important issues are omitted from the agreement.

In some cases, interior designers recommend teams of trade contractors that they themselves have assembled, and there is no general contractor, or GC. In such situations, the designer becomes the construction coordinator, with far greater involvement than when there is a GC. In that case, the designer may be responsible for soliciting bids; for selecting a range of single-trade contractors; for facilitating contracts between them and the owner; and for scheduling and reviewing their work. Unless a designer wants to submit a fixed-price bid covering all relevant trades and to obtain licensing and insurance as a general contractor, the construction contract will be between the client-owners and the relevant trade contractors, even if this means that the designer must forego the customary markup on materials such as tile selected, and perhaps even provided, by the designer.

> A designer who is not properly licensed and insured must not function as a general contractor in offering design-build services.

A contract for construction that includes design services—so-called "design-build"—may be offered by a designer who is licensed as a general contractor. A design-build business, offering one-stop shopping, improved accuracy of estimating, and efficient completion, usually offers separate contracts for design and for construction, although some firms combine the design and construction phases into one contract.[10]

"Design-build" does *not* mean construction *management* plus design services. It means that a designer has taken responsibility for the construction work *itself* by becoming the contractor. Design-build contracts are tricky, in a legal sense, and should be developed in consultation with an attorney specializing in construction law, who will also advise the designer-builder on the appropriate manner to structure a design-build business to avoid any liability that may stem from increased accountability. (The services of an architect may be required.) Perceived conflicts of interest may ensue when the traditional independence of the designer is folded into the contractor's role.

THE INTERIOR DESIGNER AS OWNER'S SURROGATE

In cases where a client or owner is in another city—preparing to relocate, perhaps—or engaged in long-distance commutation, an interior designer may function as the owner's designated representative, making decisions on behalf of the owner. In those cases, the interior designer is functioning not merely as a consultant, but as an owner's surrogate. It is not uncommon for a wealthy, busy client with far-flung interests to provide an interior designer with a budget and a mandate to create a certain kind of home—perhaps a *pied à terre* (lodging for occasional use) in a lively urban setting or perhaps a country home in a wilderness location. A designer entrusted with the responsibilities of an alter ego, or other self, usually has completed previous projects for the client and has a well-developed familiarity with the client's taste.

An out-of-town client may ask a designer to function as a surrogate to create an interior setting.

THE INTERIOR DESIGNER AS WITNESS

The designer is not a party to the standard construction contract between an owner and a contractor. However, designers not only help to prepare contracts but are present as witnesses at contract signings. This presence focuses attention on the designer's later role in reviewing ongoing work, helping to ensure that a realistic schedule is projected, and ascertaining that no corners are cut with materials or procedures. An owner and a contractor may be meeting for the first time at the contract signing; already, then, the designer, who knows both and has likely brought them together, is functioning as intermediary.

Designers are not parties to construction contracts but help to prepare them and witness signings.

The Master Contract

The novice interior designer who is called upon to provide a construction contract for a client's negotiation and signature may find the prospect daunting. Much is at stake. It would be expensive and risky to prepare a construction contract from scratch. Even an attorney would not attempt that, but would use a template that incorporated the wisdom and experience of previous contract writers. The development of a unique master construction contract is a "major project involving both considerable time and expense."[11] Once it is in your computer, you can print it whenever you need it, nicely formatted. However, you also have the option of using a purchased standard contract as the master; and, indeed, this is an option that designers frequently exercise. Like any unique master a designer may develop, a standard construction contract permits the inclusion of customized material; it functions as a "wrapper" for the named, enumerated documents contained within each contract. Thus, a contract for construction is actually a set of documents.

A particular agreement is developed from a standard or master contract.

The Contract Documents

In addition to the basic Agreement between Owner and Contractor, the documents consist of scope statement and specifications, drawings, conditions, addenda, and amendments, including a negotiated payment schedule. The general contractor's bid may also be folded in.

The contract documents consist of:
- **The basic agreement.**
- **Scope statement and specifications.**
- **Drawings.**
- **Conditions.**
- **Addenda.**
- **Amendments.**
- **The GC's bid.**

The contract thus constituted includes the languages of owner, contractor, and advisory parties such as interior designer, architect, or the client's or contractor's attorney. Differences in these languages reflect the relationship structure that the contract represents; they function as a trigger for the healthy negotiation that results in a contract deemed fair and workable by all parties.

Project Description and Scope Statement

All project descriptions and scope statements (and the specification sets that derive from them) are organized as a response to the unstated question: What type and quality of work needs to be done to bring the project premises into conformity with the interior designer's (and client's) vision? Crucial to the usefulness of scope statements is the quality of observation behind the writing. Did the designer carefully observe the existing conditions prevalent in the premises to be worked on? Did the designer carefully think through the work that needs to be done? Are the estimates of the areas to be worked on accurate and plausible? It is helpful for the designer to break the project down into sections or categories of greater or lesser priority, indicating work that could be postponed or removed if there is a budget problem. As discussed in Chapter 6, the scope of work may be divided into phases representing the likely progress of the job. Since the scope statement is created earlier than the specifications, the designer needs to be forward looking in writing it. In general, the orderly and thorough performance of work is furthered by specifications that are consistent with the scope statement and read as a logical outgrowth of it.

Specifications for Construction

Specifications are formally defined as "that portion of the Contract Documents consisting of the written requirements for materials, equipment, systems, standards and workmanship for the Work, and performance of related services."[12] Frequently running 50 to 100 pages for a comprehensive renovation of a two-bedroom apartment,[13] specifications set forth the quality or grade of work to be performed within a previously agreed-upon scope.

The specs should be consistent with the scope statement and read as a logical outgrowth of it.

Because of the legal ramifications of specification writing, virtually all designers use as templates the master specifications created by experts that describe standard materials and methodologies. You can browse one compilation of specs, including standard construction details, at http://www.aecinfo.com. Manufacturers also provide sets of guide specifications to assist designers who wish to specify their products. For instance, if you wanted to specify polished concrete masonry units for a fireplace surround or a foyer, you might rely on the products and guide specifications of E. Dillon & Company of Swords Creek, Virginia. It is to be found at www.edillon.com. Of course, you would have to edit these and other guide specifications for your project. E. Dillon[14] provides useful tips on how to do so:

> The E. Dillon & Company guide specifications will need to be edited by the specifier for a specific project and to reflect the products, options, and applications being used. The guide sections have been written so that most editing can be accomplished by deleting unnecessary requirements and options. Depending on project requirements, some additional information will need to be added by the specifier. Options are indicated by [ ]. Notes to assist the specifier in selecting options and editing the specification guides are printed in bold and indicated with ****. For final editing, all brackets and notes will need to be deleted from the guides. For example:
>
> **** Premier Line Polished Face CMU units can be provided with one or more vertical scores per face.****
>
> Face pattern: Polished, smooth, flat face [scored with [one] [____] vertical false head joints].

Guide specification sets confirm designers' sense of correct practice and help them protect themselves in the event of a lawsuit. The writing designer is responsible for the coherence of specs for each project, for their accuracy, and for their precise correlation with drawings, samples, and other visual materials.

Use master and guide spec sets as templates to create your own.

THE LANGUAGE OF SPECIFICATIONS

In the specifications for a given project, the designer states the precise requirements for quality construction in each particular instance. So important is the language of specifications that, in any legal dispute that may arise, the words are considered to take precedence over the drawings! Therefore, it is very important for the designer to get those words right, to say everything that needs to be said, and to say it all clearly, but not to say more than is necessary.

As you can see in Figure 7.1, specifications are usually *streamlined*—that is, phrased concisely, with unnecessary articles and pronouns omitted. The use of

Figure 7.1
The Modulite illuminated ceiling system is an extremely versatile interior skylight. Modulite's pyramidal design and miniature scale are ideally suited for multiple or single-unit applications in limited space.
Excerpt from Manufacturer's Specifications for Modulite Skylight Ceiling, American Decorative Ceilings. ©2000 American Decorative Ceilings, http://www. americandecorative ceilings.com. All rights reserved.

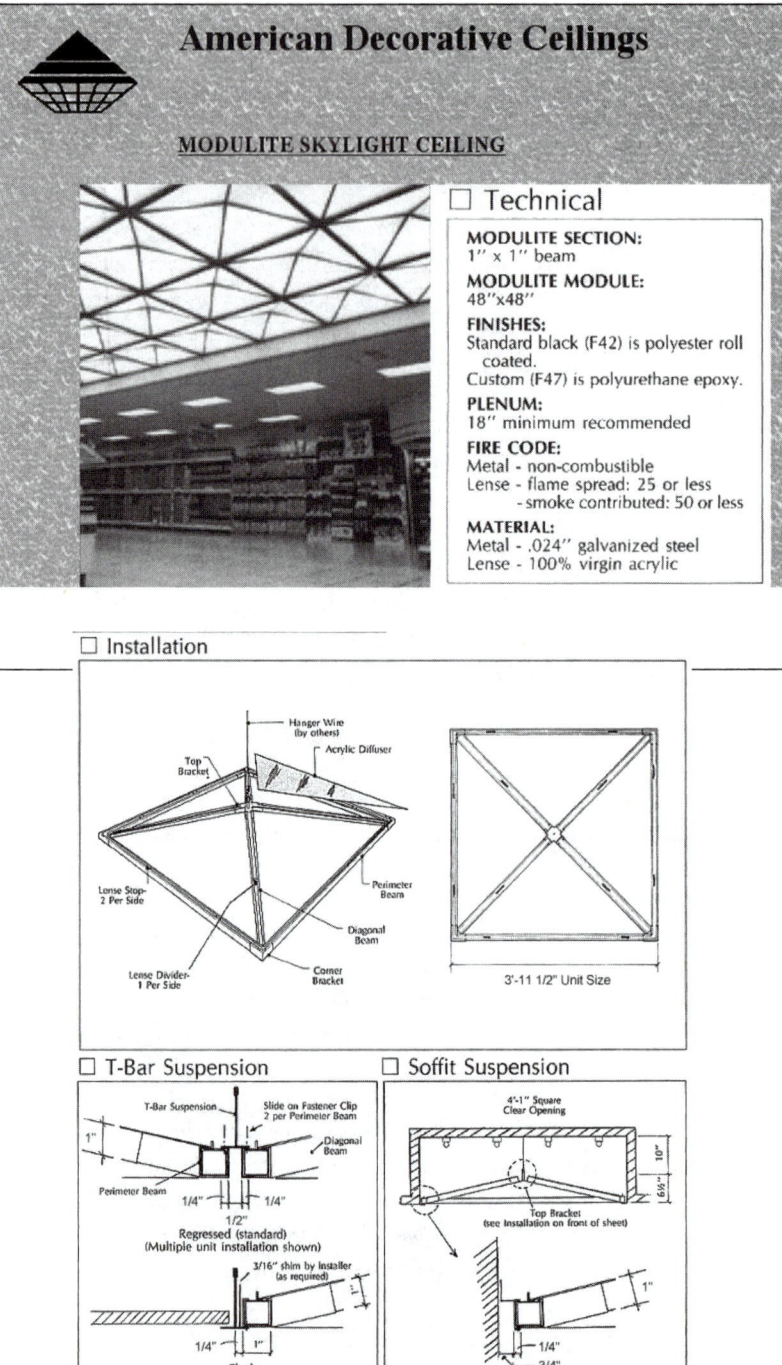

Figure 7.1
(continued)

SPECIFICATION

PART 1 - GENERAL (See typical "General" section of "Typical Specification")

PART 2 - PRODUCTS

2.01 MANUFACTURER

A. Illuminated ceiling system shall be "Modulite" model number LML44-F42 (if finish is other than black, insert appropriate number from Section 2.02G. below), as manufactured by American Decorative Ceilings, Inc.; 4158 E. 71st St.; Cleveland, Ohio 44105; Telephone number (216) 341-2222, Fax number (216) 341-8501.

2.02 MATERIALS

A. All suspension members to be constructed of the following:

    1. Material: 24 Gage galvanized steel with zinc plating to inhibit rust.
    2. Finish: Two part polyurethane epoxy.
    3. Profile: 1" x 1" beams as indicated on Installation Drawings.
    4. Edge Trim Profile: As indicated on Installation Drawings

B. Perimeter beams shall be of standard lengths, formed into channel sections with stabilizing returns on top of section for uniform rigidity. Dimensions of beams as indicated on Installation Drawings.

C. Diagonal beams are of same profile as perimeter beams.

D. Corner brackets to be factory fabricated from the same materials as Perimeter Beams are installed at all corners for smooth uniform transitions. Insert beam members into connectors as indicated on Installation Drawings, and secure with exposed decorative tek-screw provided by ceiling manufacturer.

E. Acrylic diffuser to be manufactured from 100% virgin acrylic, with a maximum temper set of 25, and a roll stress relief of 5. Minimum thickness to be 0.080", color to be milk white, and sizes to be factory pre-cut.

F. Lense stops and lense separators to be provided by the manufacturer at locations per Installation Drawings. Said brackets to ensure the proper alignment of lenses with the metal suspension components.

G. Finish to be (black (F42)), (white (F41)), (medium bronze (F44)), or (custom color (F47)) (strike out all non-applicable finishes)

2.03 FABRICATION

A. Fabrication of glazed acrylic diffusers and metal suspension system to be factory cut, mitered, and notched. All intersections are to be factory mitered for easy abutting joints. ONLY MINOR FIELD FABRICATION WILL BE ACCEPTED.

B. Fasteners through-out shall be electroplated galvanized steel of proper design and strength to accomplish fastening purpose.

PART 3 - EXECUTION (See typical "Execution" section of "Typical Specification")

Proofread
streamlined specs
for coherence.

for, *of*, and other prepositions may be minimized. Streamlining usually places the subject first, foregrounding keywords for quick reference. Sometimes a colon replaces the words *shall be* or *to be*, which are included by inference. Proofread carefully to make sure that coherence has been maintained in brevity.

Like other technical writing, specifications are precise and factual. Quantities, amounts, materials, and procedures are clearly spelled out. Because the primary audience for specifications is highly knowledgeable, the designer employs technical and trade terms that accurately and quickly convey meaning. Abbreviations are used to save time and space but are clearly defined.

In the simple examples below, from the plans for a residential townhouse renovation in New York City, the words *gypsum* and *spackle* are not explained. Readers are assumed to know that gypsum is the common mineral (hydrated calcium sulphate) used to make cements, plasters, and *sheetrock*, or gypsum wall board, while spackle is a powder (containing gypsum plaster and glue) that when mixed with water forms a paste used to fill cracks and holes in plaster or sheetrock walls.

TOWNHOUSE CONSTRUCTION SPECIFICATION:
EXAMPLE # 1
gwb   new gypsum wall board. New 5/8" FC (firecode) GWB walls. Tape and spackle smooth so that when viewed from any angle wall is flat. Prime with Benjamin Moore Latex Quick Dry Prime Seal. Finish with two coats Benjamin Moore Regal Wall Satin. Provide 10 square-foot color SAMPLES in place as required. Color to be specified (no more than 3 colors per room).

TOWNHOUSE CONSTRUCTION SPECIFICATION:
EXAMPLE #2
mr gwb   new moisture-resistant gypsum wall board. New 5/8" FC (firecode) MR GWB walls. Tape and spackle smooth so that when viewed from any angle wall is flat. Prime with Benjamin Moore Latex Quick Dry Prime Seal. Finish with two coats Benjamin Moore Regal Wall Satin. Provide 10 square-foot color SAMPLES in place as required. Color to be specified (no more than 3 colors per room).

Note that in each of the townhouse specifications, the writer has started at the beginning and proceeded in sequential steps to the end, creating an orderly process analysis (see Chapter 3). The townhouse specifications do not need to refer to drawings or other visual materials, as in Figure 7.1, where such references are needed.

Townhouse specification examples 1 and 2 may appear to be identical. The second one, however, is for moisture-resistant gypsum wallboard, known in the building trades as "green board," whereas the first is for ordinary gypsum wallboard. Otherwise, the two specifications *are* identical. The writer is restating best-practice procedures in order to ensure quality and to provide the client with legal protection against shoddy workmanship. Likewise, the phrase "no more than three colors per room" is repeated to protect designer and contractor against client indecision and excessive fussiness that would result in unbillable hours of handholding. It is not necessary for this kind of writing to be inventive, only accurate, thorough, and precise.

Specification writing, you will note, combines description with *prescription*, the writing of authoritative rules or instructions. Most of us are familiar with the instructions that come with computers, toasters, washing machines, automobiles, and other devices and mechanisms that require a precise method of operation. As an aid to clarity, many instructions are formatted as numbered lists to emphasize that the order in which tasks are performed matters. For consistency among quantities of specs and to ease information retrieval, related groups of numbered specs are frequently divided into numbered sections dealing with General, Product, and Execution specs. The instructions in the simple townhouse specifications are not formatted so elaborately; but consistent with their prescriptive purpose, the required procedures are presented as sequential steps in the order in which they likely will be performed.

Like other instructions, specs are often written using the *imperative*, or command, mode—"tape and spackle," "finish with two coats"—to announce that the instruction is not meant to be contested. A command sentence contains no subject, only a verb. It says "do it," without saying who is to do it, although "you" is implicit in the command. The "you" presumed to be reading the specifications is a contractor, fabricator, or vendor who is legally responsible to the owner for performing the specified actions exactly as instructed. It is also possible to write specifications in the *indicative*, or objective mode. ("The contractor will tape and spackle.") However, the imperative mode conveys the designer's responsibility to prescribe correct methods and materials of high quality.

Correctness and quality are especially important when writing specifications that affect people's safety and health, such as those for fire doors, staircases, balconies, and plumbing fixtures. The Web site for IIDA pro-vides a page of useful links facilitating building code research to help inte-rior designers write specifications that conform to code in various localities. They are to be found at http://www.iida.com/legislation/codeOrglinks.html.

The number of drawers in a built-in chest may not be as consequential as the number of windows required for a room in a given locality, but clients expect accuracy in small matters as well as large. A client who has ordered a pickled-pine floor inlaid with fruitwood-stained maple wants the best-qual-ity woods and adequate coats of finish to create the desired coverage and sheen. Likewise, if no roller marks are acceptable on a painted wall, then it is best to say so in specifications and accompanying notes, leaving no doubt in the minds of contractors.

THE ORGANIZATION OF SPECIFICATIONS

The language of specs:
- Is precise and factual.
- Employs technical and trade terms.
- Uses abbreviations but defines them.
- Uses sequential steps to provide orderly process analysis.
- Refers to drawings as needed.
- Ensures quality by stating best-practice procedures.
- Combines description with prescription.
- Uses numbering to aid in classification and retrieval.
- Uses the impera-tive to convey authority.

Much of the language of any designer's specifications, or specs, will likely be taken from sets of master specifications, which are typically classified under the sixteen categories of work used in the CSI Master Format (Figure 7.2).

Compilations of specs classified in this manner are found at http://www.aecinfo.com and in catalogs such as *Sweet's*. Most of the Construction Specification Institute Format categories are logical from the standpoint of those who must actually perform the work, for example, *Category 16: Electrical*. Other categories may not be. *Category 05: Metals* groups the manufactured metal studs used in the construction of walls with stainless steel brackets custom-welded for hardwood cabinets. This grouping may not make sense to a GC, since the cost of the studs would be included in the formula for pricing walls by square-foot area, while the brackets would be fabricated by a subcontractor. That is to say, the coherence of the "Metals" category may seem purely abstract to the contractor, with no prac-tical use in the experiential realm in which work must be priced, assigned, and performed.

If specifications are not organized in a manner that facilitates general contractor's pricing, they may need to rearrange the specifications and clas-sify them within their own categories. A contractor who misses something in this act of translation and thus underbids the job may run out of money needed to complete the project in a timely manner. Clients have legal reme-dies should this occur, but if their homes or offices are not ready by the specified move-in dates, they may justly blame not only the contractor, but also the designer.

In general, the orderly and thorough performance of work is furthered by a classification of specifications that is consistent with the scope statement and clarifies the nature and extent of the work to be performed. Some typical spec classifications are trade- or work-based; room-based; and hybrid.

TRADE-OR-WORK-BASED SPECIFICATION SETS   The CSI format categories represent division by trades, for example, painting, general construction, plumbing, electrical work, and so on. This breakdown is particularly useful for a large project. Small but important specialty items in a particular part of a space such as, say, custom-fabricated radiator grilles in the dining room may be grouped under the heading "Special Projects."

ROOM-BASED SPECIFICATION SETS   Specs may also be divided and classified by room or area of the project premises, for example, the residence, bathroom, kitchen, TV room, and so on. This breakdown makes sense on a walk

> Typical classifications of construction specs are:
> * Trade or work-based
> * Room-based
> * Hybrid

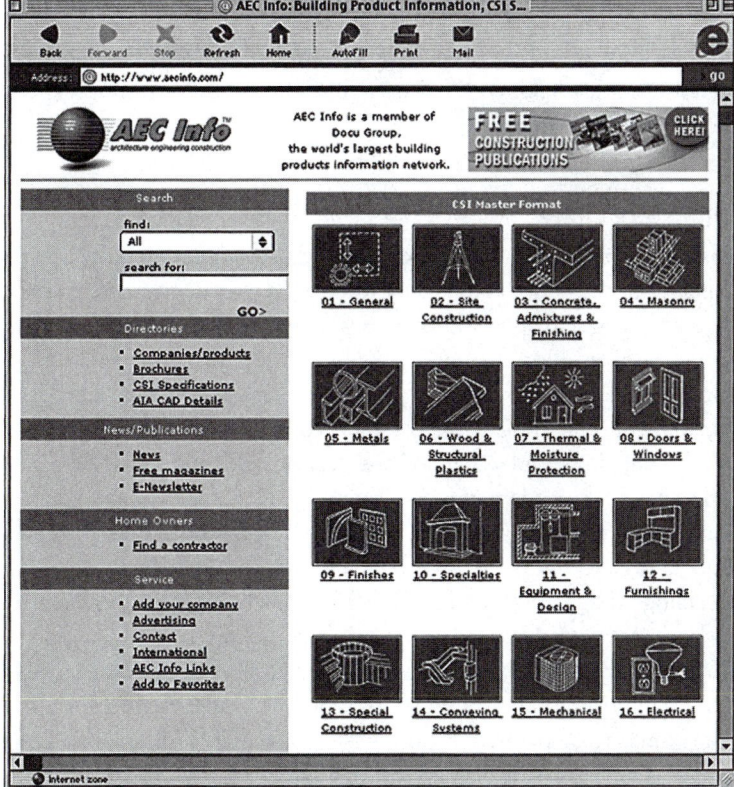

Figure 7.2
The master format of the Construction Specification Institute (CSI).
Courtesy, AEC Info, member of DocuGroup. *http://www. aecinfo.com*

through the premises and is easily comprehensible to all involved in a project, which can facilitate discussion. However, it is more appropriate for small projects than for large ones; it can lead to confusing repetition for large projects. For instance, there may need to be painting in every room. If there is no painting schedule, general contractors must pull out the painting specs for each room, assemble them in their own "painting" classification, and then generate a bid based on what they would have to pay the painting contractor for the total amount of painting involved in the project.

HYBRID SPECIFICATION SETS   The hybrid classification divides specs by room or project area as well as by trade or work category, without undue concern for the niceties of parallel construction that are paramount in most other kinds of writing. A flexible hybrid breakdown avoids repetition and makes it less necessary for GCs to translate specifications into categories meaningful to them. For instance, even if most of the specifications are organized by room, it makes sense to group painting, plumbing, and electrical work under appropriate trade-based headings on their own schedules. Be sure to provide adequate cross-referencing if your classification is hybrid. For instance, in a specification set for "Office 1," you might indicate that painting is specified on the painting schedule.

Schedules and Other Drawings

Schedules show the full scope of a given type of work in a graphically simple manner.

Specifications are frequently correlated with *schedules*, or sets of related work-performance items tabulated by room and by trade to create graphically simple and effective displays both representing and breaking down the full scope of any given kind of work. Schedules are part of *the drawings*, "the graphic and pictorial portions of the Contract Documents showing the design, location and dimensions of the Work, importantly including," in addition to schedules, "plans, elevations, sections, details . . . and diagrams."[15] The drawings for a residential renovation might include, for instance, a door schedule and a window schedule. There might also be a plumbing-fixture schedule that is accompanied by *cut sheets*, images and descriptions copied from catalogs like *Sweet's* of items such as toilets, sinks, or shower stalls. Similarly, an appliance schedule might be accompanied by cut sheets showing images of a refrigerator, a kitchen range, and a dishwasher.

There is almost certain to be a finish schedule, indicating how each plane of each room is to be painted or otherwise finished, including walls, ceilings, and floors. The treatment of the walls, ceilings, and floors of any closets or built-in shelf units or cabinets would also be specified.

Note that the simplified excerpt from an imaginary finish schedule presented as Table 7.1 contains the abbreviations *gwb* and *mr gwb*. These refer the contractor to the two townhouse specifications mentioned earlier in this chapter for gypsum wallboard and moisture-resistant gypsum wallboard. There are also references in Table 7-1 to *T-1* and *T-3*. These abbreviations refer the contractor to tile specifications (not shown) that would prescribe the finish of surfaces designated T-1 and T-3, respectively.

The precise elements of a project are best represented in linear fashion in the specifications lists, while the full extent of a type of work is correlated to the specifications more graphically in schedules. Still other elements are best represented in a plan. The nature and complexity of a particular project will dictate the most effective way to represent its various elements. For instance, a small, partial renovation may require only ten electrical "points," or intervals at which boxes interrupt the wiring system for ultimate connection of electrical devices such as outlets (receptacles for plugs), switches, dimmers, and light fixtures. (Some appliances, such as air conditioners and heaters, may also be "hard-wired" through boxes rather than plugged in after move-in by the client.) The insertion of these ten points may easily be described in the scope statement and specifications; no other documentation is required.

A more complicated electrical system may have hundreds of points, or thousands. For instance, a complete renovation of a two-bedroom apartment may require the wiring of two hundred or more points![16] There may be separate wiring systems for telephony, computers, cable TV, and audio speakers, all to be installed by the electrical contractor. These points are usually indicated with symbols on a plan, so that the designer, the GC, the electrician, and others involved with the project can see at a glance what is needed and where it is needed.

Contractors will base their fixed-price bids on the designer's drawings, specifications, and scope statement, so it is crucial that these documents be accurate, thorough, and well observed. The bidding process is discussed more fully later in the chapter. When a bid for construction has been accepted, the documents on which it is based are folded into the master agreement and become part of it.

TABLE 7.1   FINISH SCHEDULE

	FLOOR	WALL: NORTH	WALL: EAST	WALL: WEST	WALL: SOUTH	CEILING
Bathroom	See T-1	See T-3		mr gwb	mr gwb	mr gwb
Bedroom 1	gwb					

Excerpt from Simplified Fictional Finish Schedule

General Conditions

The work that is enumerated in the contract documents has been priced and will be executed under a set of *conditions*, or assumptions on which rest the validity of the agreement. The general conditions establish policy in matters relating to such issues as disputes—whether serious arguments are settled in court or by arbitration—and *warranties* (guarantees that the work is properly executed and free of defects). The conditions establish the duration of a warranty and what it encompasses. Other matters typically covered in the general conditions of a construction contract[17] include:

- Compliance with local codes
- Responsibility for obtaining any necessary building permits
- Ownership of plans
- Changes to the scope of work—submission, administration, and approval
- Insurance (who carries how much)
- Responsibility for existing hazardous conditions
- Termination or cancellation of the contract
- Responsibility for payment of lawyers' fees if a dispute arises
- Liens (the right to another's property if an obligation is not discharged)

These and other conditions spell out the terms under which a contract applies. As shown in Table 7.2, the General Conditions set forth in AIA document A201-1997 are arranged by numbered paragraph within fourteen articles. (The CD-ROM presents additional material from this document.)

The difficulties that many general conditions were written to counter will not arise in most projects. Conditions such as those governing the discovery of hazardous materials, the client's failure to pay the contractor, the contractor's hiring of inadequately skilled labor, or the client's dismissal of the designer may appear to be far-fetched if the project goes well; but they will set the ground rules if it does not. Attorneys have written standard construction contracts in a pessimistic manner, so that parties to an agreement, confident that their interests are protected if things go wrong, can focus on forging a good work relationship based on trust and hope.

Contracts vary in the thoroughness and complexity of the general conditions attached to them. Many are not as comprehensive as those represented by the table of contents in Table 7.2. The simplest construction contracts available are published by purveyors of legal forms such as Blumberg. Sold in retail stationery stores, the Blumberg construction contract is a skeletal document about a page in length. It contains no general conditions and is suitable only for very small jobs. More comprehensive is the five-to-six-page form contract available through the American Association of Home Owners.

The construction contracts developed by the AIA (American Institute of Architects) are widely acknowledged to be comprehensive and fair-minded, with general conditions covering a host of contingencies. They are generally used for projects requiring the participation of a registered architect. AIA form A201, which is correlated with the AIA contract document A101, contains 44 pages of *general conditions* and is suitable for a construction project of any size, including the largest. (These are the general conditions represented by the table of contents in Table 7.2) A simpler AIA document, A107, contains a contract and general conditions within 11 pages and is suitable for projects of lesser scope. Document A105 contains a contract and general conditions in four pages and is suitable for projects of very limited scope.

TABLE 7.2   TABLE OF CONTENTS AIA DOCUMENT A201-1997.
GENERAL CONDITIONS OF CONTRACT FOR CONSTRUCTION

TABLE OF ARTICLES

1. General Provisions
2. Owner
3. Contractor
4. Administration of the Contract
5. Subcontractors
6. Construction by Owner or by Separate Contractors
7. Changes in the Work
8. Time
9. Payments and Completion
10. Protection of Persons and Property
11. Insurance and Bonds
12. Uncovering and Correction of Work
13. Miscellaneous Provisions
14. Termination or Suspension of the Contract

Adapted from www.aia.org.

If no architect is playing a role in a construction project and an interior designer who is not an architect is coordinating construction on a client's behalf, the interior designer will of course rely on a contract from another source.

The general conditions of any standard contract may be supplemented by special conditions inserted by the designer, the contractor, or the client, who is typically advised by an attorney when signing a contract for a sizeable project. Contracts with fewer, less well-detailed general conditions invite attorneys to write supplemental conditions that are partisan in nature and divisive in impact. However, for simple contracts governing smaller projects (see Figure 7.3) a vast superstructure of general conditions is inappropriate. (The full contract for Figure 7.3 is featured on the CD-ROM.)

Negotiation reconciles legitimate competing interests and results in amendments to the standard contract

Figure 7.3 Excerpt from Sample Renovation Contract for a Small Project. Provided as a Public Service to Consumers by Canada Mortgage and Housing Corporation (CMHC). All rights reserved, 2001. Reproduced with consent of CMHC. All other uses and reproductions of this material are expressly prohibited.

---

6. CHANGES IN WORK

The owner may make changes by altering, adding to, or deducting from the Work, with the Contract and Contract Price being adjusted accordingly. Changes to the Work require a written Change Order Form, signed by both the Owner and the Contractor.

a) **Extras** will be calculated in the following manner (check one):

1) _____Material cost plus hourly rate of $ _____

2) _____Labor and material cost plus _____%

3) _____A lump sum to be agreed on in advance by both parties.

Extras are payable upon (check one):

1) _____Signing the Change Order

2) _____Invoicing pursuant to the Change Order

3) _____Completion of work specified in Change Order less _____% holdback in all cases.

b) **Deletions** will be calculated on a cost less _____% basis, to be deducted from the relevant or next scheduled payment.

Amendments

No matter how well a designer has prepared a construction contract for signing, there will be negotiation to reconcile legitimate competing interests that cannot be fully predicted by a standard contract. Each construction job is different in terms of scope, program, and specifications. There are more than 250,000 general contractors in California alone.[18] Though some operate as franchisees, for the most part their businesses are run in highly individualized ways, with little standardization, though contractors are subject to state and local regulation and are generally required to be licensed. Clients, of course, are fully as diverse and individual as contractors. The designer functions as an intermediary to smooth out differences between the parties to a construction contract and to reconcile their interests.

Amendments, or changes in the printed contract, are sometimes typed in over carefully crossed-out lines of the printed document, and initialed by both signatory parties. Some short amendments are written and initialed in the margins of previously prepared contract pages. Longer amendments are spelled out on separate pages. Provisions that modify, change, delete from, or add to the general conditions are sometimes classified as *Supplemental Conditions* and may be inserted by the owner's attorney, the contractor or the contractor's attorney, or the designer.

CLIENT'S SUPPLEMENTAL CONDITIONS

As advised by an attorney, a client may wish to delete or renegotiate terms deemed too advantageous for the contractor. Supplementing one recent contract for a house renovation, for instance, was a change in paragraph 2.2.5 of Article 2 of the General Conditions of A201-1997, which reads:

> Unless otherwise provided in the Contract Documents, the Contractor will be furnished, free of charge, such copies of Drawings and Project Manuals as are reasonably necessary for execution of the work.

The supplemental conditions provide for the following modification:

> 2.2.5 The owner will furnish the Contractor with three (3) copies of written material and one (1) reproducible set of Drawings at no cost.

This modification sets clear limits on the copying of contract drawings to suit the needs of a large construction crew and—with the addition of a reproducible set of drawings— places the burden and expense of reproduction on the con-

Supplemental conditions may be inserted by a designer, contractor, or client, advised by an attorney.

tractor. The owner is relieved of an obligation that could be a costly nuisance and might be difficult for, say, a two-career couple to fulfill.

DESIGNER'S SUPPLEMENTAL CONDITIONS

The designer's supplements to the same contract include a number of clarifications to Section 1.1 of the General Conditions document A201, which contains Basic Definitions. A new paragraph, 1.1.8, is inserted, which contains Miscellaneous Definitions. Among these are the following:

> 1.1.8.4   The term *provide* means to furnish and install, complete and in place, including all accessories, finishes, tests and services as required to render the item so specified completely ready to use.

> 1.1.8.5   The term *furnish* means procurement of fabrication of materials, equipment or components, or the performance of services to the extent indicated. Where used in respect to materials, equipment or components, the term shall include delivery to project site, but is not intended to include the installation of the item, either temporary or final.

> 1.1.8.6   The term *install* means the placement of materials, equipment, or components, including the receiving, unloading, transporting, storage, and installing, and the performance of such testing and finish work as is compatible with the degree of installation specified.

These supplemental definitions lower the risk of misunderstanding by all parties to the project. They help to ensure that no one involved in the construction project is given leave by loose language to act like the Red Queen in Lewis Carroll's *Alice in Wonderland*, who said that a thing meant whatever she wanted it to mean.

CONTRACTOR'S SUPPLEMENTAL CONDITIONS

The contract for the same residential construction project was further modified by the contractor's supplemental conditions. He stipulated, for instance, "The owner shall pay all utilities." He further stipulated, "One working telephone line is to be provided on the job site for the use of Contractor's personnel. Contractor will provide the phone/fax instruments and will reimburse the owner for any long-distance calls."

By the first of these modifications the contractor avoids the administrative hassle of *prorating*, or dividing proportionally, the power-service bills. By the second, the contractor hopes to avoid the difficulty and delay that might be caused by time spent waiting for the phone line to be installed. It becomes the owner's burden to arrange for installation well before the arrival of the contractor's crew. Negotiation might ensue over such a request. For instance, the owner might suggest that the contractors use their cell phones, to which the contractor might respond that timely completion of the project requires a fax, which operates through a land line. The owner might then insist on a pay phone, which might or might not be acceptable to the contractor, though the decision would most likely be based on convenience rather than cost. "Utilities and phone service are charged back as overhead if they are not paid directly by the client, so what is at stake here is efficiency," explains GC Peter Martin.[19]

As the client's intermediary, the interior designer may need to explain issues raised by the contractor so that a climate of trust can be established. Understanding the practical issues that affect a contractor's ability to perform his or her job help a designer better serve the client's and the project's interest.

> The designer explains issues raised by the contractor so that a climate of trust can be established.

Clients may bridle at a contractor's wish to delete contract phrasing such as "time is of the essence," a legal term that gives teeth to other enforcements of time limits within a contract. Many attorneys are reluctant to provide an exact definition of this term. It suggests that if the job is completed a day behind schedule, there has been a breach of contract and the client is no longer obliged to pay for the completed work. Contractors may feel that they should not be held solely responsible for delays that may have been caused by factory delays, proliferating change orders, or client indecision. The client's attorney may be loath to give up this phrasing, and spirited negotiation may ensue.

The contractor may also wish to delete any blanket waiver of liens inserted into the contract. As explained in Chapter 6, a *mechanic's lien* gives a contractor who practices any trade—not necessarily fixing cars!—a right in the client's property if the obligation to pay for work is not discharged. A lien placed on a client's house, for instance, would mean that an unpaid contractor would be paid from the proceeds of a sale of the house before the owner realized any gain. A *waiver* would mean that the contractor agreed to forgo the right to place such a lien. An owner may pressure a contractor into forgoing this simple legal protection—the most important one the contractor has. The contractor might agree to a blanket waiver in order to be awarded a contract,but could claim coercion later. In negotiation, an owner may back down on blanket waiver but request waivers of lien from individual trade contractors during the course of the building project as evidence that they have been paid by the GC. Some states require waivers to be signed by general and trade contractors as progress payments are made over the course of a job. This prevents exaggerated claims after final completion. (It is worth noting that many states permit designers to file mechanics' liens in the event that they are not paid by their clients. These liens are discussed in Chapter 6.)

OWNERSHIP OF DRAWINGS AND MODELS

Many clients would like to retain drawings, models, and other parts of the designer's work product, sometimes for sentimental or documentary reasons. If, however, the client sold or gave the plans to others, who then used them as the basis for further construction, the designer might be exposed to liability. Furthermore, a designer is prevented from reselling or reusing any plans that a client has been allowed to retain. This may suit a client who wants the assurance of a unique office, home, or other space. In the long run, however, it may be very expensive for a designer to provide such assurance. The language in the construction contract that relates to the designer's work product should echo and conform to similar language in the designer-client agreement (see Chapter 6). If the designer retains ownership, the contractor needs to return materials such as drawings and models as soon as possible. The designer may insist that the contractor insure the designer's plans and models while using them if they are valuable.

NEGOTIATING THE PAYMENT SCHEDULE

> The most important amendment to be negotiated often is the payment schedule.

In most cases, by the time negotiation begins, the fixed price for a given construction project has already been accepted, based on a contractor's bid, which is in turn based on the drawings and specifications provided by the design team. Frequently there are few surprises as the parties proceed to agreement. Often the most important amendment that needs to be negotiated is the payment schedule, which dictates the manner in which the general contractor will be paid for the agreed-upon construction work. Assuming a payment at the beginning and a "holdback" at the end of the work, the typical agreement will specify one of three bases for progress payments: milestones of completion; calendar intervals; or percentage of completion.

> Three typical payment schedules are milestones of completion, calendar intervals, and percentage of completion.

MILESTONES OF COMPLETION   This method of compensation releases progress payments when previously agreed upon milestones have been reached. At the milestone known as *substantial completion*, most of the contractor's remaining compensation will be released. (A construction job is deemed substantially complete when major systems are functional, the space is usable for its intended purpose, and only minor deficiencies or defects remain to be resolved.) A portion of the total due the contractor (the *holdback*) is retained until the milestone known as *final completion* has been attained, based on the completion of *punch-list* tasks. The punch list may include such items as missing light-switch plates, "windows" (poor coverage in the paint job), and so forth. When the tasks on the punch list have been completed, full and final payment is made to the contractor, whose warranty still applies if new problems emerge.

The milestones-of-completion payment schedule (Figure 7.4) is frequently used with one-trade contractors—for instance, for a "brush and trowel" job executed by a painting contractor who subcontracts any necessary plastering. Sometimes, after an initial payment, progress payments are scheduled on a third-third-third basis, with final payment, again, due when the punch list has been completed.

CALENDAR INTERVALS   The easiest payment schedule to administer is based on calendar intervals. After an initial payment, the contractor is paid on the fifteenth of every month or at other suitable intervals, with a portion of the money reserved for the completion of the punch list. This payment schedule requires a safety mechanism, such as designer approval, that will protect the client in the event that work proceeds more slowly than it should.

PERCENTAGE OF COMPLETION   The most complicated payment schedule to administer, percentage of completion is also the most precise in matching the dispersal of funds to the work that has actually been accomplished. It is especially appropriate for larger jobs or more costly ones and provides good protection against contractor failure, dispersing enough money but not too much.

In negotiating any payment schedule, the designer's role as intermediary is crucial. On the one hand, the client wants to maintain leverage as the amount of work still to be completed grows ever smaller, for fear the contractor will slight a paid-out project in favor of newer ones with more money in them. On the other hand, the contractor needs a good cash flow to maintain the forward momentum of the project without *financing* it, that is, having to borrow money at interest to complete it. To avoid problems throughout the project, a savvy designer will work with both parties to the contract to establish a payment schedule with which they are comfortable.

COST-PLUS   In specialized cases, construction work is not contracted on a fixed-price basis, but on a *cost-plus* basis. With such a contract, costs are

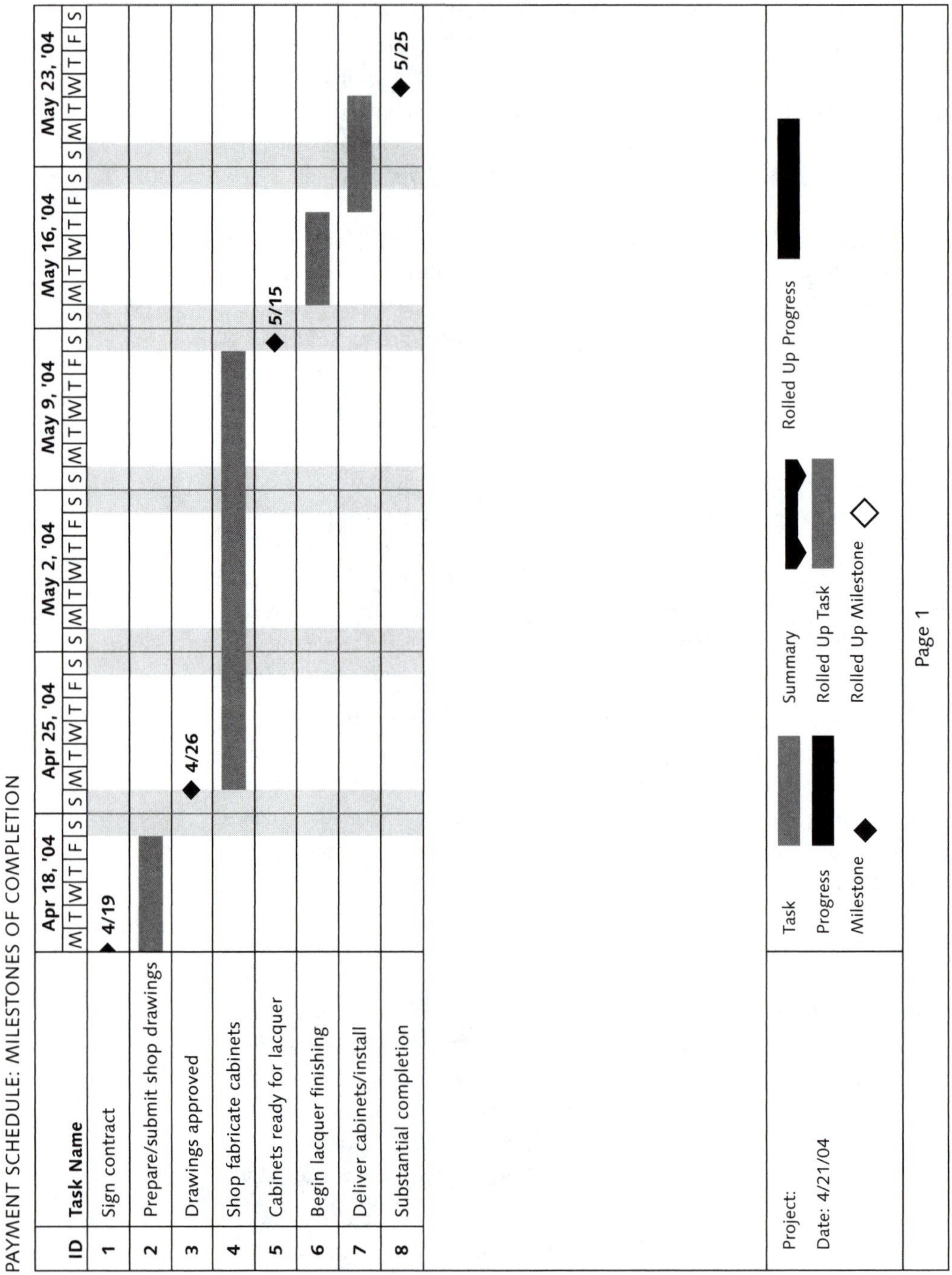

PAYMENT SCHEDULE: MILESTONES OF COMPLETION

ID	Task Name	Apr 18, '04	Apr 25, '04	May 2, '04	May 9, '04	May 16, '04	May 23, '04
1	Sign contract	◆ 4/19					
2	Prepare/submit shop drawings	▮					
3	Drawings approved		◆ 4/26				
4	Shop fabricate cabinets		▮▮▮▮				
5	Cabinets ready for lacquer				◆ 5/15		
6	Begin lacquer finishing					▮	
7	Deliver cabinets/install					▮	
8	Substantial completion						◆ 5/25

Project:
Date: 4/21/04

Task ▮ Summary ◣▬◢ Rolled Up Progress ▬
Progress ▮ Rolled Up Task ▮
Milestone ◆ Rolled Up Milestone ◇

Page 1

Figure 7.4 On this chart, milestones are indicated by the ◆ symbol.

passed through directly to the client. In addition, contractors paid on this basis charge a fee based on costs (cost plus negotiated markup) or a percentage of overhead and profit (10 to 15 percent overhead, according to Linda W. Case, plus 10 percent profit[20]). Because the markup that contractors are typically allowed by no means guarantees profitability, they will define as many items as possible as "costs." Clients will wish to narrow the range of items defined as costs.

Wages and other labor costs of those employed exclusively on the project are typically negotiated as costs. So is payment of partial salaries for time spent by the contractors' employees on project-related work performed in a shop, on a site, or en route transporting workers, equipment, or materials. Some other items typically negotiated as costs are:

- Payments to trade contractors
- Relevant costs for materials, supplies, tools, and equipment
- Taxes and permit and other government fees
- Related expenses for such items as telephone and courier service
- Insurance costs
- Administration costs covering such matters as billing and change orders

A cost-plus contract provides a way of proceeding with a complex construction project that is too unpredictable for a fixed-price bid. However, it can be very difficult for client and designer to control spiraling costs with this contract structure. A contract for cost-plus work is a difficult negotiation that a novice interior designer should not undertake on the client's behalf without the assistance of an attorney.

Do not attempt to negotiate a cost-plus contract without the assistance of an attorney.

Addenda

When unforeseen and unforeseeable difficulties emerge in the course of performing project work or when a client experiences a change of mind or wishes to enlarge the scope of a project, a *change order* is created by the designer or the contractor. If approved, it is signed by owner, contractor, and designer, and is inserted into the contract as an *addendum*, or addition. (*Addenda* is the Latin plural of *addendum*.) The original signed contract should have spelled out the exact manner in which change-order applications are made and administered.

Change orders are often the subject of intense negotiations between owner, designer, and contractor. The process of composing them, submit-

Keep careful track of submitted change orders to avoid problems with timely completion.

ting them for approval, and keeping track of the manner in which they modify the contract can be a central factor in the evolution of the contract relationship. If change orders have not been properly submitted and approved, contractors have no assurance that they will be paid for work represented by changes in the scope of the project. They may be unwilling to proceed with crucial elements of the project that dramatically affect timely completion. Designers need to keep track of submitted change orders in their logs and to follow up on any that have not been properly pursued through acceptance or rejection. This important part of the administrative work supporting a project is covered more fully in Chapter 10.

Contracts for Fabrication

Even if no construction is required on a project's premises, the interior designer may need to procure and supervise the fabrication of customized or custom-made items to complement those chosen for purchase from various manufacturers' product lines. For instance, the designer might specify teakwood kitchen cabinets built with wooden pegs rather than with nails, in the traditional Japanese manner, by a highly specialized cabinetmaker. Or the designer might specify that a slipper chair in a bedroom be recovered by an upholsterer in a fabric chosen by the client from among swatches provided by the designer, with new cushions filled with goose down.

In the case if the teakwood cabinets, the cabinetmaker would be hired and paid by the GC, as part of the agreed-upon responsibilities, in the context of a larger construction job. If there is no larger construction job, however, there is no general contractor, so agreement would need to be reached directly with the cabinetmaker. In the case of the slipper-chair upholstery, which would not be part of a construction project under any circumstances, it would also be necessary to reach agreement directly with the fabricator. In both these cases, the question for the designer is *who* reaches agreement with the fabricator?

Determining the Parties to the Contract

Unless fabricators are willing to contract directly with the client—some work only with designers—and unless the designer is willing to forgo or reveal the markup customarily charged, the designer must come to agreement with fabricators and pay them, then apply for reimbursement by the client. It is important to build in protection against customer dissatisfaction that might result in an unwillingness to reimburse the designer for custom-created merchandise. Most problems can be avoided[21] through:

- Clear, thorough specifications.
- Phased client approvals based on samples.
- Progress visits to the fabricator's workplace.
- Fabricator's submission and designer's review of shop drawings.
- A substantial deposit requirement from the client.
- Pass-through payments from the client at each approval.
- Good, clear communication.

Of course, the soundest precaution a designer can take is to refuse the role of financial intermediary where fabrication is concerned. Although it is possible to manage the risks that designers incur when contracting with fabricators, there is a great deal of latitude for misunderstanding in these relationships. Tad Crawford and Eva Doman Bruck urge designers to "insist that the client contract directly with the fabricator," even if the designer is to submit designs and work directly with the fabricator. "What duties the designer performs are billed to the client on an agreed-upon basis, either as a fee, an hourly rate, or a markup."[22]

> If you are paying a fabricator for reimbursement by a client, build in protection against customer dissatisfaction.

Specifications for Fabrication

For fabrication as for construction, clear specifications play a crucial role in ensuring quality, which is important whether client or designer contracts with the fabricator. If the cushion-filling specification is loosely written, merely calling, say, for "good-quality" filling, then either goose down or poly foam may meet the criterion. The designer needs to closely specify not only the materials to be used for a custom-created item, but also the methods used to execute the work; the stages at which approval must be solicited; and the furnishing of samples as appropriate. For instance, the Japanese cabinetmaker might be directed to use straight, clear boards of high-quality teak from nonendangered trees and to submit a sample of the wood he or she had chosen before proceeding with fabrication.

The designer's role in specification for fabrication is to clearly communicate the quality of design and the design intent. Designers "recommend" methods and materials that they have experienced as proper for achieving the desired quality and intent. They defer to fabricators' expertise if quality and intent are preserved. Shop drawings are important in this regard. Both the fabricator's timely submission of drawings and the exact nature of the approval process should be clearly governed by the terms of the contract with the fabricator.

A poorly written specification is a problem waiting to happen. For instance, suppose that the maker of the teakwood cabinets customarily uses pegs of the same wood as any cabinet planes being joined by the pegs. A designer who was not accustomed to peg joinery and who did not find much guidance from standardized specifications might not have produced any specifications regarding the pegs. Yet the client may have been supposing all along that the pegs would be of a contrasting wood, so that the uniqueness of the cabinet design and construction would be readily apparent. If no sample of the peg joinery had been requested, the difference between the cabinetmaker's work process and the client's expectation might not show up until the cabinets had been delivered. It would certainly be prudent for the designer to have insisted that the client approve the cabinets before they were installed!

No cabinetmaker would be willing to take the cabinets apart and put them back together again with different-colored pegs—especially not for the previously agreed-upon price. Now the designer may have to engage the client in some patient discussion to win acceptance of the cabinets; or, if you as the designer had a use for the cabinets, you might elect to purchase them for yourself and to ask the fabricator to make a new set that conformed to the client's expectations. Yet this might not be practical, for the cabinet-maker might have taken other jobs and might be unable to manufacture, deliver, and install new cabinets before the client's move-in date. Painting the peg heads darker with an artist's brush may be feasible; but the fabrica-tor may not be eager to undertake this time-consuming, precise work with-out additional payment that the client may make only grudgingly.

Clear, accurate specs prevent problems with fabricators. Clearly, it is best to write thorough and accurate specifications in the first place, to make progress visits to the shop if at all possible, and to request adequate samples and shop drawings at any and all stages of the work when changes are possible and practical.

Procuring and Evaluating Bids

Whether the designer or the client contracts with the fabricator, it will most likely be the designer's responsibility before coming to agreement to pro-cure several *bids*—fixed-price proposals for stipulated work based on spec-ifications prepared by the designer. Only fully qualified fabricators with whose work the designer is familiar should be invited to bid, and the same specifications should be presented to each bidder.

When reviewing and evaluating bids (Figure 7.5), it is prudent to find out how long each bid will be considered current. (The fabricator or other contractor may insist on submitting a new, higher bid if there is protracted delay between the sub-

Weber Design

Online Bid Submittal

CONTRACTOR INFORMATION

Company Name _____ Contact _____
Mailing Address _____
Phone #'s: Office _____ Mobile _____ Project Designer _____
Type of Service _____ Date _____ E-mail _____

PROJECT INFORMATION

Job or client name _____ Job number _____
Type of Job _____
This bid includes
- Materials only
- Labor only
- Materials & labor
- Other _____

Description of work to be done: (It is not required here, but if you like, you may also attach your standard proposal to the document and we will incorporate it into the contract documents that will form the contractor agreement that we will send you for signing.) _____

_____
_____
_____
_____
_____

Bid Price _____

Options pricing _____
_____
_____
_____

378 WILLOW LANE • CLARYVILLE, NY • 12725
PHONE AND FAX: 845-555-6789 • E-MAIL: ALVIN@WEBDESIGN.COM

Figure 7.5
Online bid
submission form.

mission and acceptance.) In addition, be sure that the issue of taxation has been clearly spelled out. (Sales or other applicable taxes should be included in the price quotation, or it should be stated that there will be an additional charge for tax.)

EXTRA CHARGES

Always ask bidding fabricators about extra charges.

When considering a fabricator's or other contractor's bid, inquire about any extra charges that may not have been spelled out. For instance, will there be charges for any of the following?

- Change orders?
- Using materials provided by the client or the designer?
- Slow approvals?
- Shipping of samples or of finished products?
- Delivery of the finished products?
- Late progress payments?
- Canceling an order?

DIFFERENCES IN PRICE QUOTATIONS

Allow for appropriate substitution of materials and methods.

Neither fabricators nor construction contractors may be willing to furnish extensive line items in their bids, since these provide entry points for downward negotiation. However, careful interviewing can elicit a sense of differences in materials, methods, and general approach that may account for differing price quotations.

In specification, it is customary to use the phrase "or equal" to allow some latitude for fabricators to provide similar quality items with which the designer may not be familiar, but which the fabricator can acquire at competitive pricing. To allow for this, the specifications should require bidders to submit substitutions for the specified materials and methods along with their bids. This allows bids to be compared fairly, and it heads off any claim of "deficient" specs that a fabricator may have in mind as a way of increasing profits without providing the agreed-upon quality. If a careful review of bid documents reveals missing or inappropriately substituted specs, the designer needs to be aware that the contractor may try to claim unforeseen costs or conditions later on as a way of making more money. Figure 7.6 is a specification that allows a mason to substitute stone from a vendor other than Dillon for a fireplace surround, providing the substituted stone is appropriate for the project.

It is important that you be able to explain to clients why fabricators' price quotations for the same job may differ. Clients may not have a clear understanding of the concept of quality as it relates to the performance of work.

PART 2 – PRODUCTS

2.1   ACCEPTABLE MANUFACTURERS

A.   Dillon & Company, P.O. Box 160, Swords Creek, Virginia 24649
      800-234-8970

B.   Manufacturers of equivalent products submitted and approved in
      accordance with Section 01630 – Product Substitution Procedures.
      Designer reserves right to reject.

C.   Substitution request based on aggregate, color, polished surface, and
      gloss, even though structural characteristic, shapes, and materials are
      equivalent.

Figure 7.6 Specification permitting substitution. *Adapted excerpt from section 04221, Guide Specs for Polished Face Concrete Masonry Units, E. Dillon & Company. http://www.edillon.com/products/premier/04221PF.doc.*

While a client can reasonably expect that both low-end and high-end upholsterers sew straight seams, it is not reasonable to expect that the low-end upholsterer attach the pillow trim by hand rather than by machine if "hand" was not specified. "Quality" usually means good of its kind within specifications. It does not usually mean the finest conceivable or even the finest available.

Many designers make a practice of accepting the middle of a group of three or more bids, throwing out the low and the high. Bids should not be accepted or rejected solely on the basis of a rule of thumb, but should be rigorously compared to see what work has actually been priced. The designer needs to make sure that a fabricator or contractor has been meticulously responsive to the specifications. The high bid may represent the most careful and accurate response, and the lower-bidding fabricators or contractors, if selected, may end up cutting corners to cover their costs.

Be leery of conspicuously low bids, and work with your clients to educate them about the risk that a conspicuously inexpensive fabricator may have been *lowballing*—quoting a deliberately low price—in order to get the job, fully intending to jack up the price with change orders. Likewise, a conspicuously high bid may signal the fabricator's intention to subcontract the work and to charge a markup as an administrative fee.

THE ISSUE OF CHARACTER

For any work requiring a fabricator or other contractor to enter a client's occupied home, the reliability and character of the workers should be a key issue, considered as carefully as cost and work quality. The fabrication or

When evaluating bids, accept or reject on the basis of rigorous comparison.

Be leery of conspicuously low bids.

construction team that is interacting with your clients should possess social skills such as politeness, friendliness, and helpfulness. They need to respect client preferences in matters such as smoking. Without express permission, they should never, ever, use anything belonging to the client. Above all, they should have a record of honesty and personal integrity.

To ensure the hiring of reliable fabricators and other contractors, employ only those who have been given high marks by previous employers whose opinions you trust and respect. Do not rely on hearsay or respond without further research to ads in the Yellow Pages or elsewhere. Always check references! Strive to maintain good relationships with vendors whose work and character you deem excellent, so that you may call on them again and again.

Employ only fabricators and contractors recommended by previous employers whom you trust.

CULTIVATING RELATIONSHIPS

Let validating bids qualify those who supply them for future employment.

Avoid asking fabricators (or other contractors) to submit bids solely to validate to a client the price quoted by a fabricator whom you have pre-selected on the basis of known quality and reliable personal characteristics. It is time-consuming and thus costly to prepare bids. A fabricator will feel exploited if a bid is solicited in a situation in which another bidder is already "wired" to the job. The fabricator may refuse to prepare bids for you in the future.

Of course, you may have a hard time convincing your clients that fewer bids do not mean higher prices. If you must obtain validating bids, then it is best to be open about what you are doing, asking for these bids as a favor. In the future, you can return the favor by seeking opportunities to promote validators as favored bidders for other suitable projects. Your experience of working with them on their validating bids thus becomes a qualification process whereby they are pre-selected for future jobs.

The good reputation of many designers is closely linked to their excellent relationships with first-rate fabricators and contractors. Protect these relationships. If fabricators and other contractors are fairly treated, they are more apt to be generous in a pinch. For instance, if no manufacturer's product line included a stain color light enough to satisfy a client for custom-made kitchen cabinets, some fabricators might concoct a custom stain at no extra charge. They would be less willing to do this if the designer had not treated them well in the past, and they had no expectation that they would be treated well in the future.

Protect good relationships with reliable contractors and fabricators.

Customizing the Fabrication Contract

When a bid for fabrication has been accepted, the next step is the preparation of a contract. This will likely be the designer's responsibility whether the agreement is between designer and fabricator or client and fabricator. To be sure that all relevant contingencies are covered, you would be advised to customize a standard contract such as the one presented in Crawford and Bruck's *Business and Legal Forms for Interior Designers.*[23] A standard fabrication contract, prepared by an attorney such as Tad Crawford, covers a wide range of business contingencies and can be customized by you, the designer. If the fabricator prepares the agreement or confirms your order on a standard form, be sure that it satisfactorily addresses the issues that are covered in the master agreement that you customarily rely on.

As in a construction contract, customize the standard contract with a fabricator.

Negotiating with Fabricators

Whoever is responsible for initial preparation of the contract, designers must be prepared to negotiate with fabricators as with construction contractors. Many of the contingencies covered in a standard contract will be acceptable to a reputable vendor. For instance, serious dispute is unlikely over a clause stating that the risk of loss is borne by the fabricator until the job is delivered, although the fabricator may raise prices to cover the cost of any extra insurance required to encompass the entire delivery process. The cabinetmaker will understand that if a fire breaks out in the shop while your client's kitchen cabinets are under construction, the cabinetmaker is solely responsible and must still deliver cabinets according to specifications, although it would be a hardhearted designer or client who held the cabinetmaker to the original delivery date. (The contract should specify a time limit for extensions of the delivery date based on events beyond the fabricator's control. For the protection of your client, it may also be prudent to specify that the fabricator must carry a given amount of insurance that would cover the loss and re-fabrication of damaged works in progress.)

Even the most reputable fabricators are likely to contest such standard attorneys' formulations as a time-is-of-the-essence clause, which would make late delivery a breach of contract. As discussed earlier in this chapter, many if not most feel that such clauses penalize them unfairly for tardiness caused by factors beyond their control.

WARRANTIES

Fabricators may wish to limit the time the designer has to inspect the fabricated item(s) and to report defects. From the client's point of view, defects may not emerge until there has been an opportunity to use the product. From the fabricator's point-of-view, use may create defects that a fabricator should not be asked to repair without further charge. It may be unreasonable to expect an upholsterer to repair tears in cushion covers that mysteriously appear after three months of hard use by an owner's children and dogs. Yet fabricators or other contractors should be willing to place the products they have created under warranty—that is, to guarantee them for a certain amount of time and to make reasonable repairs of product defects within that amount of time. If the seams on a cushion cover are parting, revealing the muslin that encases the cushion, the upholsterer must make a repair. The designer needs to establish warranties—and warranty periods— that are both meaningful and fair. (The appropriate warranties will be evident on a per-project basis.)

Establish a meaningful and fair warranty.

QUALITY STANDARDS, SAMPLES, AND APPROVALS

It is important to explicitly state that the fabricator must meet a *quality standard* consistent with the client's expectation and based on the specifications. This puts the upholsterers clearly in the wrong if they shave costs by using duck down for cushions rather than the goose down that was specified. Likewise, the kitchen cabinetmaker is in the wrong if he or she uses crooked, knotty boards rather than straight boards free of knots, as specified.

The contract should explicitly spell out what *samples* and shop drawings are to be prepared and furnished at various stages of the fabrication process. Samples ensure good quality and protect against the possibility that clients will change their minds, as frequently happens. For instance, the client for the kitchen cabinets might realize when checking a sample that the stain called "honey" is much darker than has been apparent from the manufacturer's chip. The client might ask for a lighter stain color. If no lighter color is available from that manufacturer, the designer and the cabinetmaker might collaborate on finding another quality stain manufacturer whose product line includes a lighter color, which would in turn need to be sampled.

If appropriate samples are submitted to the client for *approval* before the next relevant phase in the project goes forward, the client and designer can correct any problems that have arisen. Indeed, approvals should be required at every appropriate stage of the job and linked to the furnishing of samples. This is crucial for involving the client and ensuring acceptance of the work.

Submitting samples to the client ensures quality and wins acceptance.

FURTHER NEGOTIATION GUIDELINES

Here are some further guidelines to aid in the negotiation of successful contracts with fabricators:

- Clearly state the *basics*, such as names and addresses of the parties and the price agreed upon for the work.
- Name and enumerate the *specifications*, drawings, and other documents folded into the contract, and state the number of pages in each.

- Specify the *contractual term*. The fabricator must be willing to provide the items fabricated by the time the client requires them, either for move-in or to enable other work to be performed. For instance, if custom-fabricated radiator covers are to be painted with the rest of the room in which they are installed, they must be delivered before the painter arrives on the project premises.
- The contract should include the manner in which the fabricated item is to be packaged for *delivery*, the delivery date and location, the nature of any insurance covering delivery, and the manner of delivery (for instance, delivered to the freight entrance of an apartment building via the fabricator's own van, but carried to the apartment by separately hired workers). Many a fabricator prefers not to accept responsibility for delivery, but will load the item at the shop for no additional charge. There may be an extra charge if the fabricator pays freight charges and insurance for delivery.
- The contract should explicitly state when you or your client will be required to render *payment* for the fabricated items. Is it upon delivery? Within 30 days? Within 60 days? If a deposit is required, the amount needs to be specified as well.

If you are supplying a fabricator with *materials* on behalf of your client, you will need to specify who pays for the return of any materials not needed. It should also be stated whether the fabricator needs to provide insurance for them, and if so, how much. For instance, if you provided the fabric for upholstering the slipper chair in your client's bedroom, does the upholsterer need to insure it? Perhaps not, if it is only a small amount of fabric that is neither rare nor valuable, and if designer and client agree on the risk. You would be more apt to require insurance if, say, an order had been placed for hundreds of custom-manufactured desks for which you had supplied, on behalf of your client, many board feet of valuable lumber custom-ordered and shipped at your expense from a source in Indonesia—especially if you had not yet been paid by the client for the cost of the lumber plus your markup.

Writing Contracts for the Long Term

In amending standard contracts for construction and fabrication to reflect negotiations between clients, contractors or fabricators, and designers, you

Write contracts for construction or fabrication in plain English.

will need to practice the plain English writing skills discussed in Chapters 1 and 6. Contracts for the performance of work must mean what they say, whether they govern the crafting of a single, exquisite table or the partitioning of a huge, open office space. Every word counts. It is not easy for someone untrained as an attorney to foresee the ramifications of each and every linguistic turn. This is why it makes sense to draw on master specifications and to base agreements for construction or fabrication on standard contracts that have been created or carefully examined by attorneys. It also makes sense to have an attorney look at each customization of a master contract, though this may seem expensive for smaller jobs.

In general, be suspicious of unusual requests affecting those parts of the contract that provide standard, or *boilerplate*, legal protection against the use of deceptive business tricks. Be leery of a fabricator or contractor who asks for a waiver of warranties. It is a mistake, however, to be inflexible in matters facilitating the smooth and easy communication that makes work go smoothly and well. If a fabricator or contractor prefers to handle "written" change orders via e-mail, with hard copy to follow, perhaps you can accommodate this if you are comfortable with electronic messaging and check your e-mail on a regular basis. Your contracts should ensure that your interests and those of your clients are protected against a variety of painful contingencies. However, your contracts should not be straitjackets that prevent adequate movement. Legal agreements can manage risk; they cannot eliminate it. In the end, the best guarantees against trouble are clear writing and the personal character of all parties to an agreement.

Discussion Questions

1. For what kinds of projects can you foresee inserting into a construction contract each of the following kinds of progress payments?

- Milestones of completion
- Calendar intervals
- Percentage of completion

Provide a clear rationale for your responses.

2. How can you reconcile your need to obtain the lowest possible price and highest quality for a client with your need to maintain good long-term relationships with trusted fabricators and contractors?

Exercises

1. Divide the United States into regions and assign one region to each student or to a small group of students. Let each individual or group go to http://www.iida.com/legislation/codeOrglinks.html. Follow the appropriate links for research that will help you write specifications that conform to code in "your" region. Print out your research. As an entire-class group, choose five types of specification. How does code affect them in the different parts of the country investigated by the various groups of students?

2. Let each student go to http://www.aecinfo.com. Find specifications within each of the five types identified by your class in Exercise 1. Adapt them as needed, given the code research for "your" region. Format and prepare your document in a manner suitable for presentation to a client.

3. For an imaginary kitchen renovation, prepare an appliance schedule containing specifications for five appliances. Tabulate the schedule and provide references in it to cut sheets photocopied or printed from paper or online catalogs.

4. Interview a single-trade contractor. Obtain descriptions of two situations that resulted in a conflicted project outcome. What caused the conflicts? How might they have been avoided? Working in small groups in your class, compare and contrast the research that you did. What common factors can you identify? Choose one person from each group to report to the entire class. Again, compare and contrast. What common factors can you identify? What inferences can your class as a group draw?

8

Contract Administration:
Fixtures, Furnishings, and Equipment

Many interior designers—particularly those who specialize in residential work—earn a good portion of their professional income by purchasing fixtures, furnishings, and equipment (FF&E) on behalf of their clients. Although many designers who specialize in contract design (for corporate and institutional markets) simply hand the client a list of specifications, designers of all stripes and sizes offer services related to *procurement*, the acquisition of needed products from vendors. In Chapter 6, we look at how contracts express the ways in which designers bill their clients for performing such services. This chapter discusses the role of writing with respect to the procurement process itself, that is, the administration of orders for fixtures, furnishings, and equipment.

Specifications for Procurement

Procurement begins with the designer's vision, which is realized through specifications, or "specs" (see Figure 8.1). Sometimes specifications are used as a guide to purchasing by the client or the client's representative.

Sometimes a designer works with a client who contracts with a vender for FF&E at a cost that has been determined in advance, either through bidding or negotiation (using, for instance, AIA Contract A175 ID-2003, which is featured on the CD-ROM). Sometimes the designer takes the client shopping with the list of specifications in hand; sometimes the designer acts as the client's purchasing agent. For the purchase of FF&E, specs determine the quality or grade of workmanship desired and clearly and precisely represent a product's features. Specifications can be either simple or complex, closed or open, depending on the designer's project.

Simple Specs

A small design firm working with residential or small-business clients may submit a simple list of products to be purchased. Such a list reflects the

Figure 8.1
Designer considering specification choices based on her collection of swatches.
Courtesy, Michael Brady Inc.

client's wish that the designer function almost as a personal shopper, making choices for or with the client and preventing costly errors in taste and judgment. Simple specifications reflect a good working relationship between designer and client. Still, they must lay down an accurate track record to protect the designer in case of disagreement.

Simple specs must be as accurate as complex specs.

Complex Specs

For a large corporate or commercial project, the *complex specifications* may be elaborate and numerous and are typically written in a manner that permits competitive bidding. Complex specifications are often organized according to a standard system such as *Masterformat™*. This system was developed by the Construction Specification Institute (CSI), a nonprofit organization that has developed not only a standardized format for the preparation of specifications, but a common language as well. The CSI specification system is based on a "detailed numbering system, organized by materials, trades, functions and space relationships."[1] Its use reduces the chance of omitting important information for complex projects. It also makes it easier for a writing designer to make changes during the procurement process. No matter how complex (or simple), specifications may be either closed or open.

Complex specs may be closed or open.

Closed Specs

A specification written for a specific product for which no substitute would be acceptable is called a *closed specification*. For instance, a particular model of Viking range may be specified for a kitchen renovation. (If substitutions are not allowed, a vendor who submits them anyway may have to pay for the additional time it takes a designer to evaluate alternatives.)

Open Specs

Open specs with the words "or equal" permit substitution.

An *open specification* "usually has the words *or equal* incorporated into [it]."[2] If a specification is *open*, a vendor submitting a bid may substitute products that are very similar to what has been specified. For instance, an appliance dealer might propose the substitution of a Thermador, General Electric, Bosch, Gagenau, or KitchenAid range for the Viking specified. Since product differences are often subtle, alternates can be very time-consuming for designers to evaluate. It is customary for open specifications to include "definitions of what procedures will be followed concerning the submittal of alternates."[3] Requests related to substitutions may need to be submitted before the end of a bid period and may need to contain detailed descriptions of products proposed for substitution.

Varieties of Formal Specification

In addition to being either open or closed, specifications are of four varieties: proprietary, performance, reference, and descriptive.

PROPRIETARY SPECS

In a *proprietary specification*, the designer stipulates the manufacturer's name and the model or part number. For instance, a kitchen designer might specify MLL39TCRXY, a Modulux 24.9-cubic foot, side-by-side refrigerator with a dispenser for ice cubes, crushed ice, and water (see Table 8.1). Such a specification is not only proprietary but closed. When used by a large design firm with a specialty in commercial or industrial design, a proprietary specification functions as a *base bid* that helps the designer evaluate various suppliers' bids on the same product. A proprietary specification is the easiest variety to write, according to Christine Piotrowski, since "in many cases the designer only needs to provide the basic . . . information of manufacturer, product number, and finishes." (For instance, the designer might specify "stainless steel" for the finish of refrigerator MLL39TCRXY.) "When more detail is needed," Piotrowski explains, "manufacturers often provide" it; the designer then transfers the additional information to the specifications with little or no rewriting.[4]

Proprietary specs state maker and model.

TABLE 8.1 EXAMPLE OF SPECIFICATIONS

MODULUX 24.9-Cu.-Ft., Side-by-Side Refrigerator with Dispenser, Model # MLL39TCRXY

APPROXIMATE DIMENSIONS (HxDxW)	$69^3/4"$ by 33" by $35^3/4"$
CAPACITY	
Total (cubic feet)	24.9
Fresh Food (cubic feet)	15.33
Freezer (cubic feet)	9.53
Shelf Area (square feet)	22.4

Proprietary specifications permit a designer to save drawing time by furnishing exact and predictable dimensions early in the project. (The approximate dimensions, or HxDxW, of Modulux refrigerator model MLL39TCRXY, for instance, are 69³/₄ by 33 by 35³/₄ inches.) Since alternatives are not evaluated, the project schedule is compressed if the designer's specifications are proprietary. These specifications also permit the designer to control quality. (Modulux model MLL39TCRXY may have been well rated, for instance. Another manufacturer's comparable model may not have been.) A proprietary spec prevents the contractor from substituting less expensive products than the client and designer might desire.

On the negative side, proprietary specifications may make it harder for the client to save money by selecting less expensive alternatives. Proprietary specs also make it harder for the contractor to provide products of equal or better quality that are more readily available or have provided better results for the contractor's clients in the past. For this reason, most government agencies, among other clients, require that proprietary specifications, be written "open," that is, with an "or equal" clause.

PERFORMANCE SPECS

Based on "qualitative or measurable statements,"[5] *performance specifications* typically require that vendors submit test data with their bids. Since no model number, manufacturer, or trade name is specified, a performance specification is open and nonproprietary. Any product that meets the performance criteria is acceptable, so a specification of this type opens up the bidding process.

How does a performance specification function? *Consumer Reports* has found that "a refrigerator's usable capacity is typically about 60 to 80 percent of its nominal capacity."[6] A kitchen designer specifying a refrigerator for a family of active cooks with a small kitchen might insert a performance spec stating that the usable capacity of the refrigerator must be at least 75 percent of its nominal capacity, as measured by *Consumer Reports*. The various vendors in the client's region might submit qualifying bid prices for several refrigerators from different manufacturers.

Performance specs are based on measurable criteria.

If a designer cannot use a proprietary spec, performance specs may afford a good measure of control. Yet performance specifications must be written carefully and comprehensively and so can be time-consuming to create. The bids they generate may also be time-consuming to evaluate. In this process, it is possible for error to creep in that may be costly to rectify. The designer may lose control of the design concept; for instance, a client may respond favorably to a low-priced refrigerator that has good usable capacity but is inappropriate for the designer's visual concept. An obscure brand that meets the performance criteria and is favorably priced may turn out to be difficult to repair because it is not backed up by an adequate service network. The client may ultimately blame the designer.

REFERENCE SPECS

Like performance specs, *reference specs* are open and nonproprietary. A reference specification "usually utilizes established standards, such as the standards of the American Society for Testing and Materials (ASTM) and the American National Standards Institute (ANSI) rather than . . . performance [or other] criteria for required products."[7] To take an ever-so-simple example, a residential designer might specify a refrigerator with an *Energy Star* designation, meaning that it is 10 percent more efficient than required by July 2001 regulations stipulating that new refrigerators must meet "efficiency standards up to 30 percent more stringent than those in place" previously.[8] Although this example refers to a high standard, it is more typical for reference specifications to establish a minimal standard. If that is the case, the designer must be sure that the quality referenced is sufficiently high for the project in question. Reference standards, Piotrowski points out, are more widely used in construction than for interior design projects in which specifications are primarily for fixtures, furnishings, and equipment. Their most typical interior design use, she observes, may be for "wall and floor products and installation."[9] In general, reference standards are useful for establishing a quality basis and can save the designer a lot of effort. It would be time-consuming to specify, let us say, all the performance criteria that underlie the Energy Star designation.

Reference specs are based on established standards.

DESCRIPTIVE SPECS

Like a performance or a reference specification, a *descriptive specification* does not rely on the name of a manufacturer, a product name, or a model number to represent the desired product. Instead, the descriptive specification represents the product in terms of its features, which become the criteria on which bids must be based. It is then up to vendors to propose products from various manufacturers that satisfy the criteria.

Descriptive specifications must be both precise and comprehensive. At the Web site of the fictional manufacturer Modulux, you might find a long list of specifications—perhaps two printed pages—for Model #MLL39TCRXY. Table 8.1 displays an excerpt from those fictional specifications.

It is obviously much easier for a designer to simply specify Modulux Model # MLL39TCRXY—a proprietary specification—than to write a full

Descriptive specs are based on product features.

descriptive specification, even if the data for that specification are provided by a manufacturer (as in this case), which they cannot always be. For instance, a contract designer may create descriptive specs for open office systems that must be assembled from several manufacturers' product lines and custom-priced for the project under bid.

Descriptive specifications have clear advantages. They are open and are apt to generate a healthy range of bids when vendors for particular products are sparse. Although writing descriptive specs can be time-consuming, it is much easier for an interior designer to compare bids if the desired features for a given product type have been fully spelled out than it would have been to compare "or equal" substitutions that have what Piotrowski calls "subtle differences."

Descriptive specifications can incorporate performance criteria. For instance, a descriptive specification for a refrigerator might include the performance criterion that 75 percent of nominal capacity must be usable. A combination of descriptive and performance criteria may enable a designer to better control a project.

If descriptive specs are not precise and comprehensive, with clear detailed drawings supported by notes and recommendations, bids may be submitted, accepted, and executed in a manner that does not adequately support the design concept. For instance, suppose that it were not clearly specified that the edging around a laminate conference tabletop for a corporate office must be bull-nosed. The manufacturer's flat or milled edging may not be visually appropriate. Yet once the table has been delivered, it may strain the schedule and budget to ship it back to the vendor and to reorder and re-ship a table with bull-nosed edging. The vendor may not have bull-nosed tables in stock, or the cost may be higher. The designer may be left with a dilemma of unpalatable options—either incurring schedule and budget problems or accepting a table that undermines the design concept and may ultimately contribute to client dissatisfaction.

A table with the wrong edging may be the subject of wrangles, but it is unlikely to yield a lawsuit. If the designer had neglected to specify built-in antistatic control for carpeting laid in the family waiting rooms of a hospital and the resulting static interfered with life-support systems in nearby patient rooms, the designer's jeopardy might be greater and a lawsuit more likely.

Writing Specifications

Specifications may be written in either the indicative or the imperative (command) mode. Chapter 7 presents examples of construction specifications written in the command mode. Yet often, as Christine Piotrowski has pointed out, interior designers choose to use the indicative mode.[10] Here is an excerpt from a specification sample presented in Chapter 7 that is written in the imperative or command mode, as is typical for many construction specifications:

> Tape and spackle smooth so that when viewed from any angle wall is flat. Prime with Benjamin Moore Latex Quick Dry Prime Seal. Finish with two coats Benjamin Moore Regal Wall Satin.

In the command mode, the verbs in the sentences do not have any subjects. Orders are given: not "you will do this," or "he shall do this," but simply "do this." Rewritten in the indicative mode, the command-mode sentence, "Tape and spackle smooth so that when viewed from any angle wall is flat," might read: "Contractor shall tape and spackle smooth so that when viewed from any angle wall is flat." The sentence style is still *elliptical*, or spare, with no articles or pronouns, but now it is no longer "bossy." (Note the proprietary specifications of Benjamin Moore paint in the two sentences written in the imperative mode.)

Piotrowski notes that *shall* designates a command, while *will* implies a choice.[11] This is debatable. As noted in Chapter 6 of this book, legal-writing expert Richard Wydick[12] believes that both *shall* and *will* convey a range of indeterminate meanings. Yet traditional, standard grammar supports Piotrowski.

Traditionally, *shall* in the first and second persons signifies ordinary future intention, while *will* signifies, for those persons—that is, *I* and *you*—firm intention. In the third person—*he*, *she*, or *it*—*shall* traditionally signifies ordinary future intention, while *will* signifies firm intention. Since specifications are written in the third person, *shall* is the stronger verb, though few people nowadays may know why this is so; increasingly, as Wydick is aware, *shall* and *will* are used interchangeably. Language use mutates over time; interior designers, like other people, need to be alert to the evolution that is always taking place. Since the use of *shall* rather than *will* is customary among interior designers for specifications, that is one more reason to prefer it. Usage that is customary is always clearer to readers than usage that is *idiosyncratic*, or highly personal.

Whether writing specifications in the command or the indicative mode, the designer needs to be clear, precise, and unambiguous in the use of language. Many design firms use standard specifications, hire specification specialists for particular projects, or designate someone employed by the firm

Imperative: Tape and spackle wall. Indicative: Contractor shall tape and spackle wall.

To save space, spec writing style leaves out articles and pronouns.

The language of specs is precise, clear, and unambiguous.

to specialize in the preparation of specifications. All these practices reduce the possibility for error, as does software that performs the work of specification for the designer.

Automating Specification

Automation is appealing to interior designers preparing specifications for large or complicated projects for their corporate, institutional, and residential clients.

To cite one example, ARCOM makes available Masterspec Furnishings software that the company describes as a "comprehensive, automated procurement specification system created especially for interior design professionals working with furnishings dealers and vendors. It includes data-sheet-format specifications that cover furniture, fixtures, and miscellaneous furnishings typically contracted after interior construction is complete."[13] With this software, interior designers can prepare purchase-order requirements that are integrated with furnishings contracts between owners and suppliers. They can create notes for technical and coordination issues. They can also access lists of manufacturers' products and current contact information.

Or a designer might choose Tectonic Studio, at https://studio.tectonic.com, a Web-based software tool that simplifies and streamlines the specification process. It features "a comprehensive library of commercial interior finishes, color-true product imagery, and accurate, up-to-date specifications."[14] It permits searches by attributes and values such as dominant or accent color. Electronic swatches and sample boards are generated through a designer's choices within the software, which can then be sent via e-mail to people who do not have the software. By clicking on any product, specifications are displayed and can be printed. So far so good (and Tectonic does more, as we shall see); but specification is only the beginning of the procurement process.

Varieties of Purchasing Paperwork

Each *purchase order* (a formal request that someone supply something in return for payment) yields a slough of documents that keep track of what has been ordered and where it is in the procurement and billing process. Purchasing paperwork includes not only the purchase order, but also the purchase log, the purchase-order index, and vendor- and shipper-generated paperwork.

The Purchase Order

The most characteristic type of paperwork connected with the purchase of FF&E is the purchase order (Figure 8.2) itself. As Tad Crawford and Eva Doman Bruck explain, "The purchase order serves as a notice to vendors, manufacturers, and other suppliers . . . to begin work on a specific assignment or to deliver goods. Most vendors will not proceed without a written purchase order."[15] The purchase order, or PO, is useful to the interior designer as well as to the vendor. It is a comprehensive record of each order and can be used to verify that no mistakes have been made at the vendor's end. Many electronic systems generate purchase orders, ranging from business stalwarts QuickBooks and Filemaker to design-specific software such as MasterSpec Furnishings, Tectonic Studio, Design Manager, and IBS. It is possible for an interior designer to customize Microsoft Office PO templates (available through the MS Office Web site), (see Figure 8.2 and CD-ROM for a sample purchase order). It is also possible for a design firm to create a purchase order from scratch, using Microsoft Word or another word-processing program. If you don't have a computer, you can create a PO form on a typewriter and photocopy it as needed. Alternatively, you can have a commercial printer create form sets with your firm's name imprinted on them.

Debbie Green, advising window-treatment designers, endorses the practice of printing all computer-generated POs on yellow paper to signify wholesale pricing. Some designers hand-write or type POs on multicolored form sets to create copies of POs in at least two colors: white for the vendor; and two copies in some other color for in-house use in the pending purchase-order file and the project binder or client active file.[16] A colored copy may also be sent to a warehouse that will be receiving shipment to let its workers know the order is in the pipeline. If you are pressed for time or are printing purchase orders from a printer that is shared by others in your design office, it may not be practical to painstakingly print copies of each PO on different colors of paper. You may find that it works best to simply print on standard paper (usually white) the number of copies you need, then stamp the word *COPY* diagonally across all but the PO designated as the original.

Identify PO copies with colored paper or by rubber stamping.

However you identify PO copies, your firm's purchase-order form or template should contain the time- and custom-honored elements that facilitate good record keeping and enable efficient order tracking and billing.

Elements of a PO

Your purchase order should be imprinted with the *PO date* as well as *letterhead information* consisting of your firm's contact data: firm name, address, telephone and fax numbers, and e-mail and Web addresses. The

Weber Design

PURCHASE ORDER

378 Willow Lane
Claryville, NY 12725
Phone and Fax 845-555-6789

The following number must appear on all related correspondence, shipping papers, and invoices:

P.O. NUMBER: 100

Client/Project:

Vendor Address:	**Ship To:**	**Bill To:**
Name	Name	Name
Company	Company	Company
Address	Address	Address
City, State ZIP	City, State ZIP	City, State ZIP
Phone	Phone	Phone

P.O. DATE	**PROJECT DESIGNER**	**SHIPPED VIA**	**PROJECT NUMBER**	**TERMS**

ITEM #	**QTY**	**UNIT**	**DESCRIPTION**	**UNIT PRICE**	**OTHER**	**TOTAL**

SUBTOTAL	
SALES TAX	
FREIGHT & DELIVERY	
OTHER	
TOTAL	
DEDUCT DEPOSIT	
BALANCE DUE	

Vendor's Customer #:

1. Please send two copies of your invoice.
2. Enter this order in accordance with the prices, terms, delivery method, and specifications listed above.
3. Please notify us immediately if you are unable to ship as specified.
4. **Send all correspondence to:**
   Weber Design
   378 Willow Lane • Claryville, NY • 12725
   Phone and Fax 845-555-6789

Authorized by   Date

name of the *design contact person*, or person submitting the PO, needs to be included, too. In addition, the purchase order should contain any *project number* assigned by your firm.

There should be an area for your *client's name* or *the name of the project*, for example, "Bathroom, Ira B. Watson Residence." In addition, the purchase order should contain the design firm's purchase-order number, along with the ship-to information, the vendor's address, the vendor's customer number or billing number, the order information, the terms of payment, the ship-via information, the bill-to information, and the signature. This is a lot of information, but none of it is mysterious and all of it serves a clear purpose.

DESIGNER'S PURCHASE-ORDER NUMBER

Even for projects that consist of renovating a single residential room, such as a bathroom or kitchen, it is customary for a designer to designate a range of numbers to be used exclusively for the consecutive numbering of all orders for FF&E and supplies relating to that project. For instance, Weber Design may assign the Watson bathroom renovation the 3000 range—all numbers from 3000 to 3999. That would mean that the first item ordered or purchased for the Watsons would bear the purchase-order number 3000, the second 3001, and the last 3999. For a very large project entailing the purchase of thousands of items, the range might be 10000 to 19999, or even 100000 through 199999. (Alternatively, Weber Design may assign the Watsons a client number such as 376, which would be constant for all projects. The numbered purchases for a given Watson project would be linked to their client number by a hyphen: 376-3008.)

Sometimes areas within a client's designated number range are allotted to different types of purchases. For the Watson bathroom project, Weber Design may allocate the numbers between 3000 and 3499 to the purchase of construction-related materials such as paint, tile, and fixtures (that is, plumbing and electrical fixtures and hardware). The numbers between 3500 and 3999 might be used for furnishings and equipment: a heated towel bar, shelving, toothbrush rack, a medicine cabinet, towels, shower curtain, rugs and mats, framed botanical prints, plants and cachepots, and so on. You may think that Weber has allotted too large a range of numbers for a single bathroom, but many design firms prefer to err in the direction of caution. After all, the universe of numbers is infinite. When a project has long been completed, its range of numbers can be recycled. If there is no client number, a designer who reuses PO number ranges can add letters in front of them to clarify the project designation. For instance, the Watson bathroom might have the letters WB in front of each purchase-order number: WB3000, WB3001, and so on.

> The designer's PO number is designated by project and may be linked to a client number.

SHIP-TO INFORMATION

This part of the PO tells the vendor where to ship what you, as designer, have ordered. It might be the address of the project premises; it might be the address of a storage facility; it might be your own office. It might be a fabricator's shop; for instance, you might have upholstery fabric shipped to the upholsterer's shop. Of course, the address should be complete and accurate. Some additional explanatory notes may also be required. The last thing you want is for shipments to be misdirected and thus not delivered in a timely manner.

VENDOR ADDRESS

This section contains the company name, mailing address, e-mail address, and phone and fax numbers of the vendor that will be filling the order, including the name of the *vendor contact person* for the order.

The vendor may assign a customer number.

VENDOR'S CUSTOMER NUMBER OR BILLING NUMBER

If your firm has been assigned a customer or billing number, it should be entered on all POs submitted to a given company. This will aid in timely and accurate billing and will help keep your account current.

ORDER INFORMATION

This section is frequently formatted as a table with columns but no rows, to allow for flexible item entries. This section is sometimes titled *Specifications*. The column heads should include:

- *Item Number*   With reference to this order only. Will always begin with "1" and proceed in sequence through each item ordered.
- *Quantity (QTY)*   The amount of each item ordered.
- *Item Name and/or Code and Description*   Including finishes, colors, sizes, and other special information. If drawings, sketches, or swatches are attached, note that here. It may also be appropriate to mention catalog page numbers.
- *Unit Price*   Price per item.
- *Other*   In this column, note discount or other relevant pricing information such as the vendor's markups for rush and overtime orders.
- *Extension* (item total column)   QTY multiplied by unit price as modified by the information in the *Other* column.

After the last total has been entered in the extension, or item total, column, the item totals are added up to create the *subtotal*, the amount owed for merchandise units before applicable add-ons. Applicable *tax* is then added on, based on a percentage of the subtotal. Applicable *freight and delivery charges* are also added on, along with any appropriate *charges for installation* of items such as wall units. A *total* is generated which represents the subtotal plus all add-ons. From this is subtracted the amount of any *deposit* that has been paid. The final figure is the *balance due*—what the interior designer owes the vendor.

TERMS OF PAYMENT

A PO typically contains a box or other space designated for stating the terms on which payment is due. For instance, the terms of payment might be "50 percent deposit, balance due upon receipt of delivery." Or the terms of payment might be "Collect," meaning collected upon delivery. (For large orders, most suppliers will in fact require deposits and may ask for bank and business references as well.)

SHIP-VIA INFORMATION

Your purchase-order form needs to have an insertion window for the designated shipper of the items ordered—for example, United Parcel Service.

BILL-TO INFORMATION

If the vendor's *invoice*, or statement of money owed, is to be sent to anyone other than the interior designer who is issuing the PO, the name and address of that person is entered in the "bill-to" section, along with phone and fax numbers and an e-mail address. According to Tad Crawford and Eva Doman Bruck, most vendors prefer to bill the designer rather than a third party.[17]

SIGNATURE

Each PO needs to be signed by a person with authority to issue it, usually the interior designer or project manager. Because a PO is legally binding even if the designer has made an error in the order, the savvy designer will have gotten the client's written go-ahead before signing and issuing the PO; but this is typically tied to phased approvals, so it may not be necessary for the client to approve each individual purchase order.

The Purchase Log

While the purchase order contains all the information that a vendor needs to fulfill, bill, and ship a particular order, it does not contain all the information that the issuing designer needs to track each design-project component

The log tracks purchases through pricing, ordering, delivery, and storage.

through the procurement process. Nor does it gather together information about all purchases initiated for a given project. It is therefore advisable for an interior designer to create a purchase log for each project in order to facilitate the tracking of all items ordered. The purchase log will typically include spreadsheet sections for simplified specifications. It will track each purchase through the pricing, delivery, and storage phases of the procurement cycle.[18] Table 8.2 featured in the text and on the CD-ROM, shows an excerpt adapted from a sample purchase-log form created by Tad Crawford and Eva Doman Bruck. *Their Business and Legal Forms for Interior Designers* comes with a CD-ROM containing not only the purchase log but other forms (including a purchase order) that you have the right to download, customize, and use if you have purchased the book and CD-ROM. You could also use procurement, spreadsheet, word-processing, or other relevant software to create a report that logs and tracks POs.

The index helps organize and find purchase information.

The Purchase-Order Index

To further clarify the organization of your purchase records, you may find it useful to create a pending purchase-order index for your PO file.[19] As you can see from the example shown in Table 8.3, featured in the text and on the CD-ROM, a PO index tabulates data under headings such as date, vendor, project number, total order amount, and PO number. A purchase-order index contains less information than a purchase-order log, but it enables a designer to quickly reference the range of outstanding purchases for all of a firm's projects. You could create a similar index that is project-specific. If it were filed in the front of a project binder, you wouldn't have to flip through numerous individual POs to retrieve basic information. A purchase-order index displays a "thumbnail sketch" of each PO indexed, so a designer can quickly access the number of a particular PO, its date, or its amount.

TABLE 8.2   PURCHASE LOG

			BID DOCUMENTS			PRICE TRACK				SHIPPING TRACK						STORAGE TRACK		
Item	Vendor	Contact	Drawing Ref. #	Vendor Catalog #	Swatch, Sample Ref. #	PO #	PO Total	Change Order Ref. #	Vendor Invoice Total	Order Date	Ship Date	Deliv./ Date/ Venue	Ship Via	Bill of Lading #	Receipt Date	Location	Tag #	In/Out

Adapted from Tad Crawford and Eva Doman Bruck, Business and Legal Forms for Interior Designers *(New York: Allworth Press, 2001), 80.*

TABLE 8.3   PURCHASE-ORDER INDEX FOR A PENDING FILE

DATE	VENDOR	PROJECT NUMBER	PO TOTAL	PO NUMBER

Adapted from Tad Crawford and Eva Doman Bruck, Business and Legal Forms for Interior Designers (New York: Allworth Press, 2001), 88.

Vendor- and Shipper-Generated Paperwork

In addition to the paperwork generated by an interior design firm's orders, each purchase generates vendor and shipper paperwork that must be checked against the original PO. Vendor-generated paperwork includes order confirmations and invoices. Shipper-generated paperwork includes shipping or freight bills and bills of lading.

Check vendors' and shippers' paperwork against your own.

ORDER CONFIRMATION

This form mirrors the interior designer's purchase order—or should. In it, the vendor acknowledges every important detail of the PO, including the name of the designer who placed the order, the designer's PO number, the billing and shipping addresses, the order information, and the "tag for"— the name of the client for whom the merchandise has been ordered. The order confirmation also contains new information, including the date of the confirmation, or acknowledgment; the vendor's order or invoice number; the scheduled shipping date; and the means of shipping. The designer needs to check the confirmation against the original order and update the purchase log as needed. The vendor needs to be alerted to any discrepancy between the original PO and the order confirmation.

INVOICE

An *invoice* (Figure 8.3) is a statement of monies owed for goods or services, commonly known as a bill. Venders' invoices "are usually sent at the same time the merchandise is shipped," and so may arrive before the actual shipment.[20] The vendor's invoice needs to be checked—not only against

Figure 8.3
Invoice form
created with
Microsoft
template.
*Reprinted with
permission of
Microsoft.*

Vendor Name

Invoice

Bill To:
Street Address
Address 2
City, ST ZIP Code

Ship To:
Street Address
Address 2
City, ST Zip Code

Invoice #:
Invoice Date:
Customer ID:
Project/Client:

Date	Your Order #	Our Order #	Project Designer	Ship Via	Terms	Tax ID

Quantity	Your Item #	Unit Code	Description	Discount %	Taxable	Unit Price	Total

Subtotal	
Tax	
Freight & Delivery	
Misc.	
TOTAL	
Deposit	
Balance Due	

REMITTANCE
Customer ID:
Date:
Amount Due:
Amount Enclosed:

Vender's Street Address
Address 2
City, ST ZIP Code
Country

Phone: 535-555-6789
Fax: 535-555-6789
Email: someone@example.com
Website: http://www.treyresearch.net

Vendor Name

the PO, but against the shipped merchandise—to make certain that it corresponds exactly to what was ordered and billed. The invoice also needs to be checked for any discount extended for prompt payment. If the billing is correct, the designer will pay the vendor's invoice and will invoice the client within ten days of accepting the shipment.

SHIPPING OR FREIGHT BILL

Sent separately from the merchandise a short time after it has been shipped, the *shipping* or *freight bill* invoices the shipping or freight service. Note that this bill is sent by a different vendor—the shipping or freight company—than the supplier of the merchandise.

BILL OF LADING

A statement of how many items are in a particular shipment and who is entitled to receive it is called a *bill of lading* (Figure 8.4) and is given to a truck driver at the loading point. Merchandise in transit from a vendor's factory or warehouse is tracked by the number assigned to the bill of lading, not by the designer's PO number. If a shipment is delayed or misdirected, the designer who is trying to locate the order needs to have on hand the number of the bill of lading, the name and location of the vendor that sent the shipment, the shipping date, the quantity and types of merchandise shipped, and the delivery venue. If the designer does not have the number of the bill of lading, it may be necessary to request it from the manufacturer. Once the designer has the number, it should be duly noted in the purchase log.

> Track shipments in transit by the bill of lading's number.

PACKING LIST

A statement about the number and nature of items in each shipment is called a *packing list* (Figure 8.5). Such a list usually accompanies a shipment, often encased in a plastic envelope affixed to the exterior of a carton or crate. Upon delivery, the quantity of items received must be checked against the quantity indicated on the bill of lading. In addition, all items should be unwrapped and inspected for concealed damage, the extent of which should be noted on the bill of lading to facilitate any claims that need to be made. Documentary photos of damaged packaging and defective items may be taken. If a claim for damages needs to be filed, copies of all relevant paperwork generated by the vendor—including the bill of lading—will be part of the claims packet, as will evidence that the shipping or freight bill has been paid. In addition, the designer will need to submit the shipper's inspection report along with documentation of any repair, re-shipping, and other expenses incurred as a consequence of the damage.

> Damage claims are based on full, accurate records and paid bills.

Date	Bill of Lading – Short Form – Not Negotiable		Page 1 of _____

Ship From

Name:
Address:
City/State/Zip:
SID No.:

Bill of Lading Number:_____

Bar Code Space

Ship To

Name:
Address:
City/State/Zip:
CID No.:

Carrier Name:_____
Trailer number:
Serial number(s):

Third Party Freight Charges Bill to:

Name:
Address:
City/State/Zip:

SPAC:
Pro Number:

Bar Code Space

Special Instructions:

Freight Charge Terms: (Freight charges are prepaid unless marked otherwise)
Prepaid: ____ Collect: _____ 3rd Party:____

☐ **(check box):** Master bill of lading with attached underlying bills of lading.

Customer Order Information

Customer Order No.	No. Packages	Weight	Pallet/Slip (circle one)	Additional Shipper Information
			Y N	
			Y N	
			Y N	
			Y N	
Grand Total				

Carrier Information

Handling Unit		Package				Commodity Description	LTL Only	
Qty	Type	Qty	Type	Weight	HM (X)	Commodities requiring special or additional care or attention in handling or stowing must be so marked and packaged as to ensure safe transportation with ordinary care.	No.	Class

Where the rate is dependent on value, shippers are required to state specifically in writing the agreed or declared value of the property as follows: "The agreed or declared value of the property is specifically stated by the shipper to be not exceeding _____ per

COD Amount: $_____

Free terms: Collect __, Prepaid __, Customer check acceptable __

Note Liability limitation for loss or damage in this shipment may be applicable.

Received, subject to individually determined rates or contracts that have been agreed upon in writing between the carrier and shipper, if applicable, otherwise to the rates, classifications and rules that have been established by the carrier and are available to the shipper, on request, and to all applicable state and federal regulations.

The carrier shall not make delivery of this shipment without payment of and all other lawful charges.
Shipper Signature_____

Shipper Signature/Date	**Trailer Loaded:**	**Freight Counted:**	**Carrier Signature/Pickup Date**
This is to certify that the above named materials are properly classified, packaged, marked and labeled, and are in proper condition for transportation according to the applicable regulations of the DOT.	_ By shipper _ By driver	_ By shipper _ By driver _ By driver/pieces	Carrier acknowledges receipt of packages and required placards. Carrier certifies emergency response information was made available and/or carrier has the DOT emergency response guidebook or equivalent documentation in the vehicle. **Property described above is received in good order, except as noted.**

Figure 8.4 Bill of lading form created from a Microsoft template. *Reprinted with permission from Microsoft.*

Vendor

Packing Slip

Address
City, State ZIP Code
Phone: Fax:

Order Date: Date:
Order Number: Customer Contact:
Purchase Order: Customer Account:

Ship To: **Bill To:**
Name   Name
Company   Company
Address   Address
City, State ZIP Code   City, State ZIP Code
Phone: Phone:

Product	Description	Unit Type	Order Quantity	Ship Quantity
		TOTAL	**0**	**0**

Comments:

Please contact the Customer Service department at 1-800-555-0100 with any questions or concerns.

THANK YOU FOR YOUR BUSINESS!

Figure 8.5
Packing slip created
from a Microsoft
Excel spreadsheet.
*Reprinted with
permission of
Microsoft.*

Information Management

Any designer handling the procurement process for a client must organize a great deal of information that links specification to purchasing and order tracking as well as to bid management, if bids have been solicited. All these functions must be linked to the design firm's general billing and accounting practices. Most designers develop a system for managing information. Information management systems in use by interior designers range from a simple paper filing system to computerized procurement-management systems such as Franklin-Potter's Design Manager software or Tririga's Web-based Intelligent Business System™ (IBS).

Paper-Based Procurement Records

All-paper records are practical for very small firms.

The simplest and least expensive way for a design firm to manage procurement is with an all-paper record system. This may be the most practical choice for very small firms, solo practitioners, or start-up firms, including those with niche practices.

THE PENDING PURCHASE-ORDER FILE

At the Web site www.minutesmatter.com, which is geared to the needs of small design firms specializing in window treatments, Debbie Green describes a simple paperwork-organization scheme designed to work in tandem with QuickBooks accounting software, although Green claims it will work even for designers who do not have a computer. She suggests that a firm organize information into five paper-filing categories:

* Business files
* Active client files
* Pending unpaid-bill files
* Client proposal files
* A pending purchase-order file

Green's firm maintains only *one* file for all purchase orders, filing them in numerical order.[21]

> All purchase orders are printed on yellow paper to signify wholesale pricing. As an item is ordered for a client, we issue a purchase order in QuickBooks. When placing an order, we always obtain the [supplier's] reference number, expected ship date, and cost. A purchase order should be reprinted if any changes are made. When an item is

received, the purchase order is pulled. The information on the packing slip is verified against the purchase order. The packing slip is then stapled to the back of the purchase order and filed in the client [active] file.

Since this system numbers purchase orders for all of a designer's current jobs consecutively, without establishing a special range of numbers for each job, it is suitable for very small firms with relatively uncomplicated projects. Keeping all pending purchase orders in one paper file yields a highly portable procurement-administration system, one that is compatible with the "files-to-go" approach Green describes elsewhere on her site. Her approach allows a window-treatment designer to work from a car, driving from appointment to appointment with a plastic milk crate full of hanging folders in the back of her vehicle.[22] A small design firm—even a solo designer who, for fabrication purposes, is tied to a workroom—can successfully cultivate a seminomadic business style, traveling light and moving relatively fast, although the preponderance of papers in the other four filing categories—business files, active client files, pending unpaid-bill files, and client proposal files—presumably remain at the workroom-linked home office, along with QuickBooks and the computer, if the designer has one. (Sometimes the pending-purchase file is known as a "tickler file," because the designer may need to make gentle inquiries—"tickle" the vendors—to keep orders moving.)

> A tickler file helps the designer keep orders moving.

THE PROJECT BINDER

As discussed in Chapter 10, a fairly sizeable project may be run from a three-ring binder devoted exclusively to the project in which are stored not only the paperwork related to procurement, but telephone logs, meeting minutes, and other documentation that is important for the realization of a design project. This binder is consulted in association with plans, drawings, swatches, and other resource and reference matter that does not lend itself to being filed with $8\frac{1}{2}$-by-11-inch papers and so is stored differently. The more documentation a design project involves, the more attention a designer or a designer's staff must pay to the issue of organization. As purchase orders proliferate, tracking them must be accomplished manually in a paper-based system. This may be a daunting task for large or complicated jobs.

> A project binder organizes all paper records for a project.

Electronic Procurement Records

The complexity of the procurement process—particularly with larger projects—leads many designers to invest in computer software that will reduce the volume of paperwork. "Do design, not paperwork" is the motto of Franklin-Potter's Design Manager. (You can find a comprehensive listing of other software for the interior design industry at www.dezignare.com.)

DEDICATED DESIGN MANAGEMENT SOFTWARE

Design Manager is specifying, purchasing, tracking, billing, and accounting software created specifically for interior designers[23]:

> All of the functions are integrated, meaning that an entry in one portion of the software will automatically update all the other portions. For example, if you enter a vendor's invoice, Design Manager will update the purchase order, tracking, invoicing, and accounting information so that all portions of the software maintain accurate records.

According to Franklin Potter,[24] here is how the software works:

- *Specifying* The designer inputs project information once to produce proposals, purchase orders, and invoices.
- *Purchasing* Once the proposal is approved, purchase orders are generated automatically.
- *Order tracking* As the orders progress, Design Manager tracks the status of each piece and each vendor.
- *Billing* Client invoices are generated automatically, from the designer's project specifications. Sales tax, freight, and client deposits are factored into the final invoice.
- *Accounting* The fully integrated accounting system gathers information as project work progresses to produce accounting journals, financial statements, and account reconciliations.

In the *specifying* phase, the software contains numerous features to help a busy designer minimize the paperwork connected with purchase management. For instance, Design Manager permits long descriptions—up to a page and a half for each item in a project—and allows a designer to list items and summarize by room locations. The program instructs the computer to extend unit cost by quantity, calculate costs based on buying terms, and mark up the cost or discount the retail to calculate the price to the client. The software further permits the designer to combine purchases from many vendors into a single item on the proposal and client invoice. In addition, Design Manager permits the designer to use different wording in proposals and purchase orders. "This helps eliminate client price shopping and allows

Dedicated software can help designers with purchasing and other paperwork.

detailed instructions to be seen only by the vendor."[25] Clearly, the individual who designed that feature had some practical experience!

In the *purchasing* phase, the spec information is transferred to the purchase order, which the designer can edit, expanding the description with details that are pertinent to a given vendor. Design Manager automatically generates separate purchase orders, or "POs," for items from different vendors and shipping addresses. When a single proposal item requires purchases from several vendors, the designer can create POs for each of them. "Up to ninety-nine vendor POs can be linked to a single item on the proposal." At the same time, the software consolidates all items for a project from a given vendor into a single PO based on the name of the vendor and the ship-to address.

The software provides an equivalent amount of assistance to the designer in the *order-tracking* phase, giving the designer instant access to:

- What was proposed to the client
- What was ordered from vendors
- Deposits received from clients
- Deposits sent to vendors
- Back orders
- What clients owe the designer
- What the designer owes to the vendors

In the *billing* phase, the software assists with freight and sales-tax processing, warns the designer of incipient billing errors, and permits selective invoicing, so that a designer can invoice clients for individual items, for all items on a proposal, or for the total project. Also supported are credits and partial billing of items.

In the *accounting* phase, Design Manager maintains a detailed historical audit trail covering "decades of information and millions of transactions." It helps the designer keep track of what vendors are owed and helps determine who gets paid what when. It records and tracks client deposits and payments so that a designer can always generate a complete record of the monies received from a client and can demonstrate the manner in which it was applied to a project. In addition, the software keeps tabs on which vendors are holding how much of a designer's deposit money.

An electronic system like this one is a far cry from the single pending purchase-order file described by Debby Green, or even from a collection of purchase orders and other procurement documents manually filed in a project binder. Informal or formal training may be required for the designer to fully integrate purchase-management software into office operations.

Once the learning curve has been negotiated, the software permits the designer to keep track of a great deal of information—and to generate purchase documents as needed—without being overwhelmed by paperwork. With such a system, information is stored on the design firm's own computers, where, needless to say, it must be appropriately backed up—electronically and on paper. For some large or complicated projects, a Web-based system may be more appropriate. In such a system, information is stored, maintained, accessed from, and backed up on large computers outside the design firm.

Large projects may require a project Web site.

DESIGN-BUILD SOFTWARE LINKED TO CAD AND THE INTERNET

On November 28, 2001, Tririga, Inc., which styles itself "a leading provider of software for the hospitality, aerospace, and design/build industries," announced a joint initiative with AutoDesk, Inc, the leading design software company. The two companies had developed a bi-directional link between AutoDesk® Architectural Desktop 3.3 (ADT) and Tririga Intelligent Business System (IBS) that would provide a way to extend "model-based design intelligence" throughout a project's life cycle.[26] But even without the bi-directional link to ADT, Tririga's IBS was already positioned to provide Web-based procurement-management services to designers and builders of many stripes, including the designers of executive aircraft interiors.[27]

What is the nature of the IBS software? According to Tririga president and CEO Anthony A. Marnell III, it is the first technology that automates "the *entire* design and build process—from CAD design and engineering to development, procurement, and ongoing maintenance."[28]

> Starting at the design phase, the software adds a layer of intelligence to traditional CAD drawings—a level that is extended to support every stage of the process—from developing specs, to analyzing costs, to managing bids, to issuing purchase orders. This intelligent information is stored online in a searchable database. . . . [Everything] is available in real-time to worldwide partners over the Internet. . . . [who] can . . . share knowledge on a global scale. At the same time, asset managers can access a centralized system for information, with all project history and legacy data at their fingertips. The information is accessible anytime, from anywhere, which facilitates communication across time zones and serves the needs of the emerging global economy.

According to Tririga, its IBS platform "offers a powerful solution for the commercial interiors industry to centrally manage and streamline large-scale development, renovation, facility improvement, and capital expenditure projects."[29] Tririga refers to its software platform as "enterprise class"; and, indeed, it manages purchasing on a very large scale. Early in 2001, for instance, hotel-and-casino magnate Stephen Wynn selected IBS to "support the design specification and FF&E . . . procurement phases" in the development of the $1.6 billion Le Reve, a "next-generation resort" in Las Vegas that will have 45 floors, 2,455 luxury rooms, and a 4-acre lake. According to Todd Nisbet, executive vice-president of Wynn Design and Le Reve's project manager, "We were looking for a way to integrate all the interior-design specifications and purchasing requirements and put [them] all online so that we could have efficiency."[30]

Wynn Design needed efficiency! For this project, in addition to its own employees, more than 50 specialty design firms and approximately 300 subcontractors connect to the Tririga system.[31] The database is accessed by "restaurant and retail space designers, architects, [and] environment engineers," as well as interior designers.

Of course, the project database must be protected by password. Suppliers and designers bidding on Wynn contracts must be approved before obtaining access. When they have negotiated the Internet security checkpoints, they find applications that present Wynn's bidding information as contract forms. They can submit bids by filling out the forms online. "Once a vendor is chosen, the system will automatically roll the winning proposal's data straight into a purchase order from Timberline,"[32] the specialized accounting software that links purchasing commitments to design and construction budgets.

In the past, Wynn's administrative employees spent 80 percent of their time using word processors to retype complicated design contracts every time a bid was accepted. The new system eliminates much of that work, introducing significant cost efficiencies for Wynn Design and its parent company.[33]

VENDOR-DRIVEN SOFTWARE

Wynn Design's procurement system brings vendors to a project-specific Web site. There are also arrangements that bring interior designers to electronic procurement systems maintained by vendors. The designer may patronize a walk-in design center, utilize a vendor's CD catalog, or order on the Internet.

Some designers use electronic procurement systems maintained by vendors.

WALK-IN CENTERS   To take just one example, the Expo Design Centers operated by Home Depot offer special trade services to kitchen and bath designers at selected centers. At these competitively priced walk-in centers, interior designers can work with their Expo counterparts to tour showrooms and assemble selections. On-site software assists with pricing a designer's selections and generates a floor plan, elevations, a 3-D perspective, and layouts for plumbing and electrical work. When the final selections have been made, the designer writes one check and receives a completely itemized bill. Expo coordinates ordering to avoid any delays in deliveries, installs much of what the designer has ordered, and coordinates with the contractor for the rest.[34] These services may be particularly useful for designers who execute projects in regions other than the ones in which they are based, since the design center acts as the designer's agent with the contractor.

CD CATALOGS   Companies such as Cooper Lighting place their electronic catalogs on CD-ROM. Designers who use the catalog frequently can download the entire catalog to their hard drives. Designers who use the catalog intermittently can download only the files needed to access catalog data from the CD-ROM. The catalog software displays specs in Adobe Acrobat Reader and facilitates ordering from Cooper.

ONLINE ORDERING   In addition, designers may order many products through Web sites like that maintained by Tectonic Studio (https://studio. tectonic.com), which is discussed earlier in this chapter. After the specification phase, order forms can be created and orders placed through the designer's e-mail program.

Of course, in selecting software to automate the procurement process, design firms of all sizes are looking for ways to cut down on paperwork. Let us not forget Franklin-Potter's motto for its Design Manager software: "Do design, not paperwork."

Writing Purchase Documents

Virtually all designers would agree that paperwork such as filling out procurement forms is not "design." But can it be called "writing"? While it may seem that "writing" is involved in procurement only in the sense that intelligible marks are being made on paper or displayed on screens, the inscribing of records connected with orders and accounts is not a degraded version of a complex cultural practice. The opposite is true; in the view of historian Georges Jean,[35] the complex practice of recording ideas, memories, and feelings that we call *writing* has humble origins in the keeping of ancient accounts:

> As far as we know, [writing] began in ancient Mesopotamia, the land between the Tigris and Euphrates rivers (modern Iraq). This area was, around the 3rd millennium BC, divided into Sumer in the south and

Akkad in the north. . . . Beyond the officials of the royal court[s], the priests, and the merchants, the population of Mesopotamia consisted largely of shepherds and farmers. . . . [The] first inscriptions found on clay tablets from Sumer . . . list sacks of grain and heads of cattle. The first written signs were therefore used for agricultural accounts. . . . From its humble beginnings as an accounting system, writing gradually became, among the people of Mesopotamia, first a form of memorandum, then a system for recording spoken language, [then] an alternative medium for communication, thought, and expression.

Jean further reminds us that writing was "born of practical necessity," because reliable records of accounts could not be kept orally.[36] We need reliable records for the same reason that people needed them in Mesopotamia 3,000 years ago: to create a clear accounting trail that can be agreed upon by various parties to a transaction or series of transactions. Accurate, careful record keeping created harmony among ancient people, and it serves the same function in our own complex society; indeed, the more complex the transaction, the more important it is to be precise, patient, and thorough in documenting it.

> Writing was born 3,000 years ago of the need for accurate records, which are still important.

Purchasing to fulfill interior design contracts is vastly more complex than exchanges involving sacks of grain and cows. Yet accurate record keeping will facilitate harmony between clients, designers, vendors, shippers, and warehouse personnel. Even if a design firm tracks purchases with sophisticated software, the system is no more reliable than each individual who puts information into it. The secrets of successful writing for procurement are simple and time-honored: be sure that your records are accurate, precise, and thorough; spell carefully; and check and re-check at every step of the way for consistency, clarity, and responsiveness to other relevant documents.

Discussion Questions

1. Proprietary specs are easy for designers to write and yield rigorous control over quality. Why and under what circumstances would designers write other kinds of specs?

2. Would you rather work in a large firm in which the procurement process was completely automated or in a very small firm in which procurement was handled manually? Using techniques you learned in Chapter 3, write a two-page comparative analysis examining the grounds for this choice. Save your analysis for use in connection with Chapter 9.

Exercises

1. Using the formatting features of your word-processing program, create a purchase form that contains the full range of PO elements that have been identified in this chapter. Be sure to include the graphic identity that you created for your firm in exercises for Chapter 4. In small groups, critique one another's PO forms for professionalism and functionality.

2. Go to the Web site of an appliance manufacturer. If you wish, narrow your search to a particular price range or category of finishes. Select four appliance types and one product within each type. On the purchase order you prepared for Exercise 1, manually enter proprietary specs for all four products.

In addition, print out the complete descriptive specifications for each of your four products. Using a search engine such as Google, find three other vendors of each of the appliance types you have selected. Choose an alternate product that closely matches the descriptive specs for each product for which you printed specifications.

Prepare a five-minute oral report describing your experience and what you learned about specifying products.

3. Interview an interior designer to find out how his or her firm handles the procurement process. What kinds of specs are written? How does the firm handle paperwork? Does the firm maintain paper files, electronic files, or both? Share what you learn in a class discussion.

Writing in the Design Office

9

There are now design firms that, in the words of Lewis Jay Goetz, IIDA, AIA, "do not own a t-square. Most of the staff might not even know what one is."[1] With the shift to *CAD*, or computer-aided design, have come other technological shifts, most notably to e-mail, that are profoundly changing the nature of communication within design offices. Goetz points to the expansion of technology in four areas: marketing; design and presentation; business and finance; and communication. According to Goetz,[2] the fourth area is the most important.

> Sophisticated landline telephone systems, cell phones, palm devices, faxes, e-mail, videoconference, teleconference, Internet and now Instant Messenger are the devices we use to communicate with personnel, clients and consultants. . . . [The] tools alone do not necessarily make communication better, but they do give us the ability to respond faster and to start solving problems sooner.

Technology and Communication

Technology in the design office hardly diminishes the importance of language. Integrating CAD into the office of Rill & Decker in Bethesda, Maryland, meant creating a "verbal culture" where designers "constantly confer."[3] The elements of this culture can range from "a yell across the office" to a lengthy formal report, but it is e-mail that keeps information constantly flowing, e-mail that facilitates, not only tele-commutation, tele-collaboration, and relationships with clients who live half a world away from a project site, but ordinary work within the design office.

A designer away from the office can access faxes, drawings, photos, and any other information stored on an office server through a program like Symantec's PC Anywhere. Or the designer can access information—including renderings of 3-D models—posted to a project Web site. Finally, a designer can take a laptop to a meeting in a client's office. "Revisions are quick with CAD," says Dan Beert, IDEC, IIDA. "A designer may do them instantly, right in the client's office. Or a CAD-savvy member of a client's facilities department may work directly on a drawing, which is then e-mailed back to the designer's home office. Increasingly, CAD drawings are e-mailed around the globe to various collaborators, creating a 24/7 design process."[4]

The technologically sophisticated design office is one in which "team members must stay in touch," according to Beert. "Information is continually crossing boundaries." In this fluid, fast information environment, we chuckle at the formalities of old-fashioned office communication with its ponderous conventions dating to an era when memos were dictated to secretaries, who then typed them. In our speeded-up era, most decisions must be made immediately and recorded as they happen. Paper-based writing continues to have its important uses, particularly as research becomes more central to the interior designer's task. Yet only e-mail seems fast enough to respond to the rapidly shifting exigencies of ongoing design and project-management work.

Writing E-Mail

Some designers would prefer to believe that the fast, light messaging called e-mail is not in fact "writing," which they see in cultural opposition to the designer's way of getting visual—compressing a great deal of information into an image that another designer can read rapidly and wordlessly. Much of a designer's intra-office verbal communication consists of what Beert has called "alerts and reports." There may not seem to be much "writing" in an e-mail communication that reads: "I've revised the ceiling plan for the second-floor office space. See me if you have any questions." Yet a message like this is written in good English, clear, plain, and understandable. In fact, solid, easy-to-read e-mail conforms to the writing conventions that are sometimes called *Netiquette*, or e-mail etiquette.

Because the turnaround time is rapid, e-mail is more conversational than is paper-based communication. There are many casual e-mail situations in which grammatical perfection and correct punctuation may not seem to matter. However, you need to be aware of the more formal situations in which meticulousness is important. As Kaitlin Duck Sherwood points out, "[an e-mail] correspondent [doesn't] have normal status cues such as dress, diction, or dialect, [and] so may make assumptions based on your name, address, and—above all—facility with language."[5] Here are some guidelines that will help you send the right message when you e-mail[6]:

E-mail may be casual; but it needs to be written in good, clear, plain English.

E-mail Format and Style Guidelines

- Use punctuation eliminating periods apostrophes and commas is a false time economy the resulting email is hard to read
- DON'T USE CAPITAL LETTERS TO CREATE EMPHASIS. It's the e-mail equivalent of bellowing. don't use all lowercase letters either.
- Isr upit d [rv; vjrvlrt, whoops! Use your spellchecker, and proof *manually* as well. If you spell *from* as *form*, spellchecker won't catch it, and spellchecker doesn't always apply grammar and syntax rules appropriately either.
- Don't forget to proof the "To" line of each message, in case you inserted the wrong address or hit "Reply to All" when you meant to hit "Reply."
- Save the e-mail stationery option for form letters. Don't use it to send logos or other promotional graphics that may take a long time to download and may be illegible in some mail programs.
- Use a salutation that consists of the recipient's name followed by a comma and line space: "Mary,"
- Create a four-to-seven-line signature file listing alternate means of contacting you, such as by phone and fax. Use it as the default signature for all professional e-mails.

- Do not use fancy formatting, such as bold, italics, and color, unless you know that the recipient's mail program supports it. Show emphasis with *asterisks.* Use underscores to show _underlining_.
- Break your e-mail into short paragraphs, easy to take in at a glance and separated by a line space. Restrict the length of your sentences.
- Don't forward an e-mail with layers of text to scroll through before you get to the meat of the message. Copy and paste the relevant part into a new e-mail.
- Put your reply above the message to which you are replying. That's where it is easiest to see. If e-mails are hopping back and forth, the older text gets continually pushed to the bottom, where it belongs.

E-mail Content Guidelines

- Send attachments only by prior agreement. Although they are a fast and convenient way to transmit visual and other information, they can take a long time to download, and they take up space on the recipient's computer. If at all possible, post large graphic files to a project Web site.
- To avoid the dissemination of viruses via attachments, install and update antivirus software.
- Always include a meaningful subject line. Sometimes it's the only way a recipient can find a message when searching for one. When replying to a message but changing the subject of the conversation, change the subject line, too.
- Stick to the e-mail topic. If you need to branch off to a new topic, then put it into a different e-mail, with a different subject line, so that your recipient can file it separately. (Don't be afraid of sending multiple e-mails.)
- Do not embed sound in business e-mails.
- Whether by hitting "Reply" or by copying and pasting, include enough of the message to which you are responding to provide a context. Otherwise, a recipient who receives many messages during a day may not remember the nature of the conversation. However, quote only the smallest amount needed to make the context clear. To save bandwidth and avoid redundancy, eliminate older text that is not vital in the current context. Previous e-mails on the subject provide adequate record of the thread.

- Get to the point in the first screen. Do not make your reader scroll down to find out what you are talking about. Remember, the highest-tech people may be reading their e-mail on tiny handheld screens.
- Even if yours is a dress-down office, avoid vernacular e-mail practices such as <u>shorthand</u> ("r u gng 2 the meeting"); <u>smileys</u> (☺); <u>abbreviations</u> (LOL for laughing out loud); and <u>excessive punctuation</u> (multiple "bangs," or !!!).
- Be polite. Everyone appreciates niceties such as *please* and *thank you.*
- When writing to someone you don't know, identify yourself clearly in the first paragraph.
- Don't suppose that e-mail is a private medium. If you do not want it posted on a public bulletin board with your name on it, do not put it into an e-mail.
- Never send an e-mail when you are angry.

Under the best of circumstances, e-mails have a way of sounding more hostile than intended. This is acknowledged by Patricia T. O'Conner and Steward Kellerman,[7] authors of *You Send Me*, a book about e-mail.

> The things so many people like about e-mail—the speed, the informality, the brevity, the disengagement—give words a sharp edge. Clipped, telegraphed messages seem brusque and curt. Small slights are magnified. A tiny, half-joking pout looks like a major hissy fit. A mild suggestion sounds like a dressing down. And attempts at subtlety, irony, or sarcasm land with a thud more often than not.

Clipped, telegraphed e-mail messages can seem brusque and curt.

According to O'Conner and Kellerman, most people think e-mail is a cross between a letter and a phone call (speech). Those who think e-mail is closer to speech are more apt to ignore not only their spellcheckers, but also the pleasantries that make correspondence smooth and agreeable. People who think e-mail is more like letter writing are "pickier about the niceties—manners as well as spelling, grammar, punctuation, and such." You need to bear in mind that "the purpose of writing—whether with a pen, a typewriter, or a laptop—is to connect with others. When people write well, they connect. When they write badly, they don't."[8]

Whatever the medium, write to connect.

Writing Memos

In spite of the differences between electronic and paper-based forms of communication, there is continuity between the two media. Even though e-mail (electronic) is sent to people outside an office (Figure 9.1a), while memos (paper-based) are the characteristic form of communication within an office (Figure 9.1b), e-mail has adopted certain format characteristics of the older memo genre (Figures 9.1a and b are also featured on the CD-ROM). For instance, the format of the top matter in an e-mail—the To line, From line, Date line, and Subject line—echoes that of the top

Figure 9.1a
An example of
an e-mail

E-MAIL HEADER

From:	Sam Jenkins <Sam_Jenkins@client.com>
Sent:	Tuesday, June 29, 2004, 10:16 AM
To:	Alvin Weber <Alvin@WebDesign.com>
Subject:	Swatches for Phys-Rite Reception-Room Chairs
cc:	Nelson Rogers, Mary Warren

Al,

The swatches of fabrics from Holland House and Tanner Inc. have been messengered over to Mark Connerly. He will telephone me after the Facilities Commitee has met. I will keep you posted.

Best regards,
Sam

Sam Jenkins
Client International Ltd.
3964 Martin Drive
Glastonbury, CT 06033
860-555-6789
Sam-Jenkins@client.com
www.client.com

Figure 9.1b
An example of
the memo

INTEROFFICE MEMORANDUM

To:	ALVIN WEBER
From:	SARA FISHER *SF*
Subject:	SWATCHES FOR PHYS-RITE RECEPTION-ROOM CHAIRS
Date:	7/13/04

The swatches of fabrics from Holland House and Tanner Inc. have been messengered over to Mark Connerly. He will telephone me after the Facilities Committee has met. I will keep you posted.

cc: Jane Mandela, Roger Petry

matter in the *memorandum*, or written reminder (see Figure 9.1b), as do the copy lines, which designate the recipients of copies and blind copies.

Indeed, the copy lines that persist in e-mail can be read as vestiges of an old-fashioned factory-style office with clear hierarchies, "mechanistic values,"[9] fragmented work, and a rigorous separation of levels and departments. Receiving copies can make people feel that they are part of a group. However, who copies what to whom can also be a not-so-subtle expression of who is in the loop and who is not, who is in charge and who is not. In a more practical sense, copies are a way of making sure that everyone who needs to know about something does know about it. This rein-forces accountability and helps people do their jobs within an organizational structure.

Copy memos to include people, not to exclude them.

In the paper-based office, alerts or reminders are sent on paper memo forms, which you can easily make from templates (click File→New). It is easy to prepare them from scratch, too, for they are very plain and simple, as you can see in Figure 9.1b. For those creating their own memo forms, without recourse to templates, there are several ways to format the top matter. It can be entirely in title case (caps and lowercase), or the heads and the subject line can be capitalized while the information in the Date, To, and From lines is in title case. Usually the heads are flush with the left margin of the page.

The *Writing Guidelines for Interior Design Students* at Virginia Polytechnic Institute and State University (Virginia Tech) contain some very useful tips for memo writers:

- As in writing e-mail, it is important to state the subject in the subject line clearly and concisely. Remember, it functions as the title of the memo.
- If more than one person is designated as a recipient in the "To" or "Copy" lines, the recipients should be listed in alphabetical order.
- Memos should be addressed only to the persons who are expected to take actions as a result of receiving them.
- However well you know the recipient of a memo, don't ramble. Get to the point early on. If your memo is longer than half a page, be sure that your main points, well supported, proceed in an orderly manner.
- Each memo should end with a clear statement of the action the writer expects to be taken.[10]

Again, the memo format is used *only* inside the office. Letters that are mailed to people outside the office are written, of course, on letterhead sta-

Memos are sent
only within
a company.

tionery, with the address of the letter's recipient above the salutation, or greeting; and with a full signature at the end of the letter. By contrast, no greeting is written into the body of the memo, nor are memos signed; rather, writers of memos place their initials next to their names on the From line.

Writing the Informal Report

While brief, routine correspondence within an office may be handled either by e-mail or through paper-based memos, *reports*, or written documents detailing the findings of an individual or a group, are usually transmitted in a paper-based format unless they are very short. In general, reports are characterized as informal or formal, depending on their length, subject matter, and audience. Some reports may also be presented orally or on Web sites.

An informal report is an in-house affair. It is not intended to be widely distributed or published. It is usually no more than one or two pages long, though it can be as long as ten pages. Informal reports are key to the day-to-day operation of a design firm, presenting more information and discussion than memos, but only as much as is needed for decision making. You can use short, informal reports to:

- Elucidate problems.
- Inform about products, methods, and progress.
- Provide background.
- Make a recommendation.
- Propose an action.

Informal reports
although longer
than memos, are
concise and clear.
They are written
for readers inside
a company.

An informal report needs to be written in a manner that is concise and clear, so that all who receive it will understand it and be able to act on it. Your writing style should conform to the guidelines laid down in Chapter 1 — good, plain English. In addition, your readers will appreciate your close attention to issues of formatting.

Formatting the Informal Report

For the convenience of readers, an informal report usually includes subheads placed flush left, in title case. (Remember that all articles and prepositions are lowercase.) There is usually no punctuation after the head, and there is usually more line space above the head than below it.

Also for the convenience of the reader, you need to insert page numbers. If you are not inserting a header, place the page numbers in the upper right-hand corner or at bottom center. If you are inserting a header, do so at the left-hand top of the page and insert the page numbers on the right-hand top. You may wish to use one of the report or proposal covers that are packaged as templates with MS Word. (A customization may be viewed in Figure 4.8.) If you do not use a cover page, then the text of the first page of your report should start about a third of the way down the page and should bear at the top, centered, the title of the report.

Elements of the Informal Report

With only two basic written parts, the introduction and the discussion, the informal report is a simple genre. In the design professions, visual support material is crucial to the impact and significance of a report and must be considered an integral part of it.

Informal reports have two parts; the introduction and the discussion.

INTRODUCTION

Usually the introduction to an informal report performs one of three functions:

- Stating the report's objective
- Stating the problem and the solution discussed in the report
- Stating the context of the report

The context introduction may be expanded as appropriate to introduce a longer, more complex report.

STATING THE REPORT'S OBJECTIVE   This simple, versatile form of introduction is widely used in all manner of reports. It is perhaps best for a short report. Here is a sample objective. Note that it is preceded by a head and a colon:

> Objective: To evaluate textured-carpet purchase options for the corporate headquarters of Allied Communications.

STATING THE PROBLEM   Because it focuses on a problem and its solution, this introduction is well suited for a troubleshooting report. If its recipient is a busy project manager with a long list of problems to monitor, an introduction stating a problem permits a got-it response with the option of reading the discussion later.

Figure 9.2 presents an analysis of a sample introduction in which a problem is stated, a solution is proposed, its significance is summarized, and a recommendation is made.

Introductions stating a problem are suitable for a troubleshooting report.

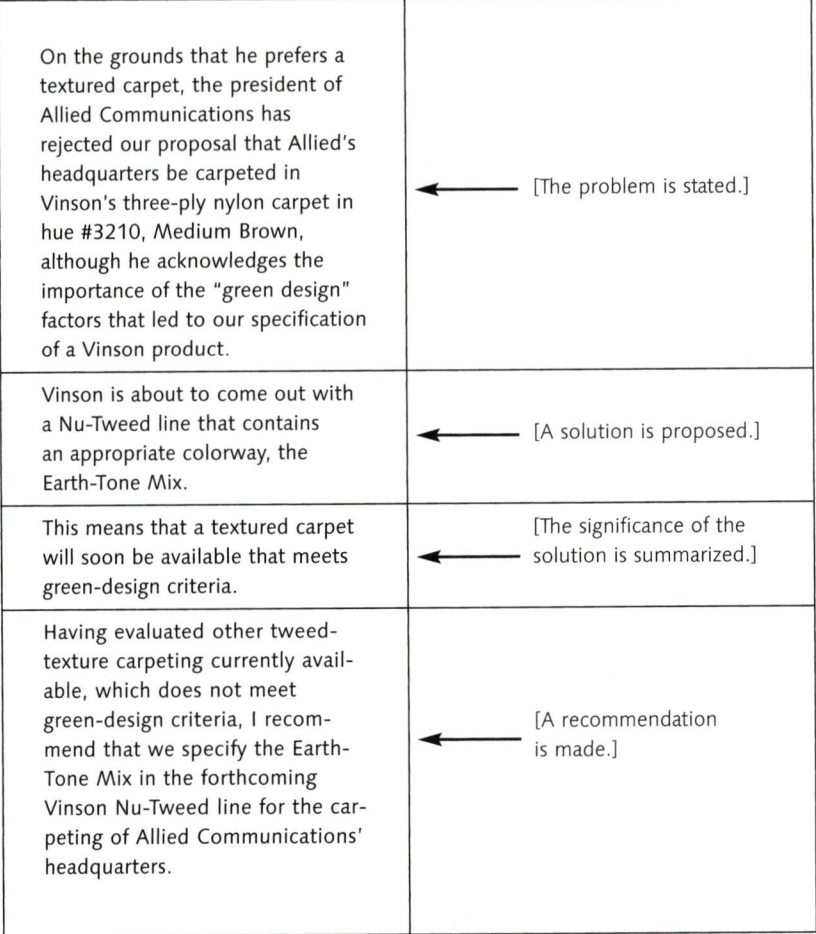

On the grounds that he prefers a textured carpet, the president of Allied Communications has rejected our proposal that Allied's headquarters be carpeted in Vinson's three-ply nylon carpet in hue #3210, Medium Brown, although he acknowledges the importance of the "green design" factors that led to our specification of a Vinson product.	⟵ [The problem is stated.]
Vinson is about to come out with a Nu-Tweed line that contains an appropriate colorway, the Earth-Tone Mix.	⟵ [A solution is proposed.]
This means that a textured carpet will soon be available that meets green-design criteria.	[The significance of the ⟵ solution is summarized.]
Having evaluated other tweed-texture carpeting currently available, which does not meet green-design criteria, I recommend that we specify the Earth-Tone Mix in the forthcoming Vinson Nu-Tweed line for the carpeting of Allied Communications' headquarters.	⟵ [A recommendation is made.]

STATING THE CONTEXT   A simple contextual introduction usually states in a single paragraph the reason for writing the report, how you obtained your information, the purpose of the report, and a summary or preview of the main points you intend to make in the discussion that follows. Figure 9.3 shows the text of a simple contextual introduction.

A simple contextual introduction provides a thumbnail sketch of the big picture. The person reading it is given a restatement of the original request, eliminating the need to sort through other documents to find it. Note that the report for which Figure 9.3 presents the introduction could not have been sent as an e-mail because the attachment, consisting of carpet swatches, is a physical object.

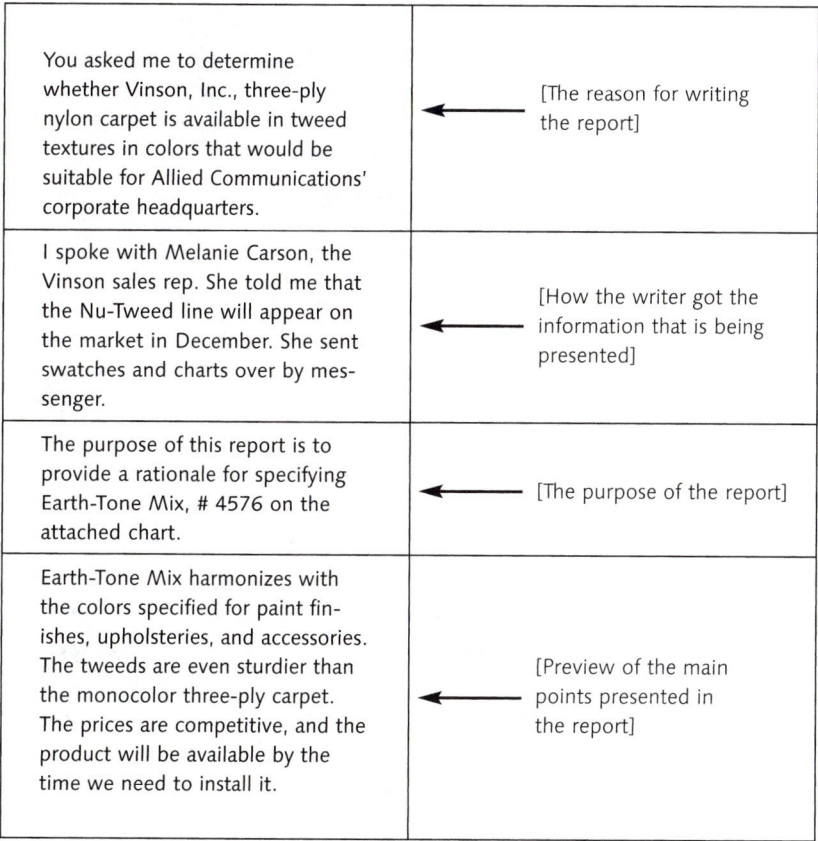

You asked me to determine whether Vinson, Inc., three-ply nylon carpet is available in tweed textures in colors that would be suitable for Allied Communications' corporate headquarters.	[The reason for writing the report]
I spoke with Melanie Carson, the Vinson sales rep. She told me that the Nu-Tweed line will appear on the market in December. She sent swatches and charts over by messenger.	[How the writer got the information that is being presented]
The purpose of this report is to provide a rationale for specifying Earth-Tone Mix, # 4576 on the attached chart.	[The purpose of the report]
Earth-Tone Mix harmonizes with the colors specified for paint finishes, upholsteries, and accessories. The tweeds are even sturdier than the monocolor three-ply carpet. The prices are competitive, and the product will be available by the time we need to install it.	[Preview of the main points presented in the report]

Figure 9.3
Analysis of writing sample: simple contextual introduction.

EXPANDED INTRODUCTION   Suitable for a relatively long and complex report is the expanded context introduction. Divided into several paragraphs, the expanded introduction usually states an objective, and may also contain either (1) an executive summary of the points to be made in the body of the report; or (2) a conclusion-and-recommendation statement. The conclusions and recommendations should correlate one-to-one with the heads that organize the discussion section.

An expanded introduction is suitable for a relatively long and complex report.

Sometimes an expanded introduction also contains a background paragraph about the methodology that generated the report or the history of the project examined in the report. The sample that follows contains both a recommendation-and-conclusion statement and a background paragraph.

Objective: To evaluate textured-carpet purchase options for the corporate headquarters of Allied Communications.

Conclusions and Recommendation

I recommend that Weber Design specify the Earth-Tone Mix in the forthcoming Vinson Nu-Tweed line for carpeting of the Allied Communications headquarters.

1. Nu-Tweed satisfies Allied's preference for textured carpeting.
2. Nu-Tweed, like other Vinson products, meets green-design criteria.
3. Nu-Tweed is available in an appropriate colorway at the same price as Vinson's monocolor 3-ply, which has been approved.
4. Nu-Tweed will be available on time to meet our installation schedule.

Background

On the grounds that he prefers a textured carpet, Jack Colson, the president of Allied Communications, has rejected our proposal that Allied's headquarters be carpeted in Vinson's three-ply monocolor nylon carpet in hue #3210, Medium Brown, although he acknowledges the importance of the green-design factors that led to our specification of a Vinson product. At your request, I spoke with Melanie Carson, the Vinson sales rep, who told me that Vinson's Nu-Tweed line will appear on the market in December. She sent swatches and charts by messenger. I also reviewed the textured-carpet research in our files and went on the Internet to see what other new products are available.

DISCUSSION

The discussion section, or body, of a report provides a fuller and more detailed treatment of the points summarized in the introduction. For instance, the writer of the preceding expanded introduction might explain in the discussion that the client prefers tweed-textured carpet because he believes that soil is less visible on it. The writer might also explain that Vinson had overcome production difficulties with the Nu-Tweed line. The detail elaborated in the discussion will be more convincing if it is amply supported by visual aids.

The body of a report provides detailed treatment of the points summarized in the introduction.

VISUAL AIDS

Well-chosen visual support permits direct, sensuous exploration of concepts. It excites and engages an audience and creates multiple points of entry into a discussion. In the design field, it may cogently be argued that the text of a report is presented in support of illustrations, swatches, and samples, rather than the other way around. For the purpose of organization, however, it makes sense to think of visual material as supporting concepts—the ideas you are presenting in written or oral reporting. Your visual support material should contribute to the richness and relevance of your discussion, not distract from it.

Think of your visual materials as support for your ideas.

Visual support material can be *paper-* or *screen-based* or *object-based. Paper-* or *screen-based information* includes charts, graphs, tables, photographs, drawings, and CAD-created models, all of which may be inserted into a document, appended to a document, viewed on a computer's monitor, or attached to an e-mail. These materials may also be posted on a Web site.

Generally, your graphics should be about one-third to two-thirds the size of a computer screen, if viewed on a monitor, or one-third the size of a printed page. All visual materials should be appropriately labeled. Contrast should not be so low or so high that detail is lost to the straining eye.[11]

Graphics should be one-third the size of a printed page, appropriately labeled, and of medium contrast.

Object-based visual support materials include textured fabric swatches and material samples such as granite that are three-dimensional and, though they can be scanned into a computer, require close visual and tactile examination. While a seemingly two-dimensional sample such as a paint chip may be susceptible to scanning, the object itself may more fully display its richness, texture, and depth of hue. Object-based support material may also include fully built models, rather than approximations of three dimensions in two-dimensional drawings.

References to visual support materials must be firmly integrated into the text of a written report. Either they can be mentioned directly within the text itself (textual reference), or they can be inserted in parentheses (parenthetical reference):

Textual Reference

As you can see from the Vinson specification sheet attached as Figure 2, . . .

Parenthetical Reference

The photographs of the Holden house reveal the extensive water damage in the kitchen and pantry areas (Figure 16).

Types of Informal Reports

Several types of informal reports are important in the field of interior design. These include the following:

- Progress report
- Brief analytic report
- Recommendation report
- Feasibility report
- IMRD report
- Outline report
- Oral presentation

Increasingly important in the electronic office is the presentation of online and other research in a Web log, or blog.

PROGRESS REPORT   Submitted on a periodic basis, progress reports tell whether work is progressing in a satisfactory manner, on budget, and on time. A typical progress report (Figure 9.4; also on the CD-ROM) contains the following sections: introduction; work completed; work scheduled; and problems.

If you were working for a sizeable contract-design firm, you might be asked to write a progress report discussing the status of a large order of custom-made furniture. You would detail the progress of the fabrication. You would indicate what percentage of the work had been finished and state any problems you had discovered. For instance, if a lathe crucial to the completion of a certain kind of millwork had broken down, you would say so in the problems section of your progress report.

Progress reports tell whether work is satisfactory, on budget, and on time.

BRIEF ANALYTIC REPORT

Brief analytic reports help solve problems.

Brief analytic reports are usually written to help solve problems that have arisen in the day-to-day execution of work. (For an extended discussion of analytic techniques, see Chapter 3.) A brief analytic report typically supports a particular solution to a problem. Often, the solution emerges from a discussion ordered in terms of criteria sorted in descending order, from most to least important. The writing designer's judgment determines whether proximity to natural light or adequate space for file cabinets is a more important factor in selecting the space for Hamilton Corporation's new branch office. Other report types based on criteria are the *recommendation report* and the *feasibility report*.

For a writing designer, criterion-based reports typically incorporate visual materials for maximum impact. As always, be careful with the placement of drawings, CAD images, samples, and other graphic elements. Consistency is important in matters such as size of images, spacing around images, and the alignment of image with text.[12]

Figure 9.4 Progress report.

Weber Design

Project_____   Project No._____
Contractor_____   Contract No._____
Project Designer_____   Date_____

MONTHLY RENOVATION PROGRESS REPORT
REPORT NO._____

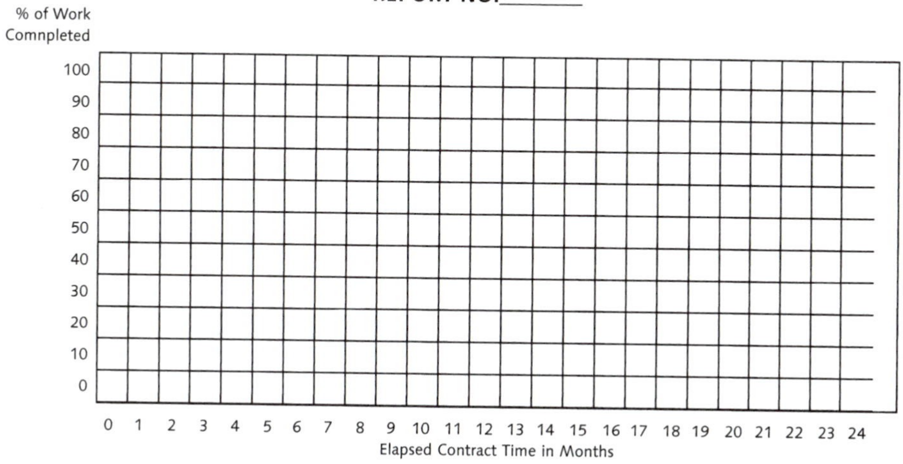

% of Work
Comnpleted

| 100 |
| 90 |
| 80 |
| 70 |
| 60 |
| 50 |
| 40 |
| 30 |
| 20 |
| 10 |
| 0 |

0 1 2 3 4 5 6 7 8 9 10 11 12 13 14 15 16 17 18 19 20 21 22 23 24
Elapsed Contract Time in Months

Contract Time Elapsed

Starting Date_____   Contract Time Calendar Days_____

Time Extension # Days_____   New Completion Date_____

% Completed_____ | % Time_____ | % Variation from Schedule_____

Problems |_____
_____
_____
_____
_____
_____
_____
_____

RECOMMENDATION REPORT

A recommendation report evaluates alternatives by criteria.

A recommendation report makes a recommendation based on a set of alternatives evaluated according to criteria. Each criterion is discussed in its own section. The criteria are stated in a manner that helps to create a standard. The criteria must each be assigned a rank as well.[13]

For instance, for a report on sustainable design and floor coverings, you might rank the following four criteria, listed below in alphabetical order, without ranking:

- Indoor air quality (VOC, or volatile organic compound, emissions)
- Resource conservation (recycling and recyclability)
- Sustainability (closed-loop manufacturing)
- Warranties and guarantees

A report might compare several products using these criteria—ranked according to a designer's priorities—with reference to the Environmental Protection Agency's Purchasing Guidelines in order to generate conclusions supporting a recommendation.[14] Use of a table as visual support would facilitate decision-making, compress the presentation of discussion, and make data more accessible to readers. (see Figure 9.5 in the text and the CD-ROM.) Floor-covering samples, as appropriate, would also facilitate decision making.

Figure 9.5
Sustainable-design
analysis grid.

Criteria	Supplier 1	Supplier 2	Supplier 3	Industry/EPA Standard
Indoor air quality				
Resource conservation				
Sustainability				
Warranties and guarantees				

Credit: Grid suggested by Nat Harrison and Lynn Preston, of Collins & Aikman Floorcoverings, "Climbing Gear: A Guide to Researching Sustainable Design," IIDA: Perspective (Winter 1999), http://www.iida.com/communications/publications/perspective/winter99/industry1.htm.

FEASIBILITY REPORT

Like a recommendation report, a feasibility report presents a solution to a problem after a number of relevant factors have been investigated. However, a feasibility report focuses on one option, investigating whether it makes sense for a project to be undertaken. For instance, a feasibility study might be undertaken to determine whether the interior of a historic house could be restored to period in a manner consistent with the amount of money collected in a fund-raising drive, examining costs and specifications. Like the recommendation report, the feasibility report is organized by criteria, with each criterion discussed in its own section and appropriately supported by visual material.

A feasibility report investigates whether a project should be undertaken.

IMRD REPORT

A widely used vehicle for presenting information gathered in the course of research efforts is the IMRD report. The acronym *IMRD* stands for the four sections usually found in this type of report: introduction, methodology, results, and discussion.

The IMRD report is widely used to present research results.

- In the *introduction* section, the report's objective is stated and contextualized very briefly with a statement of the concerns that motivated the research. Since this section appears directly under the report's title and is at the top of the first page, it is usually not necessary to top it with a head that states the obvious.
- The *methodology* section tells how you obtained your information. In it you state whom you talked to, what you read or otherwise investigated, and why. Your rundown of these matters should permit anyone else to do the same research and achieve the same results. It establishes your credibility.
- The *results* section states what you found out in the course of your research. It is often correlated closely with visual support in the form of a table or graph of data. It may also be correlated with swatches, charts, and other information provided by suppliers.
- The *discussion* section reports on the significance of your research. If your research methods affect your findings, it is important to say so. For instance, if your research into nontoxic paint in heritage colors dealt only with American providers, you might say so. The close of the discussion section may set forth a recommendation that further action be taken. For instance, having reported that the scope of your paint research was limited to American manufacturers, you might propose that the scope of the research be broadened to include foreign manufacturers.

Increasingly, research (Figure 9.6) is seen as a "primary component of the design process."[15] The IMRD is a useful vehicle, among others, for presenting in writing the results of research supported by visual materials. However, the vehicle of choice in many design firms for reporting on research—particularly materials research—is oral presentation. An IMRD or any other written report can be reformatted as an outline report to facilitate oral transmission.

Figure 9.6
The two-story source room at the interior-design firm Marc-Michaels, Winter Park, Florida, was patterned after a law library, with meeting rooms, conference rooms, and executive offices radiating out. The firm has a full-time librarian to help manage the partners' collections. "Samples of fabrics, trims, and drapes are sorted in bins by color, pattern, weight, and mood," says Marc Thee in *Worth* magazine. "The catalogs are sorted by category—furniture, lighting, flooring, commercial, and residential. The mezzanine holds tile and wallpaper samples." *Photo by Tim Sargent.*

OUTLINE REPORT

The *outline report* is an expanded outline, like a résumé, in which the outlined items are equal to the headlines that would appear in a detailed report. Information is presented in phrases or sentences, rather than in complete paragraphs, with indentation indicating levels of importance.

If an outline report is used as the basis for an oral presentation, the speaker simply follows the outline, explaining and filling in details as needed. Sometimes the outline is transferred to a series of cards for the convenience of the speaker. Sometimes the outline report is copied and distributed to audience members or projected onto a screen as a PowerPoint presentation, or both. The economy of this format is that it can condense a lot of material into a short space, but readers who have not heard the oral presentation may not

The outline report is frequently the basis for an oral presentation.

be able to "unzip" the condensed information simply by looking at the outline. (The outline report may be used as the basis for a more extended written presentation if need be. For that matter, as already indicated, a full written report can be stripped down to an outline report for oral presentation.)

Visual aids are as important a part of oral presentation as they are of written presentation in the field of interior design. In addition to a PowerPoint presentation of your outline report, or printed handouts of it, you may choose to make large, rapid drawings on a flip chart held by an easel; write on a black- or whiteboard; pass around swatches or paint chips; or provide audience members with packets of materials such as manufacturers' product-specification sheets. Because visual aids are both engaging and powerful, it is sound practice to introduce them early in your presentation, although you need to be selective in their use so as not to overwhelm or confuse audience members with too many diverse stimuli.

Introduce visual aids early in your oral presentation.

ORAL REPORT

If you have marshaled your visual support materials carefully and have based your outline on a careful organization of the points you need to make, your oral presentation should proceed smoothly. (If you find that you cannot fill in extemporaneously on your outline points, then you might consider a full scripting of your report, if only as an exercise. Reading aloud from a script can strike an audience as cut-and-dried, lacking in spontaneity, charm, and spirit.) Here are some tips to help you make oral presentation both enjoyable and effective.

In Advance
- Time your presentation, so that you will stay within the time frame set aside for your report.
- Rehearse your presentation before an audience of family or friends.
- Wear comfortable but appropriate clothing and shoes.
- A relaxed presenter is more appealing than an anxious one, so cultivate your calmness. You might try some relaxation exercises, spend some time in the company of a person you like and trust, or meditate briefly in your office or cubicle. Eat sparingly before making your presentation.

Just Before You Speak
- Arrive early so that you can get a sense of the room in which you will be presenting. Are there changes you would like to

make and can make in the air conditioning or heating? Where should you stand to get the best possible lighting for your presentation, but without direct sunlight or harsh glare in your eyes?

- Arrange chairs in a comfortable, interactive configuration, preferably a circle. (To arrange the chairs in rows before a lectern tends to promote passivity within an audience—as if its members were vessels into which a lecturer would pour wisdom.) Get people talking and laughing before you make your presentation. With less tension, they will pay better attention.
- Be sure that you have a glass of water close at hand as well as a packet of tissues.
- If you are using a laser pointer, an overhead or screen projector, or other apparatus to support your presentation, practice with it beforehand until its use is second nature to you. If you cannot use it smoothly and unobtrusively, it is better to do without it.

As You Speak

- Avoid looking down at your outline or cards. You will seem to be mumbling no matter how clearly you articulate. Hold your outline pages or cards at about chest level. Look out or around at the audience now and then. You can trust your eye to bring you back to your place in the outline.
- If you find it disconcerting to make eye contact with the members of your audience, then look just above their heads, changing your focal point frequently.
- Don't be afraid to walk around. It will make your presentation more interesting.
- Articulate clearly and forcefully.

Be sure to leave plenty of time for questions and comments when you make an oral presentation. *Synergy*, a mutually regenerative energy system, is created by the presence in a room of a small group, particularly if its members are seated in a circle. Whereas a written report, read in solitude, evokes a deep and thoughtful response, in which one person attempts to "think through" a problem, an oral presentation can bind a group into a decision-making process in which ideas spark other ideas and creative possibilities ripple in different directions. A question-and-answer period reinforces this spirit of collaborative community. It enables you to take advantage of synergy and should therefore be considered a meaningful part of any oral presentation.

Always leave time for a question-and-answer period.

BLOG

Apart from oral presentation, the reporting genre most expressive of collaborative culture is the *Web log*, or *blog*, a Web page "made up of usually short, frequently updated posts that are arranged chronologically—like a what's new page or a journal."[16] A blog is a cross between a chronologically organized log and an annotated Webography in which links are provided along with a brief commentary on what is found at the linked-to site. A blog may be created by one person, but it is the collaborative possibilities of the genre that are germane for a project-management or other design-related Web site. A sample of artist Danny Gregory's Web log is featured on the CD-ROM.

Blog pages are not like traditional Web pages, which are "atomic pieces—chunks of text connected by a handful of links. . . . [Blog] pages, more often than not, have rich structure inside the page. They aren't single chunks of information; the page contains lots of different information."[17] Within this compound page format, the blog of an ongoing project may contain updates, change orders, progress photos, and brief reports on any problems that have arisen. It may also include references to case and best-practices studies. With its characteristic links to and commentary about other Web sites, a blog is well suited to reporting on online research and making it instantly available to everyone involved in a project.

> Blogs . . . help small groups communicate in a way that is simpler and easier to follow than e-mail or discussion forums. . . . A blog can help keep everyone in the loop, promote cohesiveness and group culture, and provide an informal "voice" of a project or department to outsiders.[18]

In "keeping everyone in the loop," the blog is an ideal medium for the emerging model of contemporary design-firm organization described by Frances Duffy for IIDA's *Perspective*. As in other professions and businesses, blogging supports "new values such as egalitarianism, transparency, stimulus, creativity, lateral thinking, and accelerated responsiveness." Indeed, what could be more emblematic of "accelerated responsiveness"[19] than blogging's "instant messages to the Web"?[20] In the blogging genre, cooperation is on display and competition is visually submerged, so that blogging both creates and reflects a collaborative social reality.

In a practical sense, blogging permits the members of a small group to work together in gathering information for later use in a more structured report that is presented orally, or printed on paper for distribution within or beyond the design office. The ability to negotiate varying levels of formality

The collaborative aspect of blogging may be useful for group projects.

is a valuable skill in today's design office. The writing process that begins with annotations on a blog (or a series of e-mails) may culminate in a client presentation (see Chapter 10) or in a formal report that requires the collaborative efforts of everyone inside the office.

Writing the Formal Report

Formal reports may be lengthy and are written for distribution outside an office.

Formal reports are not only longer than the informal—usually ten pages or more—but they are more widely distributed within an office and are suitable for circulation outside as well. A formal report is likely to have a broader scope than an informal report; for instance, a formal report may investigate energy-conserving designs or techniques for designing sustainably on a low budget.[21] Formal reports on topics such as these are perceived as important and are presented in a manner that emphasizes that importance—not only to provide information but to enhance the prestige of the firm.

Elements of the Formal Report

The formal report usually begins with *front matter* that serves an orientation purpose. This is followed by the *body* of the report, which contains an introduction; the discussion broken into sections, or chapters; conclusions; and recommendations, if any. (Many formal reports culminate in conclusions.) The body of the report is followed by *back matter*, which consists of a glossary, if needed; references; and appendixes.

The front matter of a formal report orients the reader.

FRONT MATTER

A formal report is usually accompanied by *transmittal*, or cover, correspondence, which is considered to be part of the front matter, though it is not integral to the report proper. Otherwise, the front matter helps readers to perceive the structure of the report. The front matter is largely devoted to orientation materials, which typically include a title page, a table of contents, a list of illustrations, and an executive summary or abstract.

TRANSMITTAL CORRESPONDENCE   A letter or memo that directs the report to a particular reader or group of readers usually accompanies a formal report. If the report is being sent outside the office, the transmittal correspondence takes the form of a letter. If the report is being sent within the office, the transmittal correspondence takes the form of a memo. The body of either a letter or a memo would most likely contain the following types of information:

- A reference to the report by title
- A statement of the reason for sending it
- A brief overview of the report's scope and purpose
- An account of any problems that limit the report's effectiveness

In addition, the transmittal correspondence contains acknowledgments that credit all who helped with the report. For instance, a report on universal design might acknowledge the assistance of agencies assisting elderly and disabled people in your locality. If you interviewed elderly or disabled people, these individuals might also be acknowledged in the transmittal correspondence.

TITLE PAGE   Some firms have a "house" title page that is part of the stationery package. As discussed in Chapter 4, you can make your own title page from the MS Word report-cover template that is packaged with most computers. Or you can create a title page from scratch, following these guidelines:

- Be sure the title of the report reflects its contents.
- Place all elements flush left or center them, depending on the look you want.
- Use either uppercase (all caps) or title case (caps and lower case), in normal or bold formatting. If you choose title case, remember that, apart from the first word of the title, the initial letters of prepositions and articles should not be capitalized.
  - *Incorrect*   The Carpet Purchase Options <u>For The</u> Henderson College Admissions Office
  - *Correct*   The Carpet Purchase Options <u>for the</u> Henderson College Admissions Office
- Use a standard font that harmonizes with the font used in the body of the report.
- Include your name, title if you have one, the name of your firm, the date, and a report number if appropriate.

If the report was prepared for someone, put that information on the title page as well. For instance, if you were writing a report on environmentally sustainable design for low budgets and that report had been commissioned by the agency for low-income housing in your city, you would state that on the title page created for the report.

TABLE OF CONTENTS   This important "map" lists all of a report's principal sections in the order in which they occur and gives the number of the page on which each part begins. It also functions as an outline of the report, detailing its structure and the scope of its subject matter, thus making it easy for readers to find particular information in the report. Here are some simple tips for creating an effective and useful table of contents.

- Format the table-of-contents items to reflect the formatting in the body of the report, but do not use underlining in the table of contents.
- Do not put *page* or *p.* before the page numbers.
- To connect section titles to page numbers, consider the use of a *leader*, or string of dots. This old-fashioned device may be appropriate for some reports, though it is not used in books.
- Title the contents page *Table of Contents*.

LIST OF ILLUSTRATIONS   The illustration list gives the number, title, and page number for each piece of visual support material used in the report. If the sections of the report are numbered, then the illustrations should be double-numbered by section: Figure 5.3. If illustrations are included in the back matter of a report, they should be numbered in the same way as those in the report proper—either sequentially or by section. If the report contains both tables and *figures*—illustrations based on images—then prepare a separate list of each.

EXECUTIVE SUMMARY OR ABSTRACT   The summary, or abstract, conveys the full report in miniature. It tells the reader the purpose of the report and the problems it addresses, states the conclusions, and sets forth recommendations.

BODY OF THE REPORT

The body of a formal report follows the traditional or the administrative pattern.

Formal reports may be structured as recommendation reports, feasibility reports, or IMRDs, among other report types. In addition, the body of a formal report is organized according to one of two patterns: *traditional* or *administrative*.

The *traditional* pattern leads the reader through the discussion to the conclusions and recommendations. It places the emphasis on logical progression. The *administrative* pattern places the conclusions and recommendations before the discussion for the benefit of those who must put the recommendations into practice. Table 9.1 presents the structure of the formal report according to the two patterns, breaking down its content into front matter, body, and back matter. You can see at a glance that only the body varies within the two patterns.

INTRODUCTION   Generally, the introduction to the body of a formal report is divided by headings into sections dealing with purpose, scope, procedure, and background. The introduction may also contain a summary, although it may be eliminated to avoid duplicating the summary presented in the front matter.

- The *purpose* statement is clear and simple and should be written in the present tense: *This report presents the results of investigation into social factors impinging on the design of student centers at small liberal-arts colleges.*
- The *scope* statement discloses the limits of the investigation and provides an overview of its coverage by topic. For recommendation and feasibility reports, the criteria are stated, with a brief explanation of their rank order and derivation.

Table 9.1 Structure of Traditional and Administrative Formal Reports

TRADITIONAL FORMAL-REPORT PATTERN	ADMINISTRATIVE FORMAL-REPORT PATTERN
Front Matter	**Front Matter**
Title Page	Title Page
Table of Contents	Table of Contents
List of Illustrations	List of Illustrations
Executive Summary or Abstract	Executive Summary or Abstract
Body of Report	**Body of Report**
Introduction	Introduction
Discussion: Sections	Conclusions
Conclusions	Recommendations, if any
Recommendations, if any	Discussion: Sections
Back Matter	**Back Matter**
Appendixes (including glossary if needed)	Appendixes (including glossary if needed)
References	References

- The *procedure* statement is written in the past tense. It explains how you obtained your information—whom you interviewed and what bibliographic and Webographic sources you consulted. For clarity, you may need to discuss the various aspects of your procedure under headings. Or you may need to give this discussion a more prominent position in the report, setting it up under its own heading parallel in importance to the introduction.
- The *problem* statement presents the circumstances that prompted the investigation discussed in the report. A good problem statement lays the problem out succinctly, specifies its causes, and explicates its short-term and long-term significance, explaining, if necessary, how new facts put into question old ways. You may need to clarify your own involvement.
- The *background* statement provides context for the problem as well as the report, and may sometimes be combined with the problem statement. The resulting hybrid statement might be titled either *Background* or *Problem*.

DISCUSSION   Here you can find the extended discussion of factors leading to the conclusions reached in the report, divided into sections or chapters. If the report is criterion-based, each criterion will be treated in its own chapter or section, with the most important discussed first. Each section will have its own introduction, its own discussion, and its own conclusion. Visual support is introduced as needed.

CONCLUSIONS AND RECOMMENDATIONS   Generally, the conclusions section of a formal report underscores its most significant findings, which are related to specific data given in the discussion section of the report. The conclusions are often presented as a numbered list in the same order as they are set forth in the discussion, with brief comments on each conclusion. Often the conclusions are referenced with page numbers, indicating where to look for discussion in the report. Remember, the conclusions and attendant recommendations may be placed after the discussion or before it, depending on the effect that is desired.

> The conclusions in a formal report present its most significant findings in a numbered list.

Like the conclusions, the recommendations in a formal report are presented in a numbered list, with the principal recommendation listed first. If the conclusions have been clearly written, the principal recommendation should be obvious. Further recommendations may also be made, suggesting appropriate follow-through. Again, it needs to be stressed that all formal reports do not convey recommendations.

> The recommendations in a formal report are also presented in a numbered list.

Back Matter

Typically found in the back matter of a formal report are a glossary or list of abbreviations; references documenting bibliographic and Webographic sources; and appendixes containing data that are relevant but not central to the report's conclusions but rather, provide context for them.

GLOSSARY OR LIST OF ABBREVIATIONS   If at all possible, define key, special, difficult, or unusual terms within the body of the report, rather than forcing readers to frequently resort to a *glossary*, or list of technical terms, in an appendix. If your report contains so many special terms that it would impede a reader's progress for you to define them all within the discussion proper, then it is appropriate to include a glossary or a list of abbreviations in your report's back matter. For example, if your report refers to a great many government agencies by acronym (like, EPA for Environmental Protection Agency), it may not be possible or desirable to use the full name of the agency each time it is mentioned. Yet readers are apt to forget what acronyms stand for. It makes sense to list in the back matter all acronyms and the full name that each is based on.

> A glossary is an appendix defining key and technical as well as terms and abbreviations used in a formal report.

The terms or abbreviations that are defined in the glossary are typed flush left, in alphabetical order, and are italicized. Insert no period or other punctuation following them, but leave four spaces before beginning the definition, which starts with a capital letter. If the definitions are no longer than one sentence, they are not followed by a period. If some definitions contain more than a sentence, then use a period after every sentence.[22]

> *Ogee*   A molding with a profile in the form of a letter S
> *Ogee*   An ogee molding has a profile in the form of a letter S. An ogee arch is pointed and has an S-shape on both sides.

REFERENCES   It is customary to include in the back matter a list of works that illuminate the issues discussed in the report. These might be books, periodicals, or texts found on Web sites. A rich reference list adds credibility to a formal report, particularly if the items in the reference list are *annotated*, that is, supplied with brief notes about their usefulness.

Consistency and accuracy are crucial in the reference section of a formal report. Be sure you have all the relevant data and have spelled them correctly. It would be a courtesy to your reader to arrange items under category headings if your reference list is lengthy. Otherwise, format according to the style manual used by your firm, or, if you are a student, your school. Well-regarded style manuals include those published by the Modern Language

> APA style is standard for design-research publications.

Association (MLA), American Psychological Association (APA), and the University of Chicago Press. APA style is typically used in design-research publications. You can learn more about it at http://www.apastyle.org.

It is important to follow a consistent style even if it is a hybrid created from several sources. If you are in doubt about which style manual to follow, you may wish to consult John Bruce Howell's *Style Manuals of the English-Speaking World: A Guide.*[23]

APPENDIXES   Material frequently relegated to an appendix includes lengthy citations of code and tables, elaborate charts, or lists too cumbersome to include in the report. All appendixes should have true relevance to the report's subject matter. Be sure to give each appendix a title. In addition, you may wish to set appendixes in a smaller font than the text of the report proper. Remember, though, that small fonts are hard to read.

Layout of the Formal Report

A formal report may have a much more complex layout than an informal report, though both formal and informal reports should have pages numbered in the upper right-hand corner or bottom middle of each page, without punctuation. Both formal and informal reports should also make use of a header to identify each page. Apart from pagination and headers or footers, other layout issues that arise in the creation of the formal report are related to chapter divisions, page design, and heads.

PAGINATION

Assign numbers to all pages of the report proper, including those occupied by tables or figures, even if you suppress some of those numbers. For instance, the page numbers for title and part-title pages are usually suppressed. (Your word-processing program will permit you to do this with a click.) Use Roman numerals in italics (*i, ii, iii*) to paginate the front matter. The first page of the introduction should be numbered with an Arabic 1. For relatively short reports, continue the standard numbering of the report proper in any back matter. For longer reports that include many appendixes in the back matter, identify each appendix by a capitalized letter of the alphabet and number it separately—for example, A-1, A-2, B-1, B-2, and so on.

Assign numbers to all pages of the report, even if you suppress some of those numbers.

HEADERS OR FOOTERS

Phrases in the top or bottom margins of pages may identify not only the report but a section of the report.

Report on Non-Toxic Paint in Heritage Colors

Appendix A: EPA Standards

CHAPTER DIVISIONS

Begin each section of the report at the top of a new page or—in very long reports—insert part-title pages, with the title of the section centered horizontally and vertically. If the report is being printed in book layout, on both sides of the page, then begin each chapter or section on a right-hand page.

> Use headers, part-title pages, heads, and subheads to clarify formal report structure.

PAGE DESIGN

A good page design makes reading easy. Some reports may be formatted in columns, with the pages printed back to back like a book. Others will resemble academic papers, printed on one side of each page with the text spread across the page. If the report is being published in a spiral or other binding, the margins at the insides (spine sides) of the pages may need to be widened.

Most formal reports are organized not only by chapters but, within the chapters, by a system of *heads* that indicate levels of significance, as do the increasingly indented items in an outline. Clearly formatted heads and subheads make it easy for readers to grasp main concepts and subordinate points quickly.

HEADS

A typical heading system indicates three levels of importance. Differences among these levels are expressed by *formatting* (boldface, italics, and underlining); *case* (capitals and lowercase or all capitals); *font size*; and, of course, *indentation*. In general, larger size has greater visual prominence than smaller, all capital letters than capitals and lowercase, and left than indented. However, centered text is more prominent than text in either the left or indented positions. All items at a given level of organization should be grammatically parallel in construction.

> A typical system of heads indicates three levels of importance.

Writing, Research, and Creativity

Although formally reported in-depth research may seem antithetical to the creative process of design, Franklin Becker, Ph.D., who chairs a multidisciplinary department at Cornell University that includes interior designers, architects, ergonomists, and environmental psychologists, believes that design research performed by interior designers and architects increases[24] the likelihood of creating something that succeeds simultaneously on multiple levels—from how it works and looks to how much it costs and how difficult it is to manage and maintain. Information, in this context, is not a factor limiting creativity, but one liberating imagination. . . . Whether designing a home, office, hospital, or penny arcade, designers must understand, in depth, what goes on in the setting and how personal experience and public images and legend shape expectations about what should (or should not) occur in it.

According to health-care-facilities designer Rosalyn Cama, design research is useful not only in creating interior design that succeeds, but in adding "credence and color" to presentations while educating clients about "the elements of design that improve human behavior in the built environment."[25] Research, says Cama, helps designers anticipate their clients' future needs, understand their clients' values, target the right markets for their services, and redefine design objectives to better correlate with human need, human behavior, and "the relationship between our inner worlds and our physical environments."[26] (See your CD-ROM for Dutch designer John Thackara's perspective on research and its presentation.)

Social-based design research can improve both design and client relations.

Traditionally, much of a designer's research takes the form of extensive interviews with clients and other users (see Chapter 2). For both commercial and residential clients, other important research may involve fabric, trim, draperies, paint, tile, wallpaper, furniture, lighting, and flooring. However, part of the social-based design research described by Franklin Becker and Rosalyn Cama will likely be conducted in different types of literature, each with its own strengths and weaknesses. Some varieties of literature a designer might consult in the course of social-based and other design research include the following:

- *Journal articles*   Although it can take up to two years to actually publish journal articles that have been accepted for publication, journals are nonetheless considered to be good sources for up-to-date information. Reputable journals such as the *Journal of Interior Design* are *refereed* by editors who take pride in publishing only the most relevant and reliable research.
- *Books*   Since it takes much longer for a book to be published than a journal article, books are most useful where timeliness is not crucial. For instance, if you are researching the characteristics of eighteenth-century style, how recent the information is may not make much difference, since the period-style characteristics have been widely known and agreed upon for many years.

If you are researching the latest developments in polymer extrusion textiles, you may find that the information published in books is too old.

- *Conference proceedings* Often the latest research has not yet been published but may have been presented at conferences. The proceedings of conferences can help you find out who is currently doing research in areas such as ergonomics and environmental psychology. You may then be able to track down other published work by the same researchers.

- *Government, corporate, or institutional reports* The published findings of research carried out by governments, corporations, and institutions can be a very useful source of information for design researchers. For instance, ASID's useful series of published reports includes the following titles:
  - *Workplace Values: How Employees Want to Work*
  - *Aging in Place: Aging and the Impact of Interior Design*
  - *Recruiting and Retaining Qualified Employees—By Design*
  - *Sound Solutions: Increasing Office Productivity through Integrated Acoustic Planning and Noise-Reduction Strategies*

- *Newspapers* Although helpful as providers of information about very recent trends, discoveries, or changes in government policy, newspapers are intended for a general audience and do not provide enough detail for serious design or other professional research. Sometimes they provide a good starting point for research that must be largely conducted with more specialized sources.

- *Theses and dissertations* These unpublished documents, generally available only by library or interlibrary loan, can be very useful sources of highly specialized information. However, the students who carried out the research may not be as experienced and reliable as researchers whose work has been published.

- *Internet* A huge variety of information appears on the Internet. In some cases this material has not been evaluated by an editorial board and may not be reliable enough to consider seriously. Since e-publishing is a faster way to disseminate information than print publishing, however, Internet sources may be more current than print sources.

- *CD-ROMs* Most CD-ROMs are intended for a general audience and are therefore unsuitable for serious professional research. However, many bibliographies intended for use by specialists appear on CD-ROMs. They can be a very valuable research tool.

- *Magazines*   Specialized periodicals focusing on interior design can be a good starting point for design research. They frequently provide information about new discoveries that you can research as needed in more specialized sources. Some design-oriented publications, such as IIDA's *Perspective*, appear online. Among the print periodicals[27] you might consult are:
  - *Architectural Digest*
  - *Kitchen & Bath Business*
  - *Interiors & Sources*
  - *Building Stone Magazine*
  - *Hospitality Design*
  - *Facilities Design & Management*

Publications such as *Time* that are intended for the general reader are not suitable for specialized design research.

Proper research references support your argument and add credibility to your reporting.

As a researching designer, take descriptive notes on each source you study, recording its pertinence to your research topic. Be sure to save print-outs of all materials found online. They will be invaluable to you in creating a *reference list*—a list of all the sources studied—which you will likely need when you report on your research. You will also need to state the sources of all direct quotations and substantive information taken from a researched source. "No matter how authoritative the [writing] style," notes Virginia Tech's *Writing Guidelines for Interior Design Students*, "unsupported claims or assertions are ineffectual."[28] Proper research references support your argument and add credibility to your writing.

As social-based and other research becomes more critical in the field of interior design, reporting on it may be an increasingly central part of some designers' work. Those who do not do the research themselves will draw on it if they are convinced, as is Franklin Becker, that "design . . . must simultaneously consider behavioral, environmental, financial, aesthetic, and symbolic challenges as different facets of a single-minded commitment to design excellence."[29]

 ## Discussion Questions

1. How are electronic media such as e-mail changing the culture of communication in design offices?

2. What kinds of formal report might an interior design firm use to "enhance the prestige of the firm," and how would the report[s] be used?

Exercises

1. In response to discussion question 2 in Chapter 8, you prepared a two-page comparative analysis of the grounds for choosing to work in a large design firm (in which the procurement process was completely automated) or in a very small firm (in which procurement was handled manually). Now, use that comparative analysis as the basis for a brief informal recommendation report with an appropriate introduction. Your audience for this report consists of career counselors at your school who help students decide whether to apply for work at small or large design firms. In your contextual introduction, assert an understanding that other students are submitting reports on different issues relating to the differences between large and small design firms.

2. Prepare a progress report on your work for the class in which you are currently using *Writing for Interior Design*.

3. Identify and interview an interior designer who uses research in his or her ongoing practice. Prepare a three-minute oral presentation for your class based on an outline report using appropriate visual support. After all students in your class have made their presentations, choose a panel of five to respond to questions and answers from other students about the role of research in interior design.

4. In support of a project you are currently executing in a design studio class, research an interior type such as library, prison, kindergarten classroom, or photographer's studio. Prepare an IMRD report of three pages.

5. Use the four criteria in the grid established in Figure 9.5 to evaluate three floor coverings. Rank the criteria according to priorities established by your class for a client with particular profile. Write a brief recommendation report evaluating the carpet selections according to the ranked criteria, with reference to the Environmental Protection Agency's Purchasing Guidelines. Format your report as a memo to other members of an imaginary design firm.

10

Contract Administration: Construction and Installation

After contractors and vendors have been selected, an interior design project enters the contract administration phase. The administration of orders for fixtures, furnishings, and equipment has been discussed in Chapter 8. This chapter explores the ways that writing assists the designer in the construction, custom-fabrication, and installation components of an interior design project. It looks at organizational and other tools the designer employs to bring a project to successful fruition after a client has signed an agreement with a general or single-trade contractor.

One of the designer's most important responsibilities during the contract administration phase is *observation*—that is, inspection—particularly on-site observation at intervals specified in the designer's contract. Typically, observation occurs at critical points such as the beginning and end of work by electricians and plumbers. Although a principal role in verifying plans and inspecting construction may be played by a licensed architect, who is responsible for protecting the owner from deficiencies in the contractors' work, an interior designer can play an important role in monitoring the progress and quality of ongoing projects.

The designer also functions as an intermediary between client, contractors, and architect. On your CD-ROM is an interview in which interior designer Chris Frost of Atlanta describes her relationship with her client Ann Cox Porter of New York City (an educator) during the renovation of Porter's brownstone on Manhattan's West Side as well as two additional projects. Frost defined her role[1] in the contract-administration phase of the Manhattan brownstone renovation as follows:

> [My role] was to bring Ann's vision and the architect's design to life, to fit Ann's real belongings and very real family into the world she'd imagined. In addition to helping to choose colors, surfaces, finishes, lighting, etc., I acted as both translator and mediator for Ann and the others involved in the project. As an ID I can speak the language of the GC and the client.

For her part Porter describes a "seamless" relationship between herself, Chris Frost, and Carl Pucci, the project architect. "We'd have a walk-through, then a pow-wow with everyone involved present. Chris played a facilitative role, keeping the conversation positive, clarifying my wishes to the architect and the contractors, and clarifying realities to me. She was *educating* me."[2]

Porter and Frost, who have worked on three projects together as client and designer, stress the intuitive and imaginative aspect of their collaboration[3]:

> *Frost*: I love learning the design vocabulary of my clients. Ann is especially good at offering images that communicate whole sets of design solutions to me. She said, "I want my grandmother's 1930s Kansas kitchen," and a certain green came to mind.

> *Porter*: Chris responded to my questions and wishes, the hazy vision. When I said I wanted a "grandma green," she came up with twelve samples.

This is important in contract design as well as residential design, "although the relationship may not be as personal. As a client's imagined world is translated into the nuts-and-bolts realism of the contractor's world, writing has an important role to play in ensuring smooth and ample communication among all parties involved in a project. The writing may be far less visionary than the relationship between designer and client. It must be clear, direct, and precise in order to protect the vision.

The Role of Writing in Contract Administration

It is important for a designer engaged in contract administration to keep highly detailed records that enumerate particulars at every step of the way. Some important junctures at which a designer must write for the record are as follows:

1. Notify the owner and the contractor in writing, with adequate supporting detail, of your rejection of work or materials if more than a trivial cost is involved.
2. Withdraw in writing your approval of any work that is subsequently rejected.
3. Commit to writing any recommendation made to the owner in a matter of serious consequence. If possible, obtain a written response.
4. Write to the owner, peer consultants, and the contractor if you discover facts that call for changes in plans and specifications, particularly if these changes affect costs.
5. If you believe that a contractor is not in compliance with the contract in the performance of work that will prove essential to substantial completion, notify the contractor in writing.
6. If you see that serious developments may adversely affect the interests of owners or other parties, tell them in writing.[4]

These are only the most crucial junctures at which an interior designer must put into writing businesslike observations of the work in progress. These documents and many others will be placed in the project file to establish the project's record.

The Project File

The project file is the definitive record of project progress.

The *project file*, or job book, is a record-storage system that enables an interior designer to organize the drawings, material samples, and paperwork relevant to each project in a manner that makes all records available and accessible to all employees of the design firm.

As the record to which all questions will ultimately be referred, the project file tracks progress along all execution tracks and records all changes made in a project, however small. If the record is full, complete, and accurate, the designer is always prepared to speak with clients, peer professionals, fabricators, contractors, vendors, or other employees of the designer's firm. Every item that is placed in the project file should be dated, and the file should be both tidy and orderly, so that another designer in the firm could take over the project, if need be. The firm could also draw on the file if a dispute arose. In addition, the firm can show project files to prospective clients in order to demonstrate the firm's management capabilities. Finally, the firm can assess the financial viability of proposed similar projects through careful examination of existing records.

There are no hard-and-fast rules about what are appropriate components for a project file, which may contain singular elements such as a cocktail napkin on which a rough drawing and some notes have been made—entered into the project file with a date, of course! It is customary to prepare a *project file index* (Figure 10.1) for complicated files containing a large number of documents, alphabetizing the list of documents and assigning each a storage locator number such as A.1.b.2. Otherwise, most project files contain three different types of material, each stored in a characteristic and appropriate manner. *Drawings*, if large—say 24 by 36 inches—are rolled or stored in a flat file. *Material and process samples* are usually stored in boxes or similar storage units. The *project paperwork* is typically stored in manila file folders or three-ring binders.

Drawings

The drawings of record for a construction project consist of the contract set and subsequent SKs (sketches) that amend or expand the project and may relate to the Certificate of Occupancy (discussed later in this chapter).

Material and Process Samples

Material samples typically collected in connection with an interior design project include fabric swatches, carpeting samples, paint chips, tile and stone samples, and flooring samples. Process samples might include a few square inches of sheetrock covered with custom-colored plaster or a few square inches of floorboard colored with a particular stain.

Project Paperwork

The paper file includes the design contract and. copies of all relevant contracts between the client and contractors or fabricators, including plans and drawings and other documents on which the contracts are based. Also included in the project file are copies of any required building permits and the reports of building inspectors. In addition to paperwork related to the FF&E procurement process (discussed in Chapter 8), the project file may include:

The project file includes building permits and building inspectors' reports along with material more directly related to interior design.

Figure 10.1
Excerpt from a
project file index

A.	
Accessories Specifications	C.1.j
Addenda	D.1.c
Agreement—Client	A.1.d.2
Agreement—Consultants	A.1.d.2
Agreement—Contractors	D.2.b
B.	
Bid Acceptance/Rejections	D.1.e
Bidders File	D.1.a
Bid Requests/Instructions	D.1.b
Bid Tabulation	D.1.d
Billings	A.1.e
Budget—Construction	C.1.e.1
Budget—Fee	A.1.6
Budget—Furnishings	C.1.e.2
Bulletins	D.2.e
C.	
Certificates of Completion	D.2.k
Certificates of Insurance	D.2.h
Certificates of Payment	D.2.g
Change Orders—Client	A.1.d.1.a
Change Orders—Construction	D.2.f
Change Orders—Consultants	A.1.d.2.a
Client Approvals	C.1.g

- An observation diary
- Telephone logs
- Meeting notes
- Project schedules
- Time records
- Change orders and other evolving contract documents
- Routine correspondence with fabricators and contractors (including memos and printed-out e-mail)
- Progress reports

Some types of items included in the paperwork portion of the project file have already been discussed in earlier chapters of *Writing for Interior Design*. For instance, routine business correspondence is discussed in Chapter 9. Other components of the project file, such as the construction administration diary, telephone logs, meeting notes, schedules, and time records, have not been discussed in previous chapters and so are treated at greater length here. Since the written record of a project is determinative in any legal disputes that may arise, it is important to make sure that everything you commit to writing is accurate and authoritative. At the same time, it is important to keep thorough and detailed records of all that transpires during the history of a project.

> Thorough and detailed records may be determinative in a legal dispute.

Construction Observation Diary

According to Warren Foster of Construction Specification Specialists, Ltd., a diary of construction observations is a critical record for reconstructing day-by-day occurrences on a job site.[5] It may serve as a guide for uncovering problems and may prove invaluable in the event of litigation. Your record of each site visit should include the date, time of day, and summary of the work currently in progress. In addition, a diary of construction observation typically includes written comments on the following:

- Location, type, and quantity of materials placed
- Number of trades working on the site
- Number of visitors present (with names and organizations—for example, "Sam Hertzfeldt, Reliable Plumbing")
- Progress of the work
- Unusual occurrences
- Condition of the site

Figure 10.2, which appears on page 360 and on the CD-ROM, displays a construction inspector's weekly activity report. Note that it includes a reference to daily observations as well.

Figure 10.2
Inspector's weekly
activity report.

Weber Design

INSPECTOR'S WEEKLY ACTIVITY REPORT

Fill out this form each Friday and transmit one copy to the general contractor, and one copy each to the senior designer and the client.

Include only a brief general summary of the week's activities in this report since finite details are included in the inspector's daily diary. Include the following where applicable:

1. Construction progress

    a. Work starting or completing

    b. Work continuing

    c. Effect of weather

    d. Delay due to strikes, material shortage, etc.

2. Job meetings held and/or special visitors on site

3. Problems encountered and/or pending change orders

4. Contractor's schedule—the planned start of key work or phases that may require coordination of special inspections

5. Major work inspected, approved, tested, etc.

6. Information of special interest

7. Inspection hours expended this week

Complete the form even when there is NO construction activity, stating the reason and the anticipated schedule. Reports will be duplicated and distributed as needed.

Telephone Logs

Since much of the administration of design contracts takes place during telephone calls, it is important to keep a careful and accurate record of all calls. (This is particularly true if your firm does cost accounting, in which case designers may be asked to account for every ten minutes' worth of time, including time spent on the phone.) Your written record of each call should include:

- The time the call was placed.
- The number called.
- The firm called.
- The name of the person called.
- The name of the person spoken to (if different).

A good log record notes the topics discussed and any decisions made, the follow-up required, and the amount of time spent on the call. If you were unable to complete the call, your record should say why. (For example: "no answer.") If you left voice mail, your notes should indicate the content of the voice mail and the action you expect to be taken as a result of having left a message. (For example: "Left voice mail. Asked that Joan Murray call me back tomorrow to discuss the window treatments for the executive dining room.")

A well-kept telephone log (Figure 10.3; also on the CD-ROM) may be important in dispute resolution. For instance, if your written records show that you left two voice-mail messages with a client and subsequently spoke with her to request that she make a selection from the swatches you provided so that carpeting could be ordered and installed in a timely manner and if the client neglected to make a selection, you cannot be accused of negligence if the project stalls because the carpet has not been installed.

In addition to recording each call in your log, take notes throughout the call, as various topics are discussed. These notes should be written out while they are fresh in your mind and sent to the person to whom you spoke for written confirmation or approval. You will find that accurate note taking is a skill that you call on again and again in order to ensure that a project runs smoothly.

> Be sure to include uncompleted calls and voice mail in your telephone log.

> Take detailed notes on each call and confirm them with the other party to the call.

Meeting Notes

Much of the work of a design or any other business is conducted in *meetings*, gatherings that serve the common purposes of those in attendance. Meetings may be held to *brainstorm*, to *plan*, to *motivate*, to *inform*, and to *solve problems*.[6] The meetings most crucial to the successful administration of design contracts are typically held to *inform* and to *solve problems*—often both at the same time. For instance, you might hold a meeting to inform your residential client of the different types of hardware available for her bathroom in several price ranges. You might narrow the selection down to certain lines and a certain price range, and then make an appointment to visit one or more showrooms with the client.

TELEPHONE LOG

Time	Firm	Number	Called	Result	Spoken to	Discussed	Resolved	Follow-up	Duration
10:07 AM	Jaffe Paint	703-9641	Sam Jaffe	Left voice mail	N.A.	Custom paint order, Mason job	N.A.	Call Masons. Call Jaffe again tomorrow if no CB	2.0 min.
10:10 AM	Masons	325-9762	Molly Mason	Completed call	Jay Mason	Delay in custom paint order	The Masons will choose a standard paint color if the custom color cannot be delivered in a timely manner.	Get revised custom paint delivery schedule from Sam Jaffe.	28 min.

Figure 10.3 Telephone log.
A good log record notes the topics discussed, the decisions reached, the follow-up required, and the duration of the call.

Meetings are held not only with clients, but also with contractors, suppliers, and peer professionals such as lighting designers. Some meetings are *informal,* based on casual encounters that develop into something more. (For instance, while inspecting the premises of an interior under construction, you might run into a cabinetmaker installing his work.) An increasingly important variant of the informal meeting is the spontaneous *online meeting* facilitated through instant-messaging technology. Anything *but* spontaneous are the meetings scheduled in advance with clients and contractors or suppliers. These are apt to be carefully structured and are considered *formal*, even if they take place on a construction site and all those in attendance are dressed informally. An important variant of the formal meeting is the conference call.

INFORMAL MEETINGS

Short meetings based on casual encounters can be useful occasions for the exchange of information and for coming to agreement on the solution to a problem. For instance, as the cabinetmaker installs the work on a residential job site you are visiting, you may notice that a kitchen cabinet door, when open, interferes with the opening of the refrigerator door. You may ask the cabinetmaker to hang the door so that it swings in the opposite direction. You would most likely jot down a series of quick notes about the content of this informal meeting while it is going on or directly afterward. (You might also take your notes as dictation to yourself by a means of a small battery-operated tape recorder.) You would follow up by *transcribing*, or writing out, your notes afterward—in this case, perhaps, in an e-mail to the cabinetmaker that is as informal as the meeting but clear and pointed. As always, it is important to include all decisions and agreements in the project file.

> Richard, I am so glad we ran into each other at the Hawkins site. As we agreed, it is a good idea for you to re-hang the door of the base cabinet nearest to the refrigerator so as to reverse the swing. I appreciate your willingness to do this before the next walk-through with the Hawkinses. Please confirm by return e-mail your shared understanding of the decision we reached.

The record of a decision made in an informal meeting, as in any other meeting, needs to be dated and shared with each participant to the meeting, to make sure that all recall it in the same way; to provide a reminder for work that needs to be done; and to keep the project file current. Each participant should signal confirmation or approval in writing.

Written records of decisions made in any meeting need to be kept and confirmed.

ONLINE MEETINGS

Increasingly important in the business world at large are instant messaging tools that allow people to conduct online meetings even while engaged in other tasks. In early 2003, nearly "one-quarter of American employees [used] Instant Messaging at work, for the most part informally, according to a . . . survey by Osterman Research, compared with just 8 percent two years" previously.[7] It had already been predicted that the medium would grow even faster as the technology became more standardized, rather than relying on the mutually exclusive technologies of providers such as AOL, Yahoo, and Microsoft.[8]

Instant messaging (IM) first caught on as a medium of choice for students, who became accustomed to the presence of constant peripheral contact (often multiple) while performing their work. As the technology spreads, IM is proving to be especially useful in the work environment for employees who are collaborating from different physical locations. For instance, an interior designer working on a project in Detroit might stay in touch with a supervisor in Dallas through IM. Instant messaging also makes it possible for clients to receive immediate replies to their questions, rather than having to play phone tag.

Some firms limit instant messaging to use within the company. For the project file, they keep records of the "typed conversations that would otherwise disappear into the ether." Some feel that this scrutiny—however necessary—works at cross-purposes with the inherent spontaneity of the medium. However, employers in design and other firms are coming to terms with the idea of peripheral contact. Unlike the informal meeting that takes place in person, the parties to an IM meeting may not have each other's exclusive attention. In this model of contemporary multitasking, it is acceptable not only to be performing other tasks while engaged in an IM meeting, but also to be engaged in other messaging sessions as well.

Those who are new to IM must be prepared for a technology that is more demanding than e-mail, as an IM question seems to press for an immediate answer. They must get used to the often "disjointed" cadence of IM conversations in which "one person is often typing about a different subject as the other answers a previous question."[9] Those who use the technology for business purposes appreciate the time-saving etiquette of IM, which dispenses with the preliminary niceties that are part of phone meetings, or for that matter in-person meetings. They also appreciate being able to know which of their partners, employees, peers, clients, vendors, contractors, and other associates are available at a given time, as this expedites problem solving.

It may confidently be predicted that new technology will refine or supplant the IM technology described here as communication itself evolves over time.

FORMAL MEETINGS

Structured in-person meetings provide an opportunity for designers, clients, vendors, contractors, and others involved in the creation of a custom interior to exchange ideas and reach decisions in the same room and thus to move forward along mutually agreed-upon lines. Writing plays an important part in the planning and conducting of formal meetings—some writing done before the meeting, some during the meeting, and some done after the meeting.

Writing before a formal meeting may include short e-mails inviting the various participants to the meeting, although this task may also be accomplished by telephone calls, voice mail, or in person. Central to the success of the formal meeting is the *agenda* (Figure 10.4), a list of the matters (issues and problems) that will be taken up at the meeting. Usually these are arranged in an order that will facilitate discussion, with the most important matters discussed as early as possible in the meeting, when people are most alert.

The agenda does not usually contain much detail. It is an outline that succinctly conveys a clear impression of the topics to be covered. It is word-processed, checked for spelling and grammar errors, and printed in a number that will be sufficient for distribution to all parties who have been invited to the meeting, with a few extras. Preparing and distributing the agenda in advance gives people time to prepare. This is a much appreciated courtesy that also tends to make meetings more fruitful.

> The agenda as an outline for oral presentation may need to be supplemented with cards.

If the person in charge of a meeting is an experienced presenter and coordinator, an agenda may suffice as a guide to the oral presentation. If the person in charge is not an experienced presenter or if the matters to be covered are complicated, the person in charge—often but not always the interior designer—may wish to create a more detailed outline or to create a set of cards—5-by-7-inch cards will do nicely for this purpose—to aid in the orderly presentation of important issues.

If you are occupied during a meeting with progress through an agenda, it may be tempting to rely on notes jotted down after the meeting to create a record of what was discussed. However, no recollection can match the immediacy and authenticity of notes taken while a meeting is in progress. Although scrawled notes are seldom tidy and their meaning may become less clear as time goes by, they are an important part of the record trail that threads through a project file, supplementing and updating the contract documents. It is not easy to run a meeting and to take notes at the same time; many designers who run meetings assign subordinates to take notes. The more note takers, the better, to ensure that no important detail goes unrecorded in the collective memory of the firm—that is, in its project file.

Figure 10.4
Preconstruction
meeting agenda.

Weber Design

PRECONSTRUCTION MEETING AGENDA

Project Name_____Project No._____

Contractor_____Contract No._____

Date_____Room_____Time_____

1. **Introductions**: Statement of purpose (by meeting chair)—administration of construction. Each person present will introduce himself or herself and briefly explain the role he or she will play in relation to the project, if any. Also ask each person to print his or her name, organization, position in the organization, phone number, and fax number on the sign-in sheet being circulated (copies will be distributed).

2. **Explain/discuss:**
   A. Responsibility of each party involved in the project.
   B. Inspection procedures.
   C. Progress schedule. Initial and monthly update.
   D. Submittals and approvals. Contractor to project designer/ inspector to client. Designer returns approved submittals to contractor with a copy to client.
   E. Routing of correspondence. Contractor, project designer/ inspector, client. Each copies the others. Changes, disputes, complaints, claims, etc.
   F. Subcontractor status report.
   G. Payment procedure.
   H. Change order procedure.
   I. Final inspections (punch list).
   J. Contractor's guarantee.

If agenda points are written on large cards for a speaker's convenience, the speaker can take notes on the cards. If spaces are left between items, agenda pages may be used in the same manner. These notes may even provide talking points for further discussion. Still another good way to take notes is in a spiral-bound notebook. If the pages on which you take notes are bound, then you don't need to worry about numbering the pages or keeping them in order, as the binding does that for you.

Notes taken in a spiral-bound notebook cannot get out of order.

Figure 10.4
(continued)

WD Page 2

K. Notice of completion.
L. Retention payment.
M. Contractor evaluation.

3. Review:
A. Special coordination problems, utilities, traffic, parking, keys.
B. Ingress and egress to project premises.
C. Safety.
D. Utilities shut down.

4. Confirm:
A. Points of tie-in to existing utilities.
B. Existing condition of project premises.
C. Source of temporary utilities.

5. Determine:
A. Contractor's plan of operation
B. Project supervisor:_____ _____
C. Contractor's off-hour contact in case of emergency:
_____ph #_____
D. Security arrangements contemplated by the contractor.
E Starting date of project:_____

6. Resolve:
A. Questions of contract requirements.
B. Shop drawings and submittals requirements.
C. Color submittals. Who confirms for client?_____

7. Anyone have anything to add while this group is assembled?

Good meeting notes record all relevant financial and schedule details brought up in the course of discussion. They scrupulously record all appropriate names. Any and all agreements reached also need to be clearly noted. (Example: "The current light switches in the dining room will be replaced with Serapis C234 dimmers. James Wright, the electrician's assistant, will pick up the dimmers on his way to work tomorrow.") In addition, good meeting notes associate each suggestion or proposal with the person making it. This not only nails down responsibility but acknowledges contributions in a courteous manner. (Example: "Sandra Wright, the client's secretary, suggested that the front doorbell must be louder, as it is not possible to hear it in the home office when the office door is closed.")

Whereas some meeting notes record only actions taken, others include the discussion that results in actions. While notes of a professional-society chapter meeting can be limited to actions taken, job meeting notes should include discussion, so as to adequately inform those not present at the meeting but important to the project. The record of what was discussed should also be kept for legal reasons.[10] Job meeting notes often assign responsibilities, note progress with regard to milestones for completion, and record completed items.

Mary Knackstedt speaks of recapping "meetings by summarizing into a tape recorder as the meeting is about to end." According to Knackstedt, "this firms up the issues discussed and gives people a chance to add anything that may have been left out."[11] If tape-recorded end-of-meeting "recaps" are your most important record of what goes on in meetings, be careful to include a summary of the discussion leading to decisions in order to clarify that all important considerations were taken into account when decisions were made.

Notes taken during the course of a meeting are often impressionistic. The note taker struggles to record all key terms and often has no time to write in complete sentences if discussion is flowing quickly. In addition, meeting details—and the meaning of meeting notes taken in personal shorthand—can fade from memory quickly. If the meeting is lengthy and discussion becomes heated, the note taker's attention may lapse, and inadequate notes may be taken on an important issue. For all these reasons, it is important to transcribe the meeting notes as soon as possible, thus creating a detailed report of what transpired at the meeting. The more important and complicated the meeting, the more detailed the report needs to be. Notes of meetings transcribed as a written account are traditionally known as *minutes*. (If the designer has dictated meeting notes into a tape recorder, these notes, of course, would also be transcribed.) After distribution, each meeting participant must confirm in writing the accuracy of the minutes.

CONFERENCE CALLS

Like instant messaging, conference calling facilitates meetings between people who are not in the same physical location. Formal conference calls are usually arranged in advance. As with other formal and informal meetings, notes are taken, transcribed, inserted into the project file, and may be distributed to all parties.

Good meeting notes include:
- Financial and schedule details.
- Appropriate names.
- Agreements reached.
- Relevant discussion points.

Transcribe meeting notes as soon as possible to aid memory.

Conference calling involves special technology whereby more than two phone callers are connected to each other at the same time. Conference calls may be arranged through a telephone service provider or through a more specialized provider. For instance, if you or your firm had set up a free account at www.freeconference.com, you could easily schedule a conference for up to 32 callers. Although it would be possible to designate the call a one-way broadcast, in which only one caller could speak, it would typically be more useful in a design-project setting to designate the conference as a conversation, which would permit all participants to speak. They would be notified that the conference had been scheduled by an e-mail message that provided the dial-in number and an access code. The conference could be scheduled with very little advance notice, and people anywhere in the world could take part, paying the regular long-distance charge or dialing a toll-free number.[12] Using cell-phone technology, a design meeting could be held by the following:

- Client A, an attorney, speaking from his office
- Client B, a choreographer, speaking from her studio
- An interior designer, speaking from a stone yard
- The general contractor, speaking from the project premises
- A flooring contractor, speaking from the premises of another project
- A consulting architect, speaking from her firm's offices halfway around the world

In addition to actual conference calling, some less formal meetings are facilitated by "fake" conference calling. A routine two-party call can become a spontaneous "conference call" when a phone is switched to speaker mode to expand participation in a conversation. For instance, a residential client speaking with an interior designer might switch the phone to speaker mode so as to permit the participation of a spouse who is in the same room.

Fake conference calling also has formal meeting applications. For instance, a corporate client might plan a meeting in which a call to an interior designer (planned in advance for a particular day and time) was placed while a number of executives were gathered in a conference room—with the telephone instrument configured to function as a speaker.

If you are sponsoring the conference call, set up its rules before or at the beginning of the call. Typically, it is important that all participants in a conference call identify themselves whenever they speak. Without any visual

Take notes during conference calls as in other meetings.

cues or tags, it is otherwise difficult to correctly identify people who are speaking and to properly attribute their contributions to the meeting. Proper attribution is crucial for the ongoing accuracy of the project file. Your notes for this type of meeting as for all other types must reflect that fact. It is best to take your notes during the call, transcribe them while they are fresh, and send the transcription to all participants for written confirmation or approval.

WRITING STYLE FOR MEETING NOTES

Good writing style for the minutes of job-related meetings of all kinds is concise but thorough and detailed. Accuracy about statements of fact and the nature of agreements reached is paramount. If the meeting is lengthy and the topics discussed are complex, the writer of minutes may wish to designate topics and subtopics with one- and two-number decimals, as in the following example:

2.0 Reports on flooring options for employee cafeteria
2.1 Vinyl asbestos tile
2.2 Cork tile
2.3 Ceramic tile
2.4 Industrial carpet

Often these numbers correspond to topic numbers in a preset agenda. This degree of formality would typically be more appropriate for a large contract client than for a small residential client.

For both contract and residential clients, and for many small meetings as well as larger ones, it is customary to provide each participant with a copy of the transcribed notes. This distribution serves four purposes:

- To provide participants with an opportunity to correct or amplify the record
- To underscore the tacit agreement of participants with the decisions reached at the meeting
- To clarify the work that needs to be done as a result of the agreements reached
- To provide an accurate record of the meeting for the project file

Provide each meeting participant with a copy of the transcribed notes.

Nowadays the written account of what happened at a meeting is apt to be sent as an e-mail to all participants and interested parties. This means that any corrections necessary to reflect consensus about what went on at the meeting can be swiftly and easily discussed and implemented.

Even with today's user-friendly word-processing programs, transcribing the notes of meetings can be tedious. Yet this process can be crucial for the project's ultimate success. Many disputes arising in connection with design projects occur because inadequate notes were taken during the course of lengthy meetings.[13] Only by fully transcribing the notes and distributing them while the meeting is still clear in the minds of all participants can you avoid trouble that is based on different understandings of what transpired at a meeting. Only by transcribing your notes can you retain control of the record. Should relationships deteriorate to the point where parties to a dispute must resolve their differences through arbitration or litigation, the party with the neatest paperwork frequently prevails.[14]

MEETINGS WORTH WRITING ABOUT

The minutes providing an account of a meeting are important, but the substance of the meeting will not be worth recounting if it is not well managed. While a clear and comprehensive agenda sets the tone of a meeting and helps to keep it on track, interior designers need to develop meeting management skills that go beyond careful agenda preparation, note taking, and transcription. Here are some tips for holding successful meetings[15]:

- Keep the meeting short.
- Let the person who knows the most about the key issues run the meeting.
- Stay on agenda, and keep the meeting moving.
- Let each participant speak, and treat all contributions with respect.
- Don't be afraid of humor.
- Summarize at the end of the meeting, even though the material will be included in transcribed notes.

Project Schedules

"Time is God's way of making sure everything doesn't happen at once," goes a not-very-ancient saying. Most design projects are executed under time constraints, sometimes severe. For instance, residential clients may need to have a nursery finished before their baby is born. Yet it is not possible to do everything at the same time, particularly those components of the project that must be executed or installed on its premises. Single-trade contractors, fabricators, and laborers can get in each other's way. Moreover, some jobs must be performed before others. For example, walls must be torn open and new electrical wiring installed before the walls are painted!

In general, project scheduling is the responsibility of the general contractor. However, a contract administrator who understands scheduling serves the client's interests by knowledgeably monitoring construction processes and identifying potential problems.[16] It would always be the interior designer's responsibility to coordinate a construction schedule with a more comprehensive project schedule that factors in the delivery of fixtures, furnishings, and equipment as well as the installation of items such as valances, radiator covers, shelving units, and cabinetry that are fabricated off-site. On very large design projects, scheduling may be the responsibility of a project control specialist.

Three types of schedule are commonly used in design-related projects of all sizes: the *milestone schedule*, the *bar schedule*, and the *critical-path schedule*. Each type of schedule conveys information in a different manner and is better suited to presenting certain kinds of information than others.

THE MILESTONE SCHEDULE

As discussed in Chapter 7, milestones are agreed-upon events in the life of a project that define a degree of progress toward completion. The attainment of a milestone is often connected to the release of a payment to the designer and/or a contractor or fabricator (see Figure 7.4). For instance, for a construction project, when the milestone known as "substantial completion" has been reached, the client frequently releases payment to the general contractor and the designer responsible for contract administration.

This is the easiest type of schedule to create, as it does not require any special computer software but can be done with a word-processing program using columns or in a spreadsheet. Typically the milestone schedule may include both pessimistic and optimistic projections and target dates and provides an opportunity for comparison with the actual time frame. A milestone schedule (see Figure 10.5) is useful for showing how long each of a series of tasks will take and for providing a simple overview of payment due dates so that clients can mobilize their financial resources accordingly.

The milestone schedule is deemed to be particularly useful in scheduling the work of single-trade contractors such as electricians, plumbers, and painters; or in any project that is composed of small tasks that are not complexly interrelated and that follow each other in simple succession. For instance, there may be an agreement that a painter will be paid in three progress payments, each representing a percentage of completion. The designer may estimate that the painter will finish Phase 1 in two weeks, Phase 2 in three weeks, and Phase 3 in one week. This information will be entered into the milestone schedule along with projections for the completion of other tasks.

A milestone schedule shows how long each of a series of tasks will take and provides an overview of payment due dates.

MILESTONE	PROJECTED DATE	PAYMENT DUE	ACTUAL DATE
Sign contract	1-Oct	10%	
Submit shop drawings	15-Oct		
Drawings approved	20-Oct	30%	
Cabinets to lacquer shop	5-Jan	30%	
Cabinets installed	25-Jan	30%	

Figure 10.5
A very simple milestone schedule for a cabinetmaking project made with Microsoft Excel.

A milestone schedule for a large design project can be unwieldy, as demonstrated in this description by members of Carter and Burgess, consultants in engineering, architecture, planning, and the environment[17]:

> This is the way the schedule for a major project used to look—and, in many cases, still does: A thick stack of computer-printed pages, each page filled with tiny print, shows the start and end dates of individual activities. All together, over a thousand lines of text may be contained in the document. If you want to know when the water supply lines for bathroom area #6 need to be sized, you can find that out. But what is not easy to answer are more important questions: How are we doing, overall? Are any unforeseen problems with manpower or other resources ahead? What happens if we miss a deadline for a particular activity? Or for another? Would it throw the whole project off, or not?

THE BAR SCHEDULE

Some of the important questions suggested by Carter and Burgess can be made graphically clear with a bar schedule (Figure 10.6), also known as a Gantt chart, an easy-to-grasp visual format showing the amount of time that tasks will take in relation to each other. If a design firm is coordinating the delivery of carpet with the laying of a subfloor, the bar schedule can show this relationship. It can help to avoid any conflict that might be caused by, say, electricians and plumbers trying to work at the same time. Bar schedules are also useful for interior designers who wish to integrate the work of

A Gantt chart, or bar schedule, shows the amount of time that tasks will take in relation to each other.

fabricators, the delivery of purchased goods, several different kinds of installation, the work of on-site construction contractors, and the schedules of clients, and do so in a manner that is easily grasped by all project participants and stakeholders. Meanwhile, if the design office has posted a bar schedule showing various projects in relation to one another, designers in the firm can more effectively allocate their time among current projects.

Basically, a bar schedule is a graph in which one of the axes represents calendar time and the other lists tasks. By means of bars of varying lengths, the bar schedule graphically depicts the amount of time required for each part of a project to be completed. Sometimes a task is broken down into several parts, each with its own bar. For instance, a plumber may be scheduled to bring up the risers for a new bathroom before the carpenters create the walls. The plumber may continue work after the walls have been erected. Thus, the plumbing work is divided into two separate, discrete bars, with the bar representing the carpenter's work on the wall falling in between.

Bar schedules are suitable for small and medium-sized projects that do not require a detailed analysis of how one part of a process affects other parts. Bar schedules can be created manually and can also be created within spreadsheets or inserted as objects in documents created in Word. (On the Insert menu, choose Object→Create New→Graph Chart). They are the easiest

Figure 10.6
A simple bar schedule for a renovation project made with Microsoft Excel.

	Week 1	2	3	4	5	6	7
Site preparation	●●						
Demolition	●●						
Framing	●	●●●●					
Plumbing		●●●●				●●	
Electric			●●●●●				
Drywall				●●●●●●●●		●●	
Painting					●●●●●		
Final cleaning						●●	

kind of schedule to read, for they show time relationships at a glance. However, they cannot portray complex interrelationships, and their readability is diminished if too many activities need to be represented by too many bars.

THE CRITICAL-PATH (CPM) SCHEDULE

For large corporate projects requiring detailed interrelationship analysis of a complex variety of processes, design project administrators generally employ the so-called critical path method (CPM), which enables specialists to identify in a mass of data the "critical path," or chain of activities that will require the most time to complete, thus ensuring that design managers will pay adequate attention to it. Critical-path schedules (Figure 10.7) can identify resource "crunches"; help find solutions to scheduling conflicts; and plot multiple contingencies.

Carter and Burgess describe an assignment for Wal-Mart distribution centers that required the compression of a twelve-month design schedule into a seven-month period to expedite construction. This assignment required the scheduling of 1,400 activities for each facility in the distribution system. The only way to keep track of a schedule this complex is through the creation of a critical-path schedule with professional project control software such as Primavera Project Planner or Microsoft Project.

The first step in creating a CPM schedule, according to Carter and Burgess, is to hold a meeting that brings together the relevant design-project managers and a scheduling specialist. First, the major milestones are "charted out"; then it is time to "sit down with individual managers and fill in the details [so as to] figure out what the critical path is."

When the scheduling specialist has gathered all necessary information from the design managers, the data are entered into software. At this point the scheduling specialist establishes the *logic ties* that signal which tasks must be completed before other tasks can begin. The computer then "knows" the interrelationship of different activities and the resources needed to accomplish them. It uses this knowledge to work out the critical path, identify resource crunches, and help solve scheduling conflicts. This process permitted the managers at Carter and Burgess to trim down their construction schedule[18]:

> "We looked at all 1,400 activities in the prototypical schedule for the Wal-Mart distribution centers and established what activities had to be completed before another activity had to begin. For example, the mechanical engineers must size and locate the air handling units before the electrical engineers can specify the power required," says

CPM scheduling:
- Works out the critical path
- Identifies resource crunches
- Solves scheduling conflicts

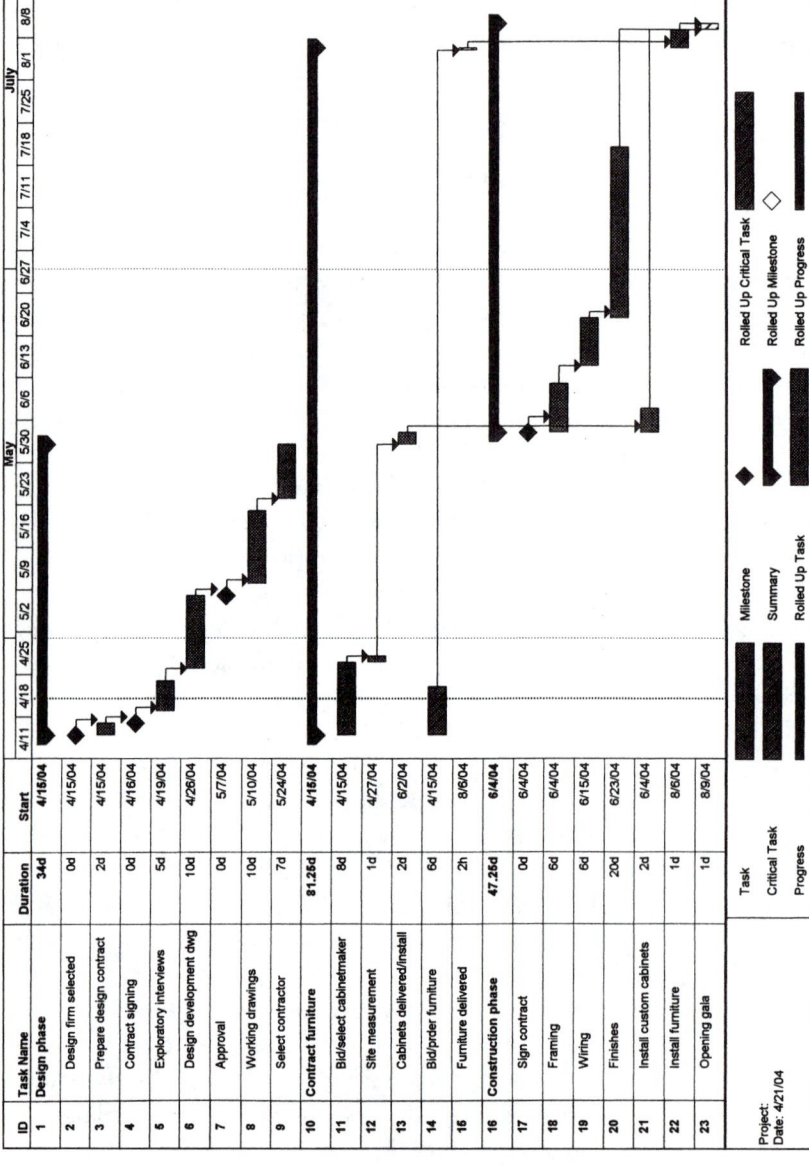

Figure 10.7 Representation of a critical path (CPM) schedule made with Microsoft Project. The critical path would show up clearly, in color, in an actual MS Project file.

Chris Stocke, P.E., Carter and Burgess division manager for distribution centers and warehouses. "This process enabled us to identify the critical activities and rearrange the sequences to eliminate unnecessary lag time. By doing that, we were able to trim five months from the twelve-month design schedule."

The initial schedule thrown off by project-control software can easily be altered to reflect the actual progress of work. Weekly status reports can be entered into the computer. "The software can then produce a variety of progress reports or charts, automatically updating and refiguring projected completion dates when individual activities fall behind or move ahead of schedule."[19] Status reports can be generated within 24 hours after the data have been collected. Thus, managers can make decisions based on very up-to-date reports.

Project-control software can customize a variety of reports, extracting different information for different managers. For instance, one design manager could receive a summary schedule report with activities grouped broadly. Another design manager might receive a detailed report about one activity. The software can also provide short-term "look-aheads" to help designers plan their work schedules. Clients, too, can receive clear, accurate reports on progress and a suitable level of information.

Tracking complex schedules is only part of what project-control software can do. Because it aids in resource management and measures overall performance, it assists in controlling costs. By integrating scheduling and cost control in easy-to-read reports, a project-control system enables more accurate prediction of the evolving likelihood of completing a large project on time and on budget.

Of course, a small interior design firm is unlikely to employ CPM scheduling or to require the assistance of a project-control specialist. Interior designers who are employed by large firms that work across a spectrum of design disciplines are more likely to encounter this type of scheduling than designers who are sole proprietors or employees of small or medium-sized firms. For interior designers employed by large multi-service firms, CPM scheduling may be an important and ever-present aspect of work performance, and the scheduling and project-control specialist an important part of the design team.

Time Records
Also important and ever-present in the work life of designers employed by large firms may be the need to keep accurate time records. (Sole proprietors

and designers employed by small and medium-sized firms benefit from careful accounting of time cost, of course, but it is much less apt to be routinely required.) In firms of all sizes, carefully kept time records support billing and facilitate internal decision making.

USING TIME RECORDS FOR BILLING

If you or your firm are billing by the hour, the importance of keeping time records is obvious. The accumulation of hours recorded by various designers within a firm will be the direct basis for billing a client, who may or may not wish to see the actual time records. If the designer is charging a fixed fee, time records help determine whether the design time estimated for each phase of the project is proving to be accurate. If the project is taking too much time to be profitable, the designer may be able to make mid-course corrections. For instance, the designer may turn off instant messaging if a client is abusing this direct access by asking too many over-anxious questions. If there has been a time-consuming error in plans drawn by a consulting architect hired by the client, the interior designer may request a fee adjustment.

USING TIME RECORDS FOR INTERNAL DECISION MAKING

A design firm of any size can use time records to aid in several important kinds of management decisions. Time records can help a firm determine the likely profitability of future projects. They can help a firm manage its personnel in a manner that rewards productivity. They can also help a firm with business planning that will foster growth and prosperity.

TO DETERMINE PROFITABILITY   Accurate time records help a design firm to determine the overall profitability of projects undertaken with specific clients or within certain categories of work. They also make it possible for a firm to compare the profitability of service offerings across a variety of projects. These comparisons help the firm set and structure fees and create project budgets. For instance, a firm may determine that it does very well with corporate projects but loses money on municipal projects, or vice versa. It may determine that specification writing is more profitable than post-occupancy services, or vice versa. The firm can then elect to charge more for less lucrative services, clients, or project types, or to change the fee structure for those services, clients, or projects. Time records also permit more accurate estimates of the time required for projects within a given category or of a certain square footage; a firm can adjust the budgets presented to clients accordingly.

FOR PERSONNEL MANAGEMENT   Well-kept time records enable a firm to determine which designers are the most productive. Those who do not have a high percentage of billable hours—that is, time that can be charged to a particular client—may be deemed unproductive and may be the first ones laid off in a lean economy. Those who meet or exceed the firm's productivity standards may be promoted or awarded bonuses. According to Christine M. Piotrowski, ASID, IIDA, a high ratio of billable hours to total time worked may "be an important issue for commercial design firms, since billing is more commonly based on an hourly rate. It is a less important issue in . . . residential firms [because they] are less likely to bill at an hourly rate."[20]

FOR STRATEGIC BUSINESS PLANNING   Careful time and other record keeping can help a firm's principals or sole proprietor determine the best strategy for future growth. For instance, a firm may decide to allocate its marketing budget to "grow" business in the sectors that had proved most profitable in the past. If projects of a certain size or type are consistently profitable for a firm, it may restructure its client mix accordingly, turning away from project types or sizes that have proven to be unprofitable in the past. For instance, a small, innovative commercial firm may decide that it cannot profitably take on multi-facility projects that require a heavy technological infrastructure and a large stable of designers to administer. A one-designer residential firm may turn down future projects with a client whose frequent changes of mind have made a past project too time-consuming to be profitable within any conceivable fee constraints. A large multi-service firm may decide to sell an unprofitable facilities-management division.

CREATING TIME RECORDS

It is customary for professional firms to keep track of quarter hours of billable time. Some firms even keep track of ten-minute segments of billable time. The consensus is that keeping track of smaller segments creates an atmosphere of micro-scrutiny and breeds employee dissatisfaction.

A typical time sheet may have columns for the date; a brief description of the task, often coded; and the time spent on the task. Management calculates the amount to be billed based on the fee rate for that employee—for example, $100 an hour—which is not usually shared with low-level employees. Time records are very often kept manually, usually on printed-out forms. In some firms, time-record forms are customized to each employee, with the amount of billable time the employee must log in a given time period entered at the top of the sheet, which typically has room to enter billable hours for a week. Alternatively, billable hours may be entered into a computer document such as a spreadsheet; or they may be kept with the assistance of specialized software that integrates time record keeping with electronic appointment and contact-management functions.

Many time record-keeping systems require the employee to categorize each billable activity with a code designating an activity type. These categories might be classified within two broad groups, one for activities related to the projects of individual clients and one for support activities that are part of the designer's overall office administration. Categories directly related to clients' projects might include "R/D," for research and development, and "D," for time spent developing a design. Support categories might include "B," for bookkeeping, and "DS," for design-support activities such as reviewing product samples and meeting with sales representatives.[21]

Time record keeping requires patience, diligence, and attention to detail. It is necessary to write clearly if you are keeping records manually. If you are typing them into a computer document, proofread immediately after each set of entries, to make sure there have been no typographical errors. Do not guess about the allocation of your time to various project codes. If you are unsure of the rubric under which a block of time should be recorded, then it is advisable to consult with a supervisor rather than guess.

When entering time records, be clear, accurate, diligent, patient, and careful.

Routine Project Correspondence

A seemingly endless exchange of bits or chunks of information characterizes the contract administration phase of many design projects involving construction or fabrication. As discussed in Chapter 9, routine project correspondence may take place via e-mail, fax, or good old-fashioned snail mail. It may be posted to a Web site. It may also take place via instant messaging. Chapter 9 provides tips for formatting and composing business correspondence, which can be an important part of a project record, demonstrating, if a dispute arises, that the designer was careful, thorough, and thoughtful. Accordingly, correspondence must be written with respect and carefully proofread no matter how casual. All the information contained in each piece of correspondence should be absolutely accurate. All correspondence should be "signed by a person with authority to stand behind"[22] decisions and statements of fact.

Routine project correspondence must be written with respect and carefully proofread, no matter how casual.

According to Warren Foster,[23] a designer's project correspondence may include:

- Routine agreements with the contractor and/or the client.
- Notes on construction methods.

- Accident reports from the contractor.
- Documentation of decisions that deviate from the original design documents.

The prudent designer will *print out* all electronic communications, however trivial, and will insert them into the project file. This ensures that important data will not be lost in the event of a computer virus, computer malfunction, media deterioration, or the computer industry's switch to new media—such as from floppies to CD-ROMs—that ultimately makes it very difficult to access older files and records. Printing out electronic communications also ensures that all files are kept in one place. (The alternative— more time-consuming—would be to scan the paper records into the computer.) Adequate backup of all electronic files should be a routine practice of each design firm, of course. As an additional precaution, computer security specialists recommend making several copies each of project and other important documents stored on your hard drive and stashing them in differing locations. This will protect you from losses caused by fire or theft, among other contingencies.

Print out electronic communication no matter how casual.

Back up all project records as appropriate.

Your most informal correspondence related to ongoing projects is likely to be with other employees of your design office. More formal will be routine correspondence with contractors, fabricators, vendors, and suppliers. (Correspondence with vendors and suppliers is discussed in Chapter 8.) Your most formal correspondence related to ongoing projects is likely to be with clients. For instance, you might send them change orders to sign.

Evolving Contract Documents

Communications that modify a construction or fabrication contract or signal important completion milestones have special legal force and must be very carefully drafted and proofed. For construction contracts, these documents include:

Pay special attention to communications that modify a contract or signal important milestones.

- Change orders
- Certificate of substantial completion
- Punch list
- Certificate of occupancy
- Certificate for payment of contractor

CHANGE ORDERS

As discussed in Chapter 7, change orders are contract documents. Accordingly, they must be approved by the owner and the appropriate contractor—for a project involving construction, very likely a general contractor. A well-written change order will describe the work that is to be changed, the nature of the change, and what kinds of work must be ordered and assigned in order to effect the change. The price of the work will be clearly stated. Sometimes contractors prepare change orders; sometimes designers do. They may be written on a form or they may be written on the preparer's letterhead stationery. Again, they must be approved and signed by both the client and the GC—that is, by the parties to the construction contract.

Change orders are numbered in the order of their creation and inserted into the project file in that order. This is important, because a large or complex job, or one with demanding clients, may have numerous change orders, some superseding earlier ones. It is also important that change orders be written with a contract-appropriate degree of specificity. (See the discussion of specifications in Chapter 7).

Among the forms offered for sale by the AIA is G701™-2000 for change orders. Many design firms and some institutional clients develop a template that is adapted for all change orders (Figure 10.8, also on the CD-ROM).

CERTIFICATE OF SUBSTANTIAL COMPLETION

Substantial completion is usually defined as the degree of completion necessary before the owners take occupancy. This means that major systems like the plumbing and electrical systems are fully functional. Finishes have been applied and overall paint coverage is good if not excellent. When these conditions have been met, the principal designer signs off on the project, often using a form from the AIA library known as G704™-2000—the certificate of final completion. At that point, a significant payment is usually released to the contractor. Upon substantial completion, application may be made for a certificate of occupancy, discussed below. However, the contractors' jobs are not finished. They have yet to deal with the punch list, completion of which will be the condition for release of the final payment.

PUNCH LIST

After substantial completion of a construction or fabrication project has been declared, a comprehensive list is prepared of all work items remaining to be completed. Although some residential contractors aim for "Zero Punch,"[24] problems arise on many if not most construction projects. Typical items are missing switch and plug plates; poorly matched adjacent areas of wood stain; poor paint coverage; and scratches on countertops or floors caused by inadequate protection of already completed areas while work was proceeding. The punch list will also include ordered items for which delivery has

---

Margin notes:

Number change orders in the order of their creation.

Substantial completion means the owners can now take occupancy.

The punch list states what the contractor must do before receiving final payment.

been delayed. The punch list (Figure 10.9, also on the CD-ROM) clearly states—item by item, with detailed specificity—the work that must be done before any request for the final payment will be honored.

CERTIFICATE OF OCCUPANCY

Known familiarly as the "C of O," or CO, the certificate of occupancy is required for legal occupation of premises. Certificates of occupancy are issued by municipalities, and the process differs from location to location. Projects requiring a CO in Bellevue, Washington,[25] are:

- New commercial and multifamily buildings.
- Substantial commercial and multifamily additions.
- Commercial tenant improvements involving a change in use.

Without a proper CO, building occupants may not be entitled to municipal services such as fire protection, water supply, trash removal, or sewer access.

The certificate of occupancy is awarded as the result of an inspection by a municipal employee for compliance with zoning restrictions; fire prevention laws; and building, energy, and any other applicable codes. The inspector may not be able to inspect or issue the certificate in a timely manner. Accordingly, punch lists do not usually include the CO. (Since inspectors are looking for substantial, or "material," violations and are concerned with minimum standards for occupancy, they will not be concerned with the minutiae of punch-list completion.)

The CO is not the interior designer's direct responsibility, but if the CO has not been awarded by a client's move-in date, the client may be unhappy with everyone involved in the project.

CERTIFICATE FOR PAYMENT OF CONTRACTOR

When the punch-list items have been completed, the designer presents the client with a signed application for payment of the contractor, frequently by means of AIA form G702™-1992, "Application and Certification for Payment." At this time, all remaining funds payable to the designer for construction administration are also released. The contractors who have been involved in the construction project will presumably close their project files at this time. However, the client is not without recourse if components of the executed job prove to be unsatisfactory. Warranties are customarily included in all contracts with contractors and fabricators. (See

Contractors' warranties protect clients after final payment.

Figure 10.8
A contract
change order
form.

Weber Design

PROJECT_____   PROJECT NO._____

CONTRACTOR_____   CONTRACT NO._____

PROJECT DESIGNER_____   DATE_____

CONTRACT CHANGE ORDER NO. _____

Note: Give complete description of work. The documents supporting this Change Order, including any drawings and estimates of cost, are referenced below and made a part of the Change Order. (Reference other documents as applicable. A copy of each shall be attached to the client's copy of the Change Order.)

C O #	Description	Extra	Credit	Days Ext
		$0	$0	0
	By signing this change order, Contractor agrees that the payment authorized by this change order is in full settlement of all claims, causes of action, and liability of any nature whatsoever which Contractor, any of its subcontractors, suppliers, or the employees of each of them may now have or may assert in the future against the Client or the Designer and the officers, employees and agents of each of them arising out of or associated with the construction of the above-referenced project. It is understood and agreed that this release extends to all claims of every nature and kind whatsoever, known or unknown, suspected or unsuspected. (A general release does not extend to claims which the creditor does not know or suspect to exist in his favor at the time of executing the release, which if known by him would have materially affected his settlement with the debtor.)			

$0	0

Chapter 7.) Within a given period of time, clients may expect the satisfaction of legitimate complaints about leaky plumbing, warped door frames, cracked tiles, or other problems. Meanwhile, the interior designer's project file may not yet be closed, for the designer will likely be coordinating installation and arrangement of the fixtures, furnishings, and equipment that must be in place before the clients, whether residential, institutional, or commercial, are fully "at home" in the project premises.

Page 2

APPROVAL RECOMMENDED	Net Extra......$0
_____	or
PROJECT DESIGNER DATE	Net Credit.... $0
CONTRACTOR AGREEMENT	
The undersigned hereby agrees to the above-described amendment of the contract	Calendar days time extended: 0
_____	
(Legal firm name of Contractor)	Copies To:
_____	
SIGNATURE TITLE DATE	• *Client*
Note: The Contractor's name shall be listed on the contract. All signatures must be signed in ink.	• *Contractor*
CLIENT APPROVAL	• *Project*
_____	*Designer*
APPROVED TITLE DATE	

Figure 10.8
(continued)

Transitional Services

The client may request additional services from the designer after the design contract has been completed. An important transitional service frequently offered by interior designers is move management. In offering this service, the designer transfers scheduling experience and skills from the design project proper to the client's projected move, scheduling packing in a manner that will permit utilization of the new premises even as moving continues.

Room Number: General	
Note/Ref	**Walls**
Window	Remove plastic scrap @ wall junction/create clean edge.
Switches	Paint cover plates silver in entry lobbies.
Paint	Check all wall/mullion transitions. Not all painted or finished. Some mullion/wall joints have trim, others are bare metal and not finished well at edge. Wall between rms. 122/123 is good.
	Miscellaneous
AT&T	Outlet boxes and faceplates not installed: hanging loose.
Blinds	Being installed.
Thermostats	Clean and close up after balancing.

Comments: Rooms 131, 132, 164, and 164A were too dark for me to see.

For instance, a corporate client's current files might be moved before older ones. For a large client, moving may be a very complex operation every bit as complicated to schedule as tasks related to the design project itself. Writing generated in connection with move management may include schedules, memos or instruction manuals, reports, and transmittal letters.

Post-Occupancy Services

Even after the client is occupying and using the project premises, there may be additional work for the designer who has been asked to perform so-called post-occupancy services. Some services of this type, such as facilities management, involve the ongoing management of the premises, including space and resource allocation. The design firm may wish to create a new project file and a new contract for an ongoing assignment of this type. This might not be necessary for more discrete and time-bounded post-occupancy services such as the preparation of a *user manual*—a set of instructions for the use of a client's premises.

A user manual (Figure 10.10) for a corporate client may be organized much like the formal report discussed in Chapter 9. It may cover everything from appropriate procedures for removing coffee stains from upholstered desk chairs to company policy on smoking to the degree of personalization permitted in office cubicles. For a large facility or a system of facilities, the report may be very elaborate. A simple user packet may be prepared for a residential client, including instruction booklets and cut sheets for all FF&E, including recommended maintenance procedures and warranties. It is also customary to include an inventory of all paint colors and other surface finishes used on the project (in case touch-ups are needed).

Project Follow-up

In addition to post-occupancy services performed at the client's behest, usually for additional fees, a design firm may follow up on a project with a post-occupancy evaluation, a project history, and a thank-you note.

Post-Occupancy Evaluation

In order to get a better sense of what works and what does not work for the clients they serve, many designers administer a post-occupancy evaluation,

VISUAL CLUTTER

Our general office appearance is adversely affected by placement of unnecessary objects on top of binder bins and filing cabinets. We urge that all product samples, models, and posters be stored out of sight when not in use. Please use discretion when displaying personal items such as photographs, mugs, stuffed animals, and humorous signs. Confine them to areas inside your own workstation.

WINDOWS

Window blinds should remain fully lowered in order to maintain a consistent look to the building. Adjust tilt of blinds to control light level. Drapery should be either fully closed or completely open.

TEMPERATURE CONTROL

Thermostats are provided to maintain temperatures in building zones or areas. Each of these areas has specific environmental needs. Please do not make adjustments to suit your personal needs. Contact FACILITY SERVICES, ext. 5732, if your area is too hot or too cold.

Figure 10.10
Excerpt from
North Ridge
General Office
Appearance
Guidelines.

or POE, after a period of time has elapsed. (On the one hand, it is unwise to wait too long, for people forget the details of their likes and dislikes as time goes by. On the other hand, enough time must elapse for people to develop a clear sense of what works for them and what doesn't.) It is customary to use the same post-occupancy *instrument*, or questionnaire designed to elicit information, for various clients, so that their responses can be compared to develop a clear picture of what works and what doesn't. "The POE is a valuable research tool," says designer Dan Beert, "much the same as a post-mortem to a doctor. It allows for better future practice."[26]

Howell Design & Build, in North Andover, Massachusetts, asks clients to complete a survey containing more than 40 questions "covering design, project communication, quality of work, and subcontractor performance."[27] Along with the questionnaire, clients are sent a gift basket containing coffee, cocoa, and company mugs. It is reported that nine out of ten respond. When the questionnaire has been completed, it is copied and distributed within the design-build company and then discussed in a company-wide meeting. If there is praise to pass around, it can be shared at the meeting. If there is blame, an appropriate and relevant team visits the client to probe the nature of the complaints.

Rather than attempting to justify performance, Howell asks clients who have complaints "how they would have handled particular situations" had they been in charge. By making disgruntled customers part of the change team, they frequently become supporters of the firm. They are more apt to refer business and to provide favorable recommendations. All information garnered from the questionnaire is entered into a database and can then be analyzed along with data from other jobs to provide information about cross-project trends.

Project Summary

When attempting to retrieve details of an archival project for catalog or other promotional purposes, it can be very useful to have at hand a simple summary of important details about the project. Firms that create such project summaries sometimes do so with the aid of a template that contains blanks to fill in with relevant information. They may use AIA form G809 ™-2001, "Project Abstract." A useful project summary may contain:

- The client's name and contact information
- The client's firm or institution if relevant

- The name and contact information of the principal designer on the project
- Names and contact information for other members of the design team
- Names and contact information for consulting peer professionals
- Name and contact information for the project photographer
- Name and contact information for the general contractor and for the principal subcontractors

Project History

A brief history of the firm's experience with the project may likewise be useful in years to come for promotional purposes. It is much easier to write a simple narrative while the experience of the project is fresh in participants' minds. To get some sense of the freshness and flavor such a history may have, take another look at the Frank Lloyd Wright description of the Johnson Wax project in Chapter 2. It contains strong narrative elements and shows not only how the project evolved but how the designer's and the firm's aesthetic philosophy evolved. Narrative techniques are further discussed in Chapters 2 and 3.

Thank-You Note

If your relationship with a client was as satisfying as that of Chris Frost with Ann Cox Porter, it will be a pleasure for you to write a thank-you note that shares your appreciation with your client. Even if you did not enjoy working with the client (and lost money on the project), it is good manners and sound business practice to thank the client for the creative and professional opportunity represented by the recently completed project. As discussed in Chapter 5, a business thank-you letter is usually typed on the design firm's letterhead, but does not contain an inside address, subject line, or attention line. It is usually no more than half a page long. Is it hypocrisy to thank a client for a job that was difficult from start to finish? Not really, when you consider that each project does represent an opportunity for a designer to grow as a professional, gaining experience that may make the next project a smoother and more fulfilling experience. Of course, you wouldn't say *that* in your thank-you letter. It will suffice to find something that you enjoyed about the client and the project, to point it out in your letter, and to sign your name. Impeccable manners are one more way to advertise your skills and abilities as a designer.

> Send a thank-you letter even if the project was unsatisfying.

Discussion Questions

1. For which kinds of projects would you use a milestone schedule, a bar schedule, or a critical-path schedule? Provide a clear rationale for each of your responses

2. Does a one-person design firm need to keep time records? Why or why not?

3. With your teacher noting all suggestions on the blackboard, discuss what members of your class would like to see covered in a post-occupancy manual governing the use of your classroom. What questions would you ask in a post-occupancy evaluation about the effectiveness of your classroom as a designed interior?

Exercises

1. Keep a telephone log of all calls you receive and place during the course of a week. Take careful and accurate notes. At the end of the week, bring your phone log to class. Exchange it with at least one other student in your class for a peer evaluation. How thorough were you? Did you clearly note all contact data and times of the various calls? Did you note the disposition of each contact attempt?

2. Prepare an agenda for a meeting of your class in which you discuss the role of writing in the work of an interior designer. Let each student provide two photocopies of his or her agenda. Your teacher will assemble two packets, each containing all the agendas, and will leave them at the reserve desk of the library or in another place where they are accessible to all members of your class. Each student must read all the agendas in the packet and select one other than his own for use by the class, providing a written rationale for the selection.

3. In each of three or four medium-sized groups, choose a moderator and let that person "run" a meeting according to the agenda selected in Exercise 2. All other members of the group will function as note takers. When the meeting has concluded, compare the notes collected by the note takers. Provide each person in the group, including the meeting facilitator, with a copy of all notes taken. Let each person prepare a set of minutes of the meeting, suitable for e-mailing. Provide each person in the group with a set of every other group member's minutes. What can you learn by comparing the minutes to the notes and to each other? At this point, open up a whole-class discussion.

4. Ask a designer who works for a large firm for a copy of the change-order template or printed form in use by the firm. Using the resources of your word-processing program, adapt the template for use by a small firm, using the identity elements you prepared for Chapter 4. Share your change-order template with your class.

5. Using Google or the engine of your choice, search for information on COs in your municipality. How does this certificate—or the lack of it—impinge on designers' relationships with their clients and their ability to fulfill commitments? Write a memo to your teacher detailing your conclusions.

11 Marketing through Promotion, Advertising, and Publicity

If your interior design work is truly excellent, won't the word get around? Surely your satisfied clients will tell their friends about your services. When prospects present themselves, you will win them with your portfolio and your capabilities packet. You have learned to write engaging, informative, dignified letters of interest and proposals. *Enough*, you may say. You don't want to demean the status of your profession with inappropriate ads or flyers. Indeed, you may be suspicious of professionals who blatantly promote their services: the plastic surgeon whose placards are displayed on buses or the "ambulance chasing" attorney whose billboard looms ominously above the high-speed expressway. If this signage is what *promotion* means, then it could do your professional practice more harm than good. Ditto *publicity*, you may think: If *publicity* means photo opportunities and sound-bite interviews, then it is for models and entertainers, not for interior design professionals. You are selling your creativity, skills, and experience, not your smile and your hairdo!

Yet promotion and publicity need not be tasteless and inappropriate. In the increasingly competitive business environment, your firm, like others, may grow more quickly and prosper more consistently if you have a solid plan for marketing. Executed with thoughtfulness and flair, promotion and publicity can become an integral part of your practice. Here are some useful definitions to begin with:

- *Marketing* is everything you do to create the context that generates business. It is not the same as selling, where goods or services are being pitched to an already-interested prospect. You are *selling* when you present your capability packet to a possible client. You would be *marketing* if you gave a talk at the local medical society on design for physicians' offices, and you left a stack of your brochures at the welcome table. Such a lecture—and your brochure in that context—would not be pitched to a particular prospect. Rather you would be raising awareness of your knowledge and skills among members of a public that is a likely source of future business.

  Marketing is indirect presentation that creates a context for *selling*, or direct presentation.

- *Promotion* is the distribution of messages that you create yourself, or pay to have created. You control the format and content of the message and sometimes pay for the space or time in which your message is put before the public.

  Promotion is the distribution of a controlled marketing message.

- *Publicity* is the art of getting a favorable message into the editorial content of print, broadcast, and other media without paying for the placement. You do not control the format or content of the message, but you gain credibility and prestige from the favorable coverage.

  Publicity means getting other people to distribute your marketing message, which you no longer control.

A good marketing plan will include both promotion and publicity. The strategies you choose should work together effectively to create what Jay Conrad Levinson calls the "metamessage," the emotional impact of your marketing, which speaks to prospective clients at the unconscious as well as the conscious level.[1] For instance, that lecture to the medical society on office design for doctors may focus on ergonomics, but it sends a metamessage about your concern for people's well-being and comfort. This metamessage is an important part of what people will take from the lecture and talk about afterward.

The *metamessage* is the emotional impact of all your marketing.

Promotion

Of course, there is truth in the hoary notion that word-of-mouth—referral—is an effective promotional strategy for a design firm. Traditionally, it is a strategy that most designers depend on, though it needs support. Over time, you can develop strategies for putting your brochure (or flyer or postcard or newsletter) directly into the hands of a greater number of potential clients by broadening your means of distribution. As your business grows and your promotional budget increases, you may decide to approach your public or publics through *advertising*—promotional messages that speak through the media, where your message must compete with other messages. You may also use your Web site to promote your business, not only by posting capability materials, but by making your site a resource for those researching interior design issues online.

Word of Mouth

Sensitivity to client needs generates good word of mouth— buzz and referrals.

Strictly speaking, *word of mouth*, or "buzz," may not qualify as promotion, since you neither created the message nor had it created, nor do you have much control over its distribution. Yet word of mouth does indeed function as promotion. Your satisfied clients create the message (often in spoken rather than written form) and put it out. They are more likely to promote you and your work if they feel that they have gotten "bonuses" of time and attention from you, so you "pay" for good word of mouth with your sensitivity to client needs. Don't be shy about asking pleased clients to tell their friends about the excellent services of your design firm. Offer your clients a tangible benefit for bringing new business your way. For instance, you might offer a 10 percent discount on the next interior design project. You can facilitate client referrals by leaving a discreet stack of business cards with each satisfied client.

Promotional Pieces

Strong support for word of mouth is provided by generous distribution of promotional pieces such as brochures, flyers, postcards, and newsletters. You don't want to be profligate, but it is crucial not to be stingy. In developing your promotional strategy, there are two sets of factors to consider: the creation of each type of promotional piece; and the distribution of the various promotional pieces.

THE CAPABILITY BROCHURE

A novice designer who is cultivating a high-end clientele may be tempted to choose a brochure that is expensively designed and printed. Die-cutting and embossing; thick, shiny coated papers; the services of a high-end graphic designer; and four-color printing may make your brochure too expensive for free-and-easy distribution. Granted, an expensive brochure may make a good impression in capability presentations. For many promotional purposes, though, you may prefer a simpler, less expensive brochure—preferably one that fits standard business-size envelopes. (Perhaps a simple folder printed in one-color ink on colored paper.)

If commercial four-color printing is crucial for your metamessage, but pricey for your budget, you might look into *gang runs*. Large printing companies that run mammoth full-color jobs on enormous presses can sometimes fit in a smaller job. That smaller job is the so-called gang run, and it costs much less than having your own scheduled run, although it won't do if you are in a hurry. Printing by gang run means that you give the printer the ready materials and the paper, and you simply wait until the opportunity arises to "gang" your job.

> A gang run, or unscheduled print job, may lower the cost of four-color printing.

The writing and design of folder, booklet, kit, and Web brochures are discussed in Chapter 4. There the brochure is considered as part of a capability presentation that elicits a sale. As a promotional tool, the same brochure needs to be considered along with its "cousins," the flyer, the postcard, and the newsletter.

> The same brochure may be used for capability presentation and promotion.

THE FLYER

A *flyer* is the simplest kind of promotional piece—a single page most often printed on one side. It can be designed in a *portrait*, or vertical, orientation, or in a *landscape*, or horizontal, orientation. The portrait orientation is more common. Whatever the orientation, the purpose of the flyer is to present factual information in a stylish manner, so as to generate interest and action. Flyers, also known as *circulars*, are used to promote everything from yard sales to hot-tub installations. Although they are sometimes printed in four colors on glossy paper, often they are the simple products of word-processing programs, perhaps printed on colored paper for extra pizzazz.

> A good flyer offers more than information.

Because design capability is a complex topic, it is usually not presented in a flyer, which is a simpler medium than the brochure. However, you might supplement your capability brochure with flyers announcing special events. For instance, you might announce with a flyer your design of sets for a theater company's current production. Perhaps you could arrange for a special viewing of the sets and host a reception in the theater, to which you would invite your clients, collaborators, and friends by means of a nicely composed flyer printed on special paper. It is always more effective to offer people something than simply to inform them.

Jay Conrad Levinson suggests the following procedure for writing flyers. "Think first of the basic idea you wish to express. Then, try to marry a picture (art or photograph) to a set of words. After you've stated your idea as briefly as possible . . . explain more fully what you are offering. Always be

Be sure to include contact information in all flyers.

sure to include information about how to get in touch with you: address, phone number, place to find you."[2]

The fundamentals of brochure writing apply to flyers:

- Use white space creatively
- Organize ideas carefully
- Let the message of print and picture complement each other
- Proofread, proofread, proofread

In Chapter 12, techniques are presented for inserting a picture into a document using your word-processing program. However, you can also use rubber cement to carefully paste the visual into the camera-ready copy you are taking to the photocopy store. Greater individualization is possible, though time-consuming. For instance, for the flyer announcing a preview of the theatrical sets, you might hand-color photocopied drawings before pasting the drawing repros onto the already copied flyers—but only if the results are of professional quality. Precision and accurate measurement are essential to avoid a slovenly look. If you have any doubt about your own capabilities as a graphic designer, stick with text, using the built-in capabilities of your word-processing program to vary font judiciously, to box information precisely, to center accurately, and so on. You might also consider the use of MS Office or other flyer templates.

Promote design services in the neutral language of informing and explaining.

Since the flyer provides less space for your message than does a brochure, you must make your case very succinctly, and you must do so while maintaining the essential dignity of your profession. Although you are *promoting*, or talking up, your design services, use the neutral language of informing and explaining (Figure 11.1). Avoid obvious promotional language, such as that found in flyers for, say, carpet cleaning or hair dye. Avoid "new" or "improved" or "exciting" or other injections of *hyperbole* ("hype"), or overstatement.

You do need to catch the attention of your readers, and to do so you can borrow two important tricks from advertising. The first is to write an engaging headline—that larger-font eye-grabber at the top of the page. The second is to translate features into benefits. For flyer purposes, these two tricks can sometimes be combined into one.

Catch the attention of readers with a feature-benefit headline.

WRITING THE FEATURE-BENEFIT HEADLINE   Let us suppose that you are participating in a panel discussion at your local public library on green design. Local designers are trying to raise public awareness about green issues relating to interior design, such as the fact that many kinds of wall-to-wall carpet are

Figure 11.1
Flyer for a design competition.

not biodegradable. They persist in dumps and landfills, and some are toxic. How can you and the library present the panel in a way that is appealing to the general public as well as to your past and future clients? First, translate the principal feature of the panel—its focus on environmental awareness—into benefits for the local community. Benefits might include preserving the look of the landscape and making the locality more attractive as a place to live. A headline might read: "How Your Indoors Creates the Outdoors." A drawing of children playing atop a pile of carpet in a dump might be placed beneath this headline. A subhead might state the title of the panel, "Green Design: Environmental Awareness and Interior Design Choices." The flyer would go on to provide the all-important "where and when" information relating to the panel discussion, including a telephone number.

Less is more in writing flyer text. People read flyers quickly. You don't need to write complete sentences, and you can present in bulleted lists information such as the names of the four designers participating in the green panel. Give "where-when" items such as time, place, and date their own lines, too.

Less is more in flyer writing.

Because a panel is the marketing focus in this example, it would be inappropriate to single out an individual among the four panelists. If an individual designer were giving a talk on green awareness, the flyer could headline, say, Michael Hujak, ASID, IIDA. By promoting the panel and the three other designers, Michael Hujak sends a different, more subtle message: that he is a player, an expert among experts. Other promotional pieces from his office with other messages will reinforce his underlying metamessage: "Michael Hujak is a talented, knowledgeable designer. Choose him for your next design project." When Michael sends the green-panel flyer to those on his mailing list, he can highlight his own name with a marker and scrawl a personal note where appropriate on each flyer he sends: "Helen—It would be grand to see you at this event. Michael."

AUDIENCE   Translating features into benefits requires an awareness of the audience for a given piece of promotional writing. For instance, a flyer for promoting a green panel directed at business people might have a headline inviting them to "Boost Profit with Green Design." The flyer might go on to say: "Four prominent interior designers tell how to choose carpet that won't end up in the toxic landfill that drives business from our region."

For an audience primarily composed of its own members and friends, a designers' organization might promote the green panel very differently. A flyer directed at peer professionals might contain no headline other than the title of the panel—"Green Design: Environmental Awareness in the Interior Design Profession"—with the name of the sponsoring professional organization above the title as guarantor of credibility and interest. Along with capsule biographies, there might be pictures of the four participating designers.

Frame benefits for the target audience.

THE POSTCARD

Many restaurants and stores display racks that offer a choice of give-away postcards, each card promotional but designed to be desirable as a personal mailing piece. Those who take the cards presumably provide the postage when they mail them to their friends, thus contributing an implicit endorsement of what is being promoted, which may be a book, a CD-ROM, a restaurant, a movie, a candy, or a beverage. The postcards themselves, if well designed, often become an object for discussion, and their broad dissemination increases public awareness of the goods or services on offer.

The company that prints the postcards also maintains the racks and charges separate fees for printing the cards and displaying them. This is good news for interior designers, for whom there is less point in marketing to a broad general public than for, say, a CD recording artist. If you decide to promote your interior design business with postcards, you will very likely choose to purchase the printing without the display. (Alternatively, you can create postcards from a template, as shown in Figure 11.2, featured on the CD-ROM, as well as in the text, and print them yourself.) Distributed to carefully targeted audiences, postcards can tell a clear, simple story about design excellence provided that the photograph or other image presented on the picture face of the card is well chosen and the graphics are of high quality.

THE PICTURE FACE   Many designers select a photograph for a postcard from those displayed in their capability brochures or portfolios. An example of a postcard from the Interior Edge is featured on the CD-ROM. Regardless of whether the photograph was taken by you or by a professional photographer, the selection should present your success at the kind of project you

Postcards tell a clear, simple story with well-chosen images and high-quality graphics.

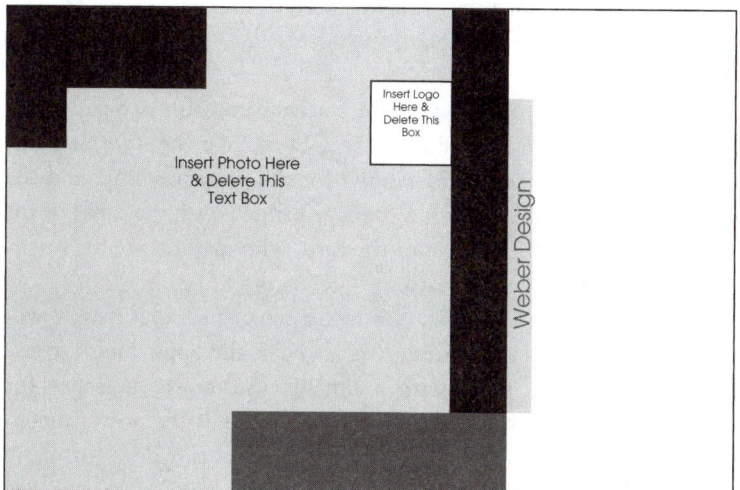

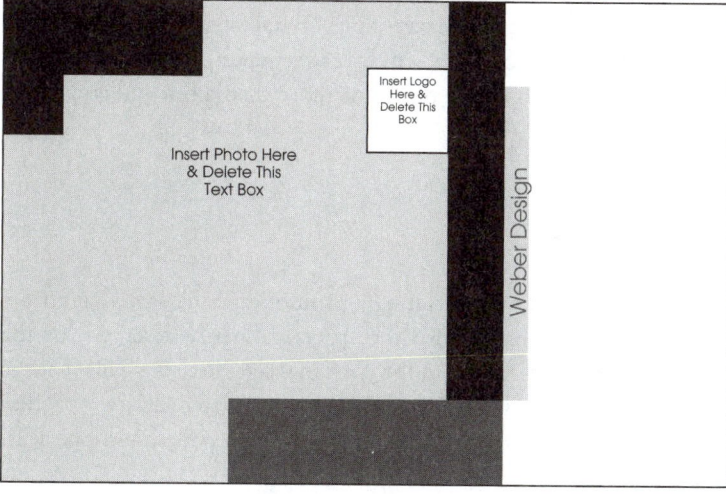

Figure 11.2
Picture face of a two-up postcard template available at ww.avery.com. In the white space, you could put a brief amount of text promoting your firm.

would most like to do; and the photo should be one for which you have purchased the rights for this use. (There is more on this subject later in the chapter.) It is possible to create a postcard that is a composite of several different photographs showcasing different design capabilities. But a larger, single photograph often reads better, particularly if the image is not all that you want on the picture side of the card. Since the purpose of the postcard is to associate your name, or the name of your firm, with the project represented in the image, you may want the name of your firm and your logo to appear on top of the image (though not right in the middle of it) so that it can be regarded only in association with your name. Unless you are adept with image-manipulation software, you will need to hire a freelance graphic designer to help you with the design of the postcard.

THE MESSAGE FACE   A postcard's *message face* usually contains two panes (see Figure 11.3 featured in the text and on the CD-ROM): the *address pane*, which is used for the recipient's address and for the postage stamp; and the *message pane*, which may be used for a message printed with the cards or for a message created later by the sender of the card, who may be you or someone to whom you have passed the card.

If you preprint the message pane, you lower the chance that people will actually mail your postcard to a friend. You also lose the opportunity to use the postcard as a mailing piece with a timely customized message—for instance, to announce that you have won a design prize. If the postcard is to function merely as a large business card with a photo—as it does for many practitioners in the interior design and related professions—then it is not important that it be usable as a mailing piece by those who receive it from you. You might as well preprint the message pane, composing a very brief adlike text that distills the essence of your firm in a few punchy points, since, with readable font size, you won't have room for more than a few bullets' worth of information:

- Excellent design
- Reasonable fees

You do have the option of preprinting a promotional message that covers not only the message pane, but also the space ordinarily reserved for the address pane. This means more room for your message. It also means that the card can be mailed only in an envelope. You may want to order two batches of postcards—one with text preprinted in one or both panes, and one with both panes left blank.

COPYRIGHT AND ACKNOWLEDGMENT   Copyright and acknowledgment for the image on the picture face of the postcard are usually printed somewhere on the message face of the card, along with any credit required for a graphic designer. If you have not purchased all rights to the photograph you are using, professional photographers will require that their copyrights be published in close proximity to the photo along with their credits: Photo by Janet James. © Janet James, 2003. If you have purchased all rights to the photo, then you would print the photographer's credit but

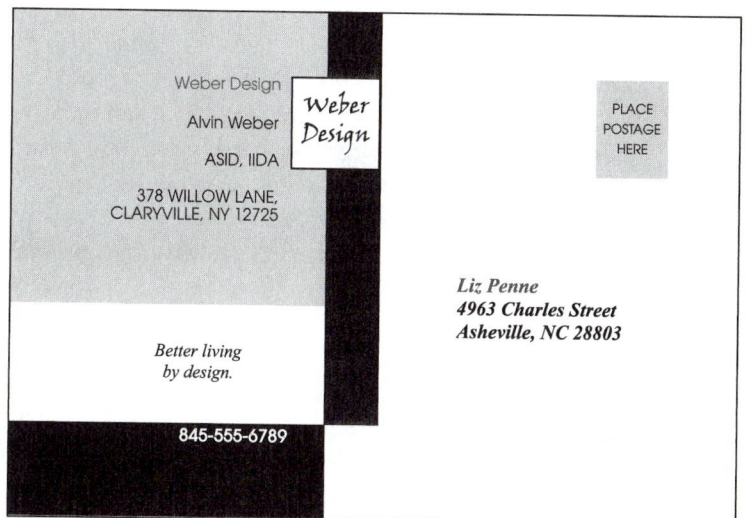

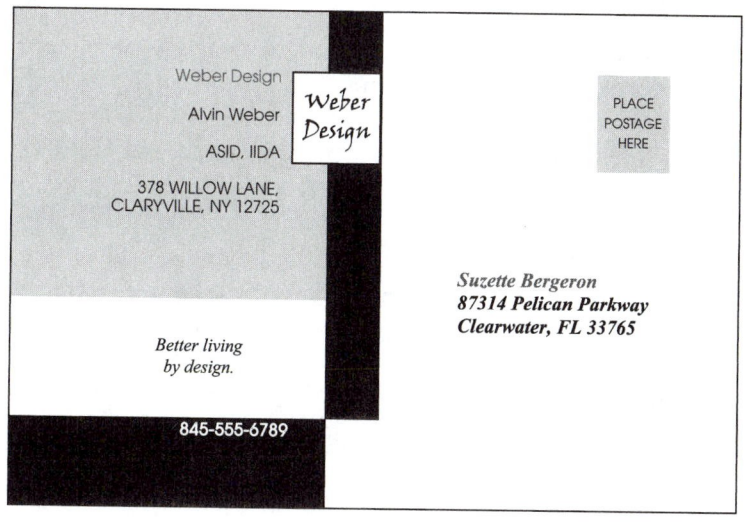

Figure 11.3 Message face of a postcard created from an Avery two-up template. Note preprinted message pane.

your copyright notice, since you would then own copyright: Photo by Janet James. © George Designer, 2004.

PERMISSIONS   To use a project photo, you may need permission not only from a professional photographer, if you have used one, but also from the owners of the home or proprietors of the business that is represented in the photograph. Even if you have permission to use a photo, do not publish the names of clients or give their addresses unless expressly permitted to do so.

THE NEWSLETTER

A private, limited-distribution news periodical is called a *newsletter*. It is an effective way to stay in touch with previous clients; to impress new prospects; to inform vendors, contractors, and collaborating professionals; and to boost morale within a middle-sized or large design firm. For easy readability and eye appeal, a newsletter is usually laid out in columns, and you don't need to be a technical genius to execute such a layout. Whereas the most sophisticated results are achieved with dedicated programs such as Quark, programs like Microsoft's Office contain templates that provide simple, crisp-looking results. Such a template permits you to choose from one-, two-, or three-column formats, with a choice of several font sizes and styles for headlines. Typical is a two-column format on each of two sides of one page. Some newsletters use four sides of two pages, but newsletters do not usually run longer than that. They are geared to the reading needs of busy people whose patience is easily exhausted, and they must compete for the reader's attention with newspapers, magazines, and other media.

NEWSLETTER CONTENTS   One of the best ways to figure out what to put in your newsletter is to look at other newsletters. This research will give you a richer sense of the options available to you. Obviously you want to let clients, would-be clients, and professional friends know about the good work your firm is currently doing or has recently done. Professional achievements such as awards are good candidates for coverage in your newsletter, as are hirings and promotions within your firm. Be sure to describe any role that you or your design associates may play in civic affairs, such as membership on your town's planning board or volunteer work on the restoration of a historic house.

Of course, the newsletter shouldn't *all* be about you, even if yours is a one-designer firm. Strive for diversity of content. Interviews with vendors, suppliers, or collaborating professionals may be of interest to your readers. Features generating reader involvement, such as a question-and-answer

Be careful to print the photographer's credit and copyright, and always get permission to use an image of a client's premises.

Strive for diversity of content in your newsletter.

column, are often popular. Try to give the recipients of your newsletter a reason to save each issue. For instance, a residential designer might provide tips on the maintenance of features such as texturized-concrete kitchen countertops. News of any product recalls affecting your clients might be welcome, as would information about relevant new technologies or improvements in old ones. You may even decide to reprint articles from the promotional materials of your suppliers if they provide interesting information on current trends in the world of interior design.

> Give newsletter recipients a reason to save each issue.

Many newsletters print personal news about the birth of children, anniversaries, graduations, engagements, weddings, and the like. This may or may not be appropriate for the image—and metamessage—you are trying to project. Whether or not to print such information is based on your knowledge of customs in your geographical area. The same may be said for editorials by a firm's principal designer on regional development strategies, local or national politics, or the changing seasons. By looking at other newsletters published in your area and for your market, you can get a better sense of whether or not personal, political, or philosophical touches would be welcome to readers.

Whatever the content of your newsletter, it is important that it come out often enough to be taken seriously, although not so often that it is an imposition. Generally, if the choice is between a more elaborate newsletter that does not appear very often and a simpler one that comes out more frequently, it is better to publish more frequently. Four times a year is an often-cited minimal frequency for holding your readers' respect and attention.

> A simple newsletter that comes out frequently is better than an elaborate one that comes out infrequently.

NEWSLETTER STYLE   Although a newsletter is written for promotional purposes, it will have more credibility if it is written in a manner that is not immediately interpreted as promotional. As for flyers and brochures, the neutral language of explaining and informing is appropriate. Beware the lure of the sprightly tone, as it easily verges on inappropriate cuteness. You may wish to emulate newswriting in certain respects, such as the objective manner and the top-down structuring of articles. Later in this chapter, in the publicity section, the fundamentals of newswriting are presented.

> In newsletter writing, beware the sprightly tone.

THE ILLUSTRATED NEWSLETTER   Any newsletter is more exciting to look at and more appealing to read if it is illustrated with photographs and other images. For an interior designer, images are essential for conveying the look and feel of in-progress and completed projects. However, the newsletter need not and should not duplicate the look of your capability brochure. While it will certainly contain photos of finished projects, it may also contain process photographs. In addition, candid photographs (snapshots) or portraits may

> The newsletter should not duplicate the capability brochure.

illustrate an interview or document a designer's presence at a professional conference. News photos may also be appropriate—for instance, a picture of a designer receiving an award from a professional or civic organization. All photographs should be published with appropriate credit and copyright.

Color photographs are always a plus for an interior design firm, but four-color printing is relatively expensive. It is less costly to print in one color—usually black—on white or colored paper. This would restrict you to black-and-white photographs, even if you were printing in, say, sepia—in which case the black of your black-and-white photos would print as brown. It is sound economy for a designer to publish a capability brochure in full color, but the newsletter and flyers in a single color. It will probably make sense for you to routinely take, or have taken, two sets of project photos, one color and the other black and white. (The black-and-white photo will be useful for publicity purposes as well; see the discussion of publicity later in this chapter.)

Try to control the cost of photos you use in your newsletter, as it may have a much shorter useful life than, say, a brochure or postcard. Although you might hope that your newsletters would be saved and re-read many times, basically each is current only until the next one comes out. This is why it is sound economic sense to deploy in a newsletter photographic images for which you do not have to pay, either because a previous agreement permits this use or because you took them yourself or in-house. Of course, any photographs that you take yourself should be of near-professional quality. In Chapter 4, you will find some useful tips on taking interior photographs with a digital or 35-millimeter camera. If you are currently a design student, by all means choose studio photography as an elective if you are able to do so. It may be useful to you in the future and will look good on your résumé!

In addition to photographs, many newsletters contain line drawings, graphs, and charts. A newsletter may be a good opportunity to showcase your skill at creating plans, elevations, axonometric or perspective drawings, and bubble diagrams, either freehand or with the assistance of a computer. You will probably not be generating graphs and charts as a regular part of your design practice. However, if you are reprinting an article from a vendor's promotional materials, you may wish to use any graphs and charts associated with the article—with proper permission and acknowledgment, of course.

A digital camera and a scanner are good investments for a designer who publishes newsletters. They make it easier to publish an illustrated periodical. Current design students may be able to avail themselves of this equipment through the central computer facility at their universities. Commercial photocopy centers such as Kinko's offer scanning and image-creation services, as do most freelance graphic designers.

Consider publishing a brochure in full color, but a newsletter and flyers in black ink on colored paper.

Have two sets of project photos taken, one color and one black and white.

A digital camera and a scanner are good investments for a designer publishing newsletters.

Once images are stored on your computer, the newsletter templates in your word-processing software provide boxes into which you can handily insert the images, though you will probably need a bit of practice to create balanced-looking columns with appropriate-sized pictures that are clear and bright. (Chapter 12 provides some assistance with the rudimentary editing of photos and their insertion into documents.) For greater layout flexibility and sophistication, some interior designers master a dedicated layout program so that they can publish in more complex and individualized formats than those available with standard office software. However, you may discover that the newsletter and other templates available for word-processing software are adequate for most purposes, particularly if you are a novice designer or have a small office.

OUTSOURCING YOUR NEWSLETTER   Even with templates, desktop publishing is time-consuming. Assuming that you have developed the necessary skills, it still might take half a workweek or more to lay out a four-page newsletter; write, format, and proof the text; select, edit, and insert the photos; and organize the entire newsletter.[3] A large, busy design office might hire a newsletter service to put out its publication. The design firm would provide "copy," or text, and art for the two outside pages; the service would fill in the two inside pages from its stock of relevant features. (The use of a newsletter service would mean that interior design firms in other regions or markets could be publishing newsletters with contents that duplicate yours in some respects. Most services will not sell the same newsletter to two customers in the same market.)

Another alternative permitting a more individualized approach is to hire freelancers to put out the newsletter using your ideas and artwork. A typical freelance team hired to produce a newsletter includes a writer and a graphic designer. If you have tried your own hand at newsletter writing and publishing, your experience will help you to evaluate the product created by such a team.

DISTRIBUTION

It is one thing to have a handsome promotional piece in hand, quite another to get the piece to those whom you wish to reach. Tried-and-true distribution tactics for promotional pieces include making them available as handouts and "take-ones." Some promotional items are suitable for display as posters and "stand-alones," particularly if enlarged. Promotional pieces may become mailing pieces, either traditional ("snail mail") or electronic. They may also be re-formatted for posting on your Web site.

HANDOUT   The word *handout* alarms some designers. They shrink at the prospect of standing on a busy corner handing to any and all passers-by their brochures, flyers, or reprints of publications in which their work has been featured or in which their awards have been announced. This caution is justified. You need to be much more selective than, say, a car wash about targeting the recipients of your handouts. Start small! Your clients are a good target audience for you to begin with. Make sure that each has a modest stack of your brochures and other handouts. Vendors, contractors, and other professionals such as architects, engineers, and landscape designers should also have several copies of each of your handouts. In return, you should be prepared to accept and help circulate their handouts.

Swap handouts with vendors, contractors, and other professionals.

By supplying your brochure or other promotional pieces to clients and collaborators, you make it easy for them to refer you to their friends, relatives, clients, and customers. All they need to do is pass along your promotional materials. No need to search for your phone number, or for the words to describe your skills and abilities.

Don't forget that your business card is a pocket-sized handout, suitable for passing around on any and all occasions. You should not consider yourself dressed to go out if you do not have a small stash of business cards somewhere on your person. You might want to consider handing out double-sized business cards, folded in half. The outside of these "brochure cards" contains standard business-card information. The inside has a headline and summarizes important capability information—for instance, your firm's design specialties. You have half as much space to fill with text as you would in a postcard's message pane—or a small display ad. Format carefully, using bulleted lists rather than complete sentences.

Take your business card everywhere you go; it's a pocket-sized handout.

As discussed in Chapter 4, CD business cards are not much larger than standard business cards, but they can contain your full capability brochure, your résumé, and more. You can link the projects mentioned in your résumé to larger sets of photos and drawings than can appear in a paper-and-print brochure, thus fully displaying your skills, abilities, and experience to a wide range of uncommitted prospects within your marketing range.

TAKE-ONE   The word *take-one* refers to the practice of leaving a pile of promotional materials so that passers-by may each conveniently take one. Sometimes such a pile is left by a cash register or other point of purchase (POP). POP materials may be left in a special display box or rack, but a simple pile of flyers, brochures, or postcards is adequate.

Leave piles of take-ones in carefully targeted locations.

Placement of take-ones is crucial. It would not necessarily help to leave your firm's capability brochure at the local greengrocer, fond as you might be of the fine, fresh produce. It would also probably not help to leave your brochures at the local hardware store, although prospective clients may be picking up supplies there. Rather, it would make sense to target your prospective clients more closely. A small stack of brochures or postcards in an aesthetically compatible furniture store might generate interest in your firm's services, particularly if you have designed a vignette or model room for that store. You might also arrange to place stacks of your promotional materials in a model home or apartment you designed for a developer or real estate agent, perhaps next to a stand-alone poster.

Other good places for interior designers to stock take-ones are home or garden shows and designer showcases. A booth, table, or model space at a trade show, as well as any exhibit that showcases your capabilities and inimitable approach are also good places to stack a pile of take-ones.

POSTERS AND DISPLAY   Some promotional pieces—flyers among them—are suitable for display as wall or stand-alone posters, particularly if enlarged (which you can have done at any photocopy center) and printed on sturdy stock. It is best for a poster to be accompanied by a nearby pile of take-ones, so that interested parties don't have to write down the information presented on the poster. You can have a poster laminated on foam-core at a copy store if you want it to function as a stand-alone display. For full stand-alone capability, ask to have an easel backing.

To stand alone, a poster needs an easel backing.

SNAIL MAILING   Nobody likes to receive unsolicited promotional materials, and you would not market your design services by sending out brochures or flyers in envelopes addressed to a "resident." Yet a carefully cultivated mailing list and regular snail- or e-mailings will keep your firm's services in people's minds. If your mailings are thoughtful, well designed, and informative, they may be welcomed by those who receive them. Even if you rely heavily on e-mail as a business strategy, it is wise to maintain a snail-mailing list. You can send your carefully formatted brochures and other promotional pieces only by snail mail; their electronic equivalents will be less individualized. Send a brief, handwritten, personal note with snail-mailed promotional pieces; a touch of individual attention fosters a sense of personal connection.

Send a handwritten note with a snail-mailed promotional piece.

At the core of both snail- and e-mailing lists are the people who are already interested in your services. Key here are your previous clients. Around this core you can add to the list in all the creative ways you can think of. For instance, if you give a talk or participate in a panel discussion, pass around a sign-up sheet for your mailing list. Include on your list the vendors, contractors, architects, engineers, and landscape designers with whom you have completed projects, as well as those with whom you would like to work. Keep track of how you found out about the latter. If your first contact is via snail mail, you can send with your brochure a brief flattering note saying something like the following:

Dear Mr. Cebretti,

The quality of your architectural work for the Mason House deeply impressed me when I read about it in the January issue of *Metropolitan Architecture*. I would like you to know about the work of my firm, Mary Jones Interior Design. I would be honored by the opportunity to collaborate on a future project.

Sincerely,
Mary Jones

Purchase a mailing list printed on labels rather than ordinary sheets of paper.

Many businesses, large and small, purchase mailing lists, and such lists may be good value for the money if they are both appropriate and *clean*, that is, free of duplicate or outdated addresses. Any list that you purchase should be well targeted and should not have been used too often for marketing interior design services. It is sensible to purchase a snail-mailing list printed on a set of mailing labels rather than on ordinary paper. You'll save a lot of time! If you have purchased unlimited use of the list—rather than one-time use—you can buy it in electronic format, on a diskette or a CD-ROM, to generate multiple sets of labels.

In deciding the size of your mailing list, consider the "drudge" factor.

Bear in mind that it is time-consuming to get out a traditional snail mailing. There is a great deal of repetitive work to do: folding the mailing pieces, stuffing the envelopes, affixing the postage and labels, and sealing the envelopes. This "drudge" factor needs to be taken into account when you consider what size list to buy. If you are a novice designer getting out the mailing yourself or you have a small firm where one or two assistants pitch in on every aspect of the firm's work, you may find that a mailing even to 500 people—small as mailings go—is a considerable challenge. And let's not forget the cost of postage! When the mailing is a certain size, you become eligible for the bulk rate of the U.S. Postal Service—but then you need to sort the mail by zip code, another time-consuming task. No matter how eager you are to enlarge your design practice, you may have trouble with a mailing list of 20,000 names, or even 2,000. It may be better to purchase a randomized smaller list—say, every fifth name from the larger list.

Swap lists with other professionals at the same level of development.

Rather than paying for a list, it might make sense for a novice designer, a solo practitioner, or a small design firm to swap lists with a compatible practitioner or firm in a related profession. The swap partners' level of professional development should be similar. Swap for a manageable list that is roughly the size of your own. If the swap agreement permits more than one use of the list and you cannot get it on CD-ROM or diskette, then ask for label sets—rather than a mere list of names and addresses. You can photocopy the list before sticking the labels onto the envelopes. Then photocopy again onto a new set of same-sized labels for a follow-up mailing.

Swaps carry some risk. Clients who signed up for your mailing list may not appreciate receiving mailings from other sources. (This is also a high risk with purchased lists.) A safer option may be co-mailing, which permits you to maintain control of your list. *Co-mailing* refers to the practice of supplying a piece for inclusion in someone else's mailing, or accepting a mailing piece from someone else. Barter and reciprocity make co-mailing an economical promotion strategy, particularly if a projected mailing is light in weight and the co-mailing piece can be added without increasing the postage for each envelope.

Co-mailing builds good will among professional friends and helps you create a network, but it is unwise to accept a co-mailing piece sight unseen, even from a well-respected professional. A good architect or engineer is not necessarily a good graphic artist or writer of flyer text!

You need to be careful about the details of the co-mailing agreements you enter into. It may seem appealing to have your brochure sent to every new home purchaser with whom a particular real estate agent has a relationship. But do you really want to send the real estate agent's blatantly commercial brochure to each of your clients? You can limit the type of mailing piece you accept for co-mailing. For instance, if you designed a room in a model house for a real estate developer, then the developer's invitation to preview that house might be appropriate for your clients, and of interest to them, particularly if a handwritten note from you underlines your connection to the model house. Another option is a co-mailing relationship based on purchase rather than barter and reciprocity. This would mean that you paid to "piggy-back" on someone else's mailing, rather than bartering for that person's co-mailing as a direct swap.

Tactics like list swapping and co-mailing are not the only ways to keep costs down for traditional mailings. You might also choose self-mailing pieces whenever possible. A postcard is a good example of a *self-mailer*, or promotional piece that does not require the use of an envelope. If a flyer is printed on only one side, then it can be folded in three, message-side in, and stapled shut or sealed with a small sticker, thus becoming a self-mailer. Newsletters may also be self-mailing, as may very simple brochures. (Be sure to choose sturdy paper.)

COMPUTERIZED MAILERS   In the long run, one of the best ways to keep down the cost of mailing is to computerize the whole process as fully as possible.

> Co-mailing lets you maintain control of your list; but do not accept co-mailing pieces sight unseen.

> Self-mailers keep the cost of mailing down, but should be made of sturdy paper.

Unless your mailing list is very small, keep it in a *relational database program* such as Claris Filemaker rather than in the simpler address-book program that is bundled with most computers. With proper backup, a computerized database is far easier to manage than the same set of addresses on index cards, in a paper address book, or on scraps of paper.

Maintain a computerized mailing list in a relational database.

Fully relational database programs permit you to put together any number of mailing lists based on selection from your master list according to a number of criteria. For instance, you might decide to create a list that is composed of clients from the past five years in certain zip codes. You can then print the list you have selected on whatever size labels you choose. You can store thousands of names but select only a manageable and appropriate number for each mailing. You can sort the list, so that the labels will print according to zip code, which will help you take advantage of bulk-mailing rates. Labels are faster to print than the postcards themselves because you can use auto-feed to print label sheets. Unfortunately, only premium-priced printers will auto-feed a stack of postcards. Most printers require that postcards be manually fed, one by one.

A good database program has uses that go far beyond the mailing of your promotional materials. In the Webography on your CD-ROM is the URL for the Filemaker Web site, which shows an impressive variety of applications designed by program users to customize Filemaker. You can take advantage of these existing customizations, or create your own.

ELECTRONIC MAILING   Far cheaper and easier than traditional mailing is electronic mailing of promotional pieces. No more envelope stuffing! Although e-mail is not suitable for elaborate materials such as an illustrated newsletter or your capability brochure, it is appropriate for mailing simple, ephemeral materials such as flyers. Here are some tips for successful electronic mailing:

- Without prior agreement, do not send print materials as attachments, even though you could save your formatting that way. Since most viruses are sent as attachments, some recipients delete messages containing attachments without opening them.
- You can compose a carefully formatted e-flyer, using colorful fonts on a colorful background, illustrated with photos or other images, within the body of an e-mail. But some of your graphics will appear as you created them only for readers whose e-mail programs are set to execute HTML. To be sure your flyer is legible to all recipients, format a nonillustrated

plain-text version, creating emphasis by such simple means as capital letters and lines of asterisks or pluses. Chapter 12 details the format options for a plain-text résumé; the same options are suitable for a promotional piece.

- By its very nature, e-mail is best suited to short, fast communication. Large e-mails download slowly, clogging people's accounts and creating resentment. Because image files are large, you may annoy some of your recipients if you send them your gorgeous project photos by e-mail, whether as attachments or as insertions into the body of an e-mail.

- Use a mailing program such as Eudora that permits you to attribute multiple e-mail addresses to one group name, such as "IDEC Conference 2004." However, keep your master e-mailing list in a database program, so that you will have more flexibility in constructing sublists for various purposes. You can then copy and paste lists of names from your database program to your e-mail program's address book, giving each list a group nickname.

- Place multiple recipients of a large electronic mailing into the BCC, or blind carbon copy, line of an e-mail. This way, your carefully nurtured address list cannot be forwarded all over the Internet and indiscriminately used for *spamming*, or unsolicited advertising.

- Fit all important information into the first screen of the e-mail. People who receive a lot of mail may not bother to scroll down when reading promotional e-mail.

POSTING ON A WEB SITE   Because image files are e-mail-account cloggers, an illustrated capability brochure or newsletter is best posted on a Web site. If you do not have a full Web site, you might look into any option for free personal pages offered by your school, if you are a student, or by your Internet service provider (ISP), either of which may provide simple site-creation facilities online. Avoid any host that extracts commercial utility from the appearance of generosity by infecting "free" sites with a plague of annoying pop-up ads. Find a host that uses free pages to promote traffic with a minimum of distraction from third-party advertising on individuals' pages.

> Post a brochure or newsletter with large image files on a Web site.

If you are setting up a simple site for yourself, stick to the basics. (The following tips for creating display ads are also useful in constructing a simple Web site.) You can create Web-like formats in PowerPoint and convert them convincingly to HTML. You will probably need help from a Web-site designer to create complex interlinking sets of pages with sophisticated

In designing Web pages, strike a balance between clear, detailed images and fast loading.

graphics. It is important to strike a good balance between clear, detailed images that contain relatively more information and are therefore larger and slower to load into visitors' computers, and the desirability of fast loading so as not to try a visitor's patience. Chapter 4 discusses some other considerations you would need to weigh when formatting your capability brochure for online display.

Your capability brochure is not the only document that will benefit from being posted online. You can post any case studies you have written or articles you have published—or, better yet, post excerpts and invite visitors to e-mail requests to receive the complete studies or articles via snail mail.

You will get more mileage from each issue of your newsletter if you post it on a Web site after it has been snail-mailed to your list. You can then link from within the online version of your newsletter or from its margins to other pages within your site or to valuable and relevant sites elsewhere online. You can post any discussion that has been generated by the newsletter. You can post information of interest that could not fit into your newsletter, including more extensive collections of photographs. (Again, be sure to get appropriate permissions and to publish adequate source citations, copyright notices, and captions.) Online posting may give your newsletter a completely new life in its cyber-format—enough that you may wish to promote the Web-enhanced newsletter in separate snail and e-mailings to your list; you can enlarge the list by inviting your Web-site visitors to sign up.

Post online an enhanced version of your newsletter.

Advertising

While you are responsible for the distribution of promotional pieces such as newsletters, brochures, and flyers, advertisements are distributed by the media in which an advertiser has paid for time or space. The possibilities for *advertising*, or paid placement of commercial messages, include:

- Radio and TV ads
- Outdoor advertising (billboards and buses)
- Listing in directories
- Print ads (classified and display)
- Online ads

Despite changing mores, a residual stigma attaches to the advertising of professional services, whether those of attorneys, physicians, dentists, architects, or interior designers. Interior designers who sell products may be bolder in their advertising strategies than designers who are primarily selling services. Despite increasing competition, radio and TV ads as well as outdoor advertising are not in noticeably frequent use by interior designers in most parts of the country. The focus in this section is on directories and on print and online ads.

Directories

The directory you are probably most familiar with is the telephone directory. The white pages are not really a form of advertising, since everyone appears in them and you cannot find a product or service that you require if you do not already know the name of the provider. The Yellow Pages, however, *are* a form of advertising, and you pay to be listed there. Many designers purchase the standard Yellow Pages listing, in which the name of each design firm appears in small bold type along with an abbreviated form of the street address and the telephone number. Designers who sell products may purchase a more prominent space in the Yellow Pages. All listings in the Yellow Pages are *classified*, or arranged by category. This has a leveling effect that encourages price competition. However, listing in the Yellow Pages provides a basic visibility that may result in business.

> The Yellow Pages promote visibility, but also encourage price competition.

You may also wish to consider being listed in more specialized directories—for instance, a directory of businesses operated by alumni of your school, or any directory published by a professional organization to which you belong. Many directories offer a choice between a simple listing or a display ad of the type discussed a bit later in this chapter. These large ads may be of special interest to designers selling products. They can also make a small or new firm seem more important.

Print Ads

Although the Yellow Pages might be considered a print medium, so-called "print ads" are typically placed in media such as newspapers and magazines. Newspapers are the advertising medium of choice for most small businesses. They tend to be affordable and offer a great deal of flexibility: you don't have to book the ad space until a few days before the ad is to appear. The medium can be problematic for an interior designer for two reasons: newspapers are broadly targeted within their geographical range, and the quality of color reproduction tends to be poor at best.

> Newspapers are the ad medium of choice for most small businesses.

Magazines are more prestigious ad venues than newspapers. They are read for a longer period of time, cost more to purchase, and are more carefully targeted to their demographics—a plus for designers. In addition, the fine color printing and thick, glossy stock of many magazines shows hues and tones well—another plus for designers. However, the fancy printing process means long lead times, and it is generally expensive to advertise in magazines. Print ads for either medium—newspapers or magazines—fall into two categories; classified ads and display ads.

CLASSIFIED ADS

"Classified" ads are published under category headings with other ads for similar services. This type of advertising is economical and can be very effective, since serious shoppers go directly to the relevant ads for a given category. Like classified directory listings, classified media advertising can have a leveling effect, since each ad is surrounded by ads for similar services. It is important for a creative and highly individualized business such as an interior design firm to construct the classified ad very carefully, bearing in mind that shoppers may be browsing for price as much as for quality.

Typically, a classified ad is all text. It may be formatted by the advertising department of the publication that is running the ad. Here is a classified ad for interior design services that appeared in *New York* magazine.[4]

> **Former Bloomingdale's Designer**—Will beautifully transform your space. Creative. To Budget. Sasha Designs: 212-555-6789

Copy for a classified ad should be short and clear and convey essentials.

You may have noticed that this ad has a headline equivalent—an attention-grabbing bold-font ad-topper. Although it is short (classified advertisers pay for each word), it is not too short. The words are clear and carefully chosen to convey essentials. "Former Bloomingdale's Designer" supplies credibility, since this chic department store is well known in the metropolitan New York area for its model rooms. "To budget" suggests sensitivity to clients' pocketbook considerations without appealing to bottom fishers. The telephone number provides the all-important contact point.

Those who are willing to pay a little more can purchase classified display ads. Such an ad has a box around it and larger, darker type than an ordinary classified ad (See Figure 11.4). It may also include color and images—two big pluses for interior designers. (One striking image may be enough, particularly for a small ad. The image could be a photo, a line drawing, or a symbol.)

DISPLAY ADS

A *display ad* in the classified section or elsewhere in a publication is carefully formatted to exhibit your message in an attractive and appealing way. The manner in which the ad's content is displayed is as important as the content itself, and the display and content interact in complex ways. Special skills are involved in creating the ad's *copy*, or text; and other skills are employed in the *art direction*, or visual preparation of the ad, including the all-important layout. Designers, like other would-be advertisers, often employ professionals with expertise in both areas, especially if the advertising space is expensive to buy. It is also possible to receive help from the staff of a publication, though such help does not usually result in an individualized ad created with an understanding of what is appropriate for a design business. The composition and formatting of small display ads can be adequately managed by a painstaking designer-writer using word-processing software. But the subtle typography and careful kerning on display in Figure 11.5 is executed with a professional graphic designer's flair and expertise.

AWARD-WINNING DESIGNER

BFA from Parsons School of Design, and
studied in France. Quality, beauiful design.

John Hafferle, ASID
914-555-6789

Figure 11.4
Example of a
simple display ad.

WRITING THE COPY

Most display and classified ads contain two types of copy, the headline and the body copy. The *headline*—the big type in the ad—states the creative idea in a catchy way that will interest people in reading the rest of the ad. This idea needs to be one that will speak to the needs of clients. It is not enough to say, "Excellent Design Services." "Excellence" may well be a *feature*, or attribute, of your design services; but this feature is best marketed in tandem with a *benefit*, or tangible good, for prospective clients. For a residential interior designer, the "benefit" of excellent design services might be beautiful, livable interiors and a more appealing lifestyle. This benefit may be expressed in a brief, catchy, to-the-point headline like "Better living—by design."

The text in an ad that is below the headline is the so-called *body copy*. It is usually set in a smaller typeface than the headline. The body copy presents the details, and it needs to be clear, easy to read, and engaging. In some ways, advertising copy is closely related to poetry. Although it is sometimes written in complete paragraphs, it is often broken up into small blocks of text that are deployed on the page so that they are easy to read, and the eye goes naturally and quickly from one bit of text to another. Bulleted lists are a frequent component of ad copy, which typically "speaks" sentence fragments rather than complete sentences. You can use subheads to organize the text and to clarify the relative importance of information. Don't forget to

> The headline of a display ad should convey features as well as benefits.

> Break body copy into small blocks of easy-to-read text.

include contact information, such as the name of your business, your address, the URL of your Web site, and your phone number.

DESIGNING THE AD

In her book *Marketing Your Remodeling Services*, Carol Davitt cites graphic designer Cindy Kamens on the use of design principles in advertising.[5] Here are some of their suggestions:

- Maintain a balance between variety and confusion.
- Develop a clear layout with a consistent style.
- Use boxes and horizontal rules to set off critical information.
- Create emphasis with initial capital letters.

Use no more than three fonts in a display ad.

Use no more than three fonts in your ad, advise Davitt and Kamens. Style the heads and subheads in the same typeface; you can use a different one for the body copy. The headline needs to be set in **bold** or *italic* type—in the largest size you will use in your ad. The subheads—set in somewhat smaller type—can also be bold or italic. The body copy should be smaller in size than any of the subheads, but not be too small. Ten- or twelve-point type is standard. According to Jay Conrad Levinson, the font size of body copy in your ad should be no smaller than the type used in the editorial portions of the publication in which the ad is to appear.

You don't necessarily need a large ad. You can call attention to a small ad with a special border, thus reducing the cost of advertising.

Making Print Ads Pay

The body copy of a print ad should be no smaller in font size than the type used in the editorial contents.

The selection of advertising media is an art and a science. One simple rule of thumb may suffice for novices: advertise in publications where other interior designers advertise, but not necessarily in immediate proximity to their ads. (You may actually wish to avoid special-interest sections, despite the prestige of advertising in them. Like the Yellow Pages, they foster pure competition, often based on price.) Make sure that your ad stands out by virtue of its size, its ingenuity, its appropriateness to the publication and the target audience, and its placement within the medium. Then, when you find something that works, stick with it. You can use the same ad, in the same position, in the same medium, many times over. You can probably get a frequency discount based on the number of insertions.

When you find an ad that works, stick with it.

To make ads pay, keep the initial cost down and make maximum use of the ad once it has run. To keep the cost down, Jay Conrad Levinson suggests buying space in regional, rather than national, publications. Make maximum use of an ad that has run by purchasing merchandising materials, such as reprints or display cards, to be used for promotional purposes; or you can make your own.

REGIONAL PUBLICATIONS

The advertising examples presented in this chapter appeared in regional, rather than national, publications. Figure 11.5 represents an ad that appeared in *New York* magazine, while Figure 11.6 represents an ad that appeared in the Westchester edition of the *New York Times* newspaper. *New York* is a regional magazine devoted to metropolitan New York City; there is no national edition. The Westchester edition of *The New York Times* is a "zoned" or localized edition of the *Times*, arguably a national newspaper and certainly one that has influence well beyond the metropolitan area.

Figure 11.5
A well-designed display ad from the *New York* magazine.

New York bills itself as New York City's "Critical Guide to Everything." Many other urban areas have glossy, four-color magazines similar to *New York* that are devoted to their city's cultural life, leisure pursuits, and shopping and service offerings. Because such publications narrow the demographic focus to culturally alert potential clients within easy commuting distance, they attract advertising by interior designers, though the advertising space may be expensive enough that a classified ad will have to suffice.

The Westchester edition of the *Times* targets an affluent suburban county, an upscale market that is sophisticated and knowledgeable about design services. Advertising in the Westchester edition costs much less than advertising in the regular edition (because fewer households are reached), but it has the prestige of an ad in the regular edition. For interior designers interested in working in the New York metropolitan area, such an ad buy may be excellent value for the money, particularly if the firm's office is in Westchester County. It is worth investigating to find out what regional advertising opportunities are available in your own practice area. Ask publications' advertising departments not only for a current rate card, but also for information about their readers.

Figure 11.6
An ad from the Westchester edition of the *New York Times.*

SMW INTERIOR DESIGN

Let us redesign your rooms with focus on your own Furniture, Art and Accessories.
• Fixed Prices Per Room • Same Day Services
Call for Brochure & Information:

Doing More for Less

You may be able to practice even more significant economies. Sometimes so-called remnant space is available after a magazine has sold most of the display-ad space in a regional edition at the full rate. You may be able to purchase some of the remnant space at a much lower rate if you ask the advertising sales department to phone you when it becomes available. (This is not an economy for impatient people or for those who want an ad pegged to a particular event.) You can maximize the impact of any ad buy if you avail yourself of the merchandising materials offered to advertisers.

MERCHANDISING MATERIALS

Most magazines offer their advertisers "merchandising," or sales, materials—easel-back cards, reprints, and other useful aids. These inexpensive materials are useful as display pieces and as enclosures in your promotional mailings, since advertising in prestigious publications conveys credibility. Even if you have advertised only once in an elegant magazine, you can display its merchandising materials to enhance your prestige. One buy may be a worthwhile purchase even if you have to pay for your ad at the "open" rate offered to advertisers who do not commit to a schedule of multiple ads.

If reprints and other sales and promotional materials are not available from the publication in which you advertised, simply photocopy your ad and use the copies as handouts, mailing pieces, or take-ones. You can also enlarge the ad and use it as a poster for display purposes.

ONLINE ADVERTISING

Like other advertising, an online ad presents a promotional message in a space that has been purchased. In addition, the online ad serves the crucial function of *click-through*, bringing visitors from the site where the ad has been placed to the advertiser's own site. In the world of e-commerce, the posting of ads is often a commercial proposition. However, money need not necessarily change hands. Swapping makes sense for some designers, though others believe that ads on a professional site are distracting and inappropriate. Certainly sites swapping ads should be compatible, and the ads should be similar in size and aesthetics.

An online ad can be very intrusive, with flashing animations and *pop-ups*, or constantly opening windows. More compatible with a designer's professional demeanor are simple button and banner ads.

A *button* is a compact ad—often in the form of a logo with text—that is intended to be placed in the shoulder space of a Web page, that is, the margin surrounding the principal content space in use for the page proper. For instance, there may be button ads in the left shoulder column of a Web magazine page with a text column occupying the center and right spaces. A *banner* ad is horizontal in format. It has been designed to go at the top of a Web page; the eye travels to it before traveling to the principal content of the page.

Whatever the format, an online ad needs to be appealing enough to viewers that they are willing to abandon the site they intended to visit in order to click through to the advertised site. Many sites that accept ads require that a click on an ad open a new browser window, so that the site hosting the ad remains in an open window and is easily revisited without users having to hit the Back button. You may wish to do the same if you decide to accept ads, whether purchased or swapped, on your site.

An online ad for an interior design firm should be appealing, discreet, and unintrusive.

Online Promotion

Placing brochure contents online allows for an unlimited number of capability presentations without the designer's having to spend time on as-yet-uncommitted clients. In theory, this leaves more time for committed clients and for the design work itself. The Web site will not perform this function if it is no sooner built then left to sit in lonely splendor in cyberspace. A Web site needs to be visited to do its job; but a designer needs to encourage visits without appearing to engage in an unseemly clamor for attention.

Use print ads and promotional pieces to drive traffic to your Web site.

The use of print ads and promotional pieces to "drive" *traffic*, or visitors, to Web sites is common in a wide variety of businesses. In addition to, or instead of, the street addresses of their firms, more and more designers mention the addresses of their Web sites in print ads and on promotion pieces, including business cards. Savvy designers also include the URLs (addresses in cyberspace) of their sites in the signatures of their e-mails as "hot" or "clickable" links.

SEARCH ENGINES

The most powerful means of bringing visitors to a site are search engines and links from one site to another. As discussed in Chapter 4, it is important to register your site with the principal search engines such as Google and Yahoo. It is crucial that the keywords of your site be a good match with the actual search categories of would-be visitors. The keywords should accurately reflect the content of your site as well.

Once your site is listed on some of the principal search engines, it will be picked up by the others, who need to maintain their competitiveness through an equally thorough inclusiveness. You do not need to avail yourself of the services advertised online and through e-mail that offer to post your site on hundreds of search engines for a price. The online application form at most search-engine sites is a simple one. Because of the importance of accuracy, it is wise to fill it out yourself. Then wait a while, without any confusing reapplication, to see if your site has been included. You can test your inclusion by entering your firm's name in the engine's search box. To see how easily others can find you, enter a relevant search term such as:

"Interior designer" + your town

The quotation marks tell you to search for the whole phrase "interior designer," not both individual words. The "+" tells you that the name of your town or city must also be present. (Not all search engines require the "+.") Of course, you must include *interior designer* and the name of your town among your keywords, or your site will not come up on the engine when those are the search terms.

If a search on the probable terms that visitors may use returns a large number of site names, yours may be very far down the list—perhaps pages into it—if there isn't much traffic on your site or there aren't many links to it. (These are two ways that search engines rank sites.) It is possible to pay for better ranking on some search sites, perhaps by advertising on them. The best way to improve your ranking is to increase the number of visitors to your site through supportive marketing practice and to link your site to others as extensively as possible.

LINKING TO OTHER SITES

To *link* means to post the address of another site on yours. Actually, ads that "click through" when you place your mouse on the graphic are a type of link; but the no-frills link is textual, with the address visible or embedded in the code that underlies the clickable link. *Cross-linking*, or link swapping, is a "webby" tradition and is an elegant and unobtrusive way to drive traffic around, particularly to noncommercial sites. The way it works is simple: On your Web pages, you post links to other people's sites. In return, they can post links to yours. But even if they don't, they may post links to other people's sites, who post links to other people's, who post links to yours, and so on. Insofar as this works—and it does, actually—the Internet fulfills its potential as a "net" or "web," in which all points are connected and everyone's interests are served.

Links can be posted on the content pages of a Web site—so-called "deep links"—or on the home page, or on a dedicated links page. Wherever they are posted, collections of links amount to private referral directories; they reflect your taste and quality standards, so you need to choose them carefully. As the fruits of valuable research time, good links are a welcome service to visitors and thus make an important contribution to your metamessage. Even if you hire someone to design and code your site, it is smart to do your own links research, or at least to supervise the research carefully. (If a new browser opens when visitors click on a link in your site's pages, they should be able to return to your "source" page quickly.)

When you have posted a link to another site on yours, you or your Webmaster may e-mail the proprietor or Webmaster of the other site, letting him or her know that the link has been posted and suggesting a cross-link, which may or may not be granted. It is definitely worth asking. The more sites linked to yours and the more traffic there is to your site, the higher your position will be on pages of the search engines that rank by number of links. However, even if there is no cross-link from a given site, it is shortsighted to play tit-for-tat by removing that link from your site. It is good for your image and your business to post links to other sites that you deem valuable.

If your links are carefully chosen and thorough, your visitors may get in the habit of checking your site first when doing research on an issue

> Improve your Web site's search-engine ranking by increasing the number of visitors to your site.

> Good links on your site are a welcome service and will bring you repeat visitors.

related to interior design. Thus, your Web site will come to generate its own traffic—and word of mouth about its value will enhance your reputation as a designer.

Publicity

Whether online of off, *promotion* communicates your message directly to the person ultimately receiving it; *publicity* communicates your message indirectly, through the media. A publicist, or paid publicity consultant, makes clients' messages available to people who create the editorial content of print and online publications, radio and TV programs, and other media. Editors, reporters, and other content providers use the publicist's input as part of the basis for their research and writing, but they also consult other sources. Their first responsibility is to report objectively to their readers, and they put together their stories with that in mind. Very few stories that appear in the media are unedited versions of publicity materials. This lack of control does not mean that publicity has no value for the marketing designer. On the contrary, publicity should be an integral part of any designer's marketing plan.

Publicity has two great virtues: its placement is free, and it is entirely credible. You may pay for the display ad next to the review of a restaurant for which you designed the interior. However, you do not pay for the review that mentions the pleasing effect of the ambience that you created with lighting, color, texture, and good use of space. Precisely because the kudos in the review have not been bought and paid for, they are credible in a way that advertising and other forms of promotion cannot be. Naturally you would say wonderful things about yourself! It is quite another thing to have experienced and dispassionate writers praising you. That is why an article on, say, a corporate-office project appearing in a magazine on contract interiors can do so much for a design firm's prestige.

A review of an already completed project is an example of what journalists call a *feature* story—one that has a relatively timeless cultural or human-interest significance. A news story is one that has a timely urgency. It is based on currently happening events. A good news story, however, has a human-interest "hook," while a feature story is often pegged to a news event.

Design firms do not generate a great deal of what would pass in a newspaper as front-page news. However, if you receive an unusual or large commission, win a prestigious award, deliver a lecture in a highly regarded venue, or open a new firm, these events may be treated as news by local media as well as by design trade publications.

Publicity aims to get across your message via the editorial content of print and online publications, radio and TV programs, and other media.

Here's how the publicity process might unfold for one hypothetical design project: If you designed the interiors for an opera-house renovation, a publicist might send out a press release mentioning your involvement in the project and heralding the gala inauguration of the opera house. The opening night of the first opera presented in the reopened house might be treated as a news event—one worthy of the front page of the local paper. Your work might receive a warm mention, which would be valuable in underlining your metamessage and in bringing your work to the attention of prospective clients. You might quote selectively from the news article in the next edition of your brochure.

A week later, the same newspaper might run in its arts pages a review of the renovation work—in which your contribution figures prominently, along with the work of an engineer, an architect, and an acoustic consultant. Weeks or months later an interview with you on the acoustic aspects of your design work might be published in the Sunday magazine supplement. Photocopies of these feature articles would be useful promotional pieces for years to come—and this without the sought-after publication in a sophisticated trade or shelter magazine that might come later, along with an annual award from a trade magazine to which you (or your publicist) submitted the project. The award would be even more valuable than a review to you and your colleagues. Its trickle-down effect would be felt throughout the firm, especially by those who had a hand in the project and were credited for this.

Publicity has a powerful impact; yet its basic tools are simple and unprepossessing. They are the press release, the press kit, the press list, the telephone, and the photograph.

The Press Release

The press release might be described as a self-generated news story. Some designers cut corners by creating combination press release–flyers, but it is better to create two separate documents. The press release (Figure 11.7) has a sober, unformatted appearance; and it is written to speak to editors and writers as peers, using news style, which is composed of the following elements:

> A press release is typically written in wire-service style, with information presented in descending order of importance.

- The first five words are the most important.
- The most important facts are given first, in descending order of importance, in both individual paragraphs and in the article as a whole.
- It is written in the third person.
- The writing is objective, as if by an impartial observer.

- There is no use of the passive voice.
- Numbers do not begin sentences.
- The journalistic questions—Who? What? When? Where? Why? and How?—are answered in the course of the article.
- There are no unnecessary words.
- No sentence may depend for its meaning on what follows.
- There are no contractions or abbreviations.

News style is also known as "wire-service style," after the giant syndicates that dominated news gathering before the advent of the Internet. It was created for the convenience of editors, and you demonstrate your savvy by using it. Because information in news-style writing is presented in descending order of importance both in individual paragraphs and in the piece of writing, or *article*, as a whole, editors can easily tailor the article to their space needs, either by cutting the ends of paragraphs or by cutting complete paragraphs from the bottom of the article.

In addition to being written in wire-service or news style, the press release has some of the following characteristics:

- Except in unusual cases, it is less than two full 8½″-by-11″ printed-out pages, double-spaced, with standard margins. It is written on high-quality paper. It is not written on letterhead stationery.
- It is written in paragraphs and complete sentences.
- The journalistic questions Who? What? Where? When? are all answered in the first paragraph. The questions How? and Why? are answered soon after.
- It has an interesting headline typewritten in capital letters and may include subheads to help organize the material.
- The name, street address, telephone number, fax number, e-mail address, and Web-site address of the contact person, as well as those of the design firm, if they are different, are typed at the *top* of the first page, along with the date of the release. If there is no special date given for the news that is being released, then the material is FOR IMMEDIATE RELEASE.
- The availability of photos is indicated at the close of the *copy*, or body of the press release, which is signified by writing ### or *THE END*, centered, between two one-em dashes, like this:

—THE END—

- Since the press release is not heavily formatted, the release prepared for print and paper may also function as the e-release.
- Spelling has been checked for accuracy, and all facts have been checked as well. The release has been carefully proofread by more than one reader.

FOR IMMEDIATE RELEASE

AMERICAN SOCIETY OF
INTERIOR DESIGNERS
CONTACT: MICHELLE SNYDER
PUBLIC RELATIONS MANAGER
(202) 675-2369 OR MSNYDER@ASID.ORG

ASID ANNOUNCES 2002-2003 STUDENT AWARD WINNERS

(WASHINGTON, July 15, 2003)—The American Society of Interior Designers (ASID) is pleased to announce the recipients of the 2002-2003 Student Chapter Awards. The honorees—outstanding student chapters and faculty advisors who help make ASID student membership a valuable investment for the next generation of interior designers—were selected by a jury comprised of practicing designers from the ASID Washington Metro Chapter.

The Mount Mary College chapter (Milwaukee) was honored with the top award of Outstanding Student Chapter of the Year. The award recognizes student chapters that have provided exceptional service to their members, professional chapters and communities. "This year the Mount Mary College ASID Chapter decided to reinvent itself and, in the process, initiated a series of new and exciting programs and services for its members," said ASID President-Elect Linda Elliott Smith, FASID. "The chapter is an excellent example of a chapter that . . . went way beyond its own expectations." Chapter activities in 2002-2003 included:

- establishing new career services such as "Lunch 'n Learns" led by ASID Industry Partners, student-led workshops on vital design topics, tours of design firms, and a student mentoring program
- designing, in partnership with the ASID Wisconsin Chapter, a successful design solution for the Serenity Inn—a home for recovering alcoholics in Milwaukee
- participating in numerous charitable events to benefit the community, including distributing homemade Valentine cards and flowers to residents of community homes for the elderly and joining in the Milwaukee-area breast cancer walk.

Figure 11.7
Excerpt from ASID
press release.
*Reprinted with
permission of ASID.*

Publicists often prepare blanket mailings of press releases to their entire snail and e-mail press lists. These may be accompanied by a brief cover letter suggesting a broadly useful *angle* of vision—a way of looking at a project that organizes all its elements around a central, interesting theme. There is usually no time to tailor each letter to its recipient, as job applicants would tailor their cover letters to prospective employers. Publicists follow up the initial mailing with telephone calls in which they refine the angle of vision.

The Press Kit

After sending a press release and following up with a phone call, a publicist may then send more information to interested parties. To publicize a design firm, additional materials may consist of:

- Photocopies of previous articles or reviews that feature or mention the design firm's work. (Ask for *offprints*, or separately printed versions of the article that appeared in the publication.)
- A cover letter on the design firm's letterhead stationery
- Photographs and drawings
- The design firm's capability brochure and other promotional materials
- A *narrative* biography of the principal designer (or designers) of the firm that puts résumé information into brief story form
- Case studies, where relevant (see Chapter 3)
- Articles that the designer has written and published in professional or trade publications or elsewhere

These materials, artfully arranged in a colorful double-pocket folder with a designer's business card in the display slits, are known collectively as a *press kit*. It can function as an extended press release, or as a promotional piece. If you were to host a special reception for the press, you might have a table at which these kits, packaged beforehand, were given to members of the press in order to whet their interest. For instance, if you had designed office interiors for a corporation that held a press conference on the opening of its new headquarters, your firm might make its press kits available along with those of the corporation. To such an event you would invite writers, editors, and media program people selected from your press list.

The Press List

Whether you are functioning as your own publicist or collaborating with a hired one, you will need to create over time, through research, a *press list* of local and national media. It will contain the names and addresses of media organizations—for example, the *Detroit Free Press*—as well as the names of your contacts and their telephone numbers, fax numbers, and e-mail addresses. You can build your press list by consulting reference works that list media in the pubic library or by buying or swapping lists. You can also build it by becoming a media watcher. Jot down the names of journalists who have written articles or presented radio or TV programs that suggest they might be interested in the work of your firm. These men and women can be reached via contact information for their media that you can find in the library.

> Build a press list by consulting reference works and watching media. Store the list in your database.

The press list may be kept in a database program along with the rest of your mailing list. If you have a "notes" field on your database records, then you can write "press list" or similar words there. You can use these words as a search term that will permit you to call up all the names on your press list at one time. If your database program is fully relational, the names on your press list can also be called up by region if you enter a search term based on geographic location or zip code.

In the "notes" field you can enter the *lead time* of each publication or program—that is, the amount of time in advance your material must be submitted. Because of the complexity of the color-printing process, glossy magazines may have a lead time of six months. The lead time of a newspaper may be no more than a week. If you group lead times according to whether they are short or long, you can enter the appropriate search term to call up all the press-list records in the *short-lead* group or all in the *long-lead* group. In this way, you can use your database program to help you get your materials out in a timely manner.

You can also keep notes in your database program about particular journalists' interests and their previous coverage of interior design and other relevant issues. These notes will prove invaluable when you are trying to build a relationship with a journalist.

In addition to notes based on your own observations, pay close attention to the ASID booklet *Professional Exposure: How to Get Design Work Published*. This publication lists contact information for more than 25 publications that accept interior design work for publication.

The Telephone

Personal contact is a very important part of publicity. Media content providers receive hundreds of press releases a day. Most of the e-releases are deleted after a cursory reading, and the print-and-paper releases may be filed in the "circular file," or wastebasket. Although press releases are written to

Follow up on press releases with phone calls.

be interesting and to serve the needs of writers and editors, they do not usually "sell" a story in and of themselves. That is best accomplished by a friendly, knowledgeable follow-up call. The publicist might inquire whether the journalist had received the release, needed more information, would like to join the publicist for lunch, or was interested in setting up an interview with the principal designer of the firm.

In telephone calls publicists strive to individualize the angle of vision presented in the cover letter sent with the press release or press kit, relying on their knowledge of each journalist's interests and drawing on any notes they have kept. They not only stay in touch with the journalists already on their press list, but also reach out to media and journalists they may not have had occasion to *pitch*, or sell a story to, in the past.

A skilled publicist will strive to cover all the angles, not just the obvious ones. For instance, your design of new interiors for the opera house is not only an interior design story, but it also has broader implications. If improved acoustics make the hall better for singers and musicians, the publicist will pitch that angle to music publications, to the arts pages of the local newspaper, and to the cultural reporter on the local TV show. If you are a young designer, MTV may be interested in doing a feature on you. If you are an older designer, the AARP magazine may want to interview you. There may be a hometown story, and one or more alumni stories—so many story possibilities, in fact, that a professional publicist spends most of his or her days on the telephone "pitching." That is one reason that working designers may have difficulty being their own publicists.

It is awkward to tout a designer's own projects. It is even more awkward to offer one's self as an interview subject. If your budget permits, hire a publicity firm to avoid dealing with this awkwardness and to benefit from the firm's media knowledge.

Or, if you find that you are more comfortable briefing editors, writers, and program people on projects in which you played no active role, trade publicity services with other designers in your firm. In such an arrangement, each designer performs as another's publicist, thus avoiding the discomfort and embarrassment of self-publicizing, particularly in telephone and face-to-face conversations. If yours is a one-person or small firm, you might consider sharing a publicist with similar-sized design firms or with peer professionals such as architects, engineers, or landscape architects. Some firms relegate publicity contact work to a carefully trained assistant, and this may be a niche that you can profitably aspire to occupy if you are about to graduate from an interior design program.

If you are functioning as a publicity contact person, you can make your work easier by following a few basic guidelines:

- Don't insist on talking to the top woman or man when you phone a publication or radio or TV station where you don't know anyone. Very often a receptionist can direct you to the person who might be interested in your story, so explain yourself politely to the person who answers the telephone. Find out who at the publication or station might be interested in the story you have to offer. If you are calling a newspaper about hard news, rather than a feature story, ask for the city desk.
- If you are calling a radio or TV station, don't expect to speak to the on-air personalities themselves. Address yourself to the *program staff*—the people who decide what to put on the air.
- Send along hard copies of any documents you fax.
- Submit drawings as STATS, or direct positive reproductions (PMTs).
- Submit news involving personnel changes, such as hiring or promotion of professionals, to the business section of a newspaper, where they may generate brief item-length reports.
- Don't neglect any opportunity. Every designer would like to be featured in *Interiors, Architectural Digest,* and other trade or shelter publications. An item in an alumni news column may seem trivial compared to a major award from a trade magazine. So may a write-up in the neighborhood newspaper or a review on a small Web site. However, a steady trickle of mentions in a wide variety of publications will slowly but surely enhance a designer's reputation.
- Be sure to include on the press list the publications of the regional, national, and international professional organizations to which you belong, such as ASID, IIDA, and IDEC.
- Be available. Chances of coverage diminish if the contact person of record is unavailable when an editor or a reporter phones.

Getting publicity requires a continuous, well-planned, well-executed effort, not just random, occasional activity. However, a publicist's hard work is not the only factor in generating coverage. Significant, too, is the quality of the photographs that are made available for publication.

The Photograph

Superb photographic representations of interiors require costly equipment and a specialized set of skills, so they are expensive. Yet it may be economical in the long run for designers to commission first-quality photographs of their best work. If designers or their publicists can offer magnificent four-color transparencies taken with cameras using, say, 8-by-10-inch plates, and particularly if the color separations have already been made, cost-conscious editors may be more interested in offering coverage than they would be if their magazines had to commission the photography thenselves and pay for the separations.

Good photographs increase your chances of coverage.

According to photographer Ezra Stoller, a good photograph of an interior or other architectural subject is hard to take with an ordinary digital camera or a 35-millimeter camera, even with a perspective control lens. "The smaller the camera, the tougher it is to shoot the job." Although the best results are achieved with the 8-by-10-inch camera, this splendid piece of equipment is less and less frequently used. "Who can afford to shoot and process 100 sheets of 8-by-10-inch color film per day—modest production for the good architectural photographer—at current prices? And if the photographer is using Polaroids as well, add another 30 percent to the daily material costs."[6] Stoller sings the praises of the $2^1/_4$-by-$2^3/_4$-inch view camera and the 4-by-5-inch monorail view camera—two cameras in frequent use by photographers specializing in architectural subjects. Designers are unlikely to own this equipment themselves.

Chapter 4 tells you how to achieve decent results with an ordinary 35-millimeter or digital camera. The photos you take, or have taken, with this equipment may look attractive in your brochure; they may not be of high enough quality for presentation in glossy design publications. This is why many well-established designers commission professional photographers, skilled with the requisite equipment, to shoot the interiors they have designed. According to Ezra Stoller, photography of interiors is usually commissioned on one of three fee bases:

1. *Record and exhibition rate* This is the lowest cost to the designer, who receives prints for archival use and for exhibition. The photographer owns the negatives and the rights to all other uses. He or she usually charges a day rate plus expenses.

2. *Publicity rate* This rate covers use in the editorial and program contents of the media. It also covers use in any promotional pieces that you produce. It does not cover use for advertising. At the publicity-rate level, the photographer retains control of the negatives and charges a higher day rate.

3. *All-rights rate*   Here the designer has paid a flat fee in advance for all uses he or she may make of the photographs. However, the photographer still retains control of the negatives. The day rate is now high enough to cover the photographer's presumed loss of so-called secondary sales. The designer can do as he or she wishes with the photos.

A photographer of stature will not accept *work for hire*, which means that the photographer charges a day rate, plus expenses, but loses all control of his or her work, turning the negatives over to the designer client for developing. Photographers who are not well established may be willing to work for hire, though it is unlikely that such a photographer will have invested in the expensive equipment that will yield the best results. Still, you may benefit from having a professional photographer take photos with a 35-millimeter or digital camera, since the photographer may be able to frame a better percentage of useful shots than you could yourself.

Bear in mind that it is demeaning for professional photographers to lose control of their work. Thinking of the long term, you may choose to negotiate a contract that is less demeaning than "work for hire," even if a strapped photographer in a competitive market would settle for that. For example, you could cede control of the negatives but insist on an all-rights buy at a relatively low day-rate with carefully controlled expenses. You may be able to contract for half a day's work rather than a full day's, though most photographers will not agree to an hourly rate. It may also be possible to bargain about the number of sites to be visited during the time you have paid for; but if the photographer is using an 8-by-10-inch camera, the set-up time is so lengthy that the photographer will not be able to visit more than one site.

If you can establish a relationship of mutual trust with a photographer, you will gain a strong ally in the professional world. As photographers gain experience and buy more expensive equipment, their rates are bound to rise. They may impose more conditions; but photographers, like most other professionals, are apt to treat with continuing respect those who have treated them with respect in the past.

Color photographs are not the only ones you will need for publicity purposes. Photos for newspaper reproduction should be black-and-white, with high contrast, and should be printed in glossy 4-by-5-inch or 8-by-10-inch format. Whether the photos are black and white or color, the name of the photographer and the name of the copyright holder should be supplied with each photograph, along with the name and address of the person to whom

> Establish a relationship of trust with a professional photographer.

> Photos for newspaper reproduction are:
> - Black and white
> - High contrast
> - 4-by-5 or 8-by-10
> - Glossy

the photograph is to be returned. You also need to supply captions. Each caption should include not only information about the site photographed but the names and, if relevant, professional titles of any individuals who have been photographed, for instance: Muriel Lopez, president of CanCo International. If the photographs include people, secure a model release from each individual photographed.

Putting Publicity to Work

If you or your design firm earns print publicity coverage, you can photocopy the article and use it in much the same way as the merchandising aids provided by the media in which ads have been placed. The publicity coverage in the content pages of a newspaper or magazine may need to be cut and pasted into a new layout, and possibly reduced to fit on one or at most two $8^1/_2$-by-11-inch pages. Or the publication in which the coverage appeared may supply you with offprints. A layout or an offprint can be photocopied as often as necessary. It can be used as a handout, a take-one, a mailing piece, a poster, or a stand-alone display piece. You can scan it for display on your Web site. You can include it in capability packets. Finally, of course, you can use it in future press kits to help you generate more favorable publicity.

Photocopy publicity coverage for use as a handout, take-one, mailing piece, wall or stand-alone poster, or Web-site content or for inclusion in capability and press kits.

Discussion Questions

1. If you were preparing postcards to promote your business, how would you utilize the various display panes, and why?

2. What kinds of articles are suitable for a residential or contract-ID firm's newsletter in your geographical region?

3. How might an interior design firm use links to enhance traffic to the design firm's own Web site?

4. For a beginning designer, how important is it to have professional photographs of projects?

Exercises

1. Prepare a flyer for an imaginary exhibition of the design boards and other materials you have prepared in the studio-design classes you have taken so far. How would you distribute such a flyer? Prepare a one-page rationale for your chosen methods of distribution.

2. From a promotional postcard rack or other source, select a promotional postcard that you consider effective. Prepare a two-minute oral report for your class explaining your selection. What criteria emerge as common themes from the selections made by you and your classmates?

3. Breaking once again into the same groups you formed to create identity and capability materials in Chapter 4, prepare a group recommendation report (drawing on what you learned in Chapter 9) proposing content for your imaginary firm's Web site.

4. Prepare a press release for the imaginary exhibition for which you prepared a flyer in Exercise 1.

12 Selling Yourself to Prospective Employers

So there you stand in your cap and gown, your interior design degree in hand, ready, willing, and eager to find your future in the world of work. In the data banks of your school's computer system are your GPA and your collected course lists, ready to be sent to any prospective employer. You have enthusiastic recommendations from your design professors and your previous employers. You would like to think that without any effort at self-promotion on your part, employers will be attracted like moths to the bright light you radiate. Alas, this is unlikely, no matter how stellar your performance has been on student and internship projects. How can you get that first job, and the job after that, and the job after that? Whatever your qualifications, your writing and research skills will help you present yourself to prospective employers in the best possible light.

In this chapter, we look at the strategies involved in the creation of effective résumés and good cover letters. We also look at the ways in which writing and research skills can enhance portfolio presentation and improve your performance on the licensing examination and in interviews.

Use writing and research skills to enhance portfolio presentation and improve your performance on exams and in interviews.

The Résumé

A *résumé* summarizes a job seeker's educational and other attainments, job experience, and skills. Today's résumé is often no more than one or two pages long, to accommodate busy employers. Its primary purpose is to get the job seeker an interview. One might say that it is an advertising flyer that "sells" a job applicant. Therefore, it needs to be eye-catching, carefully organized, well focused, and easy to read.

> The primary purpose of a résumé is to obtain an interview for the job seeker.

The traditional printed-out résumé is often highly formatted, though it is not customary to place it on letterhead stationery (save that for your cover letter). Italic and bold typefaces as well as underlining aid the reader's understanding; and information about the job seeker is displayed under headings and in lists for easy reference. (Avoid columns, which make it difficult to revise or to add new material.)

> Format your print résumé with italic and bold typefaces, underlining, headings, and lists; do not format in columns.

The print résumé must be re-formatted for electronic media. It may even be specially re-formatted for the interview situation, with photos of recent design projects scanned into the text. Whatever versions you choose to create, the organization of the résumé poses similar challenges.

Organization of the Résumé

There are three standard types of résumé organization: chronological, functional, and combination. Your choice of one of these three types will be governed by your sense of customary practice among people who already hold the type of job you are seeking. Your choice will also be governed by your particular set of skills and experience.

Chronological

The chronological résumé (Figure 12.1, also on the CD-ROM) organizes information within each category by sequential dating. A reader can get a clear picture of an applicant's history over a period of years by looking down the left-hand side of the résumé. Usually, each section is organized in reverse chronological order, with the most recent dates first. For instance, a recent graduate who has had two summer jobs, one the summer following his or her sophomore year and the other in the summer following his or her junior year, would put the more recent job first.

> The chronological résumé is organized by dates.

Employers like chronological résumés because they can see at a glance whether a prospective employee has been diligent and steady, with no wasted time. If your progress through school has been intermittent or if your job history is not steady, then it is wise to account for any time that

ROLAND LAURA-MARQUEZ

16901 Vail Mill Road, Apartment 7H
Tacoma, WA 98406
(253) 555-6789
roland@athena.com

Objective: To obtain an entry-level designer position and contribute to a dynamic team environment in a respected design firm.

Education: Washington State University, Pullman, WA 99164-2020, Bachelor of Arts in Interior Design, May 2004

Experience:
Harkman Roberts Design, Portland, OR
Summer Intern, Summer 2003
Redlined and drafted various CAD drawings in imperial and metric scale. Constructed presentation boards and designed small-scale furnishings for assisted-living facilities.

Hutchinson Valley Savings & Loan, Spokane, WA
Window Exhibit, May 2003
Arranged and displayed my own photographs of historic buildings throughout Washington State. Designed display modules and invitations to opening reception.

Boldface Graphic Design & Printing, Pullman, WA
Associate Designer, 2000–2004
Communicated, designed, and displayed creative graphics solutions for businesses and individuals.

Orangutan Bar and Grill, Seattle, WA
Waiter and Bartender, Summers 2001 and 2002
Food and drink–service salesperson.

Language Skills: Fluent in Spanish and proficient in Portuguese.

Activities: Student Interior Design Association 2000–2004
Public Relations Chair
Participated in SIDA Mentor Program. Organized trips, contacted firms for visits, and publicized certain seminars for student participation.

Special Skills: AutoCAD 14 and 2000, Adobe Photoshop, PageMaker and Illustrator, 3D Studio VIZ and MAX. Drafting construction documents, presentation boards.

Other: Interior Design Europe Summer Study Abroad Program, IIDA Student Charrette, IDEC Student Competition.

Figure 12.1 Chronological résumé for printing.

might otherwise appear to be "lost," particularly if yours is a chronological résumé. For instance, if you spent two years traveling around the United States, then you may wish to describe the design-related aspects of this journey—"focused on Victorian architecture, rooms, and period furnishings"—so that there will be no gap in the chronology you are presenting.

Functional

The functional résumé (Figure 12.2, also on the CD-ROM) is organized according to the skills a job seeker has acquired. This kind of résumé is particularly effective for those who have long, rich job histories or for those who are emphasizing transferable skills. For instance, a designer with a rich career may organize a résumé under headings such as residential, office, and store design. A designer who is returning to practice after several years of college teaching may organize a résumé under headings for skills polished in academic work as well as skills acquired in design jobs.

The functional résumé is organized by skills.

In the functional résumé, each item represents not a block of time, but a set of skills or an achievement. These occupy the all-important (because it is read first) left-hand side or centered lines of the résumé. The dates may be listed in parentheses at the ends of items or otherwise subordinated. (Some employers do not like this kind of résumé, because they cannot easily perceive the applicant's work history.)

Combination

A combination résumé (Figure 12.3, also on the CD-ROM) pulls together significant features of the chronological and the functional résumés. The principal sections of the combination résumé, such as the education and work-history sections, are presented in the reverse chronological format, with dates clearly listed. However, the résumé is topped by a special assets summary, or profile, that displays the range of strengths acquired in school, at work, and elsewhere. Thus, an employer can see at a glance if a job seeker has the right combination of strengths for the position being staffed. These strengths may be design specialties ("cost-effective design," "lighting design") or experience in key areas such as space planning, contract negotiation, client representation, and coordination with engineers and architects. An asset summary may also present management or marketing skills or the kind of transferable skills that would be useful in any business (See Figure 12.4 for examples of transferrable skills). However, unless you are applying for an administrative support job, do not highlight in your profile any technical proficiency you possess in non-design-related computer software. Save this for the special-skills section later in the

The combination résumé has features of both the chronological and the functional.

A combination résumé is topped by an assets summary focusing on design experience and management or marketing skills.

SARAH BLAIR
6250 Sifton Road, Apartment 278
Washington, D.C. 2007-4823
202-555-6789
sarah@athena.com

Goal: Further professional experience in interior design and historical preservation

ASSETS

- Extensive knowledge of interior design and historical preservation
- Highly organized
- Excellent supervisor
- Skilled communicator
- Proven fund-raiser

AREAS OF EXPERTISE

Design

- Coordinated renovation of Alden-James house in Bramblett Historical Park, Malden, Virginia. Complete overhaul of 2,400-square-foot heritage building. Responsible for color schemes, furniture selection, space planning, and window treatments in public-access historic rooms as well as functional spaces.
- Created interior designs for 35 model homes in 8 locations for a major residential builder. Responsible for space planning, furniture selection, color schemes, and window treatments.

Business Management

- Successfully trained group of 12 volunteers for Preservation Council of Greater Washington D.C.
- Developed standard office procedures for Franklin-Bedank, an architectural and interior design firm. Generated and maintained all project documents, contracts, and client files.
- Developed and executed direct-mail campaign that raised $100,500 for Preservation Council of Greater Washington D.C.

PROFESSIONAL HISTORY

Director
Preservation Council of Greater Washington D.C.
June 2002 to Present

Designer
Henkels Fine Homes
March 1998–June 2002

Office Manager
Franklin-Bedank
January 1994–May 1998

EDUCATION

George Washington University, Washington, D.C.
B.F.A. Interior Design   1994
Northern Virginia Community College, Alexandria, VA
A.A.S. Accounting   1992

—References furnished upon request—

Figure 12.2 Functional résumé for printing.

Cynthia Rose Marino
572 Archangel Lane
Middletown, CT 07457
203-555-6789
cynthia@athena.com

INTERIOR DESIGNER

Strengths

- Successful contract negotiations
- Cost-effective design strategies
- Creative space planning
- Effective contract administration
- Innovative use of light and color
- High-quality client presentations

RECENT PROJECTS

Interior Design Consultant   2004
Bradford Public Schools, Bradford, CT

Provided design services, including space planning and funiture and equipment selection, for four schools. Supervised installation on site.

Project Administrator   2002–2003
Waterview Condominiums, Simsbury, CT

Coordinated condominium remodeling project. Created design drawings. Maintained budgets, schedules, and all documentation. Completed project featured in Connecticut Homes, *January 2004.*

Design Coordinator   1999–2002
Artemide Displays, Boston, MA

Created designs and specifications for point-of-purchase displays. Assisted clients with selection of colors and finishes for all displays. Developed assembly instructions.

EDUCATION

Mills College, Oakland, CA, B.A. (with honors), Interior Design   1999

REFERENCES AND PORTFOLIO FURNISHED UPON REQUEST.

Figure 12.3 A combination résumé for printing.

Figure 12.4
Transferrable skills.

Communication

The skillful expression, transmission, and interpretation of knowledge and ideas.

Speaking effectively	Perceiving nonverbal messages
Writing concisely	Persuading
Listening attentively	Reporting information
Expressing ideas	Describing feelings
Facilitating group discussion	Interviewing
Providing appropriate feedback	Editing
Negotiating	

Research & Planning

The search for specific knowledge and the ability to conceptualize future needs and solutions for meeting those needs.

Forecasting, predicting	Solving problems
Creating ideas	Setting goals
Identifying problems	Extracting important information
Imagining alternatives	Defining needs
Identifying resources	Analyzing
Gathering information	Developing evaluation strategies

Human Relations

The use of interpersonal skills for resolving conflict, relating to, and helping people.

Developing rapport	Counseling
Being sensitive	Cooperating
Listening	Delegating with respect
Conveying feelings	Representing others
Providing support for others	Perceiving feelings, situations
Motivating	Asserting
Sharing credit	

Organization, Management & Leadership

The ability to supervise, direct and guide individuals and groups in the completion of tasks and fulfillment of goals.

Initiating new ideas	Coaching
Handling details	Counseling
Coordinating tasks	Promoting change
Managing groups	Selling ideas or products
Delegating responsibility	Decision making with others
Teaching	Managing conflict

Work Survival

The day-to-day skills which promote effective production and work satisfaction.

Implementing decisions	Meeting goals
Cooperating	Enlisting help
Enforcing policies	Accepting responsibility
Being punctual	Setting and meeting deadlines
Managing time	Organizing
Attending to detail	Making desicions

résumé. Reserve the asset profile for design-specific skills and accomplishments, and for skills in related areas such as marketing and communication.

The combination résumé can work well for a recent graduate whose work history has largely been in non-design jobs but who has acquired through education and internships strengths that can be effectively summarized in an asset profile.

Elements of the Résumé

Whatever type of résumé you create, your résumé will contain, not necessarily in this order, some or all of the elements[1] listed below:

> *Résumé Elements*
> 1. Heading
> 2. Job Objective*
> 3. Asset Summary, or Profile*
> 4. Education
> 5. Work Experience
> 6. Honors and Awards*
> 7. Activities and Professional Memberships*
> 8. Registration and Licenses*
> 9. Special Skills*
> 10. Relevant Personal Information (including hobbies and travel)*
> 11. References*
>
> *Optional.

HEADING

At the very top of your résumé will appear a heading that contains the crucial contact information enabling a prospective employer to get in touch with you. Included will be your name, street address, telephone number, fax number if you have one, and e-mail address. (If you don't have e-mail at home, work, or school, you can set up a Web-based account that you can access from a public library.) You may also wish to create a special account for job-seeking e-mail if your only computer access is at work. If you have a portfolio Web site, you may wish to mention its URL in the heading of your résumé. Be sure your Web site's content is appropriate for an employer to see—no pictures of your cat, no matter how well scanned and edited!

Most prospective employers will call during work hours, so it is important to include a daytime telephone number in a résumé's heading. If you do not want to receive job inquiries at a work number, you might consider the purchase of a telephone-answering device that records messages on your home phone and allows you to retrieve them from an outside line. You

Contact information appears at the top of all résumés.

might also consider cellphone service with voice mail. In either case, be sure that any outgoing message you record is appropriate for professional purposes—plain, clear, serviceable, and calm.

If you are a qualified member of one or more professional organizations, then you will put the relevant acronym(s) after your name in the heading, for example, "Marsha Jones, ASID, IIDA." ASID, of course, stands for "American Society of Interior Designers," while IIDA stands for "International Interior Design Association." Listed below are some other common professional associations that qualifying member designers put after their names in their résumés, on business cards, in business letters, and wherever appropriate:

Place acronyms representing your professional affiliations after your name in the résumé heading.

- IDEC: Interior Design Educators Council
- ISP: Institute of Store Planners
- CFID: Council of Federal Interior Designers (designers who work for the U.S. federal government
- IDC: Interior Designers of Canada
- AIA: American Institute of Architects (for interior designers who are also qualified architects)
- IFMA: International Facility Management Association
- IFDA: International Furnishings and Design Association

JOB OBJECTIVE

A job objective permits an employer to see if an applicant's goals are in line with the requirements of a job.

At the top of the résumé, beneath the heading, many people insert a job objective. This concisely written one-sentence statement allows an employer to determine at a glance whether an applicant's goals are in line with the requirements of the job to be filled. Some objectives are specific, while others are more general.

If you are a freelancer, it is crucial to have a clear, specific job objective at the top of your résumé so that prospective employers can easily spot your credentials among those of other freelancers in the résumé file. An experienced designer may also benefit from a clear, specific job description, whereas a recent graduate of a design program may wish to write a more general objective. If you have no particular job in mind, an overly specific objective can actually narrow the range of positions for which you may be considered. A carefully targeted objective, however, provides an opportunity for a job seeker to tie together skill sets so as to create a very distinct impression. For instance, consider the example in the following box:

> <u>Objective</u>: A junior designer's position that will permit me
> to use and enhance my creative and marketing skills

Here, a recently graduated designer who has worked in a furniture store while studying interior design expresses a wish to use the full range of her skills for the benefit of an employer.

EDUCATION

The most important parts of your résumé—its core—are those that outline educational attainment and work experience. Which of these two sections should come first? The answer to that question depends on which section is most impressive. For many recent graduates, hard-won educational credentials will be the stronger opening.

Under the heading *Education*, each item states the degree or certificate the job seeker was awarded, the major area of concentration, and the name and location (city and state) of the institution attended. You may also provide other facts that reflect well on you, such as a high GPA overall or within your major; but bear in mind that employers will give less weight to your grades once you have acquired work experience. After a year or two, you may wish to drop this information from your résumé in order to leave more room for the details of your postgraduate career.

Under *Education*, be sure to include each college, university, or technical institute from which you have received course credits, not just those from which you have received degrees. If you have completed course work toward a graduate degree or, of course, if you have received an advanced degree, be sure to include that information. Also highly relevant are any continuing-education units (CEU) you have attained to keep your professional-association membership current. For instance, you may have studied window films or period furniture or received training in computerized drafting skills.

If you are the graduate of a two- or four-year college, it is usually not necessary to include your high school years. Do so only if your high school GPA was exceptionally high or if you were the recipient of outstanding honors. Even then, it will probably make sense to use valuable résumé space for special skills and interests that you currently possess, rather than highlighting a past that has been superseded. Rather than listing your high school's name and location in the education section, list outstanding high school honors or achievements in the awards-and-honors section with the appropriate dates.

Under *Education*, include each school from which you received course credits, including CEUs acquired after graduation.

Once you have graduated from a two- or four-year college, do not detail your high school years under *Education*.

Sometimes college or university design graduates list the courses they have taken in their majors, but this duplicates information that will be included in any transcripts that an interested employer may request. In addition, prospective employers may assume that an interior design degree is based on the completion of a standard curriculum. Rather than listing courses taken, it may be more effective to write a brief narrative summarizing the principal emphases of the course work you pursued at the principal institutions you attended. Focus on accomplishments rather than activities.

In describing your education, focus on accomplishments rather than activities.

You may also wish to include an asset profile at the top of the résumé (see Figures 12.2 and 12.3) in order to clarify the practical implications of your design degree. Do, however, mention in the education section a double major or any relevant nonstandard course work—for example, "minor in international business" or "double major: interior design and art history." By all means, list undergraduate prizes, scholarships, and honors, either in the education section or in a dedicated *Awards and Honors* section later in your résumé.

WORK EXPERIENCE

In the work-experience section of the résumé, the job seeker provides, in reverse chronological order, all relevant information about each job held. It is customary to include some or all of the following:

- Dates of employment
- Employee's job title
- Employer
- City and state of employment
- Job responsibilities
- Employee's accomplishments
- Special projects
- Promotions
- Honors

Take credit only for projects for which you bore direct responsibility.

Accuracy is very important in this part of the résumé, as in other segments. Prospective employers will expect your version of your work history to conform in all respects to past and current employers' versions. It is best to take credit only for projects for which you bore *direct* responsibility.

A recent graduate whose job experience has been in fields other than design may feel a sense of discomfort when writing the work history. Many graduating design students would prefer to claim no work experience rather than to reveal previous job experience as a sales associate, fitness instructor, security guard, or cashier. Yet even the most creative designer employer will appreciate that, by holding whatever job, the applicant has demonstrated an ability to show up on time, get the work done in an efficient manner, and get along with co-workers. A design firm, like any other business, is looking for employees who are responsible, honest, and well organized. These work-ethic attitudes—and many creative skills—are demonstrated not only by completion of the design curriculum, but also by successfully holding down positions in the world of work. As you detail the nature of your accomplishments, brief narrative statements about each job will permit you to highlight the most positive and creative aspects of your work.

In the résumé's work section, include non-design jobs as well as design jobs.

BRIEF NARRATIVES ABOUT WORK   Only by looking very hard at what you actually did in any given job is the full scope of your accomplishment revealed. If you have kept a job log, or ongoing record of your daily, weekly, monthly, and annual accomplishments at work, it may be easier to see the strength of your qualifications. If you have not kept such a log, your presentation in this part of the résumé may benefit from brainstorming. Set yourself the goal of writing down 25 accomplishments for each of your jobs. Then see if you can organize them into categories that lend themselves to concise presentation.

Narrative job statements are usually terse. To save space, articles such as "the" and "a" may be left out. Often the subject "I" is left out. Verbs are chosen to convey a sense of power and agency. (See Table 12.1 for a list of these powerful verbs.) A designer-job seeker needs to convey the ability to generate new ideas, solve problems, analyze, critique, synthesize, and take both initiative and risks. You can use power verbs in your work narratives to suggest your creativity, flexibility, adaptability, self-reliance, self-confidence, and ability to communicate. It is particularly effective to begin skill or achievement statements with power verbs.

Leave the word "I" out of narrative descriptions. Begin skill or achievement statements with verbs that convey power and agency.

Less effective:
I reorganized the swatch library and created a catalog for it.
More effective:
Reorganized and cataloged swatch library.

The narrative for the most recent job (presumably the most important) is typically fuller than those for previous jobs.

In composing the work history, a designer with years of experience faces a different set of challenges from the recent graduate. Experienced designers focus selectively to convey the full scope of their contributions. For

Provide a fuller narrative for the most recent job than for previous jobs.

TABLE 12.1   POWER VERBS FOR RÉSUMÉS

POWER VERBS
Remember to use these verbs to describe your skills and accomplishments when writing your résumé and cover letters—in order to increase the strength of your writing and make potential employers take notice.

COMMUNICATION/PEOPLE SKILLS

Addressed	Edited	Outlined
Advertised	Elicited	Participated
Arbitrated	Enlisted	Persuaded
Arranged	Explained	Presented
Articulated	Expressed	Promoted
Authored	Formulated	Proposed
Clarified	Furnished	Publicized
Collaborated	Incorporated	Reconciled
Communicated	Influenced	Recruited
Composed	Interacted	Referred
Condensed	Interpreted	Reinforced
Conferred	Interviewed	Reported
Consulted	Involved	Resolved
Contacted	Joined	Responded
Conveyed	Judged	Solicited
Convinced	Lectured	Specified
Corresponded	Listened	Spoke
Debated	Marketed	Suggested
Defined	Mediated	Summarized
Developed	Moderated	Synthesized
Directed	Negotiated	Translated
Discussed	Observed	Wrote
Drafted		

CREATIVE SKILLS

Acted	Developed	Initiated
Adapted	Directed	Instituted
Began	Displayed	Integrated
Combined	Drew	Introduced
Composed	Entertained	Invented
Conceptualized	Established	Modeled
Condensed	Fashioned	Modified
Created	Formulated	Originated
Customized	Founded	Performed
Designed	Illustrated	Photographed

TABLE 12.1
(*continued*)

Planned	Revitalized	Solved
Revised	Shaped	

DATA/FINANCIAL SKILLS

Administered	Computed	Netted
Adjusted	Conserved	Planned
Allocated	Corrected	Prepared
Analyzed	Determined	Programmed
Appraised	Developed	Projected
Assessed	Estimated	Qualified
Audited	Forecasted	Reconciled
Balanced	Managed	Reduced
Budgeted	Marketed	Researched
Calculated	Measured	Retrieved

HELPING SKILLS

Adapted	Demonstrated	Motivated
Advocated	Diagnosed	Prevented
Aided	Educated	Provided
Answered	Encouraged	Referred
Arranged	Ensured	Rehabilitated
Assessed	Expedited	Represented
Assisted	Facilitated	Resolved
Clarified	Familiarized	Simplified
Coached	Furthered	Supplied
Collaborated	Guided	Supported
Contributed	Helped	Volunteered
Cooperated	Ensured	
Counseled	Intervened	

MANAGEMENT/LEADERSHIP SKILLS

Administered	Controlled	Established
Analyzed	Converted	Executed
Appointed	Coordinated	Generated
Approved	Decided	Handled
Assigned	Delegated	Headed
Attained	Developed	Hired
Authorized	Directed	Hosted
Chaired	Eliminated	Improved
Considered	Emphasized	Incorporated
Consolidated	Enforced	Increased
Contracted	Enhanced	Initiated

(continued)

TABLE 12.1
(*continued*)

Inspected	Overhauled	Restored
Instituted	Oversaw	Reviewed
Led	Planned	Scheduled
Managed	Presided	Secured
Merged	Prioritized	Selected
Motivated	Produced	Streamlined
Navigated	Recommended	Strengthened
Organized	Reorganized	Supervised
Originated	Replaced	Terminated

ORGANIZATIONAL SKILLS

Approved	Incorporated	Reserved
Arranged	Inspected	Responded
Catalogued	Logged	Reviewed
Categorized	Maintained	Routed
Charted	Monitored	Scheduled
Classified	Obtained	Screened
Coded	Operated	Submitted
Collected	Ordered	Supplied
Compiled	Organized	Standardized
Corrected	Prepared	Systematized
Corresponded	Processed	Updated
Distributed	Provided	Validated
Executed	Purchased	Verified
Filed	Recorded	
Generated	Registered	

RESEARCH SKILLS

Analyzed	Experimented	Organized
Clarified	Explored	Researched
Collected	Extracted	Reviewed
Compared	Formulated	Searched
Conducted	Gathered	Solved
Critiqued	Inspected	Summarized
Detected	Interviewed	Surveyed
Determined	Invented	Systematized
Diagnosed	Investigated	Tested
Evaluated	Located	
Examined	Measured	

TEACHING SKILLS

Adapted	Coached	Coordinated
Advised	Communicated	Critiqued
Clarified	Conducted	Developed

TABLE 12.1
(continued)

Enabled	Guided	Persuaded
Encouraged	Individualized	Simulated
Evaluated	Informed	Stimulated
Explained	Instilled	Taught
Facilitated	Instructed	Tested
Focused	Motivated	Trained

TECHNICAL SKILLS

Adapted	Developed	Regulated
Applied	Engineered	Remodeled
Assembled	Fabricated	Repaired
Built	Fortified	Replaced
Calculated	Installed	Restored
Computed	Maintained	Solved
Conserved	Operated	Specialized
Constructed	Overhauled	Standardized
Converted	Printed	Studied
Debugged	Programmed	Upgraded
Designed	Rectified	Utilized
Determined		

Adapted from Quintessential Careers, www.quintcareers.com/action-skills.html.

instance, a designer employed as a project manager might note the principal project or projects worked on as well as the particular role played in designing, budgeting, scheduling, and documenting. The experienced designer may also note any prizes received or publication in a design magazine. The recent graduate whose work history has been in fields other than design will need to emphasize non-design skills that can be transferred to the benefit of a designer employer.

TRANSFERABLE SKILLS   Skills acquired in any activity of life are transferrable if they are applicable to the job you hope to get. What types of skills are transferable? Apart from those based on well-developed work-ethic attitudes, some other broad categories are communication, research and planning, human relations, organization, and management.

Figure 12.4 shows skill sets included in each transferable-skill category. The example below shows how one job seeker described her experience in a field unrelated to interior design so as to emphasize her transferable skills:

Transferable skills are applicable to any job you hope to get.

Skills transferable
to design include:
* Communication.
* Research and
  planning.
* Human
  relations.
* Organization
  and
  management.

2002–2004 Sales Associate, Harper's Office Supplies. Created seasonal and special promotion window and point-of-purchase displays. Helped customers create color-coordinated desk and cubicle environments. Participated in inventory control and supervised temporary employees. Twice selected "Sales Associate of the Month."

Even if your experience in the field of design is rich, you would be well advised to display your acquisition of transferable skills in the important areas of communication; research and planning; human relations; organization; and management. A good strategic approach to job hunting highlights transferable skills not only in résumés, but also in cover letters and in interviews.

AWARDS AND HONORS

When citing
awards, include the
full name of the
award and its date.

If you have received a substantial number of awards and honors, then it makes sense to highlight them in a special section. For recent design graduates, awards may be creative—for outstanding design work completed in class or submitted for school competitions—or they may be academic, such as merit-based scholarships or placement on the Dean's List. Also considered an academic award is membership in an honorary society such as Phi Beta Kappa. It is important to state the full name of the award and to include its date: "2004, Mary Morris Kaplan Award for Scholastic Excellence," not simply "Award for Scholastic Excellence."

For experienced designers, awards may include invitations to design rooms in show houses created to attract the admission-paying public and to benefit a charity. Or they may include prizes won through competitions.

ACTIVITIES AND ASSOCIATIONS

Recent design graduates sometimes choose to list on their résumés activities such as student government, athletic teams, or school clubs. To some prospective employers, participation in extracurricular activities suggests skills that are transferable to a work environment. Experienced designers usually do not have room on their résumés for activities like sports.

Mention nonprofessional activities
that are pertinent
to the job you
hope to hold.

Many design firms favor community involvement and warmly urge their employees to get involved. If you share the beliefs of activist design firms with commitments to green design or other principles and if you would like to work for such a firm, then involve yourself in community activities supporting your beliefs. For instance, a novice or student green designer might get involved in groups devoted to conservation or environmental activism.

It is important to mention your accomplishments within each organization you join, and particularly any leadership role you may have taken.

PROFESSIONAL ASSOCIATIONS   Reserve a special section of your résumé for your membership in student or working chapters of professional organizations such as ASID. The "professional memberships" section of a working designer's résumé is an important statement of achievement and credibility. Membership in ASID and IIDA, among other professional organizations, requires successful completion of the qualifying exam of the National Council for Interior Design Qualification (NCIDQ). This is also the primary qualifying examination for interior designers in those U.S. states and Canadian provinces that have certification, licensing, or other registration statutes. It is required for designers seeking certification as contract interior designers specializing in institutional and commercial design.

Professional memberships proclaim achievement and credibility.

THE NCIDQ EXAM   The NCIDQ examination consists of six sections, most requiring that written information be translated into graphic format. These $1^1/_2$-to-$2^1/_2$-hour sections of the exam are given over two successive days each year. A candidate may retake any section not successfully completed, although all sections must be completed within a five-year period. Three of the six sections are computer-graded multiple-choice tests: Identification and Application (parts 1 and 2); Building and Barrier-Free Codes; and Problem Solving. There are also three practicum sections: Programming; Three-Dimensional Exercises; and Scenario.[2]

Good study skills and good design skills are both required for successful completion of the NCIDQ exam. Candidates may polish these skill sets by participating in STEP, the special study program for NCIDQ-exam takers sponsored by ASID (though you need not be an ASID member to participate). STEP, which stands for "Self-Testing Exercises for PreProfessionals," offers practice tests that prepare candidates for the multiple-choice sections. In addition, a STEP workshop offers exercises and other materials that prepare students for the practicum sections of the exam. The experience of working in simulated, timed exams is invaluable, according to one interior designer.[3] Practice with the Schematic and Design Development parts of the STEP exams helps to ensure success on the actual exam. Designers with the knowledge, skills, and experience to pass the exam can rehearse the time-management strategies that will ensure they do so.

REGISTRATION AND LICENSES

The registration section of your résumé should mention all licenses, registrations, and certificates you may possess that permit you to practice in the U.S. states and Canadian provinces that require them. Accuracy is crucial here. Dates should be exact, and the accrediting agencies should be accurately named.

Accuracy is especially important in the registration section of the résumé.

SPECIAL SKILLS

Include knowledge of software programs under *Special Skills*.

Included under the heading of *Special Skills* are specific, tangible skills. This is the place to mention not only knowledge of CAD, but the particular version(s) of the program that you are familiar with—for example, Autocad 2000—so as to aid employers in hiring. Here, too, you may assert your knowledge of business and other non-design software that might be useful to a prospective designer employer. For instance, you might mention mastery of 3-D modeling, image-editing, word-processing, accounting, project management, and layout or desktop-publishing software.

Non-native English speakers should not claim English as a foreign language when applying for jobs in the United States.

Mention as well any competency you possess in foreign languages. "Fluency" means that your command of the language is virtually indistinguishable from a native speaker's. To claim "proficiency" in a language suggests that you understand its grammar, though you may not be able to speak it flawlessly and may not have a large vocabulary. "Conversational" familiarity means knowledge of a few basics. The lowest competence worth claiming is the ability to read a foreign language.

No matter how hard you have worked as a non-native speaker to acquire English as a second language, it is best not to claim it as a special skill. Competency in English is taken for granted by most employers in the United States. Rather, competent speakers of English as a second language are advised to claim as a special skill the ability to speak their first languages when applying for jobs in the United States. For instance, a recent immigrant from France might say "Native French speaker" or "Fluent in French," with no mention of English as a "foreign" language. An alternative is "Bilingual, French and English."

PERSONAL INFORMATION

Appropriate personal information includes hobbies or talents relevant to the interior design field.

Some job seekers in past eras have chosen to include in their résumés such personal information as marital status, ethnicity, age, number of children, religion, height and weight, and even sexual preference. Since it is now illegal to discriminate on the basis of such characteristics, it is recommended that you not mention them. Appropriate personal information includes hobbies or talents that have relevance to the interior design field. For example, you might mention a pastime such as painting, photography, quilting, or building your own furniture, thus imparting to your résumé some flavor of your personality and providing an interviewer with a conversational opening.

You may also wish to mention relevant travel. Study abroad is especially valuable because it is considered educational, no matter what the travel itinerary. That said, a laundry list of cities and countries visited on a whirlwind tour will not impress prospective employers as much as design-related travel. Stress the ways in which your travel experience has contributed to your design education, for example: "Photographic tour of English gardens, including historic and cottage gardens."

Other personal information that may be relevant includes possession of a valid driver's license, willingness to travel, willingness to relocate, and military service. Some job seekers save these information bits to mention in cover letters if and when they are relevant. Willingness to travel is an important consideration for firms with national or international client bases.

REFERENCES AND PORTFOLIO

Listing references on the résumé is an option selected by some, though by no means all, job seekers. Many feel that they have more flexibility if one-size-fits-all references are not listed on the résumé. They then have the option to customize the reference list for each prospective employer. If references are not listed on your résumé, then it is customary to state, "References furnished upon request," although this may be omitted if you need the space for something more important.

It is courteous to check in advance with anyone you wish to use as a reference. Make sure that each prospective reference is comfortable speaking on your behalf. Also, advise your references that they may receive a call requesting a reference for you. In these ways you can prepare your references to do a good job for you.

Whether or not they have included references on their résumés, many designers will indicate that their design portfolios are available for review. Again, a simple sentence will suffice. Portfolio and reference availability may also be combined, as follows: "References and portfolio furnished upon request."

Formatting the Résumé for Electronic Media

Twenty years ago one good printable résumé was all anyone needed to apply for a job. This is no longer true. Many job applications in the design field are still made in the time-tested way, with a printed résumé and cover letter. These are sent via "snail mail" and are read by a human being at every stage of the application process. However, even if sent by snail mail, an increasingly large number of résumés are first read not by a person, but by a scanner, an input device that captures two-dimensional images and text, converting them into digital format. The scanned documents are stored electronically in a computer's database. There they are read by a computer that searches on command for keywords designating qualified applicants for a particular job.

Study abroad is always valuable, particularly if design-related.

Check in advance with anyone you wish to use as a reference.

Contemporary job seekers may need four résumés:
- For printing
- For scanning
- For e-mail or online posting
- For faxing

In addition, many job applications nowadays are made by posting a résumé online, which the employer then harvests; by e-mailing a résumé in response to an online or printed job posting; or by faxing a résumé in response to a print ad or an online job notice. These newer ways of applying for jobs have required some changes not only in the ways that résumés are delivered and read, but also in the ways that they are written.

Many experienced contemporary job seekers create four standard résumés, one printable, one scannable, one in plain text that is suitable for e-mailing or posting online, and one "bold" printable résumé suitable for faxing. (See Figures 12.1, 12.2, 12.3, 12.5, 12.6, and 12.9 for examples of these four kinds of résumés.) A fifth kind of résumé with scanned-in project photos (see Figure 12.10) is discussed in the "Interview" section later in this chapter.

THE SCANNABLE RÉSUMÉ

A résumé that is geared to the way that scanners and search engines read documents (Figure 12.5, also on the CD-ROM) is not the same as a résumé written to be printed. Here are a few tips:

- Scanners read only unformatted text. They are not reliable readers of italics, underlining, boxes, lines, bullets (especially round, hollow ones), symbols (including ampersands, percent signs, or foreign characters), pictures, or even tabs. It is a good idea to use capital letters for headings; but if you overdo it, YOU WILL SEEM TO BE SCREAMING FOR ATTENTION.
- Add a space before and after a slash so that the slash doesn't touch the letters on either side of it (example: designer / developer).
- Use a standard 12-point font, if possible sans serif, like **Arial**. Smaller type sizes won't scan well.
- Use lightweight white paper that contains no speckles, and, if your résumé is longer than a page, use paper clips rather than staples to fasten the pages together.
- Don't use brackets or parentheses in phone numbers.
- Use a laser-jet printer for greatest clarity and resolution.
- If you are submitting the résumé via snail mail, send it in a large, flat envelope, so that it will not need to be folded. (If you fold it, and a line of text is creased, the laser toner may flake off and make an entire line unreadable.)

- Put each item of your contact information—address, phone numbers, and the like—on a separate line. Your résumé may become longer once you change the fonts and spacing, but that is acceptable in the scannable version.
- Put your name at the top of every page so nothing will get lost.
- Don't be afraid of white space. Once a group of résumés has been electronically selected, people will be narrowing the selection. They will appreciate enough white space to make reading easy and pleasant.
- Make sure to salt your résumé with keywords throughout, to ensure that it will be found in a database search.

KEYWORDS IN THE RÉSUMÉ   When filling a job in interior design or any other field, employers increasingly rely on computer search functions to sort out résumés containing so-called key words and phrases like "commercial space planning" or "Studio Max." Computers do not appreciate the aesthetics of brevity and easy readability that characterize the print résumé. Nor do they respond to the punch of the action verbs that dominate printable résumés; instead, computers have usually been asked to look for the key nouns that name specific skills and types of experience. Search engines are virtual bloodhounds, willing and able to sort through long lists of these nouns to find what they are looking for. Computers, however, have no imagination. If the search is for "manager," a computer may not find "management," so the canny job seeker includes both nouns, though not, perhaps, in the same part of the résumé. The job seeker needs to be aware that a computer may rank search results by the number of times a search word or phrase is listed in each document. This means that you get extra points from the computer for artful repetition. However, you also need to take into account that sooner or later a person will read your résumé; for people, obvious repetition is a ho-hum.

Action verbs dominate print résumés; key nouns dominate scanned résumés.

TARGETED LANGUAGE   You need to speak to search engines in concrete language that is targeted to the field of interior design. Reading design magazines and conducting information interviews will help you get a better sense of the most current professional language. Pay close attention to the language of job notices and ads, since employers usually search for résumés using the terms in which their ads and notices were written. By comparing one ad or notice to another, you will begin to notice similarities in the way job needs are described. Be sure to include the words and phrases that are most frequently used. These highly searchable terms will tell you what you need to say about yourself so that computers—and prospective employers using them—will find you.

In your résumé, use the current language of interior design.

ROLAND LAURA-MARQUEZ
16901 Vail Mill Road, Apartment 7H
Tacoma, WA 98406
253-555-1212
roland@athena.com

PROFESSIONAL PROFILE
Junior interior designer with skills in space planning, palette selection, and specification of materials and finishes

Combine artistic talent with technical abilities in drafting construction documents and creating presentation boards

Savvy communicator with record of achievement in graphic design

Experience in public relations and broad knowledge of interior design field

35 mm and digital photography   Knowledge of ADA codes
Scanning   Project administration
Simple Web site construction

COMPUTER AND TECHNOLOGY SKILLS
AutoCAD 14 and 2000   Microsoft PowerPoint
Pagemaker and Illustrator   Adobe Photoshop
3D studio VIZ and MAX   Adobe Illustrator
Microsoft Access   HTML
Microsoft Project   Macromedia Flash 4
Microsoft Word

EXPERIENCE
Harkman Roberts Design, Portland, OR
Summer Intern, Summer 2003

Redlined and drafted various CAD drawings in imperial and metric scale. Constructed presentation boards and designed small-scale furnishings for assisted-living facilities.

Figure 12.5 A résumé suitable for scanning.

+++++++++

Hutchinson Valley Savings and Loan, Spokane, WA
Window Exhibit, May 2003

Arranged and displayed personal photographs of historic buildings
throughout Washington State. Designed display modules and
invitations to opening reception.

++++++++++

Boldface Graphic Design and Printing, Pullman, WA
Associate Designer, 2000–2004

Communicated, designed, and displayed creative graphic solutions
for businesses and individuals.

++++++++++

Orangutan Bar and Grill, Seattle, WA
Waiter and Bartender, Summers 2001 and 2002
Food and beverage–service salesperson.

EDUCATION
Washington State University, Pullman, WA 99164-2020—Bachelor
of Arts in Interior Design, June 2004

LANGUAGE SKILLS
Fluent in Spanish and proficient in Portuguese

ACTIVITIES
Student Interior Design Association 2000–2004
Public Relations Chair
Participated in SIDA Mentor Program. Organized trips, contacted
firms for visits, and publicized certain seminars for student partici-
pation.

OTHER
Interior Design Europe Summer Study Abroad Program, IIDA
Student Charrette, IDEC Student Competition.

Figure 12.5 (continued)

A *Key Skills* section maximizes the impact of a scanned résumé.

KEY-SKILLS SECTION   At the top of your scannable résumé, place a section that describes your skills and experience as a list of searchable words and phrases. List all the programs and software you know well. Also list specific design and other capabilities, not neglecting communications skills, organizational skills, and management skills. If you used "manager" in the *Key-Skills* section, then you can use "management" in the body of the résumé. This will help you maximize your sensitivity to search engines without your résumé appearing too repetitious to any human reader.

Convert your résumé to, plain text for e-mailing, changing its format as needed.

THE WEB AND E-MAIL RÉSUMÉ

If you decide to post your résumé at a Web site or submit it by e-mail to a prospective employer, you will need to convert your résumé to ASCII (say AZkey)—or American Standard Code for Information Interchange, also known as plain text. This is the lowest common denominator for electronic texts. Any Web browser or e-mail program can read it.

CREATING A PLAIN-TEXT RÉSUMÉ   To convert a printable résumé to ASCII, open it in a word-processing program such as Microsoft Word or WordPerfect. Then "save as" plain text (.txt). A pop-up screen may tell you that your document contains "features that are not compatible" with plain text. Click OK, then clean up the places where formatting such as bullet points and boldface have turned to gobbledygook during the document conversion. You will still have your original .doc file to print whenever you need it.

To format plain text appropriately, try changing bullets to asterisks, pluses, or dashes. Use a series of asterisks or dashes to create a horizontal line between sections (up to 60 characters). To prepare for posting on a Web site or for electronic mailing (See Figure 12.9, also on the CD-ROM), you will need to make certain other changes in your résumé as well:

- If the résumé is longer than one page and contains contact information or another heading at the tops of pages, or footers at page bottoms, remove all this. The ASCII résumé is meant to be read on a computer screen, so there is no pagination.
- Put the most important information in the top third of the document. Some employers print out only a screen shot, rather than the entire résumé.
- Review the contact information at the top of your résumé. Make sure that the correct information is still in the line where you placed it, rather than line-breaking in odd places.

- Set the margins so that the line of text is 6.5 inches long, or limit each line in the résumé to 72 characters. Most e-mail programs wrap text at 72. Lines longer than that are going to be cut off and dropped down, making your résumé look as if it had been chewed by a dog.
- Don't worry if the résumé you format for online posting is made much longer by your changes. An online résumé may contain as many as 6,000 characters—three times as many as a one-page print résumé. In fact, the résumé for online posting may be as long as four or five printed pages!

SUBMITTING THE RÉSUMÉ VIA E-MAIL   Unless specifically invited to do so, it is better not to send your print résumé as an attachment to an e-mail, although doing so would permit you to preserve its attractive formatting. From fear of viruses, many employers will not open attachments and will delete any e-mail that contains them. Your plain-text résumé is ideal for cutting and pasting into the body of an e-mail. Before you send it to a prospective employer, it is wise to send it to yourself. That way you will be the one to catch any transmission or technical problems. Be sure that the text looks good on the screen and prints out properly. If possible, e-mail the résumé to yourself at different accounts. That way you can see whether your résumé holds up when it opens in accounts set up to read mail in different ways.

> Send your e-mail résumé to yourself before sending it to others.

THE FAXED RÉSUMÉ

Facsimile is a direct, immediate means of transmission that tends to speed up the pace of business. Some experts recommend that a résumé or other document written for facsimile transmission be brief, so that it can be quickly read. Other experts suggest that facsimile, like snail mail, is a good medium for longer communications. Certainly it would be a mistake to be too discursive, and the documents you fax should be clear, concise, and easy to read.

The résumé for faxing (Figure 12.6, also on the CD-ROM) closely resembles the résumé for printing and snail-mailing. However, it may have a slightly simpler and bolder appearance, with, for instance, additional boldface.

The worst drawback of résumé submission via fax is loss of control over the final product. If the fax machine at the other end uses flimsy, poor-quality paper, then the appearance of your carefully formatted résumé will suffer. Fax, like Web posting and e-mail, can be an efficient way to submit a

> A résumé well suited for faxing has a bold, simple appearance.

ROLAND LAURA-MARQUEZ
16901 Vail Mill Road, Apartment 7H
Tacoma, WA 98406
(253) 555-6789
roland@athena.com

OBJECTIVE: To obtain an entry-level designer position and contribute to a dynamic team environment in a respected design firm.

EDUCATION:
B.A., Interior Design, **Washington State University**, Pullman, WA, May 2004

EXPERIENCE:
Summer Intern, **Harkman Roberts Design**, Portland, OR, Summer 2003
  • Redlined and drafted various CAD drawings in imperial and metric scale. Constructed presentation boards and designed small-scale furnishings for assisted-living facilities

Window Exhibit, **Hutchinson Valley Savings & Loan**, Spokane, WA, May 2003
  • Arranged and displayed personal photographs of historic buildings throughout Washington State. Designed display modules and invitations to opening reception

Associate Designer, **Boldface Graphic Design**, Pullman, WA, 2000–2004
  • Communicated, designed, and displayed creative graphics solutions for businesses and individuals

Waiter and Bartender, **Orangutan Bar and Grill**, Seattle, WA, 2001 and 2002
  • Food and drink-service salesperson (summer position)

LANGUAGE SKILLS: Fluent in Spanish and proficient in Portuguese

ACTIVITIES:
Public Relations Chair, **Student Interior Design Association** 2000–present
  • Participated in SIDA Mentor Program. Organized trips, contacted firms for visits, and publicized seminars for student participation.

SPECIAL SKILLS:
AutoCAD 14 and 2000, Adobe Photoshop, PageMaker and Illustrator. 3D Studio VIZ and MAX. Drafting Construction Documents, presentation boards.

OTHER: Interior Design Europe Summer Study Abroad Program, IIDA Student Charrette, IDEC Student Competition

Figure 12.6 Résumé suitable for faxing.

job application; but much less of your character will come through than with a printed résumé on good-quality paper.

It is important not to abuse this convenient, direct means of transmission. It is inappropriate to fax your résumé to every designer listed in the Yellow Pages or to the entire membership of a designers' organization. This is a form of "spam," or intrusive advertising, and it may be deeply resented by recipients. Résumés should be faxed only at the request of specific employers.

No matter what means you choose to transmit your résumé, it will make your case more effectively if is accompanied by a full-length, customized cover letter. As the old French saying goes, "The more things change, the more they remain the same."

Do not fax your résumé to every interior designer in the phone book. Fax it only by request.

Cover Letters

The cover letter (Figure 12.7, also on the CD-ROM) derives its name from the traditional practice of placing it on top of the print résumé, thus "covering" it, in an envelope for snail-mailing. The print cover letter—also known as a transmittal letter or letter of application—is usually a four- to five-paragraph, single-line spaced, one-page letter, direct and to the point. It is a standard business letter, with the sender's address and contact information, the recipient's address, and the date at the top. Often the sender's address and contact information have been specially formatted to create a letterhead. Microsoft's Word, among other programs, contains templates for the creation of business letterheads. (More on letterheads is discussed in Chapter 4.)

Always send a cover letter with your résumé or portfolio.

The cover letter is laid out consistently for easy reading, and visual appeal (see Chapter 5). If at all possible, it is addressed to a specific person by name. That person's name and title as well as the name of the company are correctly spelled.

The cover letter has three major objectives:

- To create favorable interest
- To provide perspective on the résumé
- To gain an interview

To achieve these objectives, the letter should include some or all of the following information:

- Current occupation
- Current field of employment
- Field of interest

Roland Laura-Marquez
16901 Vail Mill Road, Apartment 7H
Tacoma, WA 98406
(253) 555-6789
roland@athena.com

April 30, 2004

Ms. Frederica Schneider, ASID, IIDA
Director of Business Development
Rothstein-Chao Associates
84 Pacific Street, Suite 4801
San Francisco, CA 94105

Dear Ms. Schneider:

Your position announcement for a full-time junior designer piqued my interest. As a member of ASID and IIDA, I am confident that my knowledge in the field of interior design and my aptitude for the responsibilities of a junior designer make me both a qualified and a desirable applicant.

In final stages of class projects at Washington State University, I was responsible for the specification of interior finishes and materials, including color palettes. The exercise of this responsibility required familiarity with many different materials and finish options. In pursuing the Washington State interior design curriculum and in my internships, I have become proficient in AutoCAD 2000 and 3D Studio Viz. I have also acquired knowledge of DTP and image manipulation software through my work at Boldface Graphic Design.

I have a full command of the space-planning skills that are so fundamental to good design, both residential and commercial, and I am current with ADA codes.

In addition to my participation in the rigorous WSU interior design curriculum, I have been active in SIDA as the public relations chair. I coordinated off-campus trips and acted as liaison between students and working professionals, thus providing students with a better understanding of the interior design field.

I would welcome the opportunity to work with RCA as a productive team member. I believe the experience would be mutually rewarding. You may reach me at (253) 555-1212 to arrange an interview. I appreciate your time and consideration, and I will be in touch in two weeks to see if there is a possibility of joining your team.

Sincerely,

Roland Laura-Marquez

Roland Laura-Marquez

Figure 12.7 A cover letter for printing.

- Experience and education in the field
- Specific job or type of job desired

Some job seekers create a generic cover letter for all application situations, but career counselors suggest tailoring a cover letter to each job application. An interesting, well-written letter gives you the chance to present your communication skills and may gain you an interview. A poorly written letter that strikes readers as hasty or generic may cost you an interview opportunity. Some design firms reject candidates whose cover letters are poorly written without so much as glancing at their résumés! No matter how impressive your portfolio, you may not be a serious candidate for many promising positions if your cover letter does not demonstrate good writing skills, including accurate presentation of facts, good spelling, sound syntax, and clear organization.[4]

Organization of the Cover Letter

The body of the cover letter consists of three parts:

- Statement of the reason for writing
- Highlighting the job seeker's résumé
- Request for an interview

STATEMENT OF THE REASON FOR WRITING

Something prompted you to apply for the job you are seeking. Perhaps it was an ad in a newspaper or professional journal. Perhaps it was a conversation at an art opening. Perhaps it was something a senior designer said in a lecture to members of a local chapter of your professional organization. State simply and politely what prompted your application. Tell the employer what job you are interested in filling and how you learned of the opening. This introductory section of the cover letter usually contains no more than two sentences.

> Do not evaluate your accomplishments; let them speak for themselves.

HIGHLIGHTING THE RÉSUMÉ

Here you have the opportunity to customize your application to the needs of a specific employer. This is the heart of the cover letter. Remember to stress your accomplishments rather than your experience. The accomplishments you focus on should be specific and tangible. Your letter should single you out; but you are not writing the cover letter to brag, so do not evaluate your accomplishments. Let them speak for themselves and assume that a

> When highlighting your résumé in a cover letter, stress accomplishments rather than experience.

reader will regard them favorably. Above all, your cover letter needs to show a prospective employer how your skills and abilities would benefit the firm to which you are applying. If you are a recent graduate, emphasize studio work in areas that are a specialty of the firm to which you are applying.

Cultivate the "you" attitude in cover letters and other business writing.

THE "YOU" ATTITUDE   The ability to respond in a business situation in terms of others' needs rather than your own is sometimes called the "you" attitude. Displaying the "you" attitude in a cover letter means consciously trying to make a connection with the person reading the letter. It means demonstrating your knowledge of the employer's situation and telling your story in terms of the contribution you can make. One good way to demonstrate the "you" attitude is to avoid beginning the body of the letter with the word "I." Avoid beginning each paragraph with "I," too.

Apply only for jobs that match your skills and qualifications.

When responding to an ad or notice in which the job characteristics are clearly stated, it is a good idea to speak directly to these characteristics, explaining why you and the job are well suited to each other. Include in the cover letter only pertinent information, and apply only for jobs that seem to be a reasonable match with your skills and qualifications. To more effectively highlight your résumé, research the company to which you are applying and highlight accordingly. The first four items in the interview preparation checklist (Figure 12.8, also on the CD-ROM) suggest some good ways to look for information about a company to which you are applying. For example, if Henry discovers that a company specializes in restaurant design, he may highlight in his cover letter his experience as a restaurant manager.

If your previous work history does not fully support your application with design experience, emphasize transferable skills.

If you are a recent graduate and your previous work history does not fully support your application with design experience, then emphasize the transferable skills you have acquired. Like other prospective employers, designers want to hire people who can solve problems and provide satisfaction to clients or customers. They are looking for teamwork, communication skills, interpersonal skills, and leadership skills. Here is how one recently graduated job seeker highlighted her résumé in a letter of application for a junior designer's job:

> Some design work is accomplished by an individual working alone, while other parts of a design project require collaborative efforts. I work well independently as well as in groups. My first job was as a self-employed cookie baker and seller. As a member of the varsity women's lacrosse team at Metropolitan College, I learned to work toward common goals as part of a team.

Interview Preparation Checklist

____I have studied the company's literature, such as catalogs, brochures, press releases, and technical information hand-outs.

____I have visited the company's Web site and have made myself familiar with its features.

____I have researched the company in design publications, both print and online.

____I have a good understanding of the company's specialties, and its important and recent projects.

____I know who the firm's principals are, what they do within the firm, which projects they have worked on, where and how they were educated, what prizes they have won, and what has been written on or by them. I have noted areas of common interest with these individuals.

____I have conducted information interviews and read widely in design pub- lications, so I have a good sense of what is current in the field of interior design as a whole.

____I have prepared for the interview by visualizing the experience in advance and have jotted down the kinds of questions I expect to be asked as well as my answers to these questions.

____I have teamed up with other job hunters to interview each other—so we can hear hear how we sound when speaking out loud. We have given each other constructive feedback on oral interview strategies.

____I have done my transportation homework, and I know how to find the interview site in a timely manner. (Transportation homework may involve a call to the company and/or a visit to a trip-mapping Web site. In a dense urban setting that is unfamiliar to you, it may be prudent to take a cab to the interview location.)

____I have done my clothing-related homework. I have laid out and tried on an outfit that would be suitable for meeting the firm's most important client. (This will mean "business attire" for both men and women. Suit and tie are the norm for men, while women may choose a conservative suit, dress, or well-matched separates in subdued colors, with low-key acces- sories. Do not wear strong perfume or shaving lotion or jewelry that dan- gles, flashes, or makes noise.)

____I have specific salary requirements in mind. I have studied salary data for realistic figures that are relevant for my level of experience and in my geographical area.

____I have a clear sense of the information I would like to get from the interview.

Figure 12.8
Interview
preparation
checklist.

Let the cover letter supply relevant detail not in the résumé.

The cover letter should accurately reflect the résumé, but it need not cover the same ground. It can go into detail that the résumé cannot. For instance, if the prospective designer–employer specializes in art galleries and one of your projects in an advanced design class was an art gallery, then you might mention that project in your cover letter, though it may not have been mentioned in the résumé.

REQUEST FOR AN INTERVIEW

The final paragraph of the cover letter has a specific purpose: a pointed request for an interview. This paragraph should be short and should take a positive tone. Avoid a pleading manner. Rather than saying "If you desire to discuss my background and experience . . . I would very much welcome the opportunity to speak with you," say, "Please phone me at (212) 555-6789 between the hours of 9 and 5 to arrange an interview."

An e-cover letter is shorter and pithier than a printed one. Paste the résumé into the message below the signature of the cover letter, separated by asterisks.

The Electronic Cover Letter

In a time-conscious world, some job seekers omit the cover letter when e-mailing a résumé. Yet prospective employers appreciate your introducing yourself. They want to see how well you write, and they are interested in why you applied for this particular job at this particular company. It helps the employer for you to state clearly which job you are applying for and what you have to offer that makes your application notable. Like a printed-out cover letter, an electronic one provides an opportunity to inform the prospective employer of your qualifications and your potential for contributing to the company. In the electronic medium, you will want to convey your message in fewer words than in a printed-out cover letter, although a one-line letter would be too cursory.

In "The Elements of E-Mail Style," *Darwin* magazine columnist Scott Kirsner[5] recommends that cover letters and other e-mail be written in short paragraphs with white space in between so as to convey a desirable sense of "energy and urgency." Kirsner warns against e-mail letters that "consist of one long, blocky paragraph crammed with ideas."

Although much business e-mail contains neither a salutation nor a signature, it is a good idea to open an e-cover letter (Figure 12.9, also on the CD-ROM) with a greeting and to close it in a standard businesslike manner. Somewhere in the e-cover letter it is prudent to mention that your résumé is pasted into the e-mail below the signature block. Under your name in the signature block put your telephone number, street address, and e-mail address, so that it will be easy for prospective employers to get hold of you. Your résumé can be pasted in

Dear Ms. Schneider,

In response to your position announcement for a full-time junior designer, I am sending my résumé, which is inserted into this e-mail below the signature and contact data. As a member of ASID and IIDA, I am confident that my knowledge in the field of interior design and my aptitude for the responsibilities of a junior designer make me both a qualified and desirable applicant.

I am proficient in AutoCAD 2000 and 3D Studio Viz as well as DTP and image manipulation software. I have acquired space-planning skills and have been responsible for the specification of interior finishes and materials, including color palettes.

In addition to my participation in the Washington State University interior design curriculum, I have been active in SIDA as the public relations chair.

I would welcome the opportunity to work with RCA as a productive team member. You may reach me at 253-555-6789 if you have any questions. I appreciate your time and consideration, and I will be in touch in two weeks to arrange for an interview.

Sincerely,

Roland Laura-Marquez
****
ROLAND LAURA-MARQUEZ

16901 Vail Mill Road, Apartment 7H
Tacoma, WA 98406
253-555-6789
****
OBJECTIVE: To obtain an entry-level designer position and contribute to a dynamic team environment in a respected design firm.
****
EDUCATION: Washington State University, Pullman, WA 99164-2020, Bachelor of Arts in Interior Design, June 2004
****
EXPERIENCE: Harkman Roberts Design, Portland, OR
Summer Intern, Summer 2003

Redlined and drafted various CAD drawings in imperial and metric scale. Constructed presentation boards and designed small-scale furnishings for assisted-living facilities.
****
Hutchinson Valley Savings & Loan, Spokane, WA

Arranged and displayed my own photographs of historic buildings throughout Washington State. Designed display modules and invitations to opening reception.
****
Boldface Graphic Design & Printing, Pullman, WA
Associate Designer, 2000–2004

Communicated, designed, and displayed creative graphics solutions for businesses and individuals.
****
(continued)

Figure 12.9 An e-cover letter with pasted-in résumé.

Orangutan Bar and Grill, Seattle, WA
Waiter and Bartender, Summers 2001 and 2002
Food and beverage service salesperson.

****

LANGUAGE SKILLS: Fluent in Spanish and proficient in Portuguese

****

ACTIVITIES: Student Interior Design Association 2000–present
Public Relations Chair

Participated in SIDA Mentor Program. Organized trips, contacted firms for visits, and publicized certain seminars for student participation.

****

SPECIAL SKILLS: AutoCAD 14 and 2000, Adobe Photoshop, Pagemaker and Illustrator. 3D Studio VIZ and MAX. Drafting construction documents and presentation boards.

****

OTHER: Interior Design Europe Summer Study Abroad Program, IIDA Student Charrette, IDEC Student Competition.

Figure 12.9
(continued)

beneath a row of asterisks, a row of pluses, or a part-line created by holding down "shift" and the hyphen key.

Covering a Faxed Résumé

A faxed cover letter gains personality from a handwritten signature.

The cover document for a faxed résumé (see Figure 12.10, also on the CD-ROM) is often written on a special form, which can be created from a template, and looks more like a memo than a business letter. There is a memo-like heading, for instance, with "to" and "from" lines as well as date and subject lines. There is usually no salutation or greeting. The body of the fax-cover document, however, is similar to that of a letter, and its content is similar to that of other cover documents. The faxed cover letter gains personality from a handwritten signature, but it is not required.

The Interview

By whatever means the résumé and cover letter have been transmitted, the sender's goal is to gain an interview. In the setting of an actual interview, the printed-out résumé retains its traditional importance. It is customary for the job applicant to provide a print résumé for the convenience of each interviewer in a given firm—and there may be many. Bring copies of the résumé not only for the designers in the hiring department, but also for interviewers in human resources and elsewhere in the company. Keep a copy of your

---

FACSIMILE TRANSMITTAL SHEET

TO:	FROM:
Mary Parsons	**Roland Laura-Marquez**

COMPANY:	DATE:
Parsons Design	**6/7/2004**

FAX NUMBER	TOTAL NO, OF PAGES INCLUDING COVER:
(253) 555-1212	**3**

PHONE NUMBER:	SENDER'S REFERENCE NUMBER:
(253) 555-1212	**N.A.**

RE:	YOUR REFERENCE NUMBER:
Job Application	**N.A.**

☐ URGENT   X FOR REVIEW   ☐ PLEASE COMMENT X PLEASE REPLY   ☐ PLEASE RECYCLE

NOTES/COMMENTS:

In response to your position announcement for a full-time junior designer, I am sending my résumé. As a member of ASID and IIDA, I am confident that my knowledge in the field of interior design and my aptitude for the responsibilities of a junior designer make me both a qualified and a desirable applicant.

I am proficient in AutoCAD 2000 and 3D Studio Viz as well as DTP and image manipulation software. I have acquired space-planning skills and have been responsible for the specification of interior finishes and materials, including color palettes.

In addition to my participation in the Washington State University interior design curriculum, I have been active in SIDA as the public relations chair.

I would welcome the opportunity to work with Parsons Design as a productive team member. You may reach me at (253) 555-1212 if you have any questions. I appreciate your time and consideration. I will be in touch in two weeks to arrange for an interview.

Roland Laura-Marquez

16901 VAIL MILL ROAD, APARTMENT 7H, TACOMA, WA 98406
(253) 555-1212

Figure 12.10 Cover document for a faxed résumé.

résumé in front of you during an interview, so that you can respond more quickly and effectively to an interviewer's questions. To illustrate your creativity, competence, and computer skills, create a special presentation résumé.

Presentation Résumé with Project Photos

To create a résumé containing project photos, you need to have the appropriate images stored on your computer's hard drive, on a zip disk, or on a CD-ROM. If you have been taking project photos with a digital camera, you already have the electronic images you need. If your camera is not digital, then you need to scan in your photos or have them scanned at a full-service media shop. Once your project photos have been saved as electronic images, select clear and revelatory photos that work at a size you can use. Microsoft Word, among other programs, will permit you to insert images into a document and work with them in relation to text. Although Word lacks the capabilities of a full-fledged image-editing or layout program, Word enables you to improve the quality of your photos, to adjust their cropping and other features, and to position them on a page.

To insert a photo into a blank test document in MS Word, go to the Insert menu at the top of the document and choose "Picture." Then choose "From file" or "From scanner or camera." If you choose "From File," the "Insert Picture" screen will pop up. The address bar will instruct you by default to look in the Windows "My Pictures" file. You can practice picture insertion by double-clicking on any picture in "My Pictures" and inserting it into a blank document. If you right-click on the copy of the picture in the blank document, the picture toolbar appears. If you choose "format," you can crop, compress, and control for color, brightness, and contrast. Save the file as "Photo Insertion Test," so that you can return to it at any time to review your work and experiment further with the picture you have edited and saved.

You might like to try experimenting with picture and text. Type any text into "Photo Insertion Test," next to your picture. Your name will do, or "The quick brown fox jumps over the lazy dog." Now right-click on the photo again. This time choose "Format Picture," then choose the "layout" tab. Now try the different wrapping styles, and see how the text moves in relation to the picture. Be sure to save your work, for later reference and further practice. You will find on your CD-ROM, a template for creating a simple résumé with photos. The template will make it easier for you to insert your own photos into a presentation résumé. Not all printers can handle such a résumé, as quite a bit of printer memory is required. Printing your presentation résumé may involve a visit to a full-service media center.

Use the picture-insertion capabilities of your word-processing program to create a presentation résumé with project photos.

As you work with text and image, you will notice that the use of pictures cuts down on the amount of text that fits onto a page. That is why a photo-rich presentation résumé cannot substitute for an all-text résumé, though the photo résumé is a useful and appealing interview tool, a good conversational bridge to the portfolio, and a memorable souvenir to leave behind (more about leave-behinds later in this chapter).

Job Application Form

When you arrive at a company's offices, ready for an interview, you may feel that your time is being wasted if you are asked to fill out a generic job-application form with spaces for types of information already presented with painstaking care in your various résumés. Your feelings notwithstanding, you will be expected to comply with company practice, even though it means, from your point of view, a duplication of previous effort. Using your résumé as a reference, simply fill in the blanks on the form, though not before reading it first. Forms differ in the particular ways that information is organized—for instance, whether the applicant's name is written with the last name first or first name first. An initial read-through will help you avoid erasures and cross-outs. Print carefully, using all capital letters for maximum clarity. Remember, the application form, like your résumé, is part of the interview process that could lead to a job.

If you are asked to fill out a job application form, use your printed résumé as a guide.

To avoid erasures and cross-outs, read the entire application form before filling it out.

The Successful Interview

The Chinese character for "opportunity" was created by combining the characters for "preparation" and "luck." Nowhere is the wisdom of the ancient calligraphers more apparent than in the run-up to the employment interview. Figure 12.8 presents a checklist of interview preparation questions. You will note the importance of research, an important writing-related skill. Print out a copy of the checklist to help organize your preparation for each employment interview.

PREPARE FOR THE OBVIOUS QUESTIONS

All job seekers dread the prospect of difficult, unusual interview questions for which they are unprepared. Yet it is impossible to prepare for the unexpected. You would do better to expect and prepare for the obvious questions! You may be forgiven for stumbling when asked a subtle question, but if you are stymied by the obvious ones, you will certainly be crossed off any employer's short list. The questions you can expect are likely to fall into two categories—those that are typical of questions designers would be asked and those that would be asked of any job candidate in any field.

Prepare for the obvious interview questions so you won't stumble over them.

TYPICAL QUESTIONS FOR DESIGNERS   The hiring manager may ask about projects you have worked on at school or in the field. The manager may also inquire about your design philosophy; your work style; your relationship with colleagues, bosses and/or teachers; and the special projects and initiatives you are qualified to undertake. Recent design graduates may be asked about the basis for choosing the design schools they attended or the rationale for selecting a design major. More experienced job seekers may be asked how their previous experience relates to the work of the hiring firm and department, or the nature of the contribution they would like to make.

Interviewers often ask why a candidate wants this particular job; it is imprudent to come right out and say, "to eat and pay the rent," even if that is the case. A prospective employer wants to be flattered by your finding the firm attractive for its excellence and singularity.

TYPICAL QUESTIONS FOR ANY JOB SEEKER   Here is a short list of questions that experienced interviewers frequently ask job candidates in any field:

- What did you do at your last job? What were your responsibilities? In what ways and to whom were you accountable?
- What aspects of your job did you like the best?
- What aspects of your job did you like the least?
- Why did you leave your job?
- If you could have made one suggestion to your past management, what would it be?
- What have you done that you are proud of?
- Describe the best bosses you ever had.
- Describe the worst bosses you ever had.
- What is your greatest strength?
- What kinds of things bother you the most?
- What else should I know about your qualifications? Is there anything in particular you want to tell me about yourself?
- What are your career plans for the next year? The next five years?
- What are you seeking in this firm?
- What would you like to know about our company?

This list of generic job-interview questions is also featured on your CD-ROM. As noted in the preparation checklist, it is a good idea to think of answers to the typical questions—and questions you'd like to have answered—ahead of time. Then practice with a friend, having your friend select questions at random from the list.

PUTTING YOUR INTERVIEW RESEARCH INTO PRACTICE

Here are some other suggestions for conducting yourself well before and during an interview:

- Be on time. Not only should you have done your transportation homework (see preparation checklist in Figure 12.8) but you should make a point of arriving at the interview 10 to 15 minutes early. Use the extra time to relax and focus.
- Be friendly and polite. Shake hands firmly, sit straight in your chair, maintain eye contact, say "please" and "thank you," face the interviewer in a relaxed, open manner, and smile now and then.
- Treat secretaries and receptionists as carefully as you do design principals. They are far more than administrative support staff. They are often the "gatekeepers" and can be valuable allies if you are trying to follow up by contacting someone after the interview.
- Say "no"—nicely—to a cup of hot tea or coffee if offered, You do not want to be juggling a cup of scalding-hot liquid while trying to sound intelligent and focused.
- Be aware of your body language. Your tone of voice, posture, and facial expressions create an impression of your emotions and attitudes that should reinforce what you are saying with your words. Try not to fidget, slouch, roll your eyes, or look off into space.
- Enjoy yourself. Share your enthusiasm, energy, passion, and sense of humor. No need to change your personality or subdue your vitality. There is nothing appealing about indifference or passiveness. Let the interviewer see that you are authentic, honest, capable, and sincere.
- Do not try to be all things to all interviewers. Answer questions candidly. No one is qualified to do everything, and interviewers realize that.
- Present yourself in an articulate, professional manner. Speak concisely, clearly, and audibly. No mumbling and no rambling on and on and on! Use complete sentences. Avoid one-word answers and slang; and do not make racist, sexist, ageist or off-color remarks.

- Be positive. Keep the atmosphere friendly and pleasant. Don't criticize others or put them down to make yourself look good. Foreswear pettiness and personal animosity. This is especially important when answering tricky questions like "If you had one suggestion to make to your last boss, what would it be?"
- Put yourself in the position of the people interviewing you. They may be tired, pressed for time, overworked, and eager to get on with their own projects. Help them move things along. Rather than thinking ahead to your next opportunity to speak, listen actively to what is being said. When it is your turn, be alert to nonverbal cues indicating when you should start or stop talking. (A pause is often the sign that it is your turn to speak.)
- Look for common ground wherever you find it. Whenever appropriate, remark on the firm's special accomplishments. However, it is not necessary to praise each interviewing designer's projects in fulsome terms. Even if sincere, such praise can come off as unctuous.
- Don't take the interview process too personally. It has a rich personal element, of course, but the hiring manager and other interviewers are speaking to many job candidates, mostly strangers to them. It is unreasonable to expect an instant friendship to develop. Friendship may deepen in the future, but job interviews are professional interactions, and it is best to bear that in mind. Be charming and open, but not familiar.

THE LEAVE-BEHIND

Distinguish yourself from other job seekers with a memorable leave-behind.

Savvy designer-job seekers distinguish themselves from other job seekers with a memorable leave-behind. This could be a photo-project résumé or a portfolio introduction page. It could be a well-written memo, report, academic assignment, press release, specification sheet, or even (for the more experienced) a published article on a technical or design issue—for example, "Bio-Spectrum Lighting for the Healthy Work Place." Your leave-behind should epitomize the strengths that have been showcased in your portfolio, the all-important visual presentation of your design capabilities.

Portfolio Presentation

The portfolio is the principal means of presentation for designer job interviews.

The *portfolio* might be described as a capability packet for one person rather than for a firm. Traditionally the portfolio is an *album,* or book of visual materials, supported by text, the whole artfully displayed in a special binder and/or presentation case. The portfolio contents may be scanned onto a CD-ROM or posted on a Web site, but "the book" remains the principal means of presentation for job interviews and in other competitive situations.

Elements of the Portfolio

The portfolio needs to be prepared with great care and meticulous attention to detail. Although the images it contains are its core, the writing that accompanies the images is key to the success of the portfolio, which might be viewed as a "book," not only in presenting pages that are read in succession, but in presenting diverse elements that function as parts of a whole to create an overall impression of a designer's excellence. The written elements of portfolio presentation must be considered in conjunction with the other elements that comprise a successful "book."

Always submit your portfolio with a transmittal letter.

TRANSMITTAL LETTER

The portfolio is sometimes left with or sent to a prospective employer or other intended viewer. Or it may be transported to an interview situation. Even if you are presenting the portfolio in person, it should be accompanied by a *transmittal* (cover) *letter* that is similar to the letter of application previously discussed in this chapter. It states your reason for submitting the portfolio, summarizes your job qualifications, and expresses polite enthusiasm for the job or other opportunity for which you are being considered. If you have designed or commissioned a letterhead, perhaps with a logo (see Chapter 4), by all means write your transmittal letter on it. If the logo is reproduced on the introductory page of your portfolio, as well as on your business cards, your presentation will gain graphic coherence.

You can bind the transmittal letter (which may need to be matted) into your portfolio so that it won't get lost. Or you can put it in one of the side pockets of your binder or folder.

Choose your binder and case carefully.

CASE AND BINDER

The container in which you present your portfolio creates a viewer's first impression, so it needs to be well chosen and well maintained, and it should be discarded when it becomes shabby. Like the container for a firm's capability packet, it can be as simple as a two-pocket folder from a stationery or art-supply store. Or it can be more complicated—for instance, a spiral or (most typically) ring binder, alone or in a carrying case. There are many portfolio binder and case styles to choose from, including those presented in Figure 12.11.

Inexperienced presenters sometimes select the case after completing the presentation materials it will hold. However, it may be sounder practice to choose the case before preparing the materials it will contain. Whether you choose a case to accommodate the size and shape of your existing materials or format your materials to a specific case, choose a strong, well-made case and choose a practical portfolio size.

Although many design firms present original work such as boards and drawings in the 20-by-30-inch format, smaller-sized portfolios are easier to handle. Popular choices are 11-by-14-inches or 14-by-17-inches. Many designers choose the 11-by-17-inch format as the maximum board and drawing size. It is the largest size that will fit on most standard photocopying machines and equals two letter-sized pages side by side. Also acceptable are 8-by-10-inches and 16-by-20-inches You may have to simplify your drawings, eliminating detail, if you choose to reduce them for a small-format portfolio. If you must reduce to this extent, then consider providing a means for viewing your drawings in more detail—on a CD-ROM, for instance. Or you might bring along *one* or *two* rolled drawings if you feel it is appropriate for a particular interview; it would not be inconvenient to do so; and travel restrictions do not prevent you.

The work samples in your portfolio support the claims made in your résumé.

Size is by no means your only consideration. Examine such issues as corner treatment, hardware, finish, deployment of storage pockets, and the type of sleeves the case accommodates. The selection of a case needs to be determined by aesthetic as well as practical considerations. Like your speech, your attire, and your writing style, your portfolio container makes a statement about you as a designer. This statement should confirm the impression created by the work samples that are your portfolio's principal reason for being.

PORTFOLIO CONTENTS

The written portions of your portfolio tell viewers how to look at the materials you are presenting.

The contents of your portfolio should set you apart from others and express your special qualities as an interior designer. The work samples should be chosen to reflect your best efforts and to showcase the full range of your skills and expertise. They provide the visual evidence for the claims you make in your résumé, displaying your creativity, organization, technical skills, drawing ability, and knowledge of materials. Although subsidiary, the written portions of your portfolio, such as the captions, labels, titles, and statement of purpose, not only showcase your writing ability but tell viewers how to look at the materials you are presenting.

The portfolio should *not* be a collection of all the work you have ever done. Choose only your best, and choose each part with a sense of the whole presentation. Don't overwhelm the viewer. Four to six projects are enough to present, and it is a good idea to include at least one complete project presentation. Your portfolio needs to contain the following:

Show only your best work, not all you have done.

- Samples of your CAD work
- Rendered 3-D illustrations, computer or manually generated
- Perspectives, elevations, and axonometric drawings
- Working drawings and concept sketches
- Color boards
- Presentation plans
- Project photographs
- Publication offprints or reprints

Choose a definite orientation for viewing the portfolio—either vertical ("portrait") or horizontal ("landscape"). The portfolio in portrait orientation can be shown in a folio format, in which the pages are turned from left to right. It may also be shown in a flip format, in which the spine is parallel to a desk or table and the pages are flipped upward and back. A portfolio in landscape orientation works best in flip format. Select the orientation to showcase your particular design materials. Here are some other tips to help you get started:

Choose portrait or landscape orientation for viewing the portfolio.

- Begin and end with your most dramatic materials.
- Do include fabric swatches, paint chips, and other samples to provide texture and demonstrate your versatility. (Note: Any two-dimensional image—not just a drawing or photo, but any shallow object such as a fabric swatch—can be scanned into a computer as an image. For three-dimensional objects, better results may be achieved with a digital or video camera.)
- Choose a flexible format that permits you to customize your portfolio to each viewer, based on your pre-interview research.
- Use different page layouts to add variety and interest to the portfolio, creating unity with recurring elements such as background, placement of logo, and page-number styling.
- Choose relevant, striking project photographs. Arrange them so that their relationship on the page is clear, taking into account issues of flow, balance, and composition.
- Hand-letter if you are good at it. Many design firms value this skill. It is also fine to use press-on lettering or computer-generated type for titles, labels, captions, and other text. Don't get carried away. Too many fonts and type sizes make for a cluttered look that confuses and distracts viewer-readers.

Figure 12.11
Portfolio/
presentation
cases.

PORTFOLIO PRESENTATION CASE (W/O BINDER)

ADVANTAGES
Can customize with separately purchased binder.

OPTIONS
Retractable or spine-mounted handle, convertible to shoulder strap; brass or nylon zipper, exterior and/or interior pockets; outside identification; available in vinyl, canvas, or nylon with custom options (i.e., leather, suede, cork, velvet)

EXAMPLES
Design NSM Tank: Eberhard Faber/Design Convertible

Zippered presentation case (without binder) with handle and shoulder strap.

SEPARATELY PURCHASED BINDER

Seperately purchased binder with Chicago screw binding.

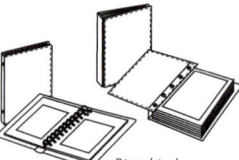

Ring binder.

ADVANTAGES
Can customize with separately purchased case; allows for more than one portfolio.

DISADVANTAGES
Components may not match.

OPTIONS
Multi-ring brass or nylon mechanism; Chicago screw binding with extention posts, expandable from $1/2"$ to $3"$; cartridge rod binder with inserts that snap in and out of book; easel book; exterior and/interior pockets; inserts available in vinyl, acetate, or polypropylene, multi-punched or welded edge, sealed on one side or three, pebbled or smooth surface.

EXAMPLES
Prat ShowBook with Chicago screw binding; Prat Compact Book; Prat Classic 102; Prat Run 110 Rod Binder; Prat Easel Slimbook.

ZIPPERED PRESENTATION CASE (BINDER ATTACHED)

Zippered presentation case (binder attached) with spine-mounted handle

ADVANTAGES
Economical and lightweight

DISADVANTAGES
No flexibility in binder options.

OPTIONS
Retractable or spine-mounted handle, convertible to shoulder strap; brass or nylon zipper, exterior and/or interior pockets;outside identification; available in vinyl, canvas, or nylon with custom options (i.e., leather, suede, cork, velvet)

EXAMPLES
Design NSM Show case Presentation Case; Design NSM Blackmaster.

Figure 12.11
(*continued*)

ZIPPERED PRESENTATION CASE WITH REMOVABLE BINDER

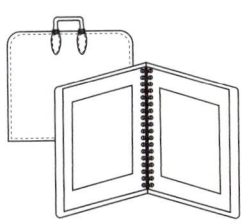

*Zippered presentation case
with removable binder.*

ADVANTAGES
Can use portfolio separately, Cna buy additional replacement albums.

OPTIONS
Retractable or spine-mounted handle, convertible to shoulder strap; brass or nylon zipper, exterior and/or interior pockets; outside identification; available in vinyl, canvas, or nylon with custom options (i.e., leather, suede, cork, velvet)

EXAMPLES
Design NSM Presentfolio; Prat Mera 300.

EASEL PRESENTATION CASE

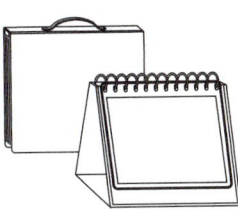

*Easel presentation case
(landscape orientation).*

ADVANTAGES
Converts to an easel for hands-free tabletop presentations.

DISADVANTAGES
No flexibility in binder options.

OPTIONS
Retractable or spine-mounted handle, convertible to shoulder strap; brass or nylon zipper, exterior and/or interior pockets; outside identification; available in vinyl, canvas, or nylon with custom options (i.e., leather, suede, cork, velvet); landscape (horizontal) or portrait (vertical) orientation; multi-ring, Chicago screw or rod welded binding; inserts available in vinyl, acetate, or polypropylene, multi-punched or welded edge, sealed on one side or three, pebbled or smooth surface.

EXAMPLES
Prat Classic - 202; Design NSM Showcase Delux Easel Album.

CUSTOM CRAFTED PORTFOLIOS

Custom crafted portfolio.

ADVANTAGES
Can be made any size, with any material.

DISADVANTAGES
Expensive.

OPTIONS
Unlimited.

EXAMPLES
Presentation Box and Portfolio book by Brewer-Cantelmo*; The Elegante, a book and case all in one; The Traygante, a sleek book/box combination.

*Brewer-Cantelmo in New York City has been in the business of making custom portfolios for over 65 years. You can choose from a variety of materials or supply your own.

- Select a legible *font,* or typeface.
- Deploy color richly, but not *too* richly. For best effect, use small doses of intense color.
- Since a viewer tends to see a double-page spread as one concept, have an even number of pages for each section of a portfolio in portrait orientation. If one section ends on the left-hand page and a new one begins on the right-hand page, a viewer may become confused.
- Employ glue that will not bleed to create unsightly blotches.
- Manipulate negative space effectively. There should be enough, but not too much.

INTRODUCTORY PAGE   The introductory page is the first right, or "recto," page in a book-style portfolio. In flip format, the introductory page is the first single page presented. Although this page is sometimes left blank, it represents an opportunity to make a clear statement about you as a designer. Sometimes a design category or specialty can inspire a specially created graphic. Cultural references or symbols can also inspire an intro-page graphic. (Layout-design applications can be used to create a collage of images, another option.) A personal logo on the intro page can contribute significantly to the coherence of your overall presentation. It may be an enlargement of your letterhead logo. Or your intro page may consist of brief introductory text placed on your letterhead stationery and centered on a portfolio page. (If the text is more than a page long, use plain paper matching your letterhead paper for the second page. The introductory text should not be more than two printed pages.)

Extra copies of your introductory text can be a good leave-behind piece. Or an entire intro page in a larger format can be photocopied and reduced to 8$^1/_2$ by 11 inches and thus converted to a leave-behind piece—an inexpensive process, even for color. Keep copies of the intro statement or reduced intro page in the side pocket of your portfolio, along with your résumé.

Use the introductory page as a statement of purpose presenting your vision.

STATEMENT OF PURPOSE   An introductory text is usually a statement of purpose that tells a viewer why the portfolio materials are being presented. It introduces your vision, your outlook on the world of interior design, and the place you see yourself occupying within it. Such a statement can provide valuable perspective on your portfolio as a whole.

DESCRIPTIONS AND CAPTIONS FOR DESIGN IMAGES   In the body of the portfolio, the various parts need to be identified and, where necessary, explained by titles, labels, captions, descriptions, and statements. These are similar to the texts described in Chapter 4 for the capability brochure. They make your portfolio self-explanatory if you are not there to talk about the projects. They explain the problem solutions represented by the images. To some extent, the texts that support your visual material play the part that you would play if you were present to talk your portfolio through.

The Talk-Through

When interviewers are ready to view your portfolio, they will usually tell you where in the office to place it, often on a desk or tabletop. If any setup is required (as for an easel presentation case), offer your assistance. Then, as invited, you can talk the portfolio through, commenting on your inspiration, influences, design concepts, and overall perspective. Needless to say, it will help you with the important presentations to have practiced your talk-through at every opportunity. Realize that effective images speak volumes, so don't over-explain.

> The texts that support your visual material play the part that you would play if you were present to talk through your portfolio.

After the Interview

Soon after the interview, while it is still fresh in your mind, debrief yourself. Write down your impressions of what went well and what did not. If you were offered the job, would you take it? What do you wish you had done differently, and how do you wish you had done it? What unanswered questions do you have?

Thank-You Letter

Whatever the results of the interview, it is good news to be invited for a conversation about the ways in which your skills and experience might benefit the interviewing firm. After an interview, it is customary to send a brief thank-you letter to the hiring manager. Although e-mail is acceptable in some situations, the thank-you is usually a short, printed-out document sent via snail mail on your letterhead. (You may read more on the business thank-you letter in Chapter 5.) Be sure to let your interviewer know how much you enjoyed the conversation. It is important to express your interest in being considered for any future jobs that arise.

Discussion Questions

1. In a whole-class discussion, brainstorm the possibilities for writing a convincing thank-you letter after a negative-result job interview. Can you as a class come up with 25 appropriate areas for gratitude? A hundred?

2. What is the difference between lying and describing the work you have done in a richly positive manner? Is there a fine line between the two? If so, how do you know when you have crossed it?

3. If you win a design competition as part of a team, how should you credit the award in your résumé?

Exercises

1. Let each student in your class bring in a set of swatches and drawings created for a studio design project. In small groups, develop guidelines for creating group portfolios from the materials brought in. Each group should prepare an oral presentation of five minutes in which all members of the group participate.

2. Prepare a two-page print résumé in the combination format; then prepare an all-text version that is suitable for pasting into the body of an e-mail.

3. Find and bring to class an ad for an interior design job that is suitable for a person of your skills and abilities. Highlighting the résumé(s) you wrote for Exercise 2, write a cover letter in which you apply for the job.

4. Conduct an informational interview with an interior design professional whom you respect, seeking not employment but knowledge of the profession and the firm's philosophy, manner of working with clients, and criteria for selecting new employees. (Make it very clear to your interview subject that you are doing research, not looking for a job.) Take careful notes. Using techniques and strategies that you learned in Chapter 9, write a brief report presenting what you learned from your interview.

Notes

Chapter 1

1. Thomas S. Hines, "Windows into Their Work: Architects as Writers." *The New York Times Book Review*, September 8, 1985.
2. Patti Fasan, "Selecting and Specifying the Right Tile for the Right Client." (Surfaces 2004 Conference, January 28–30, 2004, Sands Expo and Convention Center, Las Vegas, Nevada). Patti Fasan is a certified Ceramic Tile Consultant.
3. *The American Heritage Dictionary of the English Language*, 4th ed. (Boston: Houghton Mifflin, 2000). Consulted online at www.bartleby.com.
4. Sheila Danko, "Beneath the Surface: A Story of Leadership, Recruitment, and the Hidden Dimensions of Strategic Workplace Design," *Journal of Interior Design* (Special Issue on Narrative Inquiry) Vol. 26, no. 2, (2000): 16.
5. Ibid., 15.
6. Ibid., 21.
7. Margaret Portillo and Joy H. Dohr, "Creativity and Narrative in Eva Maddox Associates," *Journal of Interior Design* (Special Issue on Narrative Inquiry). Vol. 26, no. 2, (2000): 42. Portillo teaches at the University of Kentucky, Dohr at the University of Wisconsin-Madison.
8. Ibid., 44.
9. Ibid., 55.
10. Paul Goldberger, *Esquire*, September 1977, cited in *On the Rise: Architecture and Design in a Postmodern Age* (New York: Viking Penguin, 1985.)
11. Adapted from "Good Business Writing: Helpful Hints," a manual prepared by Gail Cain for business-writing students at the University of Sioux Falls (SD) and for various corporate clients, 2003.
12. Restoration Hardware Catalog, Holiday 2003, 68.
13. Standards adapted from Fasan, "Selecting and Specifying the Right Tile for the Right Client."
14. Cain, "Good Business Writing: Helpful Hints," 15.

15. Discussion of formality adapted from Charles T. Brusaw, Gerald J. Alred, and Walter E. Oliu, *The Business Writer's Handbook*, 4th ed. (New York: St. Martin's Press, 1993.)

16. Ibid., 30.

17. Cain, "Good Business Writing: Helpful Hints."

18. Richard C. Wydick, *Plain English for Lawyers*, 4th ed. (Durham, N.C.: Carolina Academic Press, 1998.)

19. Edward P. Bailey, Jr., *The Plain English Approach to Business Writing* (New York: Oxford University Press, 1990), 5–6.

20. Ibid., 12.

21. Ibid., 22–23.

22. Cain, "Good Business Writing: Helpful Hints."

23. Discussions of nested modifiers and elegant variation adapted from Wydick, *Plain English for Lawyers*, 52–53, 74–75.

24. From Pat Holt's "The '10 Mistakes' List," *Holt Uncensored #376*, October 9, 2003. *Holt Uncensored* is an online column archived at http://www.holtuncensored.com. Pat Holt is a former book editor at *The San Francisco Chronicle*.

25. Ibid.

26. Ibid.

27. Based on descriptions found at http://www.metmuseum.org/works-of-art/department.asp?dep=10.

28. Holt, *Holt Uncensored*.

29. Cited in, John Bayley, "Silent Music," *The New York Review of Books*, l, no. 18, November 20, 2003.

30. Robert Gunning as cited in Stephen A. Kliment, *Writing for Design Professionals*. (New York: W. W. Norton, 1998), 212–14.

31. Ibid., 214–15.

32. Wydick, 85–86.

33. Bailey, 58.

34. Book selections adapted from Martin Kohl, *The Freelancer's Bookshelf*. (New York: Editorial Freelancers Association, 1994).

35. "The Editing and Writing Process," from *Guide to Grammar and Writing*, maintained by Prof. Charles Darling for students at Capital Community College, Hartford, CT., 2003. http://ccc.commnet.edu/grammar/composition/editing.htm.

36. Ibid.

Chapter 2

1. Henry Adams, *Mont Saint Michel and Chartres* (New York: Doubleday Anchor, 1959), 96–97.

2. *Architectural Forum*, 1951, as cited in *Frank Lloyd Wright: Writings and Buildings*, selected by Edgar Kaufmann and Ben Raeburn (Cleveland: Meridian, 1967).

3. "Sight into Insight," *Harper's*, February 1974.

4. *The Languages of Art*, 1968, as cited in Sylvan Barnet's *A Short Guide to Writing about Art*, 5th ed. (New York: Longman, 1996), 17.

5. Kimberly Dovey, "Putting Geometry in its Place: Toward a Phenomenology of the Design Process," in *Dwelling, Seeing, and Designing: Toward a Phenomenological Ecology*, ed. David Seamon (Albany, NY: SUNY Press, 1993), 251–52, 254. The concept is attributed to E. Relph, *Place and Placelessness* (London: Pion, 1976).

6. Brochure, Chelsea Art Museum, May 2003. See also Light Art Collection captioning at Targetti Web site, www.targetti.com.

7. "Writing Guidelines for Interior Design Students," http://www.interior design.cavs.vt.edu/vtid/IDwriting/guides/conceptual.html.

8. Developed by Synectics Inc., Cambridge, MA, and explained by James L. Adams, *Conceptual Blockbusting: A Guide to Better Ideas* (San Francisco: W. H. Freeman, 1974), 117–118.

9. *Writing without Teachers* (New York: Oxford University Press, 1973), 55.

10. Ibid.

11. Ibid., 53–54.

12. From IDEC bulletin board discussion, IDEC@egroups. Dr. McGinnis teaches at the Academy of Art College, San Francisco.

13. Elbow, *Writing Without Teachers*, 52.

14. James L. Adams, *Conceptual Blockbusting: A Guide to Better Ideas,* 87.

15. Dan Beert, IIDA, IDEC letter to author, March 7, 2002. He draws on ideas presented at greater length and in greater detail in Donna Duerk's *Architectural Programming: Information Management for Design.*

16. "Writing Guidelines for Interior Design Students," http://www.interiordesign. caus.vt.edu/vtid/IDwriting/guides/conceptual.html.

17. Ken Coberg and Dan Bagnall, *Universal Traveler: A Soft-Systems Guidebook to Creativity, Problem-Solving, and the Process of Design* (Los Angeles, William Kaufmann, 1974), cited in Adams, *Conceptual Blockbusting: A Guide to Better Ideas*, 82, 83.

18. Virginia Polytechnic and State University, "Writing Guidelines for Interior Design Students," http://www.interiordesign.caus.vt.edu/vtid/IDwriting/ guides/conceptual.html.

19. Ibid.

20. Ibid.

21. Ibid.

22. Ibid.

23. All concept-building examples are taken from the Virginia Polytechnic Institute and State University Web site "Writing Guidelines for Interior Design Students."

24. Cited in Sylvan Barnet, *A Short Guide to Writing about Art*, 5th ed., 26.

25. "Thick Description: Toward an Interpretative Theory of Culture," in *The Interpretation of Cultures* (New York: Basic Books, 1973), 24–25.

26. "Innovative Teaching Ideas: Introduction to Interior Design," http:// idec.org/iti/deruiz_design.html.

27. Sample questions taken from "Tips on Journalistic Writing at the S & B," *Scarlet and Black Online Stylebook and Writing Manual,* http://web. grinnell.edu/sandb/stylebook/journalism.htm.

28. Listening techniques adapted from Charles T. Brusaw, Gerald J. Alred, and Walter E. Oliu, *Handbook of Technical Writing*, 4th ed. (New York: St. Martin's: 1993), 402–403.

29.   *Workplace by Design: Mapping the High-Performance Workscape* (San Francisco: Jossey-Bass), 160.

30.   Qualities of creativity identified by Michael Ray, who teaches a course in "Personal Creativity in Business" at Stanford University. See Curtis Sittenfeld, "The Most Creative Man in Silicon Valley," *Fast Company*, No. 35, January 2000, 274. http://www.fastcompany.com/online/35/ray.html.

31.   *Workplace by Design: Mapping the High Performance Workplace*, 156–59.

32.   Amy Treff, personal note to author, October 3, 2003.

33.   Excerpt from *Kid's City: A Unique Concept*. Unpublished proposal.

34.   Adapted from Becker and Steele, *Workplace by Design*, 162.

35.   Cited in Donna Duerk's *Architectural Programming: Information Management for Design* (New York: Van Nostrand Reinhold, 1993), 40.

36.   Interview guidelines adapted from *Handbook of Technical Writing*, 4th ed., by Brusaw, Alred, and Oliu (New York: St. Martin's, 1993), 345–346.

37.   "Tips on Journalistic Writing at the S & B."

38.   Ibid.

39.   *Innovation*, Spring 2003: Collideoscope Section. Jim Couch, IDSA, is the founder of Substance Design Group. E-mail: jcouch2@columbus.rr.com. http://new.idsa.org/webmodules/articles/articlefiles/spring03_riverdance.pdf

Chapter 3

1.   Adapted from Allen Danzig and Edith Schor's *Thesis: Rhetoric of the Essay*, 2nd ed. (Belmont, CA: Wadsworth Publishing Co., 1980), 127–128.

2.   Ibid., 127.

3.   Informal logic, rather than the formal logic of philosophical inquiry.

4.   Dan Beert and Gail Cummins, "Space and Multiple Intelligences: Finding the Multidisciplinary Process," paper presented at conference, Writing Across the Curriculum. Cornell University, Ithaca, NY, 1999. Beert spoke as Assistant Professor of Interior Design, University of Kentucky, Cummins as Director of the University of Kentucky Writing Center.

5.   *Architectural Programming: Information Management for Design*. (New York: Van Nostrand Reinhold, 1993), 24.

6.   Ibid.

7.   Daniel G. Riordan and Steven E. Pauley, *Technical Report Writing Today*, 6th ed. (Boston: Houghton Mifflin, 1996), 148.

8.   Duerk, *Architectural Programming*, 34.

9.   Ibid., 39.

10.   Dan Beert, IIDA, IDEC letter to the author, March 7, 2002.

11.   Duerk, *Architectural Programming*, 43.

12.   National Research Council of Canada, "Preferred Luminous Conditions in Open-Plan Offices: Research and Practice Recommendations," http://irc.nrc-cnrc.gc.ca/fulltext/ncrc43061/nrcc43061.pdf.

13.   Duerk, *Architectural Programming*, 70.

14.   Definition of sprung floor and first three implementations from "Dance Floors," http://www.calarts.edu/~dk/flooring.html. The fourth implementation adapted from "The Dance Floor" at the Web site for Catalina Island, http://www.ecatalina.com/museum/casino4.asp.

15.   Duerk, *Architectural Programming*, 70.

16. Ibid., 76.

17. http://www.umass.edu/buscomm/critanal.html.

18. Charles T. Brusaw, Gerald J. Alred, and Walter E. Oliu, *The Business Writer's Handbook*, 4th ed. (New York: St. Martin's Press, 1993), 198.

19. http://www.vcu.edu/artweb/interiors/define_ides/scope_body.html.

20. Danzig and Schor, *Thesis: Rhetoric of the Essay*, 2nd ed., 128.

21. Discussion of case study draws on the insights of Christine M. Piotrowski (ASID, IIDA), *Professional Practice for Interior Designers*, 3rd ed. (New York: John Wiley & Sons, 2002), 372–374.

22. Adapted from David McClain's "Guidelines for Business Case Analysis and Write-Up," created November 17, 2000, http://web.uccs.edu/dmclain/GuidelinesforCaseAnalysis.htm.

23. Duerk, *Architectural Programming*, 111.

24. Ibid., 111.

25. Christopher Budd, "Narrative Research in Design Practice: Capturing Mental Models of Work Environments," IDEC: *Journal of Interior Design* 26, no. 2 (2000): 59.

26. Margaret Portillo and Joy H. Dohr, "Creativity and Narrative in Eva Maddox Associates," IDEC: *Journal of Interior Design*, 26, no. 2 (2000): 44.

27. Ibid., p. 44.

28. Sheila Danko, Margaret Portillo, Ann Black, Christopher Budd, Joan McLain-Kark, and Joy H. Dohr, "Real Time Relevance," ISdesigNET: (July/August 1999), http://www.isdesignet.com/Magazine/J-A'99/FIDER/real.thml.

29. Katie Sosnowchik, "The Lessons We Learn," http://www.isdesignet.com/Magazine/03j_a/fider-lessons.html.

30. Ibid.

31. Portillo and Dohr, "Creativity and Narrative in Eva Maddox Associates," 44.

32. Danko, et al., "Real-Time Relevance."

33. Sosnowchik, "The Lessons We Learn."

34. Budd, "Narrative Research in Design Practice," 60.

35. Budd, 60–61.

36. Ibid, 61.

37. Danko, et al., "Real-Time Relevance."

38. Sosnowchik, "The Lessons We Learn."

39. Budd, "Narrative Research in Design Practices," 61.

40. Kerry Walk, "How to Write a Comparative Analysis," The Writing Center at Harvard University, 1998, http:www.fas.harvard.edu/~wricntr/documents/CompAnalysis.html.

41. Ibid.

42. Ibid.

43. Ibid.

44. Jack Sanders, "Curtain Wars," *Harvard Design Magazine*, no. 16 (Winter/Spring 2002), http://www.gsd.harvard.edu/research/publications/hdm/back/16sanders.html. Of his use of the archaic term *decorator* in this article, Sanders says the following: "The term 'decorator' ... is now considered both obsolete and pejorative: it evokes the image of

'decoration,' a culturally denigrated concept that I . . . call into question. . . . I . . . use the labels 'decorator' and 'interior designer' interchangeably, to both politicize and historicize the activity of 'decorating' domestic space." Since too small an excerpt of Sanders's essay is reproduced here for the scope of his strategy to be fully apparent, I have replaced Sanders's references to decorators with the more current term *interior designer*.

45.   Paraphrase of Charles A. Riley II's *Color Codes: Modern Theories of Color in Philosophy, Painting and Architecture, Literature, Music, and Psychology* (Hanover and London: University Press of New England, 1995), 298–299.

46.   *Technical Report Writing Today*, 6th ed. (Boston: Houghton Mifflin, 1996), 140.

47.   Ibid., 141.

48.   For our purposes in this chapter, summaries and abstracts are the same thing.

49.   From "Online Guide to Writing and Research," University of Maryland University College, http://www.umuc.edu/prog/ugp/ewp_writingcenter/ writinggde/chapter3/ch3-06.html.

50.   Adapted from "Writing Up Research: Using the Literature," Asian Institute of Technology, http://www.languages.ait.ac.th/EL21LIT.HTM.

51.   "Writing a Literature Review in the Health Sciences and Social Work," University of Toronto Health Sciences Writing Center, wysiwyg://122/http:// www.utopronto.ca/hswriting/lit-review.htm.

52.   "Writing Up Research: Using the Literature." Asian Institute of Technology, http://www.languages.ait.ac.th/EL21LIT.HTM.

Chapter 4

1.   Vilma Barr, course description for "Image: An Important Marketing Tool," a Pocket CEU [Continuing Education Unit] that is available through the ASID Web site, www.asid.org.

2.   "Business Identity," August 7, 2002, http://www.crane.com/business/ business-identity/.

3.   Olivia Bell Buehl, "Marketshare: Size Doesn't Matter," August 7, 2002, http://www.asid.org/design_basics/marketing_presentations/markets.

4.   Lexicon, "Our Methodology," www.lexiconbranding.com/process4b Appproach.html. [sic]

5.   Namelab, Inc., San Francisco, CA., http://www.namelab.com/function.html.

6.   www.lexiconbranding.com.

7.   Barr, course description.

8.   Workstage LLC, www.workstage.com/better.html.

9.   In "Top 7 Desktop Publishing Software Programs," Jacci Howard Bear also recommends Adobe InDesign, QuarkXPress, Corel Ventura, Serif PagePlus, and Adobe FrameMaker. See her capsule reviews at http://desktoppub.about.com/cs/software/tp/dtpsoftware.htm?PM=ss0 3_desktoppub.

10. Review of Microsoft Office System, Product Release Date: October 21, 2003. *ZD Net: Reviews,* http://reviews-zdnet.com/4520-3513_16-5092597.html?tag=text.

11. Carol Davitt, *Marketing Your Remodeling Services: Putting the Pieces Together* (Washington, D.C.: Homebuilder Press, 1993).

12. "Marketing Workshop/Before and After," *Remodeling* (September 2000), 40. Dr. Linda Wagner is Associate Chair of Marketing, R. H. Smith School of Business, University of Maryland.

13. August 12, 2002. *Computer Tips.* This newsletter is published by the software store Worldstart and is available through www.worldstart.com. Kinko's also publishes a good newsletter containing tips and tricks for creating effective graphic design.

14. Tom Dalton, in the August 12, 2002, issue of *Computer Tips.*

15. Janet Wagner, "Marketing Workshop: Before + After Critique of a Business Card Redesign." *Remodeling* (9/01/2002), 40.

16. Jonathan Lang, "Appendix A, Glossary of Terms," *Email Desktop Publishing Course,* posted at http://multimedia.rice.iit.edu/lesson4/dtp/appendixa.html.

17. Ibid.

18. Ibid.

19. Ibid.

20. Clifford Burke, *Printing It: A Guide to Graphic Techniques for the Impecunious* (New York: Ballantine, 1972), 84.

21. JAM. Conversation with the author, July 2003.

22. Burke, *Printing It,* 85.

23. "Make Business Cards Using Word 2002."

24. Barr, op. cit.

25. See Web site for J. Tilghman Interior Design, www.jtidworx.com, and Web site for Bauer Interior Design, www.bauerdesign.com.

26. http://www.op.nysed.gov/idbroch.htm. Web sites for other state-regulating agencies are listed at http://www.dezignare.com/interior_designers/agencies.html.

27. *The Environments Group: 2001 Annual Report.*

28. http://www.istudiodesign.com/.

29. Eastman Kodak Company (Rochester, NY, 1943).

30. Adapted from http://www.paperdirect.com/tip-p08.html.

31. Cindy Ballaro, interview with the author, September 26, 2002. Ballaro is proprietor, Marketing Matters, Charlotte NC, www.marketingmatters.com.

32. Jeanne Jennings. "For Better E-mail Results, Survey Your Audience," www.clickz.com/em_mmkt/opt/article.php/1419781.

33. UNCW University Center, Wilmington, NC. Client was Jefferies & Faris Architects, Wilmington, NC.

34. http://www.pmc.purdue.edu/pages/web/web_write_guide.html.

35. http://www.inkwelleditorial.com/e-online.htm.

36. Ibid.

37. Burke, *Printing It,* p. 87.

38.   Ibid., 93.

39.   Clodagh, *Total Design: Contemplate, Cleanse, Clarify, and Create Your Personal Spaces*; Lady Henrietta Spencer-Churchill, *Classic English, Classic Decorative Details, Classic Fabrics, Classic Georgian Style, Classic Meets Contemporary*; Conway Lloyd Morgan and Philippe Starck, Roderick N. Shade, Jorge S. Arango, and Peter Madero, *Harlem Style: Designing for the New Urban Aesthetic*.

40.   "Plumping a Career by Writing a Book," *The New York Times*, August 18, 2002.

41.   Ballaro, interview with author, September 26, 2002.

Chapter 5

1.   Jay Conrad Levinson, *Guerrilla Marketing: Secrets for Making Big Profits from Your Small Business* (Boston: Houghton Mifflin, 1984), 73.

2.   Ruth E. Gavin and William A. Sabin, *Reference Manual for Stenographers and Typists*, 4th ed. (New York: Gregg Division/McGraw-Hill Book Company, 1970), 211–215.

3.   Levinson, *Guerrilla Marketing*, 76–77.

4.   Allison Cobb, "Affinity Groups: EFA Membership Pays Off," *The Freelancer* (Editorial Freelancers Association). 27, no. 1. (September–October 2002), 6–7.

5.   Levinson, *Guerrilla Marketing*, 75.

6.   Chris Engel, panelist's untitled presentation, "Art of the Proposal" (panel discussion sponsored by the Computer Instruction Center at New School University, New York City, November 1, 2002).

7.   Levinson, *Guerrilla Marketing*, 74.

8.   Laura Mankin, "Basic Contract Law for Interior Designers" in *Business and Legal Forms for Interior Designers*, Tad Crawford and Eva Doman Bruck, eds. (New York: Allworth Press, 2001), 17.

9.   Tad Crawford, "Proposal Form," *Business and Legal Forms for Interior Designers*, 52.

10.   Art of the Proposal (panel discussion at New School University, New York, NY, 2002), announcement flyer.

11.   Gerre L. Jones, *How to Market Professional Design Services* (New York: McGraw-Hill, 1973), 110.

12.   Diane Wintroub Calmenson, "Building Relationships."*ISdesigNET*, May 1996, p. 2, http://www.isdesignet.com/Magazine/May'96/co0ver.html.

13.   Kate Hartnick, "Art of the Proposal," panelist's untitled presentation.

14.   Cynthia Rock, Senior Project Manager, Department of Capital Planning and Construction, The New York Public Library. Personal communication, March 2, 2004.

15.   Prepared by Yvonne Knighton, Small Business Technical Advisor, Federal Supply Service, April 2002.

16.   Walter Maxwell, panelist's untitled presentation. "Good Enough for Government Work: Doing Business with the Government" (Panel sponsored by Editorial Freelancers Association, New York, NY, November 19, 2002).

17.   Rock, op. cit.

18. *GSA Procurement Directory, 2002–2003.* (GSA Small Business Utilization Center, Northeast and Caribbean Region, Program Support and Human Resources Division), 20.

19. Ibid., 1.

20. Engel, panelist's untitled presentation, "Art of the Proposal."

21. Christine Erickson, panelist's untitled presentation, "Art of the Proposal."

Chapter 6

1. Adrianne Dale, Personal communication to author, January 13, 2003.

2. Christine M. Piotrowski, *Professional Practices for Interior Designers*, 3rd ed. (New York: John Wiley & Sons, 2002), 271.

3. Diane B. Worth, of the Carleton Group (Phoenix, AZ), in the course description for "The Letter of Agreement," a pocket CEU offered on the ASID, Web site, www.asid.org.

4. Tad Crawford and Eva Domain Bruck, *Business and Legal Forms for Interior Designers* (New York: Allworth, 2001), 137–142.

5. Ibid.

6. Mary V. Knackstedt, *The Interior Design Business Handbook: A Complete Guide to Profitability*, 3rd ed. (New York: John Wiley & Sons, 2002), 150.

7. Diane B. Worth, "The Letter of Agreement."

8. Crawford and Bruck, *Business and Legal Forms for Interior Designers*, 125.

9. Ibid., 126.

10. Ibid., 125.

11. Worth, "The Letter of Agreement."

12. H. Don Bowden, "ASID Update: Defining the Future," ISdesignet.com, October 2002, http://www.isdesignet.com/Magazine/ oct02/asid.html.

13. Knackstedt, *The Interior Design Business Handbook*, 152.

14. *Mechanic* in this legal term means "a skilled craftsman," not someone who repairs cars.

15. Knackstedt, *The Interior Design Business Handbook*, 151.

16. Adrianne Dale, personal communication, January 13, 2003.

17. Knackstedt, *The Interior Design Business Handbook*, 150.

18. Peter Martin, President Emeritus, Martin Construction, Inc., personal communication, December 27, 2002.

19. *Business and Legal Forms for Interior Designers*, 125.

20. The copyrighted ASID forms are licensed to purchasers for one use only, and new forms should be purchased for each new use.

21. Adrianne Dale, personal communication to author, January 13, 2003.

22. Knackstedt, *The Interior Design Business Handbook*, 149.

23. Dale, personal communication, January 13, 2003.

24. Knackstedt, *The Interior Design Business Handbook*, 151.

25. Diane Wintroub Calmenson, "Building Relationships," ISdesignet.com, May 1996, http://www.isdesignet.com/Magazine/May'96/cover.html.

26. Instruction Sheet, ID100, (ASID document, 1994), 1.

27. Martin, personal communication, December 27, 2002.
28. Personal communication, December 16, 2002.
29. Calmenson, "Building Relationships," ISdesignet.com, May 1996.
30. Worth, "The Letter of Agreement."
31. Richard C. Wydick, *Plain English for Lawyers*, 4th ed. (Durham, NC: Carolina Academic Press, 1998), 3. The critic cited is David Mellinkoff, writing in *The Language of the Law 23* (1963).
32. Wydick, *Plain English for Lawyers*, 61–62.
33. Ibid. 64. The passage cited is taken from the California Penal Code.
34. Ibid., 66, 67.
35. Ibid., 21.
36. Ibid.
37. Knackstedt, *The Interior Design Business Handbook*, 149.
38. Anecdote courtesy of Peter Martin, personal communication, December 27, 2002.

Chapter 7

1.   Joel Sanders, "Curtain Wars: Architects, Decorators, and the 20th-Century Domestic Interior," *Harvard Design Magazine* (Winter/Spring 2002), no. 16. http://www.gsd.harvard.edu/research/publications/hdm/back/ibsanders.html.
2.   This relationship and activity is illegal in some states.
3.   Tad Crawford and Eva Doman Bruck, *Business and Legal Forms for Interior Designers* (New York: Allworth, 2001), 127.
4.   Dan Beert, telephone interview with author, December 2, 2002.
5.   Linda W. Case, *Design/Build for Remodelers, Custom Builders, and Architects* (Washington, D.C.: Home Builder Press, 1992), 108.
6.   Ibid.
7.   www.asid.org.
8.   "An Interview with Bob Prest," in Case, *Design/Build for Remodelers, Custom Builders, and Architects,* 135.
9.   Case, *Design/Build for Remodelers, Custom Builders, and Architects,* 108.
10. Ibid., 85.
11. Ibid., 89.
12. American Institute of Architecture (AIA) Document A201-1997, paragraph 1.1.6.
13. Peter Martin, president emeritus, Martin Construction, Inc., interview with author, New York, NY, November 28, 2002.
14. From the introduction to the product specifications of E. Dillon & Company. http://www.edillon.com/products/premier/INTRO.doc.
15. AIA Document, A201-1997, paragraph 1.1.5.
16. Peter Martin, interview with author.
17. Adapted from Figure 6-9, in Case, *Design/Build for Remodelers, Custom Builders, and Architects,* 92.
18. Peter Martin, interview with author.
19. Ibid.

20. Case, *Design/Build for Remodelers, Custom Builders, and Architects*, 93.

21. Adapted from Crawford and Bruck, *Business and Legal Forms for Interior Designers*, 154–158.

22. Ibid., 154.

23. Ibid., 159.

Chapter 8

1. Christine Piotrowski, *Professional Practice for Interior Designers*, 3rd ed. (New York: John Wiley & Sons, 2002), 498.

2. Ibid., 493.

3. Ibid., 495.

4. Ibid., 494.

5. Ibid., 497.

6. "Refrigerators: Buying Advice," www.ConsumerReports.org (June 3, 2003).

7. Piotrowski, *Professional Practice for Interior Designers*, 498.

8. "Refrigerators: Buying Advice," www.ConsumerReports.org.

9. Piotrowski, *Professional Practice for Interior Designers*, 498.

10. Ibid., 500.

11. Ibid., 500.

12. Richard Wydick is a law professor whose book on writing for attorneys is widely used in law schools.

13. http://www.syspac.com/web/syspac/IndustryBusinessSpecific Operations/interor_design/.

14. *Getting Started: A Brief Step-by-Step Guide to Working with BlueBolt Studio* (BlueBolt Networks, 2001).

15. Tad Crawford and Eva Doman Bruck, *Business and Legal Forms for Interior Designers* (New York: Allworth Press, 2001), 88.

16. "Conquering the Paperwork Trail," http://www.minutesmatter.com/res_articles.html.

17. Crawford and Bruck, *Business and Legal Forms for Interior Designers*, 89.

18. Ibid., 78–81.

19. Crawford and Bruck, *Business and Legal Forms for Interior Designers*, 88.

20. Piotrowski, *Professional Practice for Interior Designers*, 535.

21. "Conquering the Paperwork Trail," http://www.minutesmatter.com/res_articles.html.

22. "Dress Your Business for Success," http://www.minutesmatter.com/res_articles.html.

23. "Design Manager Overview: Specifying, Purchasing, Order Tracking, Billing, Accounting, Technical Requirements." (Doylestown, PA: Franklin-Potter Associates, n.d.)

24. "Design Manager Overview."

25. Ibid.

26. "TRIRIGA and Autodesk Collaborate to Automate Design Intelligence Processes throughout the Project Life Cycle," Las Vegas, Tririga, 2001.

27. "Aerospace Concepts Selects TRIRIGA Software to Streamline Interior Design Processes for Executive Aircraft Operations," Tririga, 2001. September 10, 2001.

28. "TRIRIGA Inc Unveils Next-Generation Toolset to Automate Design and Build Processes across the Internet," Tririga, Las Vegas, June 19, 2001.

29. TRIRIGA Showcases Software to Automate Interior Design Processes at NeoCon West 2001," Las Vegas, Tririga, November 29, 2001.

30. Anne Chen, "After the Fall," *Ziff-Davis eweek*, February 4, 2002, p. 1. http://www.eweek.com/print_article/0,3668,a=21854,00.asp.

31. "Steve Wynn's Development Group Selects TRIRIGA Software to Manage Procurement Processes of Next Generation Las Vegas Resort Property," Tririga, Las Vegas, August 28, 2001.

32. Chen, "After the Fall," 2.

33. Ibid.

34. Expo Trade Services ad, Spring 2003.

35. Georges Jean, *Writing: The Story of Alphabets and Scripts*, trans. Jenny Oates. (New York: Harry N. Abrams, 1992), 12, 18.

36. Ibid., 12.

Chapter 9

1. Lewis Jay Goetz and Jason B. Wilcoxon, "Technology in the Architectural Workplace," IIDA: *Perspective* (Spring 2000), 22.

2. Ibid.

3. Joseph F. Schuler, "All CAD, All the Time," *Remodeling* (September 2002). http://www.remodeling.hw.net/industrynews.asp?archcleID-10000268098articleType-1.

4. Dan Beert, interview with author, October 9, 2002.

5. "A Beginner's Guide to Effective Email," www.webfoot.com/advice/email.top.html?shrm, 10/15/02.

6. Compiled and adapted from "Tip of the Day; E-Mail Etiquette," *Computer Tips Newsletter* (Toledo, Ohio: Worldstart, Inc., March 25, 2002, http://www.worldstart.com/guides/emailetiquette.html), from Jessica Bauer, "Writing Effective E-Mail: Top 10 Tips," www.uwec.edujerzdg/orr/handouts/TW/e-mail.htm, and from David Harris, "Electronic Mail Etiquette: Some Musings," www.cs.gueensu.ca/FAQs/email/etiquette.html.

7. Writing in the "On Language" section of *The New York Times* magazine (August 11, 2002).

8. Ibid.

9. Francis Duffy, "Office Politics," IIDA: *Perspective* (Winter 1999). http://www.iida.com/communications/publications/persective/winter99/other.politics.html.

10. Adapted from *Writing Guidelines for Interior Design Students*, Virginia Polytechnic Institute and State University, http://www.interiordesign.caus.vt.edu/vtid/IDwriting/guides/business.html.

11. *Writing Guidelines for Interior Design Students*, Virginia Polytechnic Institute and State University, http://www.interiordesign.caus.vt.edu/vtid/IDwriting/guides/pres.html.

12. Ibid.

13. Daniel G. Riordan and Steven E. Pauley, *Technical Report Writing*, 6th ed. (Boston: Houghton Mifflin, 1996), 351.

14.   Criteria suggested by Nat Harrison and Lynn Preston of Collins & Aikman Floorcoverings, "Climbing Gear: A Guide to Researching Substainable Design," IIDA: *Perspective* (Winter 1999), http://www.iida.com/publications/perspective/winter99/industry1.htm.

15.   Nancy Blossom, IIDA, FIDEC; David Matthews; Kathleen Gibson, IDEC, "Linking Interior Design Education and Practice," IIDA: *Perspective* (Spring 2002), 27.

16.   http://www.blogger.com/about.pyra.

17.   http://www.eastgate.com/Tinderbox/parts.html.

18.   www.blogger.com/about.pyra.

19.   Duffy, "Office Politics."

20.   Ibid.

21.   Stephen A. Kliment, *Writing for Design Professionals* (New York: W. W. Norton, 1998), 103.

22.   *The Chicago Manual of Style*, 15th ed. (Chicago and London: University of Chicago Press, 2003), 272.

23.   John Bruce Howell, *Style Manuals of the English-Speaking World: A Guide* (Phoenix, AZ: Oryx Press, 1983).

24.   Franklin Becker, "Good Medicine," IIDA: *Perspective* (Winter 1999), http://www.iida.com/communications/publications/persepctive/winter99/good_medicine.html.

25.   Rosalyn Cama, FASID, "Using Design Research to Create Winning Presentations," http:www.asid.org/design_basics/marketing_presentations/using_design_wining_research.asp. Cama is president of CAMA, Inc., a design firm specializing in health-care facilities, and a director of The Center for Health Design. She is a past president of ASID.

26.   Ibid.

27.   For a more complete list of magazines, go to http://www.asid.org/design_basics/about_interior_design/books.asp.

28.   "Writing Guidelines for Interior Design Students," Virginia Polytechnic Institute and State University, http://www.interiordesign.caus.vt.edu/vtid/IDwriting/guides/documentation.html.

29.   Becker, "Good Medicine."

Chapter 10
1.   Chris Frost, IFDA, e-mail to author, March 17, 2004.

2.   Ann Cox Porter, telephone interview with author, March 18, 2004.

3.   Chris Frost, e-mail to author, March 17, 2004; Ann Cox Porter, telephone interview with author, March 18, 2004.

4.   Adapted from Warren Foster, "Guidelines and Procedures for Improvement of Contract Documents" (Construction Specifications Specialists, Ltd., handout, June 25, 1990).

5.   Ibid.

6.   Mary V. Knackstedt, FASID, FIIDA, *The Interior Design Business Handbook: A Complete Guide to Profitability*, 3rd ed. (New York: John Wiley, 2002), 287. Adapted slightly.

7.   Amy Harmon, "Instant Messaging Leaves School for Office," *New York Times*, March 11, 2003, C2.

8. Ibid.

9. Ibid.

10. Steven Kliment, *Writing for Design Professionals* (New York: W. W. Norton, 1998), 95.

11. Knackstedt, *The Interior Design Business Handbook*, 289.

12. Sarah Milstein, "Calling: 32 Friends on the Phone—Taking Turns is Encouraged," *The New York Times*, March 13, 2003, G3.

13. Peter Martin, President Emeritus, Martin Construction, Inc., interview with the author, January 2003.

14. Ibid.

15. Adapted from Knackstedt, *The Interior Design Business Handbook*, 289.

16. Foster, "Guidelines and Procedures in Improvement of Contract Documents."

17. "Staying on Course with Project Control Systems," *.ISdesignet.com*, June 1996, http://www.isdesignet.com/Magazine/June'96/Projectcontrol.html.

18. Ibid.

19. Ibid.

20. *Professional Practice for Interior Designers*, 3rd ed. (New York: John Wiley & Sons, 2002), 464.

21. Knackstedt, *The Interior Design Business Handbook*, 279.

22. Foster, "Guidelines and Procedures in Improvement of Contract Documents."

23. Ibid.

24. "Big 50 Face-Off: Is a Punch List at the End of the Job a Bad Thing?" *Remodeling Magazine*, March 2003, 60.

25. City of Bellevue, WA, *Certificate of Occupancy Information*, http://www.ci.bellevue.wa.us/printpage.asp?view=977&printfriendly=yes.

26. Dan Beert, IIDA, IDEC, interview with the author, March 17, 2004.

27. Jim Cory, "A Gift Basket for Your Thoughts," *Remodeling Magazine* (March 2003), 41.

Chapter 11

1. *Guerrilla Marketing: Secrets for Making Big Profits from Your Small Business* (Boston: Houghton Mifflin, 1984), 203.

2. Ibid., 86.

3. Carol Davitt, *Marketing Your Remodeling Services: Putting the Pieces Together* (Washington, D.C.: Homebuilder Press, 1993), 83.

4. *New York* magazine, July 15, 2002.

5. Davitt, *Marketing Your Remodeling Services: Putting Together the Pieces*, 79.

6. Charles E. Rotkin, "Interview: Ezra Stoller, Architectural Photographer," *Professional Photographer's Survival Manual* (Cincinnati: Writer's Digest, 1992).

Chapter 12

1. Résumé elements adapted from *Résumés for Architects and Related Careers* (Lincolnwood, IL: VGM Career Horizons, 1996).

2. An overview of the qualifying exam and its six sections is available from NCIDQ at reasonable cost. It contains information about the exam and its rules and schedule. A useful study guide is David K. Ballast's *Interior Design Reference Manual* (Belmont, CA: Professional Publications, 1992).

3. Dan Beert, IIDA, IDEC, note to author, September 10, 2004.

4. Ibid.

5. Scott Kirsner, "The Elements of E-mail Style, *Darwin*, October 1, 2001, http://www.darwinmos.com/read/100101/ecosystem_content.html.

Index